FLASHPOINTS FOR
ASIAN AMERICAN
STUDIES

Flashpoints for Asian American Studies

CATHY J. SCHLUND-VIALS, EDITOR

Afterword by Viet Thanh Nguyen

FORDHAM UNIVERSITY PRESS

New York   2018

Library of Congress Cataloging-in-Publication Data
available online at http://catalog.loc.gov.

Printed in the United States of America
20 19 18   5 4 3 2 1
First edition

Remember that consciousness is power. Consciousness is education and knowledge. Consciousness is becoming aware. It is the perfect vehicle for students. Consciousness-raising is pertinent for power, and be sure that power will not be abusively used, but used for building trust and goodwill domestically and internationally. Tomorrow's world is yours to build.

—YURI KOCHIYAMA *(May 19, 1921–June 1, 2014)*

CONTENTS

Crisis, Conundrum, and Critique

Cathy J. Schlund-Vials

In April 1969, five UCLA students—Mike Murase, Dinora Gil, Laura Ho, Colin Watanabe, and Tracy Okida—founded *Gidra*, a radical monthly newspaper envisioned as a politically progressive, open forum for Asian American activists, authors, and artists. Christened by its creators as the "Voice of the Asian American Movement," *Gidra*—which ran from 1969 until April 1974—unfailingly showcased articles that meditated on systemic oppression at home and critiqued U.S. imperialism abroad. It likewise featured pieces that considered the possibility of cross-racial solidarities alongside the challenges of such work due to internalized racism and mainstream model minoritization. Concurrent with the West Coast institutionalization of ethnic studies as an interdisciplinary field of race-based inquiry, and coherent with the interdiscipline's rallying cry of "making education relevant," *Gidra* capaciously anticipated and significantly reflected the ways in which Asian America (as legible demographic and identifiable communal formation) was from the outset a distinctly political and expressly migratory project. On the one hand, *Gidra*'s reportage concerning anti-Asian racism, post-1965 Hart-Celler Act xenophobia, racialized U.S. foreign policy, people of color solidarities, and Yellow Power activism productively mirrored and tellingly refracted the liberatory aspirations and recovery-oriented ambitions of the Asian American movement.[1]

On the other hand, *Gidra*'s tactical engagement with progressive frames vis-à-vis revolutionary imaginings and historicized agendas—which correspondingly and contemporaneously rendered visible the parameters of mid-century social movements, civil rights era formations, and U.S. empire via disastrous wars in Southeast Asia—operate as recognizable starting points and source coordinates for Asian American studies, a field that concomitantly came into being as a direct consequence of race-based protest and racialized predicaments (e.g., state-sanctioned discrimination "over here" and state-authorized violence "over there"). Such histories and origin points analogously serve as initial moorings for *Flashpoints for Asian American Studies*, a collection that expressively commences with *Gidra*'s forward-looking mission and open-minded activist vision to consider—almost fifty years later—the possibilities of and limitations inherent in Asian American studies as historically entrenched, politically embedded, and institutionally situated interdiscipline. Unequivocally, *Flashpoints for Asian American Studies* investigates the multivalent ways in which the field has—and, at times and more provocatively, *has not*—responded to various contemporary crises, particularly as they are manifest in prevailing racist, sexist, homophobic, and exclusionary politics at home, ever-expanding imperial and militarized practices abroad, and neoliberal practices in higher education. To be sure, the title for this wide-ranging anthology is meant to suggestively illuminate various conundrums and dilemmas constitutive of a vexed twenty-first-century reality punctuated and characterized by a diverse set of "flashpoints." Connotative of "a place, event, or time at which trouble, such as violence or anger, flares up," a flashpoint demands—in the face of political calamity and systemic oppression—reflection, response, and recalibration.[2]

As *Gidra* contributor and Asian American poet/activist Amy Uyematsu avers in her opening essay, while five decades have passed since the rise of the Asian American movement and the institutionalization of Asian American studies, there remains a prevailing sense of déjà vu with regard to current events, or flashpoints; such returns, on one level, encapsulate multiple fronts, human rights campaigns, and social justice crusades: Vietnam to Iraq and Afghanistan; Selma to Ferguson; the Black Liberation Movement (BLM) of the 1970s to the present-day Black Lives Matter (BLM) movement; along with third world liberation fronts and the contemporary boycott movements involving Palestinian human rights. On another level, the recent contested election of the nation's forty-fifth president—Donald J. Trump—has quite dramatically and alarmingly engendered another "flashpoint" and rendered even more urgent these past/present contemplations. Catastrophically reminiscent of late-nineteenth- and early-twentieth-century calls to "shut the door" on Asian immigrants (via so-termed "Asiatic barred zones" and wholesale criminalization), devastatingly allusive of the World War II–era incarceration of Japanese/Japanese Americans, and calamitously redolent of fascist isolationism (e.g., "America First"), the Trump presidency is in many ways a distressingly familiar "past is prologue" administration. As a contemporary flashpoint, the administration's wide-ranging assaults against those on the margins are, even in the early stages of the Trump presidency, quite recognizable to Asian Americanists and other ethnic studies/gender/sexualities practitioners whose work endeavors to accentuate the identarian dimensions embedded in reiterative racist policy (against the undocumented and disenfranchised), xenophobic acts (emblematized by country-specific refugee bans), and sexist/homophobic initiative (via national gag orders and state-ratified bathroom laws).

These reverberations—which move between the mid-twentieth century and hover above the turn-of-the-twentieth century—frame *Flashpoints for Asian American Studies*, a project that critically charts and acutely interrogates the relevance of Asian American studies in the contemporary political moment. The diverse essays included in this volume—authored by Asian American scholars, artists, and activists, inclusive of Asian Americanist manifestos, commentaries, treatises, and expositions—are connected via their overarching consideration of the field's presentist successes and shortcomings, which make possible an attendant meditation on its future directions and unrealized possibilities.

Such connectedness is at once evident in the ways in which *Flashpoints for Asian American Studies* is dialogically linked to other anthologies that endeavor to reframe, reconsider, and re-evaluate the intellectual parameters and critical contours of Asian American studies as an interdisciplinary field of inquiry and critique. These include *Cultural Compass: Ethnographic Explorations of Asian America* (2000), edited by Martin F. Manalansan IV; *Asian American Studies: A Reader* (2000), edited by Min Song and Jean Yu-wen Shen Wu; *Asian American Studies after Critical Mass* (2004) and *A Companion to Asian American Studies* (2004), both edited by Kent A. Ono; *Asian Americans in New England: Culture and Community* (2009), edited by Monica Chiu; *Asian American Studies Now: A Critical Reader* (2010), edited by Jean Yu-wen Shen Wu and Thomas Chen; and *Asian Americans in Dixie* (2014), edited by Khyati Y. Joshi and Jigna Desai. These anthologies,

which bring together scholars from multiple disciplines (in the humanities and social sciences) and provocatively engage alternative sites
(inclusive of divergent geographies and underexplored subjectivities),
render discernible the extent to which Asian American studies is by no
means a static field but instead one marked by an expanding scholarly
trajectory.

Moreover, as a number of field collections that have recently been published or are forthcoming indicate, Asian American studies has most certainly arrived as an established interdiscipline. These include *The Routledge
Companion to Asian American and Pacific Islander Literature* (2014), *Keywords
for Asian American Studies* (2015), *The Cambridge History of Asian American
Literature* (2015), and *The Routledge Handbook of Asian American Studies*
(2016) (among others). Notwithstanding the considerable strengths of each
of these collections, and despite the value such works carry with regard
to archive and investigation, these anthologies render palpable the ways
in which Asian American studies is now a firmly institutionalized site
within the dominant U.S. academy. Such institutionalization, which carries with it the overt markers of professionalization alongside the perils
of disciplinary triumphalism, function as a point of profound departure
for *Flashpoints for Asian American Studies*, which begins with the controversial, nuanced premise that the field has incompletely fulfilled and at
times fallen short of the radical politics that undergirded its foundation
and facilitated its initial formation.

The disconnect between revolutionary activist vision, progressive poli-
tics, and moderate (or, at times, conservative) academic incorporation is explored in each of the essays that comprise *Flashpoints for Asian American
Studies*. In so doing, *Flashpoints for Asian American Studies* takes seriously
Roderick Ferguson's provocative directive in *The Reorder of Things: The
University and Its Pedagogies of Minority Difference* (2012). Explicitly, practitioners, scholars, and students of Asian American studies require, as
Ferguson notes in his analysis of ethnic studies and gender/sexuality studies, "a critical itinerary that can outline and interrogate the constitutive
contradictions of minoritized formations in the years after the sixties social movements, contradictions that have to do with the simultaneous
identifications with and antagonisms to the institutional embodiments
of power. . . . We also need analytic models that will help us imagine ways
to maneuver taken-for-granted contradictions so that their economies are
not constantly tilted toward identification but move in the direction of disidentification and on to more sustained embodiments of oppositionality."[3]
Flashpoints for Asian American Studies is accordingly guided by such a

"critical itinerary," which in its emphases on contradiction and opposi-tionality enables a wholesale reassessment of the field's past/present politics and impact.

Complicit Solidarities: Asian America
in the Twenty-First Century

These past/present politics and impacts as connected to Asian American studies (as an interdisciplinary field) and Asian America (as distinct politi-cal formation) are, as the essays in *Flashpoints for Asian American Studies* bring to light, strikingly relevant when situated within the ostensibly col-orblind logics of contemporary U.S. racial dynamics and the imperialistic practices of U.S. militarization (particularly in the Middle East and Pacific Rim). With regard to the latter, the rising tide of Islamophobia, aforemen-tioned calls to "shut the door" on Muslim and South Asian immigrants, along with the reinvigorated foreign policies that accompany recent dec-larations concerning "America's Pacific Century" cannot fully be compre-hended without attending to contradictory machinations that have historically cast Asian immigrants and Asian Americans as perilous sub-jects and would-be beneficiaries of U.S. empire (à la what Yên Lê Espiritu characterizes within Southeast Asian American studies as "the good refu-gee"). Nor can such convoluted actualities be considered without a serious examination into the ways in which U.S. knowledge production—as co-opted, corporatized enterprise and in light of the ever-growing Boycott, Divestment, and Sanctions (BDS) movement—requires a "different way of seeing" ethnic studies (and, by proxy, Asian American studies) to facilitate a prospective site of resistance and critique. In a more domestic vein, these "different ways of seeing" are especially important when contemplating present-day anti-Black racism and U.S. racial dynamics, as emblematized by the topical case of and public protests concerning New York Police Department (NYPD) officer Peter Liang.

On November 20, 2014, while on routine vertical patrol in east New York City, two NYPD rookie officers—the abovementioned Liang and Shaun Landau—entered the eighth-floor stairwell of the Louis H. Pink Houses.[4] With unlit hallways, little to no elevator service, peeling paint, and exposed, rusted pipes, the mid-rise tenement—despite its comparatively cheerful, optimistically colorful name—was among the most neglected, dilapidated, and notorious of the city's public housing proj-ects. Located in one of the metropole's highest crime areas (on Brooklyn's outer edges), the Pink Houses were constructed in 1959 and named after the former chair of the New York City Housing Authority (NYCHA) who—despite the present-day appalling conditions of his architectural namesake—furiously dedicated a working life to eradicating the city's slums through subsidized, low-income housing. In the face of constant safety complaints from tenants, in spite of repeated petitions for basic maintenance, and notwithstanding persistent NYPD officer concerns about security, the NYCHA repeatedly responded with inaction and recurrently countered with indifference: In the past three years, the NYCHA failed to replace burned-out lightbulbs, fix broken security cameras, and attend to critical building repairs.

Irrefutably, the NYCHA was not alone with regard to engendering extreme human insecurity at the Pink Houses: The NYPD—confronted with occupant objections concerning racial profiling and antagonized by resident requests that more seasoned patrols be assigned to the area—continually sent newly minted recruits who lacked the necessary understanding, compulsory familiarity, and crucial experience to deal with routine tenant engagements, more serious criminal altercations, and what even New York Police Commissioner Bill Bratton confessed was a recent and critical "spike in violence" in the neighborhood.[5] Such administrative neglect—which incontrovertibly occurred in tandem with increased state-authorized racial profiling (via codified NYPD policy) and pervasive short-sighted cop deployment (vis-à-vis the widespread use of probationary officers)—would have tragic consequences and dramatic repercussions that late November evening.

On that evening, at approximately 11:15 P.M., Liang and Landau began their nightly surveillance of the housing project. As per established vertical patrol protocol, Liang had his 9mm Glock drawn in his left hand; he steadied a small, police-issue flashlight in his right. Startled by a noise approximately one flight below, Liang—without specific target, with no visibility, and sans probable cause—discharged his weapon. Subsequently deemed an unfortunate "accident" by aforementioned Police Commissioner Bratton, NYPD's Internal Affairs, and the Brooklyn District Attorney's office, the bullet ricocheted off a wall and struck Akai Kareem Gurley, a twenty-eight-year-old father of a two-year-old girl; originally from Saint Thomas (U.S. Virgin Islands), Gurley had, like Liang (who, aged twenty-seven, was born "elsewhere," in Hong Kong), emigrated to New York at a young age.[6] Gurley and his girlfriend (a Pink Houses resident) had entered the complex just minutes after Liang and Landau; it was afterward reported that Gurley was at the Pink Houses to have his hair braided in anticipation of the upcoming Thanksgiving holiday. Suffering from shock, Gurley was unaware of the seriousness of his injuries; attempting to run from his then-unknown assailants, Gurley frantically sought refuge in the Pink Houses, though he only made it to the project's fifth-floor hallway. According to after-the-fact eyewitness accounts and trial transcripts, Liang and his partner, oblivious to the fatal detail that Gurley had been hit and unmindful that their unintended target was in dire need of emergency care, argued for almost four minutes about whether or not they should call their supervisor to report the incident. At no point did either officer provide Gurley with medical assistance, who—without basic CPR and the benefit of rudimentary first aid—quickly succumbed to the gunshot wound in his chest.[7]

Notwithstanding the specific circumstances and particular conditions that undergirded Liang's so-declared inadvertent killing of Akai Gurley, the case was—when simultaneously situated adjacent *to* and retrospectively set *against* a national imaginary of disproportionate anti-Black police violence—decidedly and ineludibly *not* exceptional. To wit, a mere two days after the Pink Houses shooting, on November 22, officers Timothy Loehmann and Frank Garmback responded to a call involving a "black male sitting on a swing and pointing a gun at people" in a Cleveland, Ohio, park.[8] The person reporting the incident clearly stressed at the beginning and reiterated at the middle of the call that the pistol was "probably fake" and that the suspect was "probably a juvenile."[9] As the officers arrived on the scene, the suspect—twelve-year-old Tamir Rice—allegedly moved his hands and reached for his waist. Officer Loehmann fired two shots; one bullet missed Rice entirely, while the other pierced the preteen's torso. As was the case in the Akai Gurley shooting, neither officer administered elementary treatment or simple medical aid; not surprisingly and quite heartbreakingly, Rice passed way the following day at MetroHealth Medical Center.[10] Indubitably, the caller's initial characterization of the pistol as "probably fake" was swiftly confirmed: Rice's "weapon" was a relatively common air gun replica filled with nonlethal plastic pellets.[11]

Placed on administrative leave, both officers—despite past complaints and previous acts to the contrary—indefatigably insisted on their wholesale innocence and tirelessly emphasized categorical nonwrongdoing.[12] Such pleas of law enforcement virtuousness were apparently heeded and believed, as made clear by a court ruling that occurred one year later: On December 28, 2015, a Cleveland grand jury elected not to indict Loehmann and Garmback. This distressing pattern of police shooting and nonarraignment—wherein prosecuting the deaths of African Americans at the hands of law enforcement are belatedly pursued, incompletely mediated, and juridically dismissed—was upsettingly foreshadowed two days after Rice's slaying and four days after Gurley's shooting, when Saint Louis County prosecutor Robert McCulloch announced on November 24, 2014, that a grand jury would—regardless of firsthand testimonials concerning racist bias and even with eyewitness accounts—not prosecute Ferguson police officer Darren Wilson on criminal charges connected to his August 9, 2014, shooting and killing of unarmed African American teenager Michael Brown. Moreover, a little over a week following the Ferguson ruling and two weeks after the Gurley shooting—on December 3, 2014—a Richmond County (New York) grand jury familiarly followed suit in its indiscriminate determination that NYPD officer Daniel Pantaleo would not face indictment for the chokehold death of Eric Garner, an African American male (aged forty-three). This juridical nonprosecution occurred notwithstanding the investigative fact that the New York City Medical Examiner's Office—from the outset and quite publicly—ruled the passing of the father of six to be a homicide.[13]

These recurring miscarriages of justice, which lay bare the state-authorized disposability of black lives via an all-too-frequent convergence of police violence and African American mortality, were contemporaneously at the forefront of the previously discussed Liang shooting of Akai Gurley. Notwithstanding recognizable registers with regard to suspicious circumstance and catastrophic end, however, Liang was—by contrast to his aforementioned law enforcement brethren—actually indicted by a grand jury on February 10, 2015, and charged with second-degree manslaughter, second-degree assault, reckless endangerment, criminally negligent homicide, and two counts of official misconduct.[14] Controversially, Liang was not only arraigned; he would—at the end of the trial—be the first NYPD officer to be convicted for a shooting that occurred in the line of duty in over a decade.[15] Liang predictably pleaded not guilty to the charges; he was—one year later, on February 11, 2016—found guilty of manslaughter and official misconduct. Two months after the verdict, on April 19, 2016, Brooklyn Supreme Court Justice Danny Chun sentenced Liang to probation (five years) and eight hundred hours of community service.[16] In the interim period between indictment and sentencing, Liang's case drew a number of reactions, principally among Asian American activists and politicians who, as will subsequently be clear, faced a peculiarly racialized conundrum.

With Liang's trial underway, more than three thousand Chinese Americans gathered at New York City Hall in March to accordingly support the Chinese American officer and register their objection to his indictment;

the following month, in April, thousands marched across the Brooklyn Bridge to Manhattan's Chinatown (in the Lower East Side) to raise awareness about the case and campaign on Liang's behalf. Integral to these protests and central to these demonstrations were problematic references to the civil rights movement (wherein Martin Luther King Jr.'s "injustice everywhere" declarations served as rallying cries) and the overriding assertion that Liang's prosecution upsettingly fit the convenient rubrics of a racially inflected scapegoat narrative. Indeed, as state assemblyman Ron Kim surmised, "Our system failed Gurley and it failed Liang. It pitted the unjust death of an innocent young black man against the unjust scapegoating of a young Asian police officer who was frightened, poorly trained, and who committed a terrible accident."[17] For many Asian American community activists, such legally inflected "firsts"—which encapsulated Liang's singular indictment vis-à-vis recent NYPD history and included above-discussed nonprosecuted shootings in Cleveland and Ferguson (among so many others)—ostensibly brought to light wrongful rebukes part and parcel of racially driven condemnations.

Even so, such protests expectedly drew quick criticism and some ire from other antiracist activists, who—under the banner of the previously mentioned Black Lives Matter (BLM) movement—had consistently levied critiques against the United States as de facto police state; these pro-Liang campaigns likewise garnered reproach from other organizations such as #Asians4BlackLives-NYC, which repeatedly stressed "solidarity with the family of Akai Gurley" and demanded that "all police officers are held accountable when they cause unjustified death and injuries in communities that are paid to protect and serve." Noting that supporters of Peter Liang "made reference to Martin Luther King Jr., the legacy of the Civil Rights movement, and the murder of Vincent Chin," #Asians4BlackLives-NYC asked, "Can we see that the death of Akai Gurley and so many black lives are linked to this history of racism in this country? Like Peter Liang, the men responsible for Vincent Chin's death never saw a day in jail. Can we see that Vincent Chin shares more in common with Akai than with Peter?"[18] These bipartisan invocations of the midcentury civil rights movement and the 1982 murder of Vincent Chin (a veritable touchstone in Asian American studies), as specifically deployed in pro-Liang campaigns, renders discernible the extent to which Asian America—as imagined political enclave and conflicted community formation—is more often than not precariously complicit vis-à-vis contemporary debates concerning rights, race, and racism.

Allusive of "involvement with others in an activity that is unlawful or morally wrong," connotative of collaborative engagement, and indicative of implicit agreement, *complicit* on one level operates as an apt adjectival modifier for Liang, whose shooting of Akai Gurley was illegal, ethically vexed, and—to varying degrees and divergent ends—consistent with a national police practice of anti-Black, racist profiling.[19] Such a term likewise functions as an appropriate descriptor for pro-Liang activists, who utilized the histories of anti-Asian racism and the civil rights movement as a means of militating against Liang's indictment. On another level, as status quo indicator, *complicity*—as paradoxically mediated in the public declarations of #Asians4BlackLives-NYC—encompasses the in-between-ness of Asian America as a distinct demographic location and heterogeneous political site. As Jay Caspian Kang in a *New York Times* article titled, "How Should Asian-Americans Feel about the Peter Liang Protests?", convincingly summarizes:

> Many Asian-Americans felt that Liang had been offered up as a sacrificial lamb to appease the ongoing protests against police violence that started two summers ago in Ferguson, Missouri. The pro-Liang protests, in turn, sparked small counterprotests by black activist, who argued that justice had been served and that a killer cop was a killer cop, period. A discomforting paradox lay beneath the whole confrontation, one that cut straight across the accepted modern vision of Asians and their adjacency to whiteness: if Liang (and, by extension, all Asian Americans) enjoyed the protection of whiteness, then how do you explain his conviction? . . . It is my belief that Asian-Americans have to form their own way of talking about race, privilege, and justice, one that acknowledges both our relative privilege and the costs of our invisibility.[20]

Kang's consideration of the Liang conundrum—which pivots on the urgent acknowledgment of "adjacent whiteness," the implicit evaluation of model minoritized Asian American privilege, and the problematics of binaried black/white invisibility—very much intersects with the nuanced queries and analyses that compose *Flashpoints for Asian American Studies*. As the individual essays bring to light, this multilayered attention to "race, privilege, and justice" necessarily begins with an acknowledgment of racial privilege or, more directly, "adjacent whiteness." This racial proximity to privilege and power—attributable to the assimilative ongoingness of model minoritization and threatened by the specter of perpetual foreignness—accentuates the current state and stakes of Asian American studies, an institutionalized interdiscipline marked by comparative paradigms, (in)visible racial projects, past/present paradoxes, and domestic/foreign polemics.

Essay Overviews

Such Janus-faced appraisals and critical juxtapositionings, which bring into focus the many contradictions of U.S. exceptionalism, are evident in Part One, titled "Ethnic Studies Revisited." As suggested at the titular level, this section examines the past, present, and future of ethnic studies via a consideration of where Asian American studies has been (as institutionalized discipline and public race project) and maps where it may be going (in light of recent student protests and the wholesale defunding of U.S. higher education). Part One begins with Amy Uyematsu's "Five Decades Later: Reflections of a Yellow Power Advocate Turned Poet," which evocatively looks back on the artist's foundational Asian American manifesto, "The Emergence of Yellow Power"; this retrospective engagement presages Uyematsu's subsequent meditation on the ways in which the aims of Yellow Power have yet to be realized despite the large-scale institutionalization of Asian American studies as viable academic focus and concentrated field. Such movement reflections foreground Timothy Yu's "Has Asian American Studies Failed?" which takes as a starting point the still-forming notion of discernible Asian American "publics." Arguing that the field's critical work—particularly with regard to deconstructing race, nation, and power—is largely restricted to narrow academic imaginaries, Yu pushes practitioners to make this labor "more public" and urges scholars to intervene far more quickly and aggressively in national discussions around race and Asian Americans.

Yu's appeal for more aggressive interventions via larger debates concerning race and racialization is divergently deliberated in Nitasha Sharma's "The Racial Studies Project: Asian Americans Studies and the Black Lives Matter Campus." Fixed to the recent "successful" institutionalization of Asian American studies at Northwestern University, Sharma advocates for the expansion of the field's ethno-racial sites as a means of making more relevant the work of Asian American studies to antiracist student activists; such relevance is incontrovertibly predicated on a need to move beyond the study of Asian populations to more clearly accentuate the field's critical centrality in social justice campaigns involving racial violence and mainstream conversations concerning contested U.S. racial formations. This politicized attentiveness to applicability, program building, and institutionalization is differentially contemplated in Cathy J. Schlund-Vials's "Planned Obsolescence, Strategic Resistance: Ethnic Studies, Asian American Studies, and the Neoliberal University." Arguing that the higher education establishment of ethnic studies was at its very inception precarious because of nonpermanent funding tracks and ephemeral faculty lines, Schlund-Vials deconstructs the politics of program formation as a means of militating against the neoliberal dynamics of what has euphemistically been characterized as "diversity management" by college and university administrators. Such stresses on the politics of program formation and the polemics of institutional obligation are further explored in Anita Mannur's "Un-homing Asian American Studies: Refusals and the Politics of Commitment," which provocatively accesses via personal administrative account the assimilative costs of curricular integration and disciplinary collapse.

Whereas Part One contemplates the institutionalization of Asian American studies and Asian American publics, Part Two—"Displaced Subjects"—includes essays that critically question the perils of field codification, the hazards of latent intervention, and the problems of field silence. Junaid Rana's "No Muslims Involved: Letter to Ethnic Studies Comrades" interrogates the constraints of U.S. race-based inquiries via a pointed critique of what is tantamount to a polemics of exclusion with regard to Palestine, the War on Terror, and pervasive Islamophobia; in so doing, Rana issues a potent challenge to both ethnic studies and Asian American studies theorists vis-à-vis radical revision and revolutionary inclusion. Such revisionary calls to shift the insular focus of Asian American studies to accommodate global politics and terrains are echoed in Asha Nadkarni's "Outsourcing, Terror, and Transnational South Asia," which initially explores the ways in which outsourcing and terror function as distinct transnational circuits between the United States and South Asia. The tracing of this particular phenomenon presages Nadkarni's subsequent assessment of contemporary discourses concerning development via British imperialism, postcolonial nationalisms, and U.S. neoimperialism. These transnational and international evaluations accordingly substantiate Nadkarni's insistence that Asian American studies must expand its global purview to better theorize the contemporary relationships between and representations of outsourcing and terror that are incontrovertibly constitutive of U.S. domestic politics and American foreign policy.

Whereas Rana and Nadkarni analogously advocate to extend the theoretical sights of Asian American studies to better accommodate for the actualities of neoliberalism and the terror-driven realities of U.S. empire, Rajini Srikanth and Candace Fujikane consider the displaced "site" of

Palestine as both organizing issue and human rights locus. Srikanth's "Asian American Studies and Palestine: The Accidental and Reluctant Pioneer" considers the perplexing aftermath of the Association for Asian American Studies' (AAAS) academic boycott of Israel. Notwithstanding the fact that the AAAS was the first academic organization in the United States to issue such a resolution, and despite subsequent BDS boycotts by the Native American and Indigenous Studies Association (NAISA) and the American Studies Association (ASA) (among others), there has—to date—been no further discussion about this "pioneering action" within the AAAS, the field's primary organizational hub. Srikanth's essay deliberates upon this silence and interrogates whether such restraint signals a field failure with regard to rights-oriented academic activism. Such silences with regard to the "displaced subject" of Palestine are correspondingly evaluated in Fujikane's "Against the Yellowwashing of Israel: The BDS Movement and Liberatory Solidarities across Settler States," which maps the intersection of Hawaiian settler-colonial politics and anti-Palestine agendas via senator Daniel Inouye's career-long support of Israel. In particular, Fujikane dismantles the strategic use of Japanese American incarceration/internment in the opportunistic elevation of Israel as alleged asylum state.

These global critiques of Asian American studies as an at times inconsistently engaged, transnationally inflected field continue in Part Three, "Remapping Asia, Recalibrating Asian America." This section opens with "Transpacific Entanglements," co-authored by Yên Lê Espiritu, Lisa Lowe, and Lisa Yoneyama. "Transpacific Entanglements" offers an analysis of what Espiritu, Lowe, and Yoneyama assert are "the often disavowed histories of U.S. war, colonialism, capitalism, and militarized empire in Asia and the Pacific Islands and the racialized figure of the 'Asian American.'" Espiritu, Lowe, and Yoneyama congruently push for a re-evaluation of the postwar period as one that was shaped by U.S. Cold War social science and problematic narratives of liberation; this tactical use of science and narrative correspondingly governs in imperialistic, militarized fashion subjects in Asia. Such rethinking of Asian subjects, which carries with it a geopolitical re-evaluation of academic politics, scholastic polemics, and governmental agendas, presages the focus of Martin F. Manalansan IV's "Tensions, Engagements, Aspirations: The Politics of Knowledge Production in Filipino American Studies." Contending that Filipino American studies as diasporic field negotiates to varying ends the vexed borders of area studies, American studies, and ethnic studies, Manalansan observes that the problems of borders are by no means limited to semantics but instead encompass issues of unequal power distribution. Indicative of a heretofore underexamined epistemic privilege, these inequalities render visible the present and future predicaments of Filipino American studies within what Manalansan characterizes as "North-South imperial relations, neoliberal university policies, and disciplinary formations."

The complicated academic relationship between "North" and "South" is productively revised to fit the likewise contested contours of "East" and "West" in Cynthia Wu's "Asian International Students at U.S. Universities in the Post-2008 Collapse Era," which addresses the ways in which Asian American studies' overriding insistence on recovering a useable resistant past via the aforementioned rights movements of the 1960s and 1970s has made it troublingly reluctant to examine relevant accommodation. As the title suggests, Wu considers how the intellectual trajectory of the field, dominated by a limited U.S.-centrism, has proved largely ineffective with regard to the twenty-first century influx of international students from Asian countries at U.S. universities. Such "East-West" reorientations assume a different register in Kandice Chuh's "Asians Are the New . . . What?," which opens with recent debates involving Asian Americans, university admissions, and affirmative action. Noting the "constitutive ambivalence that has characterized the production of 'Asian' as a racial category in the U.S. political and cultural imagination," and connecting this process of "Asian racialization" to economically determined "middleman" model minority discourses within the social ontology of the U.S. populace, Chuh calls for a critical reckoning of the model minority-identified Asian American subject. Such reckonings, in turn, enable a critical diagnosis of the continuing dominance of global capitalism as a defining feature of the U.S. nation.

Part Four—"Toward an Asian American Ethic of Care"—shifts the focus from the systemic to the affective in its diverse contemplation of embodiment, engagement, and ethos. To that end, Yoonmee Chang's "Asian Americans, Disability, and the Model Minority Myth" operates as a significant transition essay that revises Chuh's contemplation of the model minority-identified Asian American subject via a sustained critique of the ableist aspects of Asian American studies. Such ableism, as Chang convincingly maintains, obscures through minoritized exceptionalism the possibility of a disabled Asian American personhood, rendering such bodies as "impossible subjects." Seeing "otherwise" with regard to Asian American personhood and incarnation is likewise the focus of Sharon A. Suh's "Buddhist Meditation as Strategic Embodiment: An Optative Reflection," which seriously scrutinizes the relationship of Buddhism, "one of America's racialized other religious darlings," to Asian American studies, which has yet to consistently recognize religion as a legitimate site upon which to map race, gender, and sexuality. Suh argues that "the common Buddhist units of measure and authenticity"—for instance, Orientalized monks and Eastern meditation—"are uncritically reproduced in larger Asian American discourses that continue to overlook the nondevotional and nonmeditative practices of Buddhist laity." Suh's essay counters those discourses by engendering a new way of seeing meditation politics as a means of ameliorating bodily alienation and internalized white supremacy.

This shift to the ethical and contemplative, facilitated by a perceptible turn to interiority, undergirds Brandy Liên Worrall-Soriano's "What Is Passed On (Or, Why We Need Sweetened Condensed Milk for the Soul)," which engages the personal means of reflecting upon the political. In particular, Worrall-Soriano—whose recently published cancer memoir, *What Doesn't Kill Us* (2014) has received much critical acclaim—reflects upon how the field of Asian American studies, notwithstanding its preoccupations with state-authorized conflict and trauma, has historically failed to deal with widespread stigmatizations involving illness. Worrall-Soriano maps these omissions via a creative nonfiction exploration of her familial past; such forays, which assume the form of intergenerational palimpsest, bring to light the degree to which Asian American studies remains—in the face of teleology and despite critical movement—a post-traumatic stressed engagement. Such interior moves are divergently explored in Min Hyoung Song's "An Ethics of Generosity," which uses as a main contrapuntal premise the logics of neoliberal self-interest and its disastrous implications for Asian Americans and other groups of color. Song accordingly calls for a deconstruction of such logics as a means of militating against the disastrous legacies and consequences of neoliberalism; such resistance, Song successively maintains, demands a different relationship and reaction to various forms of systemic violence. Last, but certainly not least, *Flashpoints for Asian American Studies* closes with Viet Thanh Nguyen's afterword, "Becoming Bilingual, or Notes on Numbness and Feeling," which unwaveringly and unabashedly deconstructs how Asian American studies has become professionalized and entrenched, and in that sense, has both succeeded and failed.

Taken together and in drawing to a close, the essays included in *Flashpoints for Asian American Studies* accentuate a series of tensions, a set of contradictions, and a structure of possibilities that have, from the interdiscipline's inception, been at the forefront of a field that was and remains—notwithstanding various vistas and diverse sites—unwaveringly domestic and international, irresolutely transnational and diasporic, and intermittently accommodationist and activist. As significant, such wide-ranging terrains, which productively and unavoidably encompass the inconsistences of American democracy, the logics of U.S. imperialism, and the dynamics of in-flux racial formation, reinforce the political possibilities of the interdiscipline's ever-more relevant critical dimensions. These dimensions, which contain and intersect with what Lisa Lowe constructively termed "Asian Americanist critique," render pressingly palpable the necessity of the interdiscipline in what is—in the post-Obama, Trump era—an extreme and multifaceted moment of crisis.

To that end, as Lowe reminds us, Asian American culture (and politics) "is the site of more than critical negation of the U.S. nation; it is a site that shifts and marks alternatives to the national terrain by occupying other spaces, imagining different narratives and critical historiographies, and enacting practices that give rise to new forms of subjectivity and new ways of questioning the government of human life by the national state."[21] As *Flashpoints for Asian American Studies* underscores, integral to interrogating the interdiscipline's potential and limitations is the indefatigable and unending labor of envisioning "different narratives and critical historiographies" to instantiate the formation of new subjectivities, under-mined coalitions, and underexplored locales of resistance (within and outside the academy). Such reimagined investments vis-à-vis field, practice, and activism ultimately serve as a potent through-line for this volume, which takes seriously the present-day precariousness evident in multiple facets of political, academic, and everyday life.

NOTES

1. Passed in 1965, the Hart-Celler Act (known alternatively as the Immigration and Nationality Act) ended an era of Asian exclusion. The Hart-Celler Act not only increased Asian immigration overall; it concomitantly inaugurated immigration by groups previously underrepresented within Asian America, such as Koreans and South Asians. The act is credited for facilitating the first en masse migration of Asian immigrations to the United States.

2. *OED Online*, s.v. "flashpoint, n., 1," https://en.oxforddictionaries.com /definition/flashpoint.

3. See Roderick A. Ferguson, *The Reorder of Things: The University and Its Pedagogies of Minority Difference* (Minneapolis: University of Minnesota Press, 2012), 17.

4. "Vertical patrols" refer to the practice of posting officers on different floors of a building simultaneously; this practice is specific to the surveil-

lance of housing projects. The technique was originally deployed by the Chicago Housing Authority Police Department (which is now defunct) and is presently used by the New York City Police Department Housing Bureau. This is considered a controversial practice insofar as it targets low-income populations (because of setting) and is often guided by the concomitant racial profiling of those populations.

5. Snejana Farberov, "'We Cannot Repeat the 1970s': NYPD Commissioner Bill Bratton Calls for Crackdown on Gun Violence after 22 Are Shot and Killed in New York over the Weekend," *Daily Mail*, August 3, 2015, http://www.dailymail.co.uk/news/article-3184172/We-repeat-fiasco-1970s -NYPD-Commissioner-Bill-Bratton-calls-crackdown-gun-violence-bloody -weekend-New-York-sees-22-shot-three-killed.html.

6. See Hansi Lo Wang, "'Awoken' By N.Y. Cop Shooting, Asian American Activists Chart Way Forward," *NPR.org*, April 23, 2016, http:// www.npr.org/sections/codeswitch/2016/04/23/475369524/awoken-by-n-y -cop-shooting-asian-american-activists-chart-way-forward.

7. As details of Gurley's shooting came to light, the question of whether or not Liang had been properly trained in CPR emerged as a key prosecutorial consideration. On November 3, 2016, Landau testified that Liang had received approximately two minutes' worth of CPR training at the police academy. See Sarah Maslin Nir, "Officer Liang's Partner Testifies He Got Little CPR Training," *New York Times*, November 4, 2016, http://www .nytimes.com/2016/02/05/nyregion/officer-liangs-partner-testifies-he-got -little-cpr-training.html?_r=0.

8. "Hear the 911 Call about Tamir Rice: Gun Is 'Probably Fake,' Caller Says," *Los Angeles Times*, November 26, 2014, http://www.latimes.com /nation/nationnow/la-na-nn-tamir-rice-911-call-20141126-htmlstory.html. Purportedly, Loehmann and Garmback were unaware of the suspect's age when they responded to the call; this information had been left out of the original police dispatch.

9. Ibid.

10. Eric Heisig, "FBI Agent Who Gave First Aid to Tamir Rice said Cleveland Officers on Scene 'Didn't Know What to Do,'" *Cleveland.com*, June 14, 2015, http://www.cleveland.com/metro/index.ssf/2015/06/fbi_agent _who_gave_first_aid_t.html.

11. Ibid.

12. It was subsequently revealed that the Cleveland Police Department had received numerous complaints concerning police brutality and disproportionate force prior to the Tamir Rice shooting. See Timothy Williams and Mitch Smith, "Cleveland Officer Will Not Face Charges in Tamir Rice Shooting Death," *New York Times*, December 28, 2015,

http://www.nytimes.com/2015/12/29/us/tamir-rice-police-shootiing
-cleveland.html?_r=0.

13. On July 17, 2014, Eric Garner was apprehended by officers in Staten Island, New York, on the basis that he was selling cigarettes without a license. Pantaleo attempted to place Garner in handcuffs; upon reaching for his wrist, Garner pulled away. Pantaleo then placed Garner in a chokehold that lasted roughly twenty seconds. According to eyewitness accounts, Garner stated—eleven times—that he could not breathe; the officers on site eventually placed Garner on his side but offered no additional medical assistance. Garner died as a result of injuries incurred during the chokehold.

14. Jaeah Lee, "Why Was Peter Liang One of So Few Cops Convicted for Killing an Unarmed Man?," *Mother Jones*, April 9, 2016, http://www
.motherjones.com/politics/2016/03/peter-liang-police-conviction-nypd.

15. See Thomas Tracy, "NYPD Officer Peter Liang Found Guilty of Manslaughter in Fatal Shooting of Akai Gurley in Brooklyn Housing Development," February 12, 2016, *New York Daily News*, http://www
.nydailynews.com/new-york/nyc-crime/nypd-peter-liang-guilty-fatal
-shooting-akai-gurley-article-1.2528827.

16. Matt Hansen and Matt Pearce, "No Prison Time for Ex-NYPD Officer Peter Liang in Fatal Shooting of Akai Gurley," April 19, 2016, *Los Angeles Times*, http://www.latimes.com/nation/la-na-liang-sentencing
-20160419-story.html.

17. Quoted in "Former NYPD Cop Peter Liang's Guilty Verdict Leaves a Community Divided," *NBC News*, February 13, 2016, http://www.nbcnews
.com/news/asian-america/former-nypd-cop-peter-liang-s-guilty-verdict
-leaves-community-n518056.

18. Quoted in Annie Tan, "Peter Liang Was Justly Convicted. He's Not a Victim," *Huffington Post*, February 23, 2016, http://www.huffingtonpost
.com/annie-tan/peter-liang-was-justly-convicted_b_9299860.html.

19. *OED Online*, s.v. "complicit,. adj, 1," https://en.oxforddictionaries
.com/definition/flashpoint.

20. Jay Caspian Kang, "How Should Asian Americans Feel about the Peter Liang Protests," *New York Times*, February 23, 2016, http://www
.nytimes.com/2016/02/23/magazine/how-should-asian-americans-feel-about
-the-peter-liang-protests.html.

21. Lisa Lowe, *Immigrant Acts: On American Cultural Politics* (New York: Duke University Press, 1996), 29.

PART I

Ethnic Studies Revisited

CHAPTER I

Five Decades Later: Reflections of a Yellow Power Advocate Turned Poet

Amy Uyematsu

"Yellow Power," circa 1969

When militant is the only way
To guarantee we can have our say—

Yellow and red, brown and black,
The times are ripe for us to strike back.

Malcolm, Mao and Ho Chi Minh
Beacons for our revolution.

Change will ferment in that furious hour
As history is witness to yellow power.

—AMY UYEMATSU

The idea of yellow power gained popularity in the late 1960s when young Asian American activists began to organize on the West Coast. Groups with names like Yellow Seed, I Wor Kuen, Asian American Political Alliance, and the Red Guard Party were forming, and the field or even concept of Asian American studies did not yet exist. Reflecting back on almost fifty years to 1969, when I wrote "The Emergence of Yellow Power in America," I'm struck by how much Asian America has changed and yet how overall conditions of racial and economic inequality in this country have not improved. In this essay, I look back on how I came to write the yellow power article, utilizing flashpoints, quotations, and signposts that triggered key experiences and ideas. I discuss my evolution from a political activist to a poet and how being a movement "radical" in my early twenties continues to shape my thinking and writing as a now aging sansei baby boomer.

1. *Flashpoint 1969*

—January murders of Black Panthers Bunchy Carter
and John Huggins at UCLA

—February formation of the Red Guard Party in San Francisco Chinatown

—March founding of MEChA (Movimiento Estudiantil Chicano de Aztlán)

—April publication of the first issue of *Gidra*, Asian American
movement newspaper

To be a college student in the '60s was like being in a nonstop firestorm. It was the decade of American revolutions—civil rights and black power, women's liberation, ethnic studies, gay rights, counterculture. It was also the decade of a widespread anti–Vietnam War movement, with many Asian American activists taking part in peace marches along with rallies for work-ers', women's, and minorities' rights. At the same time, there was a surge of independence struggles in Africa and the third world, including the vic-tory of Cuban socialists in 1959. With the Cultural Revolution going strong in China, the teachings and writings of Mao Tse-Tung had a con-siderable impact on the American left, and many of us still have the *Little Red Book* in our libraries.

In 1969, the UCLA Asian American Studies Center was established along with the Center for African American Studies, Chicano Studies Re-search Center, and American Indian Studies Center, culminating many months of protest by mostly students of color. The first Asian American studies class, "Orientals in America," had just been offered in the spring of '69. Taking that class as a senior had a profound effect—I can even say it saved me—for it was the first UCLA course that truly spoke to me. With historian and activist Yuji Ichioka as our instructor, "Orientals in America" was an exciting, often rowdy, standing-room-only series of lec-tures, panels, and guest speakers. Yuji is now credited with coining the term *Asian American*, but in that first class the term *Oriental* was still in our vocabulary.

That same quarter I took a sociology course, "Ethnic and Status Groups in America," which complemented "Orientals in America." Our re-quired reading included *Black Power: The Politics of Liberation in America*, by Stokely Carmichael (later known as Kwame Ture) and Charles Hamilton. Inspiration and vision seemed to be at our fingertips. We were quoting Frantz Fanon's *The Wretched of the Earth*, Eldridge Cleaver's *Soul on Ice*, and, of course, *The Autobiography of Malcolm X.* We were devouring the new Asian American monthly newspaper *Gidra*, joining sit-ins and coalitions, holding conferences, demonstrating against the war, crowding to hear leaders like Angela Davis, who'd just been hired (and later fired) by UCLA.

In "Orientals in America" we learned about a historical legacy of racism against Asian Americans and formed a perspective that promoted working-class and multiethnic solidarity as well as support for international struggles against imperialism. We made connections between racism practiced by the military in the killing of Vietnamese civilians and the racism Asian American soldiers faced for looking like "the enemy." We realized that exclusionary laws against Chinese immigration were part of the same anti-Asian legal restrictions against Japanese immigrants buying land or anti-miscegenation legislation against Pilipinos. It didn't matter if we were Chinese, Korean, Pilipino, or Japanese—we were all subject to a longstanding yellow peril mentality. Karl Yoneda, a longshoreman from the San Francisco area, spoke to our 150-plus class about labor movements and the recurring exploitation of Asian immigrant workers. He reminded us "to recognize and remember that our Yellow heritage is beautiful as is that of Blacks and Browns."

2. With Raised Fists

"Say it loud—I'm Black and I'm proud."—James Brown, 1968

"Yellow Power must become a revolutionary force."
—Larry Kubota, *Gidra*, 1969

"It is a question of the Third World starting a new history of man."
—Franz Fanon, *The Wretched of the Earth*

I wrote "The Emergence of Yellow Power in America" to satisfy the final course requirements for both "Orientals in America" and "Ethnic and Status Groups in America." Between *Gidra*, Stokely's book, census data, the UCLA Powell Library (when we still had to use card files), and random class notes, I pieced together a typically rushed student essay that I never guessed would still be quoted today. Looking back, I realize it took someone young, idealistic, and ignorant to how little I really knew to write a term paper making the types of claims I did. But that was the tenor of those times. Week by week, we were picking up new ideas and developing a radical political analysis. Our angry and impassioned conviction that we were fighting for justice made us eager to "spread the word." Mike Murase published my paper in *Gidra* in October 1969, and the *Los Angeles Free Press* reprinted it soon after. That same month the new UCLA Asian American Studies Center hired me based on my article.

The term "yellow power" was a popular phrase in those early days of our movement. Larry Kubota wrote a piece titled "Yellow Power" in the inaugural April issue of *Gidra*. "Brown power" and "red power" were also frequently seen on march banners and in activist writings. The demand for "black power" was first raised by Stokely Carmichael and Willie Ricks of the Student Nonviolent Coordinating Committee (SNCC), and in a 1966 speech, Carmichael said, "What we gonna start sayin' now is Black Power!" Of course, it quickly became a byword and soon other nonwhite activists were bringing parallel calls into our own communities.

One of the key points I made in my 1969 yellow power paper was the difference between the potential voting strength of blacks and Asian Americans because of our being, at that time, a mere one half of one percent of the population. The nascent Asian American movement could not have predicted how much our population would jump, with the 2010 census showing 5.6 percent identifying as Asian either alone or in combination with one or more races. In round numbers, we went from 1.5 million in 1970 to over 15 million in 2010. Astounding growth, through steady immigration, with Asian American demographics going from mainly Japanese, Chinese, and Pilipino to Chinese, Pilipino, Korean, Indian, and nearly twenty other Asian and Pacific Islander groups.

In my own experience as a third-generation sansei, I've observed mind-boggling transformations in the ethnic profile of Los Angeles. Growing up in Sierra Madre in the late '50s and '60s, I recall nearby cities like San Marino and Arcadia being lily-white; now Chinese are the majority in those towns. According to a 2013 report by Asian Americans Advancing Justice, Los Angeles County is the "capital" of Asian America and home to the largest numbers of such groups as Koreans, Burmese, and Thais outside their home countries. Clearly, this is not the Los Angeles I knew. Based on our larger numbers, I see a profound difference in the way Asian Americans are treated and, more important, in the way we look at ourselves. Now we do have the voting clout that can decide elections—particularly in metropolitan areas around San Francisco, Los Angeles, San Jose, and New York City. After the 2012 presidential election, Stewart Kwoh, who heads the Asian Pacific American Legal Center (APALC), stated, "The Asian-American vote is becoming more important. We are the fastest growing racial group from 2000–2010, there are over 18 million in the U.S. now."

My yellow power article also discussed economic disparities within the Asian America of the late sixties. Many of us activists were from middle-class and working families, but we were concerned about unaddressed poverty, drug use, and delinquency in our communities and, inspired by the example of the Black Panthers in Oakland, tried to develop our own Serve the People programs. The so-called "successful" Asian American image continues to be reflected in higher incomes and educational levels, particularly for Chinese and Indians, but a less known fact is that Koreans, Thais, Cambodians, and Hmong have lower median earnings than the general population. Without access to data, I wrote in my student paper about "continuing racial discrimination toward yellows in upper-wage level and high-status positions." The glass ceiling that we knew existed has not changed significantly; despite our incredible educational attainment, there are still few Asian American executives, college presidents, and managers in a society that only allows us to rise so far, held beneath what some term the "bamboo" ceiling.

Asian American activists of my era rejected the image of the "silent, passive Oriental." We repudiated the stereotype the majority culture cast on us but were also critical of the "Uncle Tomism" we sometimes saw in our own communities. If I were to change one thing in my yellow power paper (and there are many areas I could revise), it is in my discussion of the supposedly quiet, fearful Asian American. We have suffered centuries of racial injustice in this society, and like other people of color, we have responded with courage, self-respect, and resistance. As early Asian American studies began to uncover our histories, both past and current, we were seeing case after case of Asians speaking out and fighting back. Pilipinos who helped to build the United Farm Workers. Young Nisei in concentration camps, the "no-no" boys, who were jailed for refusing to join the military and swear allegiance to the U.S. Chinese railroad workers who went on strike in the 1800s. Issei communists who played crucial roles in the West Coast workers movement. Coalitions between Chinese, Pilipino, and Japanese communities in Seattle to fight bills that would make interracial marriage illegal. Of course, none of this was covered in our history textbooks—we had to dig up this info ourselves. It became clear that we and other minorities have to write our true histories.

3. Gettin' It Done Collectively

"This isn't one of those blonds that anyone can pick up in a supermarket."
—Title to the preface of *Asian Women*, U.C. Berkeley, 1971

"These are critical times for Asian Americans and it is imperative that their
voices be heard in all their anger, anguish, resolve and inspiration."
—Franklin Odo, preface to *Roots: An Asian American Reader*, UCLA, 1971

As Asian American ethnic studies programs began appearing on college campuses, particularly in California and the East Coast, there were few books or articles that could be used in our classes. To fill the gap, two of the earliest publications were published in 1971 by Asian American activists at Cal and UCLA. Both books utilized existing historical articles along with new pieces on contemporary issues, interviews of community leaders, photos, and poetry.

At U.C. Berkeley, a women's collective put out *Asian Women*. A remarkable compilation of writings about Asian women both here and overseas, it reflected the broad internationalist perspective so many of us were embracing, including coverage of the 1971 Indochinese Women's Conference in Vancouver and essays on Arab and Iranian women.

In those infant years of Asian American studies, we enjoyed a certain level of freedom in how we developed our classes and programs. I was on the UCLA staff from 1969 to 1974 and did everything from being a teaching assistant to developing new courses, organizing students, and coordinating center publications. *Roots: An Asian American Reader* grew from two volumes of mimeographed articles we'd stapled together for our classes in 1970. We needed a textbook, so an editorial team consisting of Franklin Odo, Eddie Wong, Buck Wong, and myself (under my then married name, Tachiki) produced *Roots*. Our intent was to provide an eclectic collection of existing articles, movement documents (such as the twelve-point platform of I Wor Kuen), and new interviews, as well as a survey of existing Asian American literature of that time. We included poems by writers like Al Robles as well as by students. *Roots* was a collective effort of center staff and students—editors, designers, photographers, typists, and a distribution team. I recall weeks of typing up text on IBM Selectric typewriters, then laying out the articles, photos, poems, and documents on white pasteboard. Long before computers or copy machines were standard college office equipment, we were using carbon paper so we would have a duplicate. Published in 1971, *Roots* went through twelve printings and eventually sold about fifty thousand copies for the UCLA Asian American Studies Center.

It is gratifying to see how much the field of Asian American studies has flourished. According to Cathy Schlund-Vials, 2017 President of the Association for Asian American Studies, programs and departments exist at over forty colleges. Masters and doctoral dissertations related to Asian American studies or work focused on aspects of Asian America number in the tens of thousands.

When I was in high school, there was no mention of American concentration camps in my textbooks. Now there are not only history books but biographies, novels, plays, children's stories, and memoirs about the incarceration. Brian Niiya, staff member of Densho: The Japanese American Legacy Project, estimated in 2016 that camp publications number around five hundred (with this total not including films, museum exhibitions, or scholarly articles and papers). Back in 1965, my Pasadena High classmates in a twelfth-grade civics class would not believe me when I told them my parents and grandparents were sent to the camps after Pearl Harbor. Now books like *Farewell to Manzanar* appear on required reading lists. And recently, my eight-year-old yonsei grandson told me his class celebrated January 30, Fred Korematsu Day, with an all-grades assembly.

4. Aiiieeeee and More

"Think Yellow! . . . with liberty or chopsticks for all."
—Lawson Fusao Inada, *Before the War*

"As a poet I've followed the footprints of the manongs."
—Al Robles, *Rappin' with Ten Thousand Carabaos in the Dark*

"If you cut my yellow fists, I'll teach my yellow toes to write."
—Marilyn Chin, *Rhapsody in Plain Yellow*

My first experience with Asian American poetry traces back to those early movement days. Every issue of *Gidra* included poems by young activists. In "Making the Case for Asian American Poetry," Timothy Yu says, "I find that there's no more engaging way to outline a history of the Asian American movement than to track its development through poetry." When I wrote my yellow power paper, I included three poems at the end, which for me did a better job of expressing all I was going through than a dry, footnoted essay. Mike Murase published the poems in *Gidra* in August 1969. One of the poems criticized racism toward blacks within the Asian American community. Another talked about the danger of assimilating too much, which I likened to a form of suicide. Since these early efforts, I continue to find myself expressing political concerns through poetry.

My movement involvement tapered off in the late 1970s. Teaching high school math and raising a son as a single working mom took most of my time. But I was still writing poems, off and on, and in the mid-80s began serious poetry study with Zen poet Peter Levitt. My first book, *30 Miles from J-Town* (1992), was fueled largely by anger over the racist experiences shaping my youth in Sierra Madre, a small town east of Pasadena with only a handful of Asians and Mexicans. Being called "Jap" was all too familiar. One of the poems in *30 Miles* was based on the burning of a cross on our Jewish neighbors' front lawn. In another poem, I describe being kicked by a mounted New York City policeman during a 1973 protest against Nixon's bombing of Cambodia (with the closing line, "I have long black hair like the Cambodians").

The politics I formed in my early twenties shaped a worldview encompassing themes I continue to explore through verse—Asian American history and identity, with poems ranging from concentration camps to Vincent Chin, from sansei dances in the '60s to Jeremy Lin; and national and global issues, such as gun violence, failing public schools, the L.A. riots, homelessness, drone warfare. Some of my poems deal with distinctly Asian American women's themes, like double-eyelid surgery, mail-order brides, and World War II comfort women.

I am lucky to have experienced both the early years of the Asian American political movement and an ever-expanding Asian American literary movement of poets, novelists, playwrights, and more. One of my favorite authors is L.A. mystery writer Naomi Hirahara, who manages to incorporate Japanese American history and culture in all of her thrillers. Asian American writers who have had a profound effect on me are poets Lawson Fusao Inada, Janice Mirikitani, Al Robles, and playwright Momoko Iko, all of whose work can be traced back to those early movement years.

Artists and writers have always played key roles in political struggles. I recall how Lawson Fusao Inada talked to our "Introduction to Asian Americans" class in the early '70s; his poems fired us up in a way that even the most dynamic lecturer couldn't compete with. For many of us in the early Asian American movement, poetry was integral to our political education, or as activist-poet Amiri Baraka reminds us, "There is no depth to our education without art." Writers of color are the most important and exciting literary voices in today's culture. It's fitting that from 2015 to 2017, our national poet laureate was Juan Felipe Herrera, a son of Mexican migrant workers and veteran of the Chicano movement.

5. Only What We Can Carry

"Where is home? Country of betrayal."—Janice Mirikitani, *Shedding Silence*

"Yet no payment can make up for those lost years."—Ronald Reagan, presidential apology accompanying the passage of the 1988 Civil Liberties Act

In those early yellow power days, there were many sansei activists whose parents and grandparents didn't talk about the concentration camps. This was sometimes interpreted by us as being too silent or reflecting Japanese "gaman" (enduring the unbearable with dignity). But we soon came to realize that our imprisoned families constituted a small group of 120,000 with virtually no allies during that period of national hysteria. As Lawson Fusao Inada states so well in "The Legend of Protest" (from the larger poem "Legends from Camp"):

> *The F.B.I. swooped in early,*
> *taking our elders in the process—*
>
> *for "subversive" that and this.*
>
> *People ask: "Why didn't you protest?"*
> *Well you might say: "They had **hostages**."*

What's become evident in the past seventy-five years of camp research and public testimony is that there were many who protested and rioted, many who were labeled "troublemakers" and jailed at Tule Lake or deported to Japan, and there were resisters like Fred Korematsu, Minoru Yasui, and Gordon Hirabayashi, who were sent to prison when they defied evacuation orders and legally challenged the camps.

One of the most important outcomes of the Asian American movement was the 1988 Civil Liberties Act, which only resulted after a nationwide redress movement dating back to the late 1970s was able to put enough pressure on Congress to obtain a presidential apology and reparations to camp survivors. Many issei and nisei elders came forward to testify at the redress hearings. Activist Lillian Nakano remarked, "We just wanted Niseis to talk it out. And you know what? The more they did, the more angry they got."

Over the years, I've heard comments about how the camps are in the past and that Japanese Americans, including writers, need to move on. But when I do readings, I consciously try to include camp poems. According to Richard Reeves, author of the 2015 Los Angeles Times' bestseller *Infamy*, "If a few incidents of terrorism happen again, we could start to round up Muslims in great numbers as we did with the Japanese with no charges except for their religion, just as the Japanese had no charges except for the color of their skin and they looked like the enemy." In 2014 Supreme Court Judge Antonin Scalia discussed the *Korematsu v. United States* case before a University of Hawaii law school class and stated, "You are kidding if you think the same thing will not happen again."

The topic of the camps has remained in the national conversation, including a 2015 statement by then Republican presidential candidate Donald Trump that he might have supported the 1942 mass detention of Japanese Americans. Trump was immediately called out by actor George Takei, a nisei imprisoned as a boy in Rohwer, Arkansas.

Since the 2016 presidential election, we are already witnessing a disturbing rise in racist incidents and hate group propaganda. A Taiwanese Christian church in San Jose and a Korean Christian church in Oakland were both vandalized just weeks after Trump's election; swastikas were etched into glass at the San Jose church. And this past January a mosque in Texas was destroyed by fire. It's imperative that Asian American political groups, like the Nikkei for Civil Rights and Redress (NCRR), continue to speak out in public forums as the racial "spotlight" shifts to Muslim Americans and Latino immigrants. In December 2016, the Japanese American National Museum stated it "is dismayed by the latest remarks of President elect-Donald Trump that indicates he favors the creation of a registry for Muslim Americans." The Manzanar Committee asserts that "the Japanese American community, who had virtually no one to speak in our defense in 1942, has a moral responsibility to speak out now. . . . We cannot and will not allow this to happen to anyone else ever again."

6. *#Asians4BlackLives*

"I think it is very, very important that folks understand how much this country was founded on the enslavement of blacks, and how the resistance of blacks to that enslavement has been the spark plug for so many important developments."
—Grace Lee Boggs, from a 2014 Guernica interview

"Yellow peril supports black power"
—slogan on 1968 poster at Oakland rally supporting Huey Newton

In late 2015, I saw the Stanley Nelson documentary, *The Black Panthers: Vanguard of the Revolution*, which brought back memories of those beautiful young African American activists who inspired so many here and around the world. I saw this film in the same year that police killed over one hundred unarmed blacks, including the more well-known murders of Freddie Gray, Eric Garner, and Walter Scott. The film *Straight Outta Compton*, also released in 2015, depicts police brutality against young black men on the streets of Los Angeles in the '90s. In spite of our recently having Barack Obama as president (an event that many of us never imagined could occur in our lifetimes), the continuing violence of police against people of color feels like the same ol' same ol'. Only now witnesses to the crimes can capture it on their smartphones.

The Black Panthers and black power ideology provided the young Asian American movement both inspiration and direction. In "The Oriental as a 'Middleman Minority,'" (*Gidra*, May 1969), activist Alan Nishio cautioned us against being "yellow Uncle Toms" and being used by the Establishment as "an example to be followed." It's no accident that "model minority" articles about Chinese and Japanese Americans began to emerge in the mid-60s when civil rights and minority movements were becoming increasingly militant.

We were trying to dissuade members of our communities from buying into the model minority myth. In my yellow power paper, I wrote that "Asian Americans are perpetuating white racism in the United States as they allow white America to hold up the 'successful' Oriental image before other minority groups as the model to emulate." Asian Americans continue to be falsely propped up as a model minority, and too many Asian Americans don't understand how this is inherently racist and divisive. In the early movement days, we realized there needed to be more educational work within our own communities. That need is more critical than ever for the Asian Americans who are not familiar with the civil rights struggles and achievements of the sixties.

Nearly five decades later, the debate still goes on regarding our being a model minority. In a 2015 *Huffington Post* article, "What Asian Americans Owe African Americans," Christopher Punongbayan acknowledges the crucial role the African American–led civil rights movement played in improving conditions for all minorities; he argues that "Asian Americans must stand as allies to the Black Lives Matter movement." I was happy to read his stirring editorial, only to read scores of comments from Asian Americans saying that we don't owe anybody and got where we are through our own hard work. Echoes of S. I. Hayakawa.

In 2012 #BlackLivesMatter arose after the acquittal of George Zimmerman, who fatally shot seventeen-year-old Trayvon Martin. With over twenty chapters across the country, Black Lives Matter may be the springboard for a postmillennial black liberation movement. It is heartening to see social media blogs like APIs 4 Black Lives, which is designed to help Asian Americans and Pacific Islanders learn more about the Black Lives Matter movement. Or to read articles like Hannah Wang's "Black Panther, Yellow Dragon: Why Asians Need to Care about Ferguson" (*The Other*, social justice blog). Wang clearly shows an understanding of early yellow power advocates as she describes how they "stood with the black civil rights movement because they saw their causes, while differently colored, as fundamentally the same."

In a 2014 *Time* magazine opinion piece, "Why Ferguson Should Matter to Asian-Americans," Jack Linshi draws parallels between Michael Brown's death and the less reported police shootings with no criminal charges of Kuanchang Kao in 1997, Cau Bich Tran in 2003, and Fong Lee, a Hmong American, in 2006. When Vincent Chin was beaten to death by Detroit autoworkers in 1982, his killers never went to jail. Chin's story was widely publicized because of the massive mobilization that took place in Asian American communities after his murder.

Annie Tan, a niece of Vincent Chin, has criticized the large Chinese American protests that took place in February 2016 for New York City police officer Peter Liang. Liang shot an unarmed African American, Akai Gurley, with his gun discharging and the bullet ricocheting off a wall. Liang's supporters feel Gurley's death was accidental and argue that white NYC police involved in similar shootings do not get charged, but they seem to ignore the fact that Liang failed to give medical treatment to Gurley or call for an ambulance. Tan rejects the protesters' comparison of Liang to her Uncle Vincent and urges Asian Americans to "fight for the justice Akai Gurley and his family deserve."

The Asian American community debated the Liang case for many months, and in April 2016 Liang was sentenced to probation and community service with no jail time. Certain aspects of this event remind me of the 1991 murder of a fifteen-year-old African American, Latasha Harlins, by Korean store owner Soon Ja Du. Du was fined $500 and assigned probation and community service, but like Liang, she served no time in prison for the killing. The L.A. Asian American community was divided about whether Du deserved its support. I even wrote a poem about young Harlins being shot in the back over a carton of orange juice and received strong criticism from some Korean American students at U.C. Irvine, who felt Du was a victim. Both the Du and Liang controversies are much more complicated than can be detailed here, but there is an obvious need for increased political dialogue and awareness within our own communities and a willingness to confront those with racist attitudes toward blacks and other minorities. In a 2015 *Truthdig* post, journalist Sonali Kolhatkar urged, "Asians can begin by admitting that we have a problem with racism in our communities."

Shortly after the Liang demonstrations, Jay Kang wrote in the *New York Times Magazine* that despite some legitimate concerns of the thousands who marched, "the first massive, nationwide Asian-American protest in years was held in defense of a police officer who shot and killed an innocent black man." OiYan Poon, in a 2016 *Angry Asian Man* blog, asked, "What is it about Peter Liang and his conviction that is riling up a previously, generally politically apathetic population? Where were they when NYPD officers unjustly beat up 84-year-old Kang Chun Wong for jaywalking in New York City Chinatown?" I agree with younger Asian American activists like Soya Jung, who in "Igniting a Model Minority Mutiny" stated: "The Asian American movement formed to expand our collective capacity to identify and empathize not just with those who look like us, but perhaps more significantly, with those who don't look like us but who share our visions and dreams of liberation. Being Asian American means empathizing with the families of Latasha Harlins and Akai Gurley as much as we do with the families of Vincent Chin, Fong Lee, Balbir Singh Sodhi, and so many others."

In 2015, a website called Angry Asian Girls United sold shirts and hoodies that say, "Yellow Peril Supports Black Power." This slogan was photographed back in 1968 at an Oakland political rally to free Huey Newton. In the photo, the protestors include a Black Panther, two Brown Berets, and two members of the Asian American Political Alliance (AAPA), one of them holding the "Yellow Peril Supports Black Power" sign. Interestingly, this image has received recent play on social media, and in a 2015 *Huffington Post* blog, Dan Truong observed that since Ferguson, the phrase is reappearing at demonstrations against police violence.

In the past when I've heard people discuss yellow power and the Asian American movement, it has often been cast as old history and not having much relevance today. But my 1969 college essay on yellow power still gets discussed. And lately I am able to find articles, blogs, and videos on the Internet that show a growing number of younger Asian Americans voicing their anger. I'm certain that terms like "yellow peril" and "yellow power" still ring true to many who know that racism against Asian Americans persists in varying degrees—much as it did when I was young—and on a broader scale, racism against minorities is prevalent in spite of civil rights policies, voting rights acts, Obama being a two-term president, the impact of rap and hip hop music on our culture, and the seemingly higher visibility of blacks on the screen and in professional sports. Jamala Rogers, author of *Ferguson Is America: Roots of Rebellion*, says that "the same conditions that the [1968] Kerner Report found in their report—you know, poor education, lack of resources, unemployment, a racist media—all those ingredients are being stirred up right here in Ferguson, and all across the urban centers of America."

One of the images associated with the black power movement is the raised fist. When we compiled documents for *Roots* back in the early '70s, we included "Raisin' the fist" from the *Hawaii Free People's Press*. It captured what so many of us still feel—"Many people have asked what the fist symbolizes . . . . The fist stands for all the people sticking together— together tight like a fist. It means all power to the people." In 1968–1969 the Third World Liberation Front (TWLF) at San Francisco State and U.C. Berkeley was in the forefront of fighting for ethnic studies. TWLF brought together African American, Native American, Chicano, and Asian American students.

The idea of nonwhites working together alongside other progressive groups continues to be an essential strategy for bringing about change. Lessons learned fifty years ago remain true. Fighting for equality still involves marches, rallies, demonstrations with both raised fists and peace signs, and civil disobedience. In 2015 Vigilant Love, a community vigil against violence and Islamophobia, was held in Little Tokyo just days after the December San Bernardino mass shooting. This diverse coalition of ethnic and religious groups, numbering 350, included Christian, Jewish, Muslim, and Buddhist leaders. The rally was held in front of the Nishi Hongwanji building, where hundreds of Japanese Americans were lined up and taken away to camp in 1942. Organizer Kathy Masaoka spoke about not letting history repeat: "Time and again, we witnessed the questioning of the American Muslim community's loyalty just as the Japanese Americans' was in question."

It gives me hope to see a grassroots movement like Black Lives Matter gaining momentum. I'm encouraged as I consider events like Vigilant Love, the Occupy Wall Street movement, an outpouring of support for Democratic presidential candidate Bernie Sanders, months of resistance at Standing Rock, the massive women's march the day after Trump's inauguration, and ongoing spontaneous nationwide protests against Trump policies—all reminiscent of the broad-based coalitions of the sixties. Activist Eddie Wong, who was a coeditor of *Roots*, recently observed "that one significant outcome of the Obama years was proof of concept that a diverse, multi-national coalition powered by the democratic aspirations of the

African American, Latino and API masses in alliance with progressive whites could win presidential elections."

We may be witnessing the beginnings of large-scale organized resistance that harkens back to '60s civil rights struggles and reflects both the high-tech, social media culture we've become and the complex post-9/11 global reality we live in. While leaflets and protest signs are still political organizing essentials, now we have the Internet, cell phones, and social networks to help us communicate and quickly mobilize more people. As a new political movement shows signs of emerging, what role will Asian Americans play? Or, as the Pete Seeger union protest song asks, "Which side are you on?" In addition to existing economic and political inequities, minorities, as well as the majority of Americans, face dramatic and dangerous setbacks under Trump. For people of color, in particular, there are immediate and growing threats to civil rights and legal justice. The demand for black, brown, red, and yellow power—twenty-first-century style—is as urgent as ever.

> "We're gonna fight racism with solidarity."
> —Fred Hampton

> "We are winning because ours is a revolution of mind and heart."
> —Cesar Chavez

> "And I am America's conscience. And that's what they don't want to look at."
> —Russell Means

> "I think there are so many issues that all people of color should
> come together on."
> —Yuri Kochiyama

CHAPTER 2

Has Asian American Studies Failed?

Timothy Yu

Has Asian American studies failed?

That was the question I asked myself in December 2011, after reading a review in the *New York Times* of a new learning center at Heart Mountain, one of the camps where Japanese Americans were interned during World War II. In the midst of praise for the center, the review takes a surprising detour toward historical revisionism. Responding to "the explanation, now standard, that they were a result of wartime hysteria and racism," the author, Edward Rothstein, argues that internment was "more the rule than the exception" and was applied to other ethnic groups as well. Japan was "a racist, militant society" and "a number of Japanese-American organizations on the West Coast . . . were financially and ideologically devoted to the mother country and its policies." Finally, "the Japanese were known for similar espionage elsewhere." Rothstein concludes that although the internment was "racially tinged," "the context demonstrates that the relocation was a response—an extreme one—to a problem."[1]

As I sit down to write this, almost six years later, such defenses of internment have reached the national political scene. In November 2015, as numerous American politicians announced their opposition to accepting refugees from Syria, Mayor David A. Bowers of Roanoke, Virginia, issued a statement citing the internment of Japanese Americans as a precedent for turning away Syrian refugees. "I'm reminded that President Franklin D. Roosevelt felt compelled to sequester Japanese foreign nationals after the bombing of Pearl Harbor," Bowers wrote, "and it appears that the threat of harm to America from ISIS now is just as real and serious as that from our enemies then."[2] Although Bowers apologized for his statement several days later, its reverberations reached the presidential campaign. When Donald Trump, who had called for banning the entry of all Muslims to the United States, was asked repeatedly by a *Time* reporter whether the internment was wrong, he refused to answer, replying only that "I would have had to be there at the time to tell you."[3] New Hampshire state representative Al Baldasaro, a cochair of Trump's New Hampshire campaign, was far less circumspect, telling John DiStaso of WMUR that Trump's ban on Muslims was "100 percent right" and explicitly comparing it to internment: "What he's saying is no different than the situation during World War II, when we put the Japanese in camps."[4]

Such views of Japanese American interment—that it was merely a product of military necessity, that Japanese Americans represented a legitimate threat, that there were substantial reasons to doubt the "loyalty" of Japanese Americans—are, of course, the very views that were originally used to justify the internment. And they are the very views that have been thoroughly debunked by historians of Asian America, who have helped establish what Rothstein calls the now "standard" view of the camps as a product of racism. This knowledge that the camps were a racist injustice was the direct product of decades of struggle by Japanese Americans and other Asian American activists to force the U.S. government, and the nation in general, to acknowledge the injustice of internment. In the course of that struggle, the experience of internment became one of the foundational narratives of the Asian American experience. Every major history of Asian Americans takes internment as one of its centerpieces, and any student who has spent five minutes in an Asian American studies classroom should know the history of internment. So how could it be, I wondered, that everyone from *New York Times* reporters to elected officials from both parties could reject the message that internment was wrong?

The question I asked myself—and then asked aloud on my blog—was whether this ignorance of the most basic facts of Asian American history could be seen as a failure of Asian American studies.[5] Had our field had so little impact on public consciousness? Had it failed in its task of giving Asian Americans a place in the American story?

My question sparked a surprisingly strong response, and the discussion that followed included Asian American activists, bloggers, and students as well as academics. It led to a forum in the *Journal of Asian American Studies* and to a standing-room-only panel at the Association for Asian American Studies annual conference.[6] My provocation, it seemed, had spoken to a set of ongoing anxieties within our field but also to our field's largest ambitions. For of course, to ask whether Asian American studies has failed is to ask what the goals of Asian American studies are in the first place.

As the conversation went on, I realized that my question was not the traditional concern that Asian American studies had abandoned its roots in serving Asian American communities. Instead, my concern was an outward-looking one: Was Asian American studies doing enough to project its knowledge to a wider public, to reshape American discourses about race? While it seems at times that Americans like nothing more than to talk *about* Asians, Asian Americans are still rarely *heard* in such discussions. There thus seemed to be a disconnect between the substantial institutional successes of Asian American studies over the past several decades and the impact its practitioners have had in the wider public sphere. What I wanted was a more public practice of Asian American studies, one in which the insights of our field would not exist merely on the margins of political discourse but could be brought to bear on the most central political questions.

In my blog post, I offered several suggestions for how we might advance a more public Asian American studies:

Popularize the insights of our field for a wider audience
Look outward toward "mainstream" audiences
Advocacy: rapid response to public controversies involving Asian
    Americans
Cultivate public intellectuals among the ranks of Asian Americanists

Asian Americanists, of course, have been doing all of these things for years, but how, if at all, could we amplify these efforts, expanding the space for practitioners of Asian American studies to intervene in public discourse?

Whether something was already changing, or whether I simply began noticing things I hadn't before, I can't say, but in the wake of my initial observations, I thought I did begin to see more evidence of voices from Asian American studies making their way into public and political discourse. In particular, I want to highlight several events in the past few years where Asian Americans emerged, perhaps unexpectedly, at the center of public debates or controversies. In some ways, these incidents show that Asian American studies has had an impact on the public sphere but not necessarily in predictable ways. I want to emphasize two elements of these events: first, the impact of generational change on how Asian American studies influences the wider world; and second, the role of media, both traditional and digital, in linking Asian American studies to the public.

The first phenomenon was the unprecedented rise of Jeremy Lin as the first Asian American basketball superstar in 2012, which put Asian Americans at the center not just of the sports world but—for a moment at least—at the center of American popular culture. "Linsanity" became a national, even an international, phenomenon. Race was not incidental to this phenomenon but central to it, as the novelty of an Asian American star in a sport dominated by African Americans became the main storyline. Lin was hailed as a breakthrough figure, even as he was also dismissed by some as a "flash in the pan" and also, of course, made the target of racist jokes. To many Asian Americans, he became a hero, perhaps the most significant icon of Asian American masculinity since Bruce Lee.

One thing that struck me at the time was that some Asian Americanists didn't seem to take Linsanity very seriously. Asian American obsession with Linsanity seemed to concentrate among scholars and writers in their thirties and forties, who filled social media and the blogosphere with Lin-centric posts. Linsanity briefly opened up a space, indeed a hunger, for commentary on Asian Americans in the national media. And I think it's no accident that the academics who were able to jump into that space—Oliver Wang in the *LA Times*, erin Khuê Ninh for ESPN.com, myself for CNN.com—were either former journalists or bloggers. The ability to move between academic and popular audiences, and above all to respond quickly to current events, may be a kind of cross-training that many younger academics have and that even more could benefit from.

I want to touch on just one other element of Linsanity, which is the debate over how to label Lin and how Lin himself intervened in that debate. The media initially described Lin primarily as "Chinese American," but as reporters realized that Lin's parents had immigrated from Taiwan, they almost universally adopted a rather awkward phrasing, calling Lin "the first Chinese or Taiwanese American player in the NBA." The debate over how to label Lin was almost always framed in geopolitical terms, with articles referencing battles over Taiwanese sovereignty and the competing attempts of fans and journalists in both Taiwan and mainland China to claim Lin as a native son. For an Asian Americanist, of course, the problem here is almost too obvious to note: It's the myth of the perpetual foreigner, the idea that Lin "belonged" to one or the other of these ancestral origins rather than being American.

Lin himself has been diplomatic in responding to such discussions, nodding to both his Chinese ancestry and his parents' immigration from Taiwan. But Lin more frequently, and much more naturally, refers to himself simply as "Asian American." As Howard Beck of the *New York Times* reported, Lin was asked during a 2012 All-Star Weekend press conference about whether his ethnicity had caused him to be overlooked earlier in his career. Lin replied: "I think just being Asian American, obviously when you look at me, I'm going to have to prove myself more so, again and again and again. . . . But I think that's fine. It's something that I embrace, and it gives me a chip on my shoulder. But I'm very proud to be Asian American and I love it."[7]

I think it's important that Lin didn't say here what he easily could have said, which was "Perhaps I was overlooked, but now I want people just to see me as a basketball player, not an Asian American basketball player." He declined the universalizing or postracial move in favor of racial pride. And the identity he chose was not "Chinese American" or "Taiwanese American" but the pan-ethnic, racialized category of "Asian American." I want to point to this moment as a moment of success. Asian American studies, and the Asian American movement of which it is a part, has indeed succeeded in educating a generation for whom the self-identification "Asian American" comes naturally. Lin's Asian American identifications go well beyond mere naming; as media scholar Lori Kido Lopez notes, Lin is also an active participant in the Asian American online universe, making a series of videos with Asian American YouTube superstar KevJumba.[8]

I make this point as a way of counterbalancing our disciplinary inclination toward a relentless deconstruction of the term "Asian American." At least since Lisa Lowe's groundbreaking *Immigrant Acts*, we have sought to show how the category "Asian American" is internally divided, hybrid, and unstable.[9] Our embrace of transnational and diasporic frameworks has further challenged the category's boundaries. Kandice Chuh's widely cited theorization of Asian American studies in *Imagine Otherwise* as a "subjectless discourse" may make us wonder what remains to ground our discipline.[10] It's useful to remind ourselves, then, that "Asian American" still functions as a powerful point of identification, particularly for young people. That identification does not have to be understood as a monolithic one. It doesn't prevent Lin from embracing his global role as a basketball ambassador to Taiwan and China. Nor does it prevent my own students, who are passionately advocating for a strengthening of Asian American studies, from simultaneously demanding ethnic-specific classes in Chinese, Vietnamese, and Hmong diasporic studies. We should ask ourselves whether what I see as an increasing theoretical allergy to the term "Asian American" really speaks to the expansive and flexible ways young Asian Americans are using it.

The second event I want to touch on briefly is the 2014 debate in California over SCA 5, a bill that would partially reverse the ban on affirmative action at public colleges and universities enacted by Proposition 209 in 1996. After SCA 5 passed the state senate, it became the subject of heated debate. It wasn't surprising that the debate featured divisive racial politics, but rather than pitting whites against people of color, much of the national media coverage of the debate focused on the role of Asian Americans in the debate.

Many of the headlines I was seeing proclaimed that "Asian American groups" were leading the opposition to SCA 5. As many of my colleagues pointed out, this flew in the face of survey data indicating that affirmative action enjoyed something like 60–70 percent support among Asian Americans. Closer examination revealed that the "Asian American" opposition to SCA 5 was dominated by a few Chinese American groups, while numerous other Asian American groups were lining up in support of the measure. Yet the narrative was firmly established, and "Asian American opposition" came to be seen as the primary reason for the bill's eventual withdrawal from consideration in the state assembly.

How, if at all, was Asian American studies invoked in this debate, and how did Asian Americanists intervene? As Asian American activists and bloggers sought to rally support for SCA 5, they cited academic research showing the benefits of diversity for Asian American students and illustrating persistent inequities in higher education. Veteran blogger Jenn Fang of *Reappropriate* was particularly active in creating a clearinghouse for pro–affirmative action information.[11] And there were a few examples of direct interventions by Asian Americanists themselves. Political scientist Karthick Ramakrishnan published an op-ed in the *LA Times* on March 7 calling for an end to "a debate based on fear."[12] Several days later, the blog *Angry Asian Man* featured a blistering attack on the "hate, fear, and lies" of the SCA 5 opposition by OiYan Poon, who has worked extensively on issues around Asian Americans and college admissions.[13] Poon also spearheaded the use of the hashtag #NoLiesNoHate on Twitter as a way of rallying support for SCA 5, particularly among Asian Americans.

Poon's intervention may suggest a new model of academic engagement with public debates. Her piece appeared not in a traditional media outlet but on a blog widely read by Asian Americans, and her extension of the campaign onto Twitter suggests the increasingly central role of social media in activism—a topic I'll touch on again in just a moment. The role of the medium is also reflected in the tone of Poon's piece for *Angry Asian Man*, which is far from a dispassionate academic discourse: It fearlessly calls out the "bullshit" of the "haters" of SCA 5 and boldly mixes analysis and advocacy. This example suggests an increasingly powerful network among younger Asian American scholars, activists, bloggers, and journalists, and it's one that may form a model for projecting Asian American studies more forcefully into the public sphere.

We should note, though, that this is not entirely a success story either. By the time Poon's post went up on March 10, the media was already reporting that the tide was turning against SCA 5, and it was pulled from consideration in the assembly a week later. One of the problems with attempts by scholars to intervene directly in public debates is that we often just can't move fast enough; scholarship takes time, of course, but we're also generally unused to producing copy on demand and lack obvious outlets to do such of-the-moment publishing. Poon's intervention happened at light speed by our usual standards, but are there things that our field can do, institutionally, to make it possible for Asian Americanists to respond even more rapidly on matters of public concern?

Of course, the fastest-moving discourse of all is now on social media, and Asian Americans have taken a prominent role in so-called Twitter or hashtag activism. In December 2013, #NotYourAsianSidekick began trending on Twitter, with thousands of posts from Asian Americans, particularly Asian American feminists, expressing frustration with their exclusion not only from mainstream discourse but from conversations about race and gender. While the hashtag attracted widespread media coverage, from the *Washington Post* to *Time* and *Salon*, it also attracted critique from within the Asian American activist community. An article by Kai Ma in *Time* cited a tweet by veteran activist Mari Matsuda: "We theorized #NotYourAsianSidekick ideas since the 70's but kids gotta learn it from a damn hashtag. Still no Asian Am Studies at most U's."[14] Matsuda's tweet explicitly contrasted the ephemeral "success" of a trending tweet with the institutional "failure" to nurture Asian American studies within higher education.

The topic heated up again when #CancelColbert sprung up in reaction to a joke made by Stephen Colbert of *The Colbert Report* referencing his fictional "Ching-Chong Ding-Dong Foundation." (Colbert was mocking attempts by the owner of Washington, DC's NFL team to placate Native American critics of his team's name.) Launched by Suey Park, who had also initiated #NotYourAsianSidekick, #CancelColbert proved far more divisive, drawing rebukes and even ridicule from white liberals and ambivalence from many Asian American writers and activists.

While I did see some academics participating in both hashtags and retweeting some of the most popular posts, with a few exceptions Asian Americanists did not get directly involved in these heated debates. What's curious is that although many of the terms that ran through both of these conversations—feminism, racism, colonialism, orientalism—are concepts central to our work, they were being used in ways that seemed relatively disconnected from academic discourse. The connection that Matsuda suggested—between activism and Asian American studies—seemed absent. Yet thousands of young Asian Americans participated passionately in these Twitter conversations, suggesting a deep unmet need in the discourse on race. While in the cases of Linsanity and SCA 5, academics were able to find ways of participating in media and policy discourses—with varying degrees of success—the minute-by-minute unfolding of a phenomenon like #CancelColbert represents the polar opposite of the deliberate pace of scholarship. The entire controversy erupted and was over within the course of less than a week, and few academics—few people, honestly—have the energy or stamina to engage in protracted Twitter warfare of the kind such conversations demand.

Is the "success" of #NotYourAsianSidekick and #CancelColbert a "failure" for our field? Let me suggest instead that it is a challenge. There is a large and growing population of young Asian Americans out there who we are not reaching. They live online, react quickly to media controversies, are familiar with terms like "microaggressions" and "white privilege." But we can't reach them all in our classrooms, certainly not without a lot more resources being devoted to Asian American studies across the country. Without stopping being scholars—without shortchanging the vital research that we do—how can we make the lessons of Asian American studies more available, more vital, for the people who most need them: young Asian Americans themselves? The examples I've described here offer a few possible guidelines: forming stronger networks among scholars, bloggers, journalists, and activists; responding more quickly and nimbly to fast-moving political and cultural events. Individuals are already doing this. Can we, as a discipline, more effectively support and strengthen such efforts, so that the vital work Asian American studies does is projected ever more effectively into the public sphere?

The last couple of years have, I think, offered some positive signs of progress toward a more public Asian American studies. The first development has been the rise of more organized efforts to gather and present the expertise of Asian Americanists in a way that can have a more visible impact on public discourse. I'm thinking in particular of Karthick Ramakrishnan's AAPI Data project, which has been gathering social science research and survey data on Asian Americans and presenting them in media-friendly infographics that can easily be picked up by reporters or that can form the basis for social media posts or longer op-eds.[15] One possible area of future work could be to see if such efforts can be expanded to include more disciplines within Asian American studies—an effort that would require coordination across our discipline, as well as some willingness on the part of scholars in various fields to think about how to popularize their work.

We have also been reminded recently that it's possible for a single book by an accomplished scholar or writer to have a significant impact on public discourse. We might think of past examples like Ronald Takaki's *Strangers from a Different Shore*, for many years both a standard textbook in Asian American history and a more widely read popular work, or Helen Zia's *Asian American Dreams*. Erika Lee's 2015 book *The Making of Asian America*, a wide-ranging new survey of Asian American history, attracted widespread media attention and reviews in the *New York Times* and the *New Yorker*.[16] (Perhaps just as significantly, these two reviews themselves were written by Asian American reviewers.) Lee's book, framed by her own family history, is grounded in the most recent scholarship but is also consciously aimed at a popular audience, and it seems to have been successful in reaching a wide audience and in providing its author with a platform to intervene in current political debates; Lee authored a widely circulated editorial in the *New York Daily News* schooling Donald Trump on the issue of birthright citizenship and highlighting the role of Asian Americans in the history of that issue.[17]

Finally, I think we have started to see some trend toward media outlets actually turning to Asian American scholars and authors when issues relevant to Asian Americans hit the news. A small example can be found in the recent controversy over a literary anthology, *The Best American Poetry 2015*. The anthology included a poem by an author named Yi-Fen Chou, who turned out to be a white author, Michael Derrick Hudson, claiming to have adopted this Chinese name to increase his chances of publication. The ensuing uproar was, remarkably enough, widely reported in national and international media. Although the initial conversation revolved around questions of pen names and "artistic freedom"—a conversation, moreover, dominated by white writers—the loud outrage of Asian American writers, particularly on social media, at Hudson's act of "yellowface" quickly shifted the focus of the discussion to racism.

My own social media response was to write a lengthy public Facebook post in which I humorously claimed to be the real author behind the fictitious "Michael Derrick Hudson," who remained unaware that he was not real. The post came to the attention of a reporter at *Slate* who interviewed me for a story she wrote on the controversy. I was subsequently interviewed by NBC, the *Guardian*, and the *Christian Science Monitor*, while poet and professor Victoria Chang was interviewed for a widely circulated article in the *Washington Post*.

While I've written more about the Yi-Fen Chou affair elsewhere, two aspects of the controversy seem particularly relevant here.[18] First, both Chang and I came to the attention of reporters through social media (Chang had criticized Hudson on Twitter), emphasizing the role of social media as a conduit between academic Asian American studies and mainstream media outlets. Second, both of us are creative writers in addition to being academics (Chang is a professor of creative writing, while I am primarily a scholar who also writes poetry), and the media often seems more willing to give space to Asian American creative writers than to Asian Americanist scholars. Since it is rare for writers (even Asian American writers) covering Asian American issues in the media to be familiar with scholarship in Asian American studies, a stronger social media presence by Asian Americanist scholars may help create links to mainstream media, as may the cultivation of "dual threat" Asian Americanists who can work in both scholarly and creative or popular genres.

In sum, I think there are many things we can do, both individually and collectively, to help rectify the "failure" of Asian American studies to have greater public impact. We can popularize the insights of our field; we can use both traditional and social media to increase connections between academic and mainstream discourses; we can consciously work to increase our collective capacity to intervene quickly and forcefully in public debates.

Returning to the examples with which I opened also reminds us that such public interventions are themselves deeply political. Contemporary apologies for Japanese American internment may at times be grounded in ignorance, but it is a willed ignorance, one that refuses to admit to the history of racism even in the face of "official" acceptance of the idea that the internment was racist. The few insights from Asian American studies and

Asian American experience that have made it into official history and public consciousness are far from secure in their place, and it must continue to be a goal of our field to establish a public space for the lessons of Asian American studies.

NOTES

1. Edward Rothstein, "The How of an Internment, but Not All the Whys," *New York Times*, December 9, 2011.

2. David A. Bowers, "David Bowers Statement on Syrian Refugees," *Roanoke Times*, November 18, 2015.

3. Michael Scherer, "Donald Trump Says He Might Have Supported Japanese Internment," *Time*, December 8, 2015.

4. John DiStaso, "State GOP Chairwoman Says Trump's Call to Ban Muslims from U.S. is 'Un-American,'" WMUR.com, December 7, 2015.

5. Timothy Yu, "Has Asian American Studies Failed?" Timpanyu.com, December 21, 2011.

6. Timothy Yu, "Has Asian American Studies Failed?" *Journal of Asian American Studies* 15, no. 3 (October 2012): 327–29.

7. Howard Beck, "Lin's New Challenge: Media Onslaught at All-Star Weekend," *New York Times*, February 24, 2012.

8. Lori Kido Lopez, part of the roundtable "Linsanity: Media, Culture, Masculinity," Association for Asian American Studies Conference, April 18, 2013.

9. Lisa Lowe, *Immigrant Acts: On Asian American Cultural Politics* (Durham, N.C.: Duke University Press, 1996).

10. Kandice Chuh, *Imagine Otherwise: On Asian Americanist Critique* (Durham, N.C.: Duke University Press, 2003).

11. Jenn Fang, "List of #AAPI Groups & Posts in Support of Affirmative Action and #SCA5," *Reappropriate*, March 12, 2014.

12. Karthick Ramakrishnan, "Affirmative Action at California Colleges: A Debate Based on Fear," *Los Angeles Times*, March 7, 2014.

13. OiYan Poon, "Hate, Fear, and Lies: How Anti-Affirmative Action Haters are Shoveling Bullsh*t about SCA5," *Angry Asian Man*, March 10, 2014.

14. Kai Ma, "#NotYourAsianSidekick Is Great. Now Can We Get Some Real Social Change?" *Time*, December 18, 2013.

15. Karthick Ramakrishnan, AAPI Data, http://aapidata.com/.

16. Erika Lee, *The Making of Asian America* (New York: Simon & Schuster, 2015).

17. Erika Lee, "A History Lesson for Donald Trump and His Supporters," *New York Daily News*, August 18, 2015.

18. Timothy Yu, "The Real Yi-Fen Chou: What a Fake Poet Taught Us about Actual Asian Poets," *Angry Asian Man*, November 10, 2015, http://blog.angryasianman.com/2015/11/the-real-yi-fen-chou-what-fake-asian .html. This piece, written for the blog *Angry Asian Man*, was itself an attempt to put into practice some of the ideas I am raising here.

CHAPTER 3

The Racial Studies Project: Asian American Studies and the Black Lives Matter Campus

Nitasha Sharma

What is the role of ethnic studies, and specifically Asian American studies, in student activism against the corporate university? Founded by student movements in the 1960s, African American studies, Asian American studies, Latina/o studies, and Native American studies were born of a political desire for representation in higher education that privileged community and demanded structural change. Today students in campuses across the nation from California State University, East Bay to the University of Missouri and Yale University continue to make demands of administrators.[1] But they want more than representation, a seat at the table, or the promise of assimilation offered through the rhetoric of "inclusion."

At my home institution of Northwestern University, just north of Chicago in Evanston, student activists have taken administrators to task for their discourse on "diversity" that has come, in students' views, with little change in the wealthy, white, hetero- and gender-normative, and sexist cultures they experience on campus. The national Black Lives Matter movement has catalyzed student activists on my campus to become involved in innumerable issues that I discuss, below. What has been singular about their protests and activities is that they cross identity-based lines to unite around specific concerns while drawing links across issues. The activities of campus activists have ignited my rethinking of the ethnic studies project—now segmented into autonomous identity-based areas of study (including Asian American studies) as a result of increasing institutionalization—in a more holistic manner more accurately termed the racial studies project.

This essay examines the role that a broader understanding of ethnic studies has played in recent student activism occurring on my campus, one of many elite universities facing such pressures. Campus leaders—mostly minority students and including many Black women—made numerous demands ranging from divestment in coal, private prisons, and Israel and Palestine to goals directly related to the Black Lives Matter movement. I initially wanted this essay to chart how the knowledge *we* impart in ethnic studies frames student leaders' understanding of campus politics. This line of thinking, however, ended up suggesting the opposite flow: that the subfields of ethnic studies should take cues from the intersectional and connective analyses that frame the demands of students. Their transnational, cross-racial, and issues-rather-than-identity-oriented frameworks suggest a unified racial studies project, rather than a growing commitment to the circumscribed subfields we are hired into as a result of increasing institutionalization. A collective racial studies approach (commonly called "ethnic studies") could prevent the co-optation of Asian American studies that results from our institutional recognition and diversity work within the neoliberal and corporate university.

Student Activism and the Institutional Formation of Ethnic Studies

In 1968, student strikers from the Black Student Union, with the support of the Third World Liberation Front, demanded the formation of an Ethnic Studies College that was created the following year at San Francisco State University—a college that has just waged a battle over budget cuts in 2016. Ethnic studies began that same year at the University of California Berkeley, which became my institutional home when I was a graduate student transplant fleeing the constraints of anthropology at another UC campus in the late 1990s. I found support as a student of comparative race studies and benefitted from graduate students who were politically oriented (the very things anthropology discouraged at the time) and the encouragement of faculty like Ronald Takaki and Evelyn Nakano Glenn—faculty whose hires were due to the earlier student strikes. Strikers' demands included "that, in the Fall of 1969, all applications of non-white students be accepted," that faculty "chosen by non-white people as their teacher, be retained in their position," and "that 50 faculty positions be appropriated to the School of Ethnic Studies, 20 of which would be for the Black Studies program."[2] Early activists appealed for a transformed educational structure.

Their actions led to the institutionalization of the subfields of ethnic studies, which have since evolved alongside one another, albeit with uneven success and access to resources. In some cases, they are housed together under an ethnic studies or American studies umbrella, as in the case of the College of Ethnic Studies at San Francisco State University. In other cases (such as my home institution), the subfields are independent or not (at) all present. Many campuses have no Native American or Indigenous studies programs.[3]

The original demands of the 1968 student strikers appear to have been met, with hundreds of ethnic studies departments and programs across the United States and rising (if unbalanced) numbers of nonwhite students and faculty. Each year, Northwestern and similar universities issue press releases that focus on "metrics" of excellence in diversity, meaning they provide race, class, and first generation student head counts that are to reflect a progressive stance in a global world. Northwestern University also boasts a team of "Diversity Leaders" and multiple task forces, while its website offers an impressive number of reports (excluding the more damning ones) written by innumerable committees. However, institutional recognition means that faculty across ethnic studies also face pressure to publish or perish, to serve on numerous committees, and to prove their irreplaceability to campus administrators. This can lead us away from the ethnic studies project of providing counter-hegemonic understandings of the operations of power as they have created and affected various racialized groups, including a critique of the very institutions we inhabit.

What, then, does the institutionalization of terms like *diversity* and the various ethnic studies subfields mean within our current academic climate? On the one hand, Asian Americans—and increasingly Asian international students—are touted as part of the "URM" or underrepresented minority student body demographics and constitute innumerable cultural and ethnic organizations. On the other hand, administrators and student services conflate Asian Americans with White students and provide few resources for helping them to contend with their specific experiences as racialized minorities. Administrators and fellow colleagues deny tenure to Asian American studies professors across the nation, many of them women. Yet, the Asian American Studies Program at Northwestern just won the right to grant a major in the field. This happened through the efforts of committed undergraduate students who undertook years of consciousness raising about the need for the major, distinguishing Asian American studies from Asian studies, compiling hundreds of signatures on petitions, and educating people about the field. This victory was in no small part due to timing: Student activists inspired by the Black Lives Matter movement demanded this change at a time when students were holding administrators accountable for racism on campus across the United States. Student activism helps counteract the corporatization of universities that push the professionalization of our fields and the institutionalization of Asian American studies.

A Seat at the Table? Disciplining Asian American Studies

> There's been much talk lately—at academic institutions, among religious groups, and within mainstream discourse—about creating space at the table: "the table" symbolizing access and inclusion into dominant society.
>
> Nyle Fort, "A Seat at the Table: Lupita Fever and American Pathology"

Asian American studies appears to be a healthy, even thriving subfield. We have growing numbers of programs across the United States and universities like Yale that have small numbers of Asian Americanists have been motivated to increase them. The Association for Asian American Studies (AAAS) is a vibrant and growing national association with international membership that hosts a first-rate annual conference with close to one thousand attendees. In addition, Asian American studies is a part of most university and college curricula. As significant are the scholars in our field whose research critically intervenes in debates about affirmative action and the causes and consequences of war, immigration, and settlement. Our scholarship provides alternative accounts and gives voice to silenced views of world history, racial capitalism, and global inequalities. Yet, with few exceptions, our scholarship is generally only read by those with an interest in Asians in the United States.

Notwithstanding program formations and academic reputations, the field remains vexed. Returning to Northwestern, with our approved major and our growing numbers of minors and majors (over thirty), the number of tenure track lines has—since I arrived over a decade ago—remained the same at just two full lines (we all have split appointments). Numbers may be one way to gauge the health of the field: numbers of tenured Asian

Americanists, numbers of Asian American students on campus, the number of programs and departments, numbers of majors and minors, our fiscal budgets, and so on. Yet if we move away from metrics and pressures to "get butts in seats" and prioritize the immeasurables—including our politics—that once motivated the ethnic studies project, we can see why, despite our "growth," Asian American studies maintains a sense of anxiety.

Crises are not new to our field: In 1998, the controversy surrounding the decision of the Association for Asian American Studies to rescind the Literary Book Award to Lois-Ann Yamanako, author of *Blu's Hanging*, made national headlines. Our annual conference features panels centered on crisis and reflection, including "Whither the Academic in Crisis" (2016) and "State of the Field: Asian American History" (2014). Panelists discuss precarity in the age of the corporate university and misunderstandings about Asian American studies (such as conflating it with Asian studies). There are panels on the struggle to fund and staff our programs and mentorship committees addressing the perils of earning tenure. "Crisis" is thus a central—albeit by no means predominant—thematic. When it leads to careful and committed reflection, this is one of our strengths. Our self-questioning and the precarious position of Asian Americanist scholars in the university allegorizes the uncertain racial positioning of Asian Americans in the United States. And this is something that cannot be measured but instead depends upon an analysis of our politics—the very task Asian Americanists are trained to undertake.

The disciplining, or creation of autonomous Asian American studies programs, suggests the health of our field. The subject matter, methods, and motives of our field are unique and they, along with the large number of Asian and Asian American students in higher education, affect our institutional location and direction. But our separate institutional development away from an ethnic studies formation that I am now terming "racial studies" suggested by the Black Student Union in 1968 partially accounts for our devaluation. Unlike other fields and particularly African American studies, Asian American studies has not garnered the respect, resources, or levels of autonomy it could in collaboration. More troubling, however, are the political and intellectual myopias that result from our shift away from cross-fertilization of knowledge production and teaching across ethnic studies.

Ethnic studies subfields are defined by identity groups. The mission statements of Asian American studies programs define their subject: "Asian-ancestry groups" (University of California, Berkeley), "Asian Americans in the United States" (University of Maryland), and "Asian and Pacific

Islander Americans" (California State University, Fullerton). Similarly, Black studies across the nation is described alternately as the study of "the global black experience" (Northwestern University), "the experiences of people of African descent in Black Atlantic societies" (Yale University), and "African descended people in America" (Arizona State University). However, unlike the robust theoretical contributions of African American studies on, for instance, race and colonialism that are widely read and shape our understanding of *all groups*, Asian American studies has yet to move beyond the study of Asian populations to be known for our overarching concepts such as diaspora and theories of immigration. I am not suggesting that the quality of our scholarship accounts for this insularity; rather Asian American studies, like Asians in the United States writ large, are generally not heard. How, then, can we more widely circulate our findings?

In 2003, Kandice Chuh articulated the limits of identity-based paradigms with a focus on Asian American studies and Gary Okihiro similarly urges us to move beyond population-based studies.[4] Yet, the development of distinct and autonomous ethnic studies subfields within colleges and universities further entrenches the study of identity-defined groups that limits both our intellectual contributions as well as the expansive political orientations that emerge through engagement across ethnic studies. The experiences of students within my two institutional locations (African American studies and Asian American studies) reveal the impacts of an identity-based and separate study of racialized groups on a university campus in the Black Lives Matter era.

Access/Tenure Denied: Asian American Studies and Black Lives Matter

Why I would want to sit in the same place and around the same people that excluded and inferiorized me, and those who look like me, for so long? I don't want a seat at a table that was built and is maintained in the interest of consolidating power for a privileged elite. I don't want a seat at the table of white supremacy, nor do I want to fellowship at the tables of patriarchal domination, religious homophobia, or economic inequality. The table *is* the problem, not me, not black women, not us. Inviting an "exceptional" few from a historically oppressed community to "the table" is not a sign of progress. It's hegemony masquerading as progress. Symbolism is not structural change. Symbolic gestures don't fundamentally change, let alone challenge, the system of evil that created the table in the first place. The table, itself, must be destroyed.

And we *will* destroy it. We will burn it to the ground with . . .
prophetic fire!
  Nyle Fort, "A Seat at the Table: Lupita Fever and American Pathology"

The strength of Black studies across the nation relative to other ethnic
studies subfields is signified in the number of autonomous PhD-granting
departments, the number of faculty, and a general understanding of and
engagement with Black studies on and off campus. This institutional recognition is an allegory for the position of Black people in the United States
as a (hyper)recognized racial group, the one signaled by the term "race" in
mainstream U.S. discussions about "race relations." The primary association of African Americans (and not Indigenous, Asian, or Latina/o groups)
with "race" is not only a result of this country's slave past and historic Jim
Crow segregation. The ongoing, brutal, and particular forms of state and
everyday mob violence faced by Black people in the United States is unique
and sustained at crisis levels of incarceration and death.

Today, the Black Lives Matter movement founded by Alicia Garza, Pa-
trisse Cullors, and Opal Tometi is the largest and most energized and
potentially effective movement for social change since those that led to
the rise of ethnic studies in the 1960s. Their call for police accountability
for the murders of young Black men and women and the significance of
having to actually state that particular lives matter has reverberated in all
sectors of society. If segregation and the ongoing oppression of Black
people inspired national movements for civil rights and Black Power that
included student calls for Black faculty hires in 1968, the crisis faced by Black
people today led to the Black Lives Matter movement, which includes student activist groups such as Black Lives Matter Northwestern University.
Their demands have been met with open, if cautious, administrative ears.
However, if the mainstream U.S. and campus politics do not recognize
Asian Americans as racialized minorities subjected to historic and contemporary forms of exclusion and violence, how does this affect our claims
for space within the university and within racial studies, more specifically? Whence Asian Americans and Asian American studies in the Black
Lives Matter university?

In 2016, Dartmouth University denied tenure to a well-respected professor of English, representing the devaluation and misunderstanding of
Asian American studies. A nationwide cry of dissent followed with charges
of racism (redoubled in public comments about the case) and highlighted
the overtaxation and undervaluation of women of color's service in and to
the academy.[5] Misinformed comments at the end of online articles about

the case assumed the scholar was trained in Asia rather than at Princeton, an American bastion of knowledge. It revealed the stakes of particular nativist strains of racism faced by Asian Americans within the academy. This case highlights the stakes of being an Asian Americanist within traditional fields like English while holding intellectual communion across ethnic studies in a diversifying and neoliberal university.[6] At the time Aimee Bahng, housed in the English Department and an affiliate of the Women's, Gender, and Sexuality Studies, African and African-American Studies, and Asian and Middle Eastern Studies Programs, had a book forthcoming from the top press in her field and was part of the Ferguson Teaching Collective that was central to "Teaching Why Black Lives Matter" at Dartmouth University.[7] Was Bahng punished for raising her voice against anti-Black racism? More broadly, how has Black Lives Matter affected Asian American studies and students within the university? I speak to this through my appointment in both Asian American studies and African American studies and my engagements with faculty and students across the two fields.

As an anthropologist-turned-comparative race studies scholar, my career path was informed by the Department of Ethnic Studies and the Department of African American Studies and African Diaspora Studies at UC Berkeley. I taught, took classes, and interacted with students and faculty mentors from across the subfields. Ethnic studies trained me for my current split appointment with African American studies. In my individual work and teaching, it is nonetheless easy for me to forget that I am not in a unified ethnic studies department because I engage Asian American studies, African American studies, and American studies and cross-list my courses. I am likewise invested in the development of Native and Indigenous studies and maintain a relationship with Latina/o studies, which is physically housed with Asian American studies on my campus. Other than service for the broader university, I primarily interact with faculty and students across ethnic studies, which means I mostly interact with minorities and progressive Whites on a primarily White campus. I was hired alongside other ethnic studies colleagues who also have split appointments through a de facto comparative race studies and interdisciplinary cluster hire. We can relay to one department the kinds of support we may need in our other programs and vice versa, thereby building a flow of information and coalition of economic, programming, and intellectual support. Through teaching and mentorship, I get to interact with student activists, including those at the forefront of Black Lives Matter Northwestern University, who bridge these institutional divides in both their academic training and their political worldviews. Dissonance occurs when I confront those in the academy who identify strongly and singularly with the one subfield of ethnic studies to which they are attached.

The intellectual and political projects of students reflect the ways they crisscross—or do not crisscross—the various fields that study race in the United States. Over the past year, I witnessed a twofold shift among my students that includes a (re)consolidation of identity politics. Among some students in African American studies, this means that Blackness, or rather, anti-Blackness, trumps any and all other kinds of racisms (if, indeed, critics acknowledge the reality of any other kind of racism). In this view, anti-Blackness is global and foundational to the formation of society. It is the basis from which other racisms, such as Islamophobia, Native genocide, and immigrant nativism, emerge. I thus found a different reaction to my articulation of the lessons I had learned through ethnic studies: that slavery, colonialism, indentured servitude, detentions and disappearances of Brown people at national borders and prisons intersected through the demands of White supremacy and capitalism. Some African American studies students recently interpreted my presentation of comparative race studies as "anti-Black" and students, especially those moved by the scholarship on afro-pessimism, read this as a move away from the specificity and exceptionalism of the Black condition as one of abjection. The combination (but not conflation) of these intellectual and political currents also led some people on campus to assume that one's politics is reflected in what Ronald Takaki called our "racial uniform."

This retrenchment of identity politics echoed in the second tendency among a different cohort of students: Asian American studies minors who take ethnic studies classes. We have, as I mentioned, over thirty majors and minors, most of whom are Asian American and include a number of multiracial, Black, Latina, and Latino students. Notably, and quite possibly due to our Asian American Studies Program's focus on comparative race and diaspora, none of our minors or majors are White.

Our Asian American studies students in the past few years have been wrestling with their role in movements for liberation (and particularly Black Lives Matter). They also are attempting to politicize other Asian students on campus who disparage the movement and find it, along with Asian American studies, irrelevant. Asian American studies students sought guidance on when and where to enter conversations on race that were taking place on campus. Black student activists told one Asian American student that he was not a minority, he was not Black, and therefore was, like White students, there to listen rather than to speak. Students have found other ways to express their solidarity. A *desi* (South Asian American) student organized an impressive year-long series of panels titled "South Asians for Black Lives." The flier encouraged people to: "Come to a series of workshops on colorism, racial profiling, and the model minority myth to learn about anti-blackness in the South Asian American community. Let's discuss how we can be effective allies to #BlackLivesMatter as people of color!" The student, who was taking my cross-listed course called "Black and Asian Historical Relations in the U.S.," spoke with me about forming the series. Her initiative and commitment reflects broader links students made between coursework across ethnic studies and community action on campus.

My own teaching and scholarship was influenced by being a teaching assistant for an ethnic studies class at UC Berkeley, "A Comparative Survey of Racial and Ethnic Groups in the U.S.," taught by Victoria Robinson. This course was thick with the connections between the Irish indentured workers and early Chinese laborers. It taught students about refugees from Cuba and Southeast Asia. We covered the spectacle of the U.S.-Mexico border "crisis" within the context of changing economics that led to the rise of *maquiladoras* and transnational female migration from Mexico to the United States. Robinson analyzed the first and second Great Migrations as they intersected with political and industrial changes in the western and northern United States. She presented Asian Americans as more than model minority immigrants, analyzing their depictions on the silver screen and in U.S. politics. The sixteen-page syllabus (which I still have and refer to almost twenty years later) was a treasure of poems, critical questions, and short essays that summed up the major thematics of the course, alongside the reading and writing assignments.

It is no surprise that Robinson was central to the development of an "American Cultures" (i.e., diversity) requirement, which her course fulfills at Berkeley (one that Northwestern University still does not have) or that she is the director of the American Cultures Center and the American Cultures Engaged Scholarship Program. Robinson's intersecting, expansive, and multiscalar approach to various racialized groups in the United States informed my approach to teaching and scholarship. It represents what an overarching racial studies project does. It focuses on representation, but more than that it reveals the linked, uneven, overlapping, contested, and crossover relationships among groups in this nation structured by the demands of White supremacy and capitalism. To center any one group is necessarily an incomplete project.

The troubling trends I discussed above emerge from the incorporation of ethnic studies within the university (e.g., one can earn a PhD in African

American studies; many universities have Latino/a studies majors) and our rising professionalism. Being hired within a distinct unit submits faculty to pressures of having to conduct research in narrow areas and publish in field-specific venues (meaning identity-based ones, such as the *Journal of Asian American Studies, The Black Scholar,* or *Latino Studies*). It also means that ethnic studies faculty, along with those in gender, women's, and sexuality studies, "earn" (but are not rewarded for) time- and emotional-heavy service assignments as we attempt to counsel minority students underserved by the university. Student activists who struggle with self-care seek mentorship from the very faculty who face a similar structure of neglect.

Perhaps it is time to consider the death of Asian American studies in favor of an expansive racial studies project that more fully attends to race, racism, colonialism, imperialism, settler-colonialism, militarism, and the shared political project of liberation. If the autonomous structure of these programs discourages relational and time-consuming work across ethnic studies, undergraduate student activism reveals otherwise.

The Expansive Model of Student Activism

Student activists model an expansive intellectual and political project in their cross-sectional demands to the university that are informed by study across African American studies, Latina/o studies, Asian American studies, and Indigenous studies. In just the last couple of years, students at Northwestern University demanded that the university divest from private prisons, Israeli occupation of Palestine, and coal. Unshackle NU passed a resolution "about the prison industrial complex and mass incarceration's disproportionate impact on communities of color, especially Black communities. It asks Northwestern to divest from companies such as the security firm G4S that profit from human rights violations across the U.S. and elsewhere."[8] Other students (and sometimes the same ones) drew links between Palestine and the U.S.-Mexico border.

Student activism also comes from within the administration: In 2015, two students in the Associated Student Government (ASG) walked out of a function held at the university president's home to speak out about coal divestment. These same two students ran—and won (albeit not without controversy)—the 2016 ASG presidency and vice presidency despite their platform centering minority and marginalized students and class issues on a predominantly white and uber-wealthy campus. Other members of the Associated Student Government proposed a bill in 2016 in opposition to the administration's opaque and misguided hiring of Karl Eikenberry, former

U.S. ambassador to Afghanistan (a man with neither a PhD nor peer-reviewed publications that the administration was willing to circulate), whom the university provost hired to head the over $100 million Buffett Institute.[9] After his hire, Karl Eikenberry withdrew his acceptance, quite possibly because of sustained, significant, and collaborative faculty and student pressure against the hiring process. The Eikenberry Affair made national headlines, as was activism just the previous year from perhaps a more unlikely source: members of the Northwestern University football team that fought unsuccessfully to become unionized.[10] The results of student activism on campus in alliance with faculty support over the past two years have been remarkable, especially at a time of declining faculty governance and an active board of trustees that increasingly shapes the (re)order of campus priorities.[11]

But the most igniting and powerful movement this campus recently witnessed was the predominantly Black women student–led Black Lives Matter Northwestern University movement. They staged a protest that brought out over one hundred supporters and disrupted a major fundraising event held by the university president to present their demands.[12] Called "Demands of a Concerned Student at NU" or "Morty [Schapiro, University President], What's Good?" their expansive list of demands supported multiple communities.[13] They included renovations to the Black House and the Multicultural Center. They insisted on passing the overdue yet stalled "US centric diversity requirement for all majors" (similar to the aforementioned American Cultures requirement at UC Berkeley) and the development of "a Native/Indigenous Studies Department immediately."

Demand number seven of the original nineteen states: "We demand that the university implement an Asian American Studies Major by the 2016–2017 school year." And they succeeded.

It is thus in no small part because of Northwestern University's Black Lives Matter activists—many of whom had learned strategies from organizing in downtown Chicago against police violence—that Asian American studies earned a major decades after a student hunger strike that formed the program. The powerful Black Lives Matter Northwestern University movement led to a number of other immediate victories. The university has since committed to renovate and respect the autonomy of the student space called the Black House, provide resources for minorities in the STEM fields, and launched a Native/Indigenous studies hiring cluster. (In early 2017, the Mellon Foundation awarded Northwestern University with a $1.5 million grant to establish an Indigenous and Native Studies Center.) Students representing other groups also fought for the rights of Sodexo food workers and for the survivors of sexual assault, which made administrators revisit their Title IX policy.

Unlike the viewpoints of some students within our programs or those who are indifferent to ethnic studies more generally, these undergraduate student demands were expansive rather than narrow. Their persistence led the university to raise a flag with the words "Black Lives Matter" outside the student center and a two-week long series of events on topics concerning Black people. Their approach mirrors the internally diverse umbrella orientation of the national Black Lives Matter movement. Embracing the many faces of Blackness, leaders of the national movement created a video that clarified that their work on behalf of "Black Life" includes Black trans people, Black men, Black women, disabled Black people, and so on. The demands of campus activists embraced and exceeded this definition, finding the rights of Palestinians, Asian Americans, and Native peoples in addition to those of Black people central to their fight for full equality and protection from oppression. Thus, on-campus activist demands appear to be comparative, alliance-based, and intersectional, whereas the scholarship within our subfields often reflects programs of study based on populations instead of broader processes and politics.

Who Speaks for Asian America?

The activism that I have witnessed on my campus, from within student government to renegade formations that act in stealth, may have been influenced by their courses in ethnic studies. But what is more compelling is that they reflect a racial studies project, whether or not they took our classes. This perspective leads to my sense that Asian American studies should operate under the umbrella of racial studies, which includes Black and Latinx studies and critical mixed race studies and that should advocate on behalf of Native and Indigenous studies in ways that make institutional, intellectual, and political sense to Native scholars. We would continue to specialize in Asian American studies, highlighting our histories, experiences, and conceptual frameworks. The point is that when racial studies is instituted separately in the university, pressures for tenure shape our hiring and teaching practices. It can push us toward myopic studies of single racial or ethnic groups that incompletely represent broader historic and global systems of race and racism that work comparatively or, if you prefer, relationally, under White supremacy and capitalism.

It is a straw man I have built, saying that we should get rid of Asian American studies. Campuses need Asian American studies, but ideally it should be located alongside or within the other racial studies and engaged by scholars across race. There would be greater engagement with our work, as well, if we continued to develop more conceptual approaches to our material and engage in public discussions on race as guests on major news outlets. Rooting Asian American studies in a conceptual and lateral axis could give us the vocabulary for getting out of certain stalemates that have national significance such as Asian anti-Black racism and affirmative action. Why is it that conservative Asian American voices are usually the ones to earn the attention of the mainstream media? This coverage then informs others' perspectives about who Asian Americans are and what we stand for, which filters the ways that others view Asian Americans and Asian American studies.

Asian Americans were in the national news for the 2016 coverage of the trial of Peter Liang, a Chinese American police officer convicted of killing a Black man, Akai Gurley. Nearly fifteen thousand mostly Asian American protesters in New York rallied against what they considered his "unfair" conviction. Although the judge gave Liang no prison time, parts of the community felt he was unfairly scapegoated since white officers who murder Black people are not generally convicted. Yet why were these activists putting Liang's life (a person who chose to be a police officer and who did kill a young man) ahead of the death of a Black man? The myopia of Liang supporters stems from the same kinds of limited identity politics that leads not to Black Lives Matter but to the argument that anti-Blackness is the only relevant articulation of racism today.

Some Asian American journalists have attempted to make Black Lives Matter relevant by making the case that we "also face oppression." A widely cited *Times* article by Jack Linshi, "Why Ferguson Should Matter to Asian-Americans," used this line of reasoning in its subheading: "Ferguson Isn't Simply Black versus White." In the article, Linshi wants to challenge Asian American indifference about the murder of Michael Brown by stating "Michael Brown's death has several parallels in Asian-American history," including Vincent Chin (Chin's niece wrote a letter condemning the parallel).[14] These dynamics replicate particular contemporary formations of troubling rather than empowering identity politics I described as affecting some of my students. Nationally and on campus, we must move away from such identity politics: Black Lives Matter should not matter to Asian Americans because Asian Americans have also faced police violence and have died in police custody. It should matter to Asian Americans because Black lives matter.

Timothy Yu has rightly called on Asian Americanists to take greater part in national discussions on race and many scholars have done so. But our voices tend to focus on policy (immigration, education) and people (convicted officer Peter Liang) and not on general articulations of Asian Americans' political stances vis-à-vis other people of color and *as* people of color. Asian American studies can become a louder and more progressive part of these conversations through ethnic studies scholarship that illustrates the historical and ongoing forms of racism that target groups differentially.

Asian American Studies within the Collective Racial Studies Project

Racial studies reflects U.S. census categories and thus the constructs of race created through colonialism, genocide, slavery, and exclusion. But racial studies is also a political project, not one existing to "diversify" the curriculum. It articulates how power operates across race, time, and space. Asian American studies within a racial studies framework teaches us how to speak to the ways that nativism, Islamophobia, anti-Black racism, and Native erasure intersect. It is also a space within the academy where we may craft visions of the future through broadscale politics for social change. A racial studies framework explains the specificities of a particular group's histories and experiences and shows how these are rooted in shared processes of domination.

A collective racial studies project counters these specific renditions of insular identity politics in ways that expand the definition of the field of Asian American studies as the study of Asian American populations. A twenty-first-century Asian American studies is up to the task of both modeling a more expansive politics through a conceptual approach to race and power and providing our students and the wider population with the vocabulary and information about the kinds of distinct and ongoing forms of oppression that Asians in the United States face. The racial studies project was and still should be broadscale, cross-group, and globally antiracist (the kind modeled by Angela Davis, who draws links between U.S. prisons and Palestine). This includes careful research on the particular racialization of Asians through Orientalism and nativism and the ongoing exclusions and forms of violence that take place alongside specific forms of oppression faced by other communities of color.

Asian American studies is a strong, viable, and growing field. It is not the precariousness of our field within the academy that concerns me but rather the question of how we should project our growing and increasingly professionalized voice. Each spring our faculty in Asian American studies worry about our graduating seniors. How they will fare? And will the momentum of their activism on campus exit with them? Yet with the entrance of fresh faces each fall, we feel the excitement of knowing that there are students who will become deeply affected by our courses and who, through activism and sustained intellectual inquiry, will fulfill our guiding mission.

Inevitably, it is those students who most quickly feel disaffected on campus and who commit the most to changing it. While institutions are reluctant to change, these students take on the neoliberal work of being and doing diversity while attempting to fix problems not of their own making. What emerges from their work, politics, and passion is a framework not based on particular identities or populations. Rather, recent campus activists fought for structural changes that will benefit all members of the campus community. The students wove lessons from across the university, and from nonexistent programs, such as a White student who created an ad hoc Native American studies major and led the fight for Native American studies. Student action outside of the classroom provides an antidote to the limits of the subfields in ethnic studies. Students are able to take a broader approach to their studies, if they so choose, compared to the constraints of teaching within fields with tenure requirements and contract renewals based on expertise in primary areas that are increasingly institutionalized during a time of "diversity and inclusion."

We may have come to believe that, like race, institutional structures have always existed and that we and our work are defined by these institutional boundaries. But as an interdisciplinary political project, racial studies stems from what is happening in the world. And just like the Third World Liberation Front students who supported Black Student Union activists in the 1960s, our students today remind us that the whole is greater than the sum of our parts. And they are busy tearing down existing tables and replacing them with what is to come.

NOTES

1. For a list of demands from student activists at many universities, please see http://www.thedemands.org/.

2. Daniel Diaz, "Third World Liberation Front Notice of Demands," *Sutori*, accessed June 20, 2016, https://www.sutori.com/story/a-history-of -ethnic-studies.

3. Notable exceptions include Native American studies at places like the University of Oklahoma, the University of New Mexico, University of California campuses including Riverside and Los Angeles. Strengths in Pacific Island studies include the University of Hawai'i at Manoa's Pacific Island Studies Program, the Center for Hawaiian Studies, and the Pacific Islander Studies Initiative at the University of Utah.

4. Kandice Chuh, *Imagine Otherwise: On Asian Americanist Critique* (Durham, N.C.: Duke University Press, 2003); Gary Okihiro, *Third World Studies: Theorizing Liberation* (Durham, N.C.: Duke University Press, 2016).

5. This case was unique for its national coverage, including Colleen Flaherty, "Tenure Denied," *Inside Higher Ed*, May 17, 2016, https://www.insidehighered.com/news/2016/05/17/campus-unrest-follows-tenure-denial-innovative-popular-faculty-member-color, and Catherine Morris, "Denied Tenure at Dartmouth, Aimee Bahng Feels Diversity Efforts Ring Hollow," *Diverse Education*, May 18, 2016, http://diverseeducation.com/article/84350/.

6. Relatedly, the field of English's national academic association, the Modern Language Association (MLA) voted to reject the academic boycott of Israel, in contrast to the Amercian Studies Association (the de facto ethnic studies association) and the Association for Asian American Studies—which was the first of all major academic organizations to support the boycott.

7. Hannah Silverstein, "Faculty Panel Discusses the Teaching of 'Black Lives Matter,'" *Dartmouth News*, January 28, 2016, http://now.dartmouth.edu/2016/01/faculty-panel-discusses-teaching-black-lives-matter.

8. Caroline Spiezio, "ASG Passes Unshackle NU'S Divestment Resolution," *North by Northwestern*, March 3, 2016, http://www.northbynorthwestern.com/story/asg-passes-unshackle-nus-divestment-resolution/.

9. The university provost, who oversaw the hire, also stepped down shortly after the conclusion to the "Eikenberry Affair," also with no full explanation. See David Fishman, "More than 40 Northwestern Faculty Call for Withdrawal of Karl Eikenberry's Appointment as Buffett Institute Executive Director," *Daily Northwestern*, February 11, 2016, http://dailynorthwestern.com/2016/02/11/campus/more-than-40-northwestern-faculty-call-for-withdrawal-of-karl-eikenberrys-appointment-as-buffett-institute-executive-director/; Neha Reddy and Matt Herndon, "Letter to the Editor: Our Experience Challenging the Hiring of Karl Eikenberry," *Daily Northwestern*, June 7, 2016, http://dailynorthwestern.com/2016/06/07/opinion/letter-to-the-editor-our-experience-challenging-the-hiring-of-karl-eikenberry/; Nick Anderson, "How Northwestern Faculty Derailed Retired General's Global Studies Job," *Washington Post*, May 31, 2016,

http://www.chicagotribune.com/news/ct-northwestern-drops-karl
-eikenberry-20160531-story.html.

10. Dave Zirin, "The Absurd, Cowardly, and Morally Bankrupt NLRB Decision against the Northwestern Football Union," *The Nation*, August 17, 2015, https://www.thenation.com/article/the-absurd-cowardly-and-morally
-bankrupt-nlrb-decision-against-the-northwestern-football-union/.

11. For two excellent books on diversity politics on campus, see Roderick Ferguson's *The Reorder of Things: The University and Its Pedagogies of Minority Difference* (Minneapolis: University of Minnesota Press, 2012) and Sara Ahmed, *On Being Included: Racism and Diversity in Institutional Life* (Durham, N.C.: Duke University Press, 2012).

12. Amal Ahmed, "NU Students Stand in Solidarity with Mizzou, Interrupt Groundbreaking Ceremony," *North by Northwestern*, November 13, 2015, http://www.northbynorthwestern.com/story/we-have-nothing-to-lose
-but-our-chains-nu-students/.

13. Fathma Rahman, "Student Activists Add 15 Demands to Original List Sent to Schapiro," *Daily Northwestern*, January 28, 2016, http://
dailynorthwestern.com/2016/01/28/campus/student-activists-add-15
-demands-to-original-list-sent-to-schapiro/.

14. Annie Tan, "Peter Liang Was Justly Convicted: He's Not a Victim, Says This Niece of Vincent Chin," *Medium*, February 22, 2016, https://
medium.com/listen-to-my-story/peter-liang-was-justly-convicted-he-s-not
-a-victim-says-this-niece-of-vincent-chin-739168c9c944#.957koumfi.

CHAPTER 4

Planned Obsolescence, Strategic Resistance: Ethnic Studies, Asian American Studies, and the Neoliberal University

Cathy J. Schlund-Vials

Set within an all-too-real administrative imaginary of budget cuts, metric-laden assessments, programmatic justifications, and shrinking faculty lines, ethnic studies (along with women's, gender, and sexuality studies) occupies a decidedly precarious position within the so-termed corporate university. If student strikes and civil rights movements instantiated the original institutionalization of ethnic studies as a necessary interdisciplinary field of inquiry, the current state of academic affairs reflects a long-standing neoconservative, laissez-faire "planned obsolescence" (to quickly access Kathleen Fitzpatrick's provocative analytic).[1] Such planning—which took shape vis-à-vis joint appointments, "soft" funding lines, constant restructuring, and divisive resource allocations—has made possible the relatively facile elimination (or, more euphemistically, "sunsetting") of African American, Native, Asian American, and Latino/a studies programs across the country. To wit, while the midcentury emergence of ethnic studies and women's, gender, and sexuality studies represented for many a collegiate revolution via the formation of new departments and academic units, the institutional demise of these programs at the turn of the twenty-first century was nevertheless planned from the outset.

Indeed, the very forces that brought such units into institutional being—connective identity politics, organized cross-racial protest, hard-hitting antiracist critique, and multifaceted student activism—have consistently been under attack and regularly undermined notwithstanding multiculturalist pronouncements in academic plans, college mission statements, and university visions that diversity "still matters." Moreover, as Chandan Reddy constructively asserts in *Freedom with Violence* (2011), such "liberal institutionalization has sought from ethnic studies not a genealogical critique of the modern university within racial capitalism, but the development of a representative cross-racial class within the educational institution whose appearance and restricted space of effort it promotes as exhausting the meaning of racial equality. The liberal institutional promotion of a representative cross-racial class is an idealized and inverted image, a symptom of the deepening of the racial and gendered division of labor since 1970."[2] On the one hand, these strategic amnesias—characterized by the tactical deployment of Reddy's abovementioned "representative cross-racial class" and redolent in the distressing disavowal of the racist, sexist, and homophobic present—adhere to cost-benefit analyses part and parcel of the corporate university. On the other hand, as Naomi Greyser and Margot Weiss elaborate, such "multicultural or liberal pluralism is a hallmark of the revitalized corporate university," leading many to "ter[m] the intense marketization of today's university" as *neoliberal*.[3]

This economically driven codification—connotative of Reddy's symptomatic assessment of ethnic studies and denotative of oft-obscured divisions of gendered and racialized labor—simultaneously incorporates what Jeff Makovsky characterizes as integral to a higher education landscape marked by "consumerist, market-driven learning; the privatization, corporatization, and branding of the university; the decline in public spending on higher education . . . outcomes assessment and other efficiency-oriented interventions, and the casualization of academic labor."[4] To that end, deans, provosts, chancellors, and presidents regularly co-opt the language used by the likes of San Francisco State College strikers in strategic plans and academic reports, which stress, to varying degrees and divergent ends, that education must remain "relevant." These declarations prompt the defunding of humanities units, the economic devaluation of the social sciences, and the increased financialization of the STEM disciplines. Such co-optations are by no means limited to hiring justifications, budget lines, and university rescission plans. They are troublingly manifest in contemporaneous discussions about interdisciplinarity, which more often than not involve the administrative conflation of resources and superficial juxtaposition of established disciplinary loci. On the whole, these conversations time and again accentuate collaborations between distinct fields (such as science, mathematics, and literature) while disremembering the template possibilities and progressive potentialities of ethnic studies and women's, gender, sexuality studies as established interdisciplinary units.

It is within the forgetful context of the neoliberal university and against this undeniably dystopic backdrop of planned obsolescence that this essay initially considers—in admittedly pessimistic fashion—the corporatized, administrative practices of what has been classified in higher education as "diversity management"; this exploration into the current state of academic affairs presages a reading of Asian American studies as problematically homogenized, model minoritized initiative and prefigures a concluding, more hopeful consideration of the race-based interdiscipline vis-à-vis strategic resistance. As a starting point, I focus on my home institution—the University of Connecticut—where, since 2009, I have served as the director of the Asian and Asian American Studies Institute, which currently has a total of twelve jointly appointed core faculty and forty-three affiliates (this represents a threefold growth in faculty lines and 500 percent growth in affiliates over a four-year period). Accessing what Asian American studies scholar Sau-Ling Cynthia Wong evocatively termed the field's move from "necessity to extravagance," I accordingly reflect on the limitations and possibilities of administrative resistance through Asian American studies and via the multivalent lens of Asian Americanist critique.[5] If, as Kandice Chuh avers, integral to an Asian Americanist critique is the very constructedness of "Asian American" formations, such evaluations—as the conclusion of this essay makes clear—potentially prove useful in assessing the past, present, and future of ethnic studies.[6]

A Snapshot of the Neoliberal and Corporatized University: University of Connecticut

The University of Connecticut's flagship campus is conveniently located in the state's "quiet corner" (Storrs) and in "the middle of somewhere": It is roughly two and a half hours away from New York, an hour and a half outside Boston, and a mere forty minutes from Hartford, the "insurance capital of the world." While Connecticut even after the 2008 "Great Recession" remained one of the wealthiest states in the nation (it ranks fourth in terms of median household income), its capital metropole is among the poorest: One in three people live in poverty, along with half the city's children.[7] Notwithstanding the university's status as a land-grant (and, because of Long Island Sound, sea-grant) institution, tuition has gone up considerably: Most recently, in December 2015, the university's board of trustees approved a four-year, 6.3 percent tuition hike (in addition to past increases that hovered around 2–3 percent annually), making UConn distressingly cost-prohibitive for lower-income students and first-generation college students.[8] Obsessed with its self-proclaimed status as a "public ivy" and perpetually preoccupied with the *U.S. News and World Report* rankings, UConn's upper administration—as Gaye Tuchman's *Wannabe U* (2009) scathingly synopsizes—consistently seeks to reduce professor-student ratios while pursuing cost-effective nonhiring measures (which take the form of early retirements for faculty), value-saving staffing plans (for example, the en masse hiring and exploitative treatment of contingent faculty), and speculative appointments (namely, the addition of multiple vice provosts, vice presidents, and enrollment managers). The university, like its so-determined "peer and aspirant institutions," is equally fixated on productivity metrics (particularly investments in "academic analytics" and proposals for post-tenure reviews), civility (which at UConn is dubbed "collegiality" and is mediated through a seemingly endless series of task forces populated by individuals handpicked by the administration), and an intentionally vague notion of "excellence": These specific engagements and concentrations are evident in the university's current academic plan, which carries the confessedly underwhelming title "Our Time: UConn's Path to Excellence." In sum, UConn is—notwithstanding superlative declarations—sadly average and depressingly typical in its academic pursuits, its programmatic funding, and its campus-wide mission.

While this focus on the University of Connecticut may seem a bit insular, may strike one as a bit self-serving, and may hit a particularly negative chord (e.g., as an institutionally specific rant), I would argue that it is precisely the "typical-ness" of UConn that makes it a relevant site through which to map the rise, fall, and—in a more optimistic register—the potential resurgence of ethnic studies (as represented by Asian American studies). Acknowledging the specificity of different institutional frames, and recognizing my own privileged position as a tenured, full professor, I argue that in order for us to engage the ever-important question of "relevance" via Asian American studies (along with African American studies, Latino/a studies, Native studies, and gender/sexualities studies), we must take seriously the ways in which the logics of the neoliberal university and the influence of corporate culture respectively demand alternative tactics and unconventional resistive engagements. To be blunt, while student protests concerning and faculty demand for systemic change was fundamental to the mid-twentieth-century founding of identarian interdiscipline and politicized field, the role of both entities in the making of turn-of-the-twenty-first-century institutional policy has been severely diminished at best (via transience of undergraduate matriculation and administrative prohibitions on faculty governance) and potentially nonexistent at worst (for instance, the dismantling of tenure by state legislatures). Contrary to the oft-used adage that a university is "the faculty" and that we are in part here to intellectually "serve" our students, neither group figures keenly in the institution's daily operations, curricular assessments, research requirements, and annual assessments. Upsettingly and undeniably, these aspects of university life and facets of institutional lifeblood are largely determined by those afforded greater administrative means (deans, provosts, and presidents). Furthermore, as the Steven Salaita 2014 de-hiring at the University of Illinois Urbana–Champaign illustrates, such dimensions are distressingly governed by those with considerable financial assets (corporatized trustee boards, institutional "stakeholders," and big-dollar donors).[9]

As a state-supported structure and state-chartered institution, UConn's fortunes have incontrovertibly followed the course of other public Research I universities. Consistent with national trends, legislative funding has decreased and federal grants dramatically curtailed: In 2016 alone, UConn faced a $31.2 million cut in state funding; should the proposed cut have proceeded (it still remains, as of this writing, what the final outcome will be), the university would have lost a total of $139 million in annual state funding over a seven-year period.[10] Set against this dire economic backdrop, it is not surprising perhaps that—each spring—the university's president and upper administration sound calls of alarm to faculty, staff, and students about impending budget crises and unavoidable program cuts. Despite such doom-laden outlooks, at the wholesale expense of academic affairs and student support services, there is—as evident in a recent *Connecticut Mirror* exposé—always room in the budget to grow the size of upper administration along with associated salaries. Expressly, according to a June 22, 2016, *Connecticut Mirror* article, in December 2014, approximately one month after the governor cut state funding to UConn by $3.7 million, UConn's president Susan Herbst "gave three of her most senior staff members hefty pay increases over two or three fiscal years."[11]

Such generous "chickens" came "home to roost" in 2016, when it was revealed that the university had—excluding bonuses—given certain individuals in UConn's upper echelons enormous pay increases (e.g., $25,000). President Herbst alone received a "$29,500 pay raise in January, a $230,000 bonus in May for her retentions and deferred compensation, supplemental retirement and car allowance, and . . . another $40,000 bonus" in summer 2016.[12] The justification for salary increases took a paradoxically compensatory/corporate turn with the officially sanctioned assertion that these comparatively exorbitant remunerations were intended to militate against past underpayment and ensure that the university was in line with private sector practices.[13] Microcosmically analogous to the trickle-down impacts of "Wall Street" on "Main Street," such moves from "up above" have direct consequences for those of us relatively "down below." To cover shortfalls due to abovementioned state defunding and afore-discussed administrative over-expenditures, freshmen classes have continued to expand and classroom enrollment caps broadened. Likewise, international student admissions have steadily risen while support services for this population have been drastically delimited (e.g., the elimination of advisors) and oftentimes cut (immigration services). Expanded study abroad initiatives are concurrently launched (though inadequately funded) as a means of generating additional profit by targeting those individuals who can afford the flight over, the cost of tuition, and the price of residency. Last, but certainly not least, while more and more tenure cases receive additional scrutiny at the dean and provost levels, contingent faculty ranks swell post-2008 economic collapse while their respective pay rates remain at levels consistent with a pre-recession imaginary.

On one level, such administrative practices lay bare a distinct pattern of corporatization, a designation that accretes further meaning when situated adjacent to endless discussions about university "branding," which reinforce a sense that higher education is something that must be uniquely advertised and distinctly marketed in order to be profitably consumed. In reinvigorated capitalist register, on another level, if characteristic of the neoliberal university (and twenty-first-century U.S. public higher education) is what Sheila Slaughter and Gary Rhoades maintain is the assignation of "social value" through an overriding emphasis on "corporate competitiveness" as manifest in an articulated "major role in the global, knowledge-based economy," then UConn's efforts to expand its student base and internationalize its curriculum reflect market-driven assessments and render palpable profit-making agendas.[14] Integral to this exchange process is an overall valuation of social dynamics and relationships that converge on the diversification of student bodies (who assume the dimensions of tuition-rich portfolios) as a means of legitimizing the democratic claims of seemingly accessible "knowledge-based economies." Nevertheless, what remains elusive in these cost-benefit analyses and characterizations is how such human resources are maintained and, even more significantly, sustained given that the disciplines charged with diversity programming and curriculum are repeatedly ignored, under-resources, and—in the end—incontestably devalued.

Multicultural Ignorance, Diversity Management,
and the Ethnic Studies Bind

This disconnect between the asset-driven value of student diversification and the liability-laden dismissal of diversity units is brought into stark contrast when one recollects the violent histories that undergirded the original formations of ethnic studies and women's, gender, sexuality studies programs at UConn. What follows is a pattern that, until recently, encapsulated these formations: a troubling incident involving the subjugation of students hits various news outlets; the administration, after much hand-wringing and a series of missteps, creates (sans strategic plan) an institute, a center, or program.[15] After a burst of hiring, lines become nonexistent and budgets are systematically cut. In contrast to the investment-oriented rationales that guide faculty hiring in the sciences (e.g., that start-up packages exponentially lead to more grant funding and foment research productivity), and contradistinguished from those whose work benefits corporate interest and military investment, programs that do "diversity labor" represent superficial short-term engagements. The absence of racist occurrence, sexist incident, and homophobic episode is rarely attributed to the indefatigable political work done by faculty in ethnic studies or women's, gender, sexuality studies. Instead, the multiculturalist assumption is that university culture has shifted to a more progressive and liberal register; according to this teleological logic, identity-based programs are no longer needed.

To be sure, these teleologies of progress are periodically ruptured via scandal, incident, and event; and, contrary to earlier moments, such "difficult" events have been mediated not through faculty recruitment and additional resource allocation but through higher education management.[16] Despite the university's sports reputation via its "winningest" women's basketball team, and notwithstanding the demographic fact that it has a female president, UConn was, in 2013, at the center of a Title IX controversy.[17] Specifically, the institution was named in a federal lawsuit alleging that it profoundly mishandled sexual assault complaints filed by four female students; the ensuing investigation by the U.S. Education Department's Office for Civil Rights involved three additional students. Kaylie Angell, a plaintiff in the case, was purportedly told by a University of Connecticut police officer following her assault report that "Women need to stop spreading their legs like peanut butter or rape is going to keep happening until the cows come home."[18] Another appellant, Silvana Moccia, was apparently kicked off the UConn hockey team soon after she reported that she had been raped by a male hockey player in August 2011.[19] The following summer (2014), those who filed the complaint—which, incidentally, was represented by high-profile civil rights attorney Gloria Allred—were awarded a $1.3 million settlement. Responding to the landmark resolution (representative of the largest payout in U.S. university history), UConn's President Herbst stated, "The lawsuit may have been settled, but the issue of sexual assault on college campuses has not been. . . . Our hearts go out to all victims of sexual violence. The University has taken many positive, important steps in the battle against sexual assault in recent years, which are described in the joint statement, but there is still more to be done."[20] In spite of the settlement, and in the face of executive-level ameliorative rejoinder, UConn continues to occupy a vexed position vis-à-vis sexual assault: In 2016, the university was tied with nearby Brown University for the most rapes reported.[21]

Acknowledging UConn's tarnished position with regard to gender violence and sexual assault, the university has at no point chosen to increase funding and programmatic support to units that—via research, teaching, and service—had historically done feminist, antiracist, antihomophobic intersectional work. Rather, this labor was—to deliberately use neoliberal nomenclature and corporate terminology—principally "outsourced" to a newly created dean of students office and chiefly subcontracted to a freshly formed Title IX office. As this brief recapitulation suggests, while these frontline programs are quickly deemed inadequate to the task of diversity management and correspondingly rendered obsolescent, additional positions in upper administration are characterized as essential to the maintenance and growth of diversity in the university. Illustratively, UConn's aforementioned current president—Susan Herbst—issued the following statement to the institution's board of trustees on November 18, 2015. Based on a presidentially appointed "Diversity Task Force" intended to make recommendations to improve recruitment and retention of "minority faculty," and situated adjacent to student protests at the University of Missouri-Columbia, Yale University, and Amherst College wherein undergraduate demands for more faculty of color and ethnic studies accompanied allegations of systemic racism and systemized exclusion, Herbst announced plans to hire a high-level, direct-report "Chief Diversity Officer"

(CDO). Herbst admitted that while the university has made "great strides with regard to our undergraduate population . . . diversity among our faculty and staff does not come close to these undergraduate figures. As I have said since the month I arrived, faculty must put in the work it takes to recruit diverse colleagues. I wouldn't want it any other way. They know their colleagues in their fields. They know who is doing high quality work."[22]Despite the ostensible nod to faculty knowledge, Herbst initially places the responsible for diversity recruitment on those who lack financial resources and administrative means to do so; tellingly, Herbst shifts from the faculty ranks to administrative entities, announcing that the hiring of the aforementioned CDO will "educate and motivate members of this community to fully embrace diversity and inclusion as core values, not just to be talked about, but to be collectively practiced at UConn."[23] In line with the wholesale corporatization of UConn, and in tandem with its neoliberal proclivities, the person ultimately hired for this "diversity work" in 2016 was not a faculty member (though there were internal applicants) or a person with higher education experience (e.g., as an university administrator) but instead someone from the private sector (Travelers Insurance, to be more precise).

Success Story: UConn Style

This particular trajectory—from crisis-driven necessity to assessment-oriented extravagance—is replicated and reflected in the history of UConn's Asian and Asian American Studies Institute. On December 3, 1987, eight Asian American students were verbally and physically harassed while on a bus en route to an off-campus semiformal dance. Despite complaints, state, local, and university authorities failed to address—via punishment and policy—what became known as "the incident." UConn police claimed that, because the harassment occurred off-campus, the case was not in campus jurisdiction; state and local police maintained that, since the students were from UConn, it was a university matter. With no viable student support services, Asian American faculty, students, and community members staged an eighteen-month protest. In fact, two Asian American professors (Peter Liu and Paul Bock) led a hunger strike demanding redress and the institutionalization of Asian American studies. Eventually, after much back-and-forth, the Asian American Cultural Center and the Asian American Studies Institute were created in 1993 with the express intent of providing on-campus student and academic support. In spite of the racialized violence that brought the institute "into being," the program was—in

2007—slated for sunsetting following a campus-wide review, which concluded its evaluation with an overarching claim of multifaceted obsolescence: Asian Americans are not considered a minority population by the
state; years had passed since the infamous incident; and Asian American
students constitute the largest student group of color on campus (a categori-
zation that, of course, excludes international students from Asian nations).
While Asian Americans remain a hypervisible minority on campus, they
fail to register as relevant vis-à-vis contemporaneous race-based metrics,
determinedly rehearse a long-standing model minoritization. These de-
terminations contributed to a discernible paucity of faculty lines; they
likewise contributed to a sense that Asian American studies was—in a racial
imaginary marked by black/white binaries—extravagant.

Hence, whereas the University of Connecticut enthusiastically touts its
public university ranking in the *U.S. News and World Report*, its racial
politics—especially with regard to Asian American students, faculty, and
staff—access the obsolescent logics in another *U.S. News and World Report*
article published on December 26, 1966, titled "Success Story of One
Minority Group in the U.S.," that cast Chinese Americans (and, by proxy,
other Asian Americans) as "model minorities" who had achieved socioeconomic success via hard work, perseverance, and patience. Intentionally
divisive, the *U.S. News and World Report* article pits Asian Americans against
other groups of color, and such model minority frames continue to obfus-
cate possible connective histories and experiences. Such divisiveness translates surprisingly well vis-à-vis the neoliberal university landscape, which
is marked by the problematical competition for limited resources, the
polemical struggle for sociopolitical capital, and tactical clashes for upper
admin support.

All the same, this idealized characterization of Asian Americans (as
exemplary subjects and model minorities) obscures a very real history of
exclusion (anti-Asian immigrant acts), discrimination (glass ceilings), incarceration (the internment of Japanese Americans during World War II
and the detainment of Arab Americans post-9/11), and war predicated on
a dominant reading of perpetual foreignness. Situated within the context
of an Asian Americanist critique—which considers in simultaneous fashion constructed contradictions in the face of race-based master narrative
and evaluates difference despite claims of asymmetrical, multicultural
sameness—the notion that Asian Americans are model minorities who have
overcome discrimination is patently untrue yet demonstrably appealing
within a neoliberal imaginary intent on ethnic studies defunding, racial
disavowal, and educational privatization. It is in part due to the historic

and amnesiac co-optation of Asian bodies within the larger U.S. body politic that the possibilities for administrative resistance increase (albeit problematically). As a field, we are accustomed to justifying ourselves via a recovery/reclamation project of historical exclusion and ongoing discrimination notwithstanding mainstream assessments that we have, as an inaccurately conceived homogenous population, "succeeded."

As is familiar to those in Asian American studies, such "success stories" have—as promulgated by William Petersen's now infamous January 9, 1966, *New York Times Magazine* article titled "Success Story, Japanese-American Style"—converged on the World War II–era mass incarceration of Japanese and Japanese Americans. Identifying the internment as a "dark moment in history," Petersen's subsequent model minoritization of individuals of Japanese descent in the United States pivots on an ostensibly "inspirational" story of overcoming via assimilationist dedication profound rights violation and state-authorized discrimination. Such tenets of success presage the university's historical connection to the internment: In particular, the University of Connecticut was one of the few institutions on the East Coast willing to allow second-generation Japanese Americans to matriculate and eventually graduate. As is now firmly embedded in "Nutmeg State" history, the American Friends Service Committee (via the Quaker church) worked closely with community members and activists to peacefully facilitate the relocation and employment of internees; the committee and church were likewise instrumental in convincing the UConn administration to admit nineteen second-generation Japanese Americans. According to former internee Kay Kiyokawa, "My two-year stay at UConn was the most memorable experience in my life. . . . Students were very friendly and the facilities were outstanding."[24] Previously enrolled at Oregon State University, Kiyokawa was in 1942 relocated (with his family) to Manzanar internment camp. While at UConn, Kiyokawa was co-captain of the university's baseball team, played football, and was a member of Pi Beta Phi fraternity.

Notwithstanding the comparatively broad-minded aspects of this UConn "feel-good story," what emerges in more recent retellings is an identifiable assimilationist narrative that simultaneously conforms to both liberal readings and neoliberal assessments about the university. In terms of the former, Kiyokawa's admission to and subsequent graduation from UConn occurs within the political context of federally dictated unfreedom (via the internment/incarceration center); UConn vis-à-vis its university position emerges as a sociocultural "bastion of liberal thought." Such calculated emphases on liberal personhood are deliberately reiterated in the university's decade-long engagement with "human rights": To clarify, Senator Christopher Dodd (Democrat-Connecticut) has tirelessly campaigned on behalf of the Thomas J. Dodd Research Center, which is named after his father (who served in Congress and was the executive trial counsel at Nuremberg). The Dodd Center opened in 1993 (the same year as the Asian American Studies Institute and Asian American Cultural Center) and presently houses various rights-oriented archives (specifically human rights trial transcripts), the Human Rights Institute, and the Center for Judaic Studies.

With regard to neoliberal matters, Kiyokawa's recollection of his time at UConn coheres with the multiculturalist aspirations of the neoliberal university, which problematically deploys "diversity" as a means of managing and eschewing difference. The case of Japanese Americans at UConn fits the narrative requirements of such deployment insofar as it establishes an ostensible exceptionalism that renders unnecessary systemic change. These "unchanging" assessments have profoundly affected the legibility of Asian American studies as a critical, antiracist field at UConn. To surmise and summarize, administrators recounting this history will often conflate past Asian American access to current-day Asian American admission, supposing in the process that anti-Asian American racism has—despite the aforementioned 1987 "incident"—never been a problem; echoing the logics of model minoritization, Asian American faculty, staff, and students are cast as Janus-faced subjects whose past experiences with state-authorized and campus-sanctioned discrimination are integral to present-day arguments concerning and contemporary policies involving multiculturalist inclusion and equity.

Conclusion: Strategies of Administrative Resistance

I want to end in a more hopeful vein, though the story that follows begins in quite the opposite manner. Situated within the context of problematic (il)legibility, and set against a decidedly vexed multiculturalist imaginary of targeted subjects-turned-model-minorities, it is perhaps not surprising that—the same year Kiyokawa's story was published—the Asian American Studies Institute received a negative review and "sunset" recommendation. Conducted by a provost-level committee of up-and-coming upper administrators, the review stressed that the institute had in many ways performed the task of ameliorating anti-Asian racism; however, what remained unclear to the internal reviewers was the institute's "value-added" dimensions. The unit had lost a number of faculty because of nonretention (for instance, faculty moving to other positions) and tenure dilemmas (which were the consequence of disproportionate joint-appointment teaching and service loads). Despite the distinct racialized history that brought it "into being," the institute was criticized for not engaging a globally capacious agenda (more appropriately identified as "traditional" area studies); it was likewise critiqued for not having enough faculty lines even though none of the abovementioned positions were replaced.

This happened to be the first year I was employed at the University of Connecticut. What followed were a series of endless meetings with vice provosts, department heads, and deans. Notwithstanding differences in university position, and regardless of disciplinary location, the message remained the same: Why should the institution invest in a "resolved" racial project? To add fuel to the fire, the founding director resigned in protest; senior faculty rightfully refused to assume leadership positions without any promise of further funding; and, while students were willing to stage protests, the relatively small size of the unit because of a paucity of faculty lines rendered this largely ineffective. What had worked in the past— specifically letter-writing campaigns, faculty protest, and public outcry— was deemed inadequate to the task at hand: proving the unit's corporatized worth within a neoliberal university imaginary.

Such struggles with legibility have arguably accompanied not so much the formation of Asian American studies as a protest field but rather its sustainability as an interdisciplinary site. We as practitioners have been forced—for the better—to think intersectionally and act collaboratively; the dialogic dimensions of the field—with regard to questions of race, class, gender, sexuality, and citizenship—carry the potential for strategic resistance. When faced with the possibility of a sunsetted ethnic studies unit, we (as a faculty) and I (as an untenured director) knew that Asian studies was— for better and worse—more comprehensible than Asian American studies. We therefore stressed the diasporic, transnational, and international registers of the field and emphasized time and again the need for critical Asian studies (to fulfill the global dimensions of the academic plan) and comparative ethnic studies (to remain "compliant" with the university's diversity mission). Guided by "necessity," the institute returned to its Asian Americanist roots: We pursued a hiring cluster that used optics from ethnic studies (e.g., race, ethnicity, and borderlands) and applied them to Asian studies (e.g., Chinese diasporas in Southeast Asia and frontier politics on the Russia/China border).

In so doing, we moved away from justifications obscured by model minoritized racialization while embracing (strategically) the relevance of

Asian American studies as a global field of inquiry. Hence, the recent "global" turn in higher education (particularly with regard to study abroad, discursive shifts from civil rights to human rights, and international education), along with the (in)visible registers of Asian American studies as interdiscipline, offer new ways of resistively pitching and envisioning the past/present international significance of ethnic studies fields. To be sure, while "educating otherwise" remains a priority (specifically in terms of ongoing racism, sexism, and homophobia), the very constructedness of Asian American studies and the mobility of Asian Americanist critique engenders what Kandice Chuh terms the need to "imagine otherwise": to see the field's value outside what amounts to a nonviable representational politics (due to multiculturalist erasures) and recollect the local/national/global politics responsible for its formation.

NOTES

1. Kathleen Fitzpatrick, *Planned Obsolescence: Publishing, Technology, and the Future of the Academy* (New York: NYU Press, 2011).

2. Chandan Reddy, *Freedom with Violence: Race, Sexuality, and the US State* (Durham, N.C.: Duke University Press, 2011), 30.

3. Naomi Greyser and Margot Weiss, "Introduction: Academia and Activism," *American Quarterly* 64, no. 1 (2012): 789.

4. Quoted in ibid.

5. Sau-Ling Cynthia Wong, *Reading Asian American Literature: From Necessity to Extravagance* (Princeton, N.J.: Princeton University Press, 1993).

6. Kandice Chuh, *Imagine Otherwise: On Asian Americanist Critique* (Durham, N.C.: Duke University Press, 2003).

7. Mary Buchanan and Mark Abraham, "Connecticut Has More Concentrated Poverty (and Wealth) than Most Metros," *TrendCT*, May 27, 2015, http://trendct.org/2015/05/27/connecticut-has-more-concentrated-poverty-and-wealth-than-most-metros/.

8. "UConn Board of Trustees Approves 4-Year Tuition Hike Plan," *NBC* (Connecticut Local News), December 16, 2015, http://www.nbcconnecticut.com/news/local/UConn-Board-of-Trustees-Approves-Tuition-Hike-362645931.html.

9. In 2014, the University of Illinois decided to revoke a tenured job offer in the American Indian Studies program to Steven Salaita on the presupposition that he represented a threat to campus civility; such an assessment was made after Salaita had posted a series of critical tweets concerning Israel's militarized policies vis-à-vis Palestinians. Pressured by donors and pro-Israel trustees, then-provost Phyllis Wise de-hired Salaita. In November 2015, the University of Illinois agreed to award Salaita an

$875,000 settlement to drop two lawsuits he had filed and agree to never working at the institution. See Jodi S. Cohen, "University of Illinois Oks $875,000 Settlement to End Steven Salaita Dispute," *Chicago Tribune*, July 6, 2016, http://www.chicagotribune.com/news/local/breaking/ct-steven-salaita -settlement-met-20151112-story.htm.

10. "Proposed State Budget Calls for More UConn Funding Cuts," *Daily Campus*, February 3, 2016, http://dailycampus.com/stories/2016/2/3 /proposed-state-budget-calls-for-more-uconn-funding-cuts.

11. Jacqueline Rabe Thomas, "A Few Top UConn Officials Get Pay Increases Despite Tough Times," *Connecticut Mirror*, June 22, 2016, http:// ctmirror.org/2016/06/22/a-few-top-uconn-officials-get-hefty-pay-increases -despite-tough-times/.

12. Ibid.

13. Ibid.

14. Sheila Slaughter and Gary Rhoades, "The Neo-Liberal University," *New Labor Forum* (Spring/Summer 2000): 73.

15. To date, the University of Connecticut is home to the following cultural centers, institutes, and programs: the Asian American Cultural Center; the Asian and Asian American Studies Institute; the Rainbow Center; the Women's Center; the Women's, Gender, Sexualities Program; the Institute for Africana Studies; the African American Cultural Center; El Institute: Institute of Latina/o, Caribbean, and Latin American Studies; and the Puerto Rican/Latin American Cultural Center.

16. The University of Connecticut's College of Liberal Arts and Sciences attempted to engage a "diversity hiring cluster" in academic year 2015–2016; this initiative occurred in tandem with a provost-level diversity initiative. The cluster was limited to recruiting faculty who identified as African American or Latino/a. This initiative was, in the end, largely not successful insofar as it hired three such-designated faculty in a college comprised of twenty-eight departments and academic units.

17. The UConn women's basketball team has won a record eleven NCAA championships. In 2011, the University of Connecticut welcomed Susan Herbst, its first female president.

18. Pat Eaton-Robb, "Settlement in Title IX Lawsuit against UConn," *CBS Connecticut*, July 18, 2014, http://connecticut.cbslocal.com/2014/07/18 /settlement-in-title-ix-lawsuit-against-uconn/.

19. Ibid.

20. Ibid. It should be noted that Herbst received resounding criticism for her initial response to the complaint, wherein she denied the validity of it; according to Herbst, "The suggestion that the University of Connecticut, as an institution, would somehow be indifferent to or dismissive of any report

of sexual assault is astonishingly misguided and demonstrably untrue." Quoted in "Editorial: UConn President Herbst Deeply Misguided in Her Response to Sexual Assault Claims," *New Haven Register,* October 27, 2013, http://www.nhregister.com/opinion/20131027/editorial-uconn-president -susan-herbst-deeply-misguided-in-response-to-sexual-assault-claims.

21. Linda Conner Lambeck, "UConn First among Schools Reporting Most Rapes," June 10, 2016, *Connecticut Post,* http://www.ctpost.com/local /article/UCONN-FIRST-AMONG-SCHOOLS-REPORTING-MOST -RAPES-7974591.php. The official university response to the news was decidedly optimistic in its stress that the increase in filed complaints was evidence that UConn was a much more open campus with regard to sexual assault reporting.

22. Kathleen Megan, "UConn to Hire Chief Diversity Officer," *Hartford Courant,* November 18, 2015, http://www.courant.com/education/hc -diversity-uconn-1119-20151118-story.html.

23. Ibid.

24. Sherry Fisher, "Japanese-Americans Recall Special Moments at UConn," *UConn Advance,* October 27, 2003, http://advance.uconn.edu/2003 /031027/03102701.htm.

CHAPTER 5

Un-homing Asian American Studies: Refusals and the Politics of Commitment

Anita Mannur

On the morning of February 8, 2013, I woke up with considerable nervousness and excitement. It was the day my university's trustees would meet to put their final stamp of approval on tenure decisions. I had only been at my institution for four years and came up early for tenure. For most of 2012 all I heard was that I had nothing to worry about and I was being neurotic. I remember being in my chair's office while he and another senior colleague told me for the quadrillionth time, or so it seemed, that I was a slam dunk case. Despite the seeming pomp and ostensible circumstance, the day came and went. I learned nothing. I forgot that it was my mother's birthday. My mother texted me that evening from India to remind me I forgot—not because she was mad but because she didn't want my father thinking I was so self-involved that I had forgotten my mother. So, I called her and wished her a happy birthday.

Two days later, on Sunday, I checked the university website to see if there was any news on what was then called the "e-report." And there, finally—in print—were the words I longed to see. In an article titled, "Faculty Receive Promotion and Tenure" was a one-line sentence: "During the Feb. 8 meeting, Miami University's board of trustees approved recommendation for tenure and promotion effective July 1, 2013." What followed were a list of faculty members? There was my name and my department affiliation (English). I was lucky number 13. I had been hired as the first joint appointment in Asian/Asian American Studies. I was the first faculty member in the program to receive tenure, but that fact was rendered invisible. But still, eleven years after completing my PhD I had tenure, effective on my thirty-ninth birthday. As a naïve twenty-seven-year-old in May 2002, I did not think it would take me over a decade to get tenure. I wanted to get tenure before I turned forty and I just made it.

I begin with this story because it is the hinge upon which this article pivots, affectively, temporally, institutionally, and intellectually. I turn to a situated personal narrative to theorize the conditions of precarity under which Asian American studies existed in two different institutional homes to contextualize my own unexpected politics of refusal. Having spent ten years orienting myself toward a future within Asian American studies, I found myself reorienting away from the institutional formation of Asian American studies. I reluctantly became a part of its imminent institutional demise—paradoxically, it might seem, to continue the intellectual work of Asian American studies. In other words, this is a critical narrative about how I had to refuse Asian American studies to remain committed to its intellectual vision.

Tenure and the Asian Americanist

I now joke that I was on the ten-year rather than tenure track. Two postdoctoral fellowships gave me the space to write and think but took three years from my life. I was hired at the University of Illinois Urbana-Champaign as a postdoctoral fellow in 2002–2003. Though the program in Asian American studies at the time was conducting a search for a specialist in literature, I was not shortlisted, even though the initiative was designed to retain and hire diverse new faculty. When I asked for feedback, I was told by the chair of the search committee that I was not likely to earn tenure at the University of Illinois. I subsequently spent the next two years at Wesleyan University on a Freeman Postdoctoral Fellowship. At my interview, I was informed from that outset that I would not be considered for a tenure-line position; however, my role would require me to engender interest among the students in Asian American studies, develop related curriculum, and organize cocurricular programming. In return I would be mentored and they would do their best to prepare me for a tenure-line job. Of the fifty or so students I taught over the course of two years, three of the students I mentored went on to earn PhDs, one earned her JD, three have secured tenure-track positions at Research 1 universities and at least one is a high school teacher who regularly integrates Asian American studies in her courses. All of them have used their training in Asian American studies.

Four years at another tenure-track job and four pre-tenure years at my current institution ate up my thirties. Tenure, for many academics, is the ultimate goal. It confers freedom, status, and security. It removes the precarity with which one lives, particularly for the normative subject. It means having a stable home and offers a range of privileges. For me getting a tenure-track job wasn't just about attaining a form of recognition; instead, it was about the idea of feeling at home, intellectually and personally, and securing the right to stay in place, what Alicia Schmidt Camacho—in vastly different context—has described as "el derecho a no migrar."[1] I came to the United States in 1993 and lived, until 2005, as a nonimmigrant alien. I was sponsored for a green card by my family and got my first tenure-track job that same year. It was serendipitous because if that hadn't worked out, I would need a tenure-track job to sponsor me for a green card. Of the offers I received in 2005, only one provided the possibility of a green card sponsorship. It wasn't my top choice for a job. It was not the R1 job that seemed written for me. It was not the job in the ethnic studies department I so wanted to take and that for years I would regret turning down, forgetting that the strictures of U.S. citizenship prevented me from accepting it. It was at Denison University, a small private liberal arts college in the middle of Ohio where the center of town was marked by a four-way stop with a church at each corner.

Soon after I arrived, it became apparent that I had been hired because the English Department thought their chances of getting a hire would be better if they put in for a diversity hire and that this would likely have to be a temporary home. How do I know? *They told me.* The job advertisement had asked for someone who could teach either "Asian American or Latino Literature." My first year, I taught two Asian American literature classes. Both enrolled fewer students than ever before in the English Department's history. I taught another one the next year to even fewer students. After that, it was politely suggested that I consider enfolding Asian American literature into other courses: It was suggested that I teach some Asian American authors in my American women writers course, my food course, or my first-year composition course. *But, of course, it was up to me.* And just like that, after three semesters, my hopes of building Asian American literature classes were dashed. Even in the face of disappointment, I initially did not want to go on the job market again. I was comfortable and liked my life in Columbus, Ohio (a safe thirty minutes away).

Nevertheless, I became increasingly disconnected and disenchanted. After all, I had spent my time in graduate school helping to build a home for Asian/ Asian American Studies at the University of Massachusetts (my alma mater) and within the larger Five-College consortium to which it belonged. I wasn't the kind of scholar who could remain in stasis merely teaching the authors I love at an institution that had made it clear that I was valued for the diversity work I did while it remained unwilling to commit substantial resources to revise the curriculum. I wanted to build opportunities for students and create community and curriculum, particularly in the Midwest where Asian American studies meant something different and where the few students who took my classes walked away transformed.[2]

As Sara Ahmed notes, the responsibility for diversity and equality is rarely distributed evenly. One needs to think of the individual who embodies diversity within institutions of whiteness as doing a form of diversity work. Such individuals, she notes, frequently "get stuck in institutions by being stuck to a category."[3] I returned to the job market in 2007 because I wanted to become unstuck. I was the "race" person but I could not do "race work." In 2009 I was hired into the newly formed Asian/Asian American (AAA) Studies Program at Miami University, jointly appointed between that program and English as part of a cluster hire. The model upon which cluster hires are designed is to counteract the effects of institutional failure. There is an implicit recognition of the need to hire and retain faculty, particularly those of color and those teaching in underrepresented areas of the curricula. The year prior, a similar hiring initiative in History, English, and Latino/a and Latin American Studies had yielded four tenure-line hires; 2008, though, was a different story.

The financial crisis of 2008 had hit hard and all searches were on hold; the then-dean had the foresight and intellectual commitment not to cancel the cluster hire but to downsize it from three or four to two resulting in hires in English (myself) and Sociology. This position allowed and asked me to establish new curricula. Though never put in writing, I was being mentored to eventually become the program's director. I took an interest by way of regular meetings with my chair and mentor in addressing curricular needs, program development, and outreach. Within a year, I had proposed a new course, "Introduction to Asian/Asian American Studies." A year later, I was teaching a pilot section with twenty students. Three years later, the course was enrolling forty—more if I would allow students in. At the same time a new course, "China and Globalization," had been proposed and offered to similar, if not greater, success by the person hired in my cohort. Though she left academia soon thereafter, her course remained on the books. With some tweaking, we renamed it "Asia and Globalization" to allow our fledgling program of 0.5 fulltime faculty and four to five dedicated affiliate faculty to teach the course. A minor in Asian/Asian American studies was also quickly approved. Other courses were soon processed and offered at the 300 level. A unique boost to the quality of our program was the fact that we now had a handful of MA and PhD students, primarily in the English Department, interested in the study of Asian America, who could contribute to the teaching of Asian American studies. By 2015, multiple sections of these courses could be offered because of the general education needs that some of these courses served. Our small faculty was teaching between five hundred and six hundred students a year. We had a handful of minors. In our seven years, I had organized several key lectures by prominent Asian Americanists—several of whom are anthologized in this collection—who all spoke to packed audiences.[4] By these metrics, the program was flourishing, a veritable success story of Asian/Asian American studies finding a "home" in this institution.

But there is another narrative that lurks beneath this happy exterior that signals how the project of Asian American Studies at Miami was oriented toward "failure" as much as it had been at Denison. This is a narrative I can only tell because I have tenure. In "Tenured and Happy," Cynthia Wu writes, "Let's not forget the original purpose of tenure—to protect academic freedom. The writing I've produced in the past year reflects a newfound sense of ease and inventiveness. This position of stability emboldens me to take risks in my scholarship that I otherwise wouldn't have dared."[5] Like Wu, I too have a position of stability that emboldens me to take the risks that are ethical positions that people with tenure ought to be able to exercise without fear of reprisal. But, in the years after what has dubiously been come to be known as the "Salaita Affair," tenure and academic freedom are not sacred anymore. Perhaps they never were for scholars of color, critical of the neoliberal university or the racist machinations of state violence. But for me, there was a stopgap of about three years before I could voice dissent about the imminent failure of Asian American studies. Like many women of color, tenure did not grant me freedom but instead plunged me into the vortex of administration, un-homing me from the already fragile structures of a joint appointment by adding a third layer of responsibility to an already heavy work burden.

Let's, for a moment, flashback to 2013. I've just earned tenure. I'm hosting a guest speaker and during the reception for that speaker, I'm approached by a couple of faculty members to apply for the position of Director of Women's, Gender, and Sexuality Studies. My own research directly engages gender and sexuality, but as a joint appointment I have not had time in my three and a half years to build all the bridges with academic units I would like. I'm not terribly good at saying no and the offer to direct a program comes at a time when the new administration is not going to give me the opportunity to direct Asian/Asian American (AAA) Studies. Instead, that position is unilaterally handed over to the former director of the Confucius Institute, who has no academic training in the transpacific Asian/Asian American Studies vision that defined our program. That Asian American Studies is to be directed by a faculty member whose salary is paid by the Confucius Institute is politically vexed.

Since 2004, Confucius Institutes have been established on 465 university campuses in 123 countries. An article published in the *Telegraph* notes that "they are designed to project a favourable image of China's ruling Communist Party around the world through language and cultural programmes, but are allowed to restrict discussions of topics unpalatable to China's ruling Communist Party such as the occupation of Tibet."[6] This rapid expansion of China's soft power has been the source of much critique on college campuses. An AAUP statement formulated in response to the impact of globalization on U.S. colleges, universities, and academic freedom observes: "Globalization has also meant that university administrators have welcomed involvement of foreign governments, corporations, foundations, and donors on campuses in North America. These relationships have often been beneficial. But occasionally university administrations have entered into partnerships that sacrificed the integrity of the university and its academic staff."[7] The statement subsequently explores the specific impact on memorandum of understandings that are established between U.S. universities and the Confucius Institutes, noting:

> Confucius Institutes function as an arm of the Chinese state and are
> allowed to ignore academic freedom. Their academic activities are
> under the supervision of Hanban, a Chinese state agency which is
> chaired by a member of the Politburo and the vice-premier of the
> People's Republic of China. Most agreements establishing Confucius
> Institutes feature nondisclosure clauses and unacceptable concessions
> to the political aims and practices of the government of China.
> Specifically, North American universities permit Confucius
> Institutes to advance a state agenda in the recruitment and control of

academic staff, in the choice of curriculum, and in the restriction of debate.

Despite collective objections, which involved not the individual directing the unit but rather the process through which leadership and resources were allocated through the Confucius Institute, AAA starts to feel, for many of us, unmoored. The program is effectively left without an advocate who effectively understands AAA's mission.[8] We are barely off the ground before we are floundering; rather than engage our own critical scholarship, we are being asked to serve the needs of the ever-growing business school, their specific interests in Asia, and promote for the university-at-large a positive vision of Asia. In 2009 AAA had been focused on cocurricular programming focused on lectures about social justice. Under this new change, AAA was now sponsoring events to promote cultural goodwill about the people of China among American college students, what has been dubbed a form of "culturetainment" by which the diversity of China's cultures has been reduced by Hanban to a "uniform, quaint commodity," characterized by Chinese opera and dance performances."[9] Somewhere along the way the mission of social justice had been lost.

Amid this radical and unsettling shift, the program in Women's, Gender, and Sexuality Studies (WGS), a longstanding program with a commitment to social justice and intersectionality, was actively recruiting me to take on a leadership role. Before July 1, 2013, rolls around and I'm officially tenured, I've picked up another title as WGS director. For all intents and purposes I am the chair of a department that holds tenure lines, has a robust major, minor, and graduate certificate, and faculty who will need mentoring to get through to tenure. I have so many meetings that I joke with a fellow administrator that our meetings have meetings. My campus hours are so long, I've forgotten what the sun looks like. On the bright side, I always get a great parking spot because I'm on campus before sunup.

In agreeing to chair another unit—though my official title is director since WGS, along with Latino Studies (LAS), Black World Studies (BWS), Asian American Studies, American Studies (AMS), and International Studies (ITS) are programs—I had to give up some responsibilities in what is referred to as my "home" program, Asian/Asian American Studies.[10] My new teaching load of 1–1 is to rotate among WGS/ENG/AAA. A visiting assistant professor is hired to replace me in the second year of my directorship when it becomes clear that I cannot remain "stuck" to as many units as the university would like. It also becomes apparent what is to happen with AAA. It is now almost entirely staffed and taught by affiliate faculty, contingent faculty, and graduate students. There is a complete disconnect between ethics and responsibility in terms of how this program is to be sustained. In 2014, the collective pressure among the affiliate faculty to disarticulate the Confucius Institute with AAA has yielded some success. The unit has a new director, the third in five years, drawn from the tiny pool of affiliate faculty. The initial promise with which I was recruited and hired has disappeared—there is little effort at retention and the burden of running the program rests entirely with the goodwill of graduate students, contingent labor, and overworked affiliate faculty of color and queer faculty who are either joint or triple appointments.

The situation I'm describing is not unique to my university or to fledgling Asian American studies initiatives that are expected to generate revenue and student demand without full institutional support. There was no malicious intent behind appointing the director of the Confucius Institute to be the director of AAA; rather it was a cost-saving measure that was willfully ignorant of the incompatibility of the vision of these two programs. Nevertheless, this impasse signals the lack of commitment to thinking about Asian American studies as doing anything other than diversity work, let alone functioning as a viable intellectual space. As such I want to focus on the micro-level destructions that occur in the building of programs as a way of thinking about how microaggressions translate in institutional settings. As Cathy Schlund-Vials notes in her essay for this volume, institutional demise is rarely positioned as an outright goal. Rather:

> such planning—which took shape vis-à-vis joint appointments, "soft" funding lines, constant restructuring, and divisive resource allocations—has made possible the relatively facile elimination (or, more euphemistically, "sunsetting") of African American, Native, Asian American, and Latino/a studies programs across the country. To wit, while the mid-century emergence of Ethnic Studies and Women's, Gender, and Sexuality Studies represented for many a collegiate revolution via the formation of new departments and academic units, the institutional demise of these programs at the turn-of-the-twenty-first century was nevertheless planned from the outset.[11]

The aptly named "sunsetting" of programs is a micro-level destruction of programs. In Miami's case, it would be too soon to "sunset" a program that was just into its seventh year and had barely found a home. In fact, there was no physical space on campus for Asian American studies. The only home we had was a virtual one on a website, and the "home" moved with each director. Thus, the sunsetting works through consolidation. Though the previous dean had been committed to building ethnic studies, the financial crisis of 2008 had immediately put the smallest programs on the chopping block. Unless the metrics could show that these courses had the requisite numbers to maintain their autonomy, no program would be guaranteed autonomy. With no faculty lines, AAA could not sustain the numbers; without the numbers, AAA could not make the case to argue for faculty lines. AAA's best shot at survival was not to call attention to itself but to, in effect, take on the role of the model minority program and serve at the pleasure of the university's administration.

Mergers and Consolidations: Creating New Homes

The WGS program, however, posed a very different kind of challenge. With eight fulltime faculty, all but one of whom were joint appointments, and only thirty or so majors, the program had long been targeted for sunsetting. Despite contributing to the general education curriculum via courses in global and intercultural competency, the lack of undergraduate majors had put WGS along with LAS, BWS, AMS, and now AAA on the institution's radar as programs to be sunsetted via merger into a larger unit. In 2014, it was announced that AAA, along with five other programs—WGS, LAS, AMS, ITS, BWS—would be merged into a department of Global and Intercultural Studies. Though each program had held out for almost a decade, the fact that tenure-line hiring had been frozen (I was the last new tenure-line hire in 2009) had meant the programs were running on empty and highly reliant on contingent, graduate, and affiliate labor. In such situations, the neoliberal university demands that directors take on the role of compliant subjects while also holding out the promise of future hiring as the incentive. Unsurprisingly, women of color and queer faculty are often placed in a precarious position. In hindsight, it was clear that consolidation was a fait accompli—it was up to the directors to rally the troops. Program autonomy was not going to be an option and yet to eliminate programs that contributed to diversity education was not an option. When smaller units focused on the study of race and ethnicity are required to merge into a larger unit, there is also often an implicit mandate that these micro-level destructions that have long-lasting consequences are not labeled as racist, sexist, or homophobic. The faculty member or director who is charged with rallying the troops to go along with the vision of the neoliberal university that flattens out difference is often expected to "go along with the happy image of an organization" and to convey that the new vision to which we must comply is necessarily a better one with more opportunities for hiring and collaboration.[12] In this context, compliant subjects, or subjects who are seen as less unruly, are charged with doing the work of getting everyone on board to get along. Sara Ahmed describes this phenomenon as a kind of passing, whereby one passes as the "'right kind' of minority, the one who aims not to cause unhappiness or trouble."[13]

To be in a such a position when one knows that decisions have already been made and that no one individual can be castigated for destroying the integrity of ethnic or gender studies is one of precarity. The pernicious nature of the neoliberal university is that it systematically erodes the value of ethnic and gender studies but will also create scapegoats who are deemed responsible for the failure of these programs and institutions. It is more than likely that I was hired because of my ability to work efficiently and to get along well. I was a prime example of the compliant subject who passed well in the terms Ahmed describes.[14] This is, of course, an unwinnable position. Those above you will always want you to push harder to get your faculty on board; your colleagues will want you to "push back," a vague and amorphous term that is more rhetorical than practical. In such a position, one is pushing up against an institutional wall of diversity that Ahmed describes wherein "the wall gives physical form to what a number of practitioners describe as institutional inertia, the lack of an institutional will to change."[15] One of my junior colleagues chastised me for not pushing hard enough and deemed me "too nice," effectively erasing all the behind-the-scenes labor I was doing to preserve the program's vitality and to build its national reputation.

Eventually, one becomes weary. The institution counts on it. It operates under a different temporality that can wait out stubborn feelings and anger, a kind of temporality that is not increasingly unavailable to faculty and subjects who look around at the national scene and see the physical violence that countering neoliberalism does to the human body. With little to go on but anecdotal information, there is a very real toll that going up against walls takes on the bodies and health of women of color. The workspace becomes a place that triggers chronic illnesses such as migraines, weight gain, insomnia, depression. In my case, administrative bloat was literal. Institutions can wait for us to fall apart but increasingly we, as women of color, must reorient our energies and desires and say no to this kind of bodily harm.

By the beginning of 2015, the various units began the difficult task of creating a home together. But with so many different visions of a home imposed from above, consensus is hard to build. The small remained small and the big grew bigger. Programs like AAA, unsurprisingly, did not fare well in the first year. Despite three tenure-line searches, not one Asian Americanist was offered a position. Despite three tenure-line searches, not one person of color was hired.[16] Despite three tenure-line searches, not one specialist in queer studies was hired. In 2014, as part of my charge as director of WGS I had been expected to get WGS on board with joining this new department. As the longest holdouts, with legitimate concerns that a Department of Global and Intercultural Studies would marginalize queer studies and not retain the commitment to hiring faculty of color that had been WGS's mission, I had served as a go-between with the promise that one of the first hires made into the new department would be in queer studies and that the hiring and retention of people of color would be a priority. I had gone so far as to speak in front of the university senate to convince the faculty-at-large to endorse the merger because these promises had been made. When my own colleagues in my new department circumvented these promises, I refused to comply. Tired of being the compliant subject, I turned to the language of racism and sexism in calling out the hiring decisions and asked where was the commitment to diversity that had been promised if we all agreed to live in this new home. I became the bad subject for not going with the flow. I had hit the wall and the spurious applications of numbers to try to convince me that smaller programs like WGS, AAA, LAS, and BWS were being protected did not convince me or others who were not protected by tenure.

In an interview published in *Meridians* former faculty member in the English Department at Yale, Sanda Mayzaw Lwin discusses the unreliability of mathematical certainty when relying on numbers to count diversity. She notes,

> I thought of the English department where I teach and I realized that if you took two away from ten, you could be left with zero. That is, if you were to subtract me and the other junior faculty of color who is my colleague from ten, or even from all fifty or so members of the English department, you would be left with zero junior faculty of color. And I began to think about how numbers, when it comes to bodies, are not always so reliable, stable, or incontestable. In this case, $10-2=0$ faculty of color. This is why critical mass is so essential. Having a larger group of people doing this type of work changes the dynamic so that 10 minus 2 can equal 8 again. Of course we always need a critical mass of faculty of color, but it is also important to reach a critical mass not just of "physical bodies" representing diversity but

also a critical mass of people who engage with and are supportive, at the very least, of work around issues of race and migration.[17]

In many ways, what I had been looking for, and what I continue to look for, is not just a home for ethnic and gender studies, particularly Asian American studies, but a just and nonprecarious one. Certainly, this may seem Pollyanna-ish to think this is possible, but more relevant to me is the structure that animates this desire for a home.

In "Refusing Subjects and (Dis)owning America in Asian American Studies," a review of Kandice Chuh's groundbreaking *Imagine Otherwise: On Asian Americanist Critique*, literary critic Allan Isaac hones in on the place of and desire for home that Chuh investigates in her book. Isaac asks, what are the terms of national belonging that Asian American critique aspires to? Is this home "place or desire?"[18] Asian American novels provide a space to think through the desires of Asian American institutionalization precisely because of the oft-emphasized theme of securing a place to call home and a place to stay put. *A Gesture Life*, the topic of Chuh's study, focuses on the character Doc Hata, an elderly Korean immigrant who takes pride in the home he owns and only very reluctantly parts with it as he ages. As Isaac notes, "though the novel refuses a resolution with a definite home rather than a cause of lament, I would suggest that the powerful attraction for a home offers infinite elsewheres at each narration of this desire for home. That is, frustrated desire locates a focal point but each representation or re-vision of home or belonging offers multiple narrative possibilities."[19] It is useful to conceptualize the desire for institutionalization as a desire for home precisely because it is about a desire to stay put. It is about a politics of recognition and value that dares to imagine the possibility of not having to reinvent oneself again and again as so many Asian American studies programs have had to do.

Coda

As of July 1, 2016, I am no longer jointly appointed. I am a full-fledged member of the English Department. I deliberately gave up affiliate status in the very intellectual programs that most speak to my research. I did something I never expected to do. I asked to have my line moved out of Asian/ Asian American Studies and fully into English. And yet the lead up to this was met with considerable resistance, not because there was any concern for my being but because of the question of how it looked for the new department to have a senior woman of color opt out. A personal responsibility was placed on me to remain in an unhappy position because I filled many boxes. In the end, the choice for me was to choose among two literary characters as my models. Did I want to be Willy Loman, and follow the path of "being well liked" and eventually self-destruct? Or, did I want to be Bartleby the Scrivener and quietly resist?

In the end, I opted for the latter. I preferred not to be included. I preferred not to be a part of a project I could no longer believe in. As Ahmed notes, "we can be constrained even by the categories we love."[20] In my case the institutional formations of Asian American and gender studies were constraining me from doing the very work those interdisciplines had allowed me to do. But I also felt an obligation to always turn up and, as Ahmed notes, "becoming the race person means you are the one who is turned to when race turns up. The very fact of your existence can allow others not to turn up."[21] I reluctantly chose not to turn up anymore because when I turned up, it let other people off the hook. When I refused to turn up for a search committee, I had to be replaced by two people, a member of the WGS faculty and an affiliate of AAA. I had become so well stuck to multiple categories that I was the easiest go-to person for race and gender. This was certainly not what I understood intersectionality to mean.

The paradox of the neoliberal university is that it asks us to subsume our personal well-being and happiness for the greater good. And yet it is never clear what the greater good is and how exactly it benefits students or faculty. When one turns away from the academy, and from the institutional formations of gender or ethnic studies, it is often cast in terms of betrayal. And yet, as the 2016 case of Sara Ahmed's well-publicized resignation from Goldsmiths College suggests, turning away from institutional "homes" is often the only way to remain committed to the goals of gender and ethnic studies critique. Resignation in this case can be better thought of as a re-signification and a reorientation toward other kinds of goals. And so, one must necessarily ask, what if institutionalization is not the goal? One often hears about the success of Asian American studies discussed in very specific terms that privilege visibility. To gain institutional recognition is success. To measure up to the right metrics is success. To serve the university's strategic plan is success. But how does this success shore up for the Asian Americanist who was never schooled with these ideas of success in mind? I returned to the English Department in large part because it was a home to the kind of work I wanted to do. Though faculty always rotate in and out, I work in a department where I am one of five Asian Americanists. Among our tenure-line faculty, we have a pre-eminent

Latina writer, a Native Americanist, and four African Americanists. There are at least three queer-identified faculty and there are more women than men. As a department, we have little interest in hiring according to standard English literary periods. Sometimes I think we are the best kept secret among progressive English departments in the country.

In her bold essay on the strategic ways in which we might think about failure as a necessary goal, literary scholar Frances Tran advocates for a kind of unraveling that she names undisciplining. She writes: "Undisciplining encourages a shift in perspective and affect, a *dis*investment from the security of disciplinary formations and institutional paradigms of success, contained in what I have been calling the 'good life' fantasy. It proposes a different way of conceiving our scholarly activity, not as shoring up a particular interdiscipline, but rather as an unraveling that contests the constraints imposed by the academy's racialized structure of knowledge."[22] Following Tran, I submit that to undiscipline is also to un-home. To undiscipline is to refuse a home. To undiscipline is to prefer not to. To undiscipline is to recognize that failure is not failure. To undiscipline is ultimately what we perhaps should strive for to ensure a radical critique in gender and ethnic studies. To undiscipline is to allow the tenured Asian Americanist to work responsibly and to think about how to transform the discipline even as one thinks of tenure as the right to be in place.

NOTES

1. Alicia Schmidt Camacho, *Migrant Imaginaries: Latino Cultural Politics in the U.S. Mexico Borderlands* (New York: New York University Press, 2008), 4.

2. This is entirely based on my perception up until 2009. I cannot speak for institutional commitments and hiring decisions made by subsequent administrations post-2009. The fact remains that there is no major and that classes are offered sporadically in Asian American literature. More often, they are enfolded into the umbrella of ethnic literature, the rubric under which I most often taught any Asian American literary texts.

3. Sara Ahmed, *On Being Included: Racism and Diversity in Institutional Life* (Durham, N.C.: Duke University Press, 2012), 4.

4. At last count, this included, in no particular order, talks or readings by Cathy Schlund-Vials, Gayatri Gopinath, Robert Ku, Martin Manalansan, Jigna Desai, Catherine Ceniza Choy, Robert Diaz, Sangeeta Ray, Stan Thangaraj, Lisa Lowe, Cynthia Wu, R. Radhakrishnan, Neelanjana Banerjee.

5. Cynthia Wu, "Tenured and Happy," *Inside Higher Ed*, March 30, 2015, https://www.insidehighered.com/advice/2015/03/30/essay-earning -tenure-and-considering-responsibilities-faculty-life.

6. Peter Foster, "US Professors Urge Western Universities to End Ties with China's Confucius Institutes," *Telegraph*, June 18, 2014, http://www.telegraph.co.uk/news/worldnews/asia/china/10907971/US-professors-urge-Western-universities-to-end-ties-to-Chinas-Confucius-Institutes.html.

7. "On Partnerships with Foreign Governments: The Case of Confucius Institutes," Statement Issued by the American Association of University Professors, June 2014, https://www.aaup.org/file/Confucius_Institutes_0.pdf.

8. The truncated mission statement on the website notes, "Asian/Asian American Studies is an interdisciplinary program that applies a transnational and transcultural lens to critical inquiries into important issues both affecting and connecting Asia and Asian America and that prepares students to become global citizens of the twenty-first century. The program studies how the historical, socio-cultural, and political forces shape our understanding and knowledge about people of Asian and Pacific Islander heritage in the United States and in the diaspora. It aims to develop new paradigms and perspectives to close down past divisions and boundaries and to open up space for dialogue and engagement." Miami University Asian/Asian American Studies Department website, http://miamioh.edu/cas/academics/programs/aaa/academics/index.html, accessed July 31, 2016.

9. Elizabeth Redden, "Confucius Says . . . . , " *Inside Higher Ed*, January 4, 2012, https://www.insidehighered.com/news/2012/01/04/debate-over-chinese-funded-institutes-american-universities#sthash.1XrPR3mX.9wWDPAi7.dpbs.

10. Hereafter I will refer to the various interdisciplinary programs by their acronyms.

11. Cathy Schlund-Vials, "Planned Obsolescence, Strategic Resistance: Ethnic Studies, Asian American Studies, and the Neoliberal University."

12. Ahmed, *On Being Included*, 157.

13. Ibid.

14. The institutional battles I had prioritized were to secure tenure for two women of color and to facilitate the promotion of a queer faculty member. Doing this kind of labor demanded that I always had to soften moments of anger and mitigate bad feelings.

15. Ahmed, *On Being Included*, 26.

16. I should be clear that this is not about the individuals hired or their commitments to diversity and social justice. Rather it is about the process that reproduces whiteness and upends promises that are made to increase faculty diversity.

17. Nina Ha, "When Ten Minus Two Equal Zero: An Interview with Sanda Lwin," *Meridians* 3, no. 1 (2002): 5.

18. Allan Punzalan Isaac, "Refusing Subjects and (Dis)owning America in Asian American Studies," *Kritika Kultura* 12 (2009): 73.

19. Ibid., 74.

20. Ahmed, *On Being Included*, 4.

21. Ibid., 5.

22. Frances Tran, "How to Live *Un*Safely: Towards a Better Good Life for Asian American Studies," *Journal of Asian American Studies* 19, no. 3 (2016): 231.

PART II

Displaced Subjects

CHAPTER 6

No Muslims Involved: Letter to Ethnic Studies Comrades

Junaid Rana

In a 1994 essay entitled "'No Humans Involved:' An Open Letter to My Colleagues," Sylvia Wynter reflects on the acquittal of the police officers involved in the Rodney King beating in describing her now well-known critique of the severing of Black life from human life. The title, "No Humans Involved," is based on the acronym NHI, used by public officials "to refer to any case involving a breach of rights of young Black males who belong to the jobless category of the inner city ghettoes."[1] While the King case was not the first time that the NHI acronym was deployed, in policing parlance it described cases involving victims deemed by the police to have low social status and thus lower priority in order of address. As a law enforcement practice, it exemplified the principles of anti-Black racism and the use of explicit racial and social hierarchies. In what follows, I draw on Wynter's diagnostic to invoke a parallel condition: the racial figure of the Muslim and the inability to challenge racism and white supremacy for its dehumanization of Islam and Muslims. And like Wynter, I address this to my comrades in the academy, particularly ethnic studies, for the challenge that this represents in terms of the scope of our projects and research agenda. For Asian American studies, this call represents a challenge to forge a more expansive political and intellectual agenda that is part of the field's intellectual strength to include cross-racial spaces of alignment and solidarity. This offering is in the spirit of confronting an undertheorized and often taken-for-granted aspect of the politics and epistemology of the ethnic studies project. Specifically, I ask how we might forge new political solidarities with the dispossessed in an ecological and moral frame in ways that might call into question intellectual and activist boundaries. While it is a call for more study and debate, this is a chance to pivot, to assess, to shift, and it is ultimately an invitation.

At the close of Wynter's essay she writes: "The starving fellah, (or the jobless inner city N.H.I., the global New Poor or *les damnes*), Fanon pointed out, does not have to *inquire into the truth*. He *is*, they *are*, the Truth. It is we who institute this 'Truth.' We must now undo their narratively condemned status."[2] The reference to the Arabic word for peasant, *fellah*, is imagined in a planetary social arrangement that is the main subject of this sentence and parenthetically refers to Black and brown subjects of state failure as a status in which they are "narratively condemned." In other words, the damned are discursively hidden to a state in which their abject condition is abstracted from subjecthood. The present moment of contemporary theory has in some ways sought to critically include the margins into the sights of analysis, yet there is something oddly lurking in discussions of Muslims and Islam. There is an attempt in critical studies to address the domination of Arabs, Muslims, South Asians, for example, without addressing the complexity of ontology and epistemologies of difference. More succinctly, the danger is a complicity with liberal modes of thinking that would render the figure of the Muslim as simply a racialized subject without addressing issues of sociality, theology, and even alternative modes of political thought and liberation. The notion, for example, of the "damned of the land" that Fanon expands upon comes from his observations and experiences with the Algerian struggle for decolonization and a theorization of Black liberation. As I trace this confluence in this essay I raise the question of what solidarity can mean and look like in unexpected places and histories.

Recently, comparisons of the protest movements that connect the rallying cries of Ferguson to combat anti-Black racism and Palestine as a central struggle against colonial occupation emerge in a parallel historical moment in which Wynter originally critiqued policing and Black death. Emergent in this social justice relationship is a link of anti-Blackness and national liberation to the multiple layers of how other social logics are eclipsed. And more pointedly, as the visibility of anti-Black racism has prevailed as an organizing principle of modern everyday violence in the United States, Islam has emerged as a global object of violence in relationship to this logic. If Black death is necessary for liberal social life, then how does the normalization and even banality of anti-Muslim sentiment represent a shift in white supremacist racecraft? While not exactly parallel, or derivative, I argue that anti-Muslim racism is emblematic of a twenty-first-century racism that enforces white supremacy, settler colonialism, and racial capitalism in an ever-expanding practice of extraction, exploitation, and regimes of life and death. And as Blackness as a global narrative is predicated on the violence of liberal modernity, I also argue that racialized Islam is now dependent on a discourse of racial annihilation that subverts the racial logics of Blackness as a rhetoric in the flexible category of the racial figure of the Muslim. In this context, how do Asian American studies and ethnic studies reconcile war and the industries of violence of the U.S. imperial state through a global analysis of race? What might an ethnic studies critique look like that does not capitulate to a pervasive rhetoric that demonizes Muslims and that does articulate an antiracism that incorporates anti-Muslim racism? What is radical liberation for the Muslim world, given the expansive and seemingly never-ending War on Terror? If Palestine is this generation of radical activists' South Africa, and Ferguson is the model and symbol of dissent to state violence, then what are the lessons for a new internationalist vision? How might we distinguish anticolonial and decolonial practices from anti-imperial ones that craft, in Fanon's terms, a new humanity?

In what follows, I chart a genealogy of insurgent thinkers that pose questions for how to forge the possibilities of solidarity, commitment, and ethical practice, that are an experiment in the theory of decolonial liberation. These figures are by no means definitive or final but represent a sort of unthinking and rethinking of the assumptions regarding Muslims and Islam in relationship to white supremacy, racism, settler colonialism, and decolonization. In this version, these three figure represent a chain of insurgent thought that requires pause and what I hope is a refiguring of theoretical and political possibility. I have chosen them because of their chains of meaning for a reconstituted "No Muslims Involved." In this sense I refer to the low priority embedded in Wynter's original analysis, while acknowledging the symbol of "no Muslim" as a hidden presence and abstracted relationality that I describe as a spiritual genealogy. All three figures represent a hauntology of Islam (or what white supremacists call Muslim creep!) and at times reveal the secrets of such a cover—Islam for human, human for Muslim. I begin with Frantz Fanon under his oft-used pseudonym toward a rethinking of the dialectics of African/Black and Arab/Indigenous/Native. Second, I draw on Malcolm X in his post-Hajj years to offer a model in solidarity work and the tactic of revolutionary organizing. Finally, I close with the lesson of Yuri Kochiyama, who, for a short time, converted and practiced Islam and was often referred to as Sister Yuri by Malcolm and other Muslims. These three figures provide biographical examples for how we might rethink Islam as a politics of left critique and in crafting intellectual models to theorize a much more expansive notion of solidarity and liberation. I close with a brief rumination on what a Muslim Left might look like and an analysis of the connection of Islam to radical movements for social justice and internationalist liberation.

Ibrahim Fanon

There is a rumor that Fanon converted to Islam. In 1959 Fanon was the target of a car bombing and assassination attempt in Rome.[3] As he lay in a hospital bed for unrelated injuries sustained in a separate accident, he is reported to have escaped attempts on his life based on having read a newspaper report that referred to a patient under the name of Dr. Ibrahim Omar Fanon and as "the Libyan."[4] Accompanied by Tunisian and Algerian bodyguards, it is now clear that the attackers in Rome were most likely the far right settler organization called the Red Hand, or in French "Main Rouge," operated by the intelligence service of the French government.[5] As biographers of Fanon surmise, this pseudonym, "Ibrahim Fanon," was a conventional nom de guerre, an alias to maintain anonymity during wartime. Similarly, Fanon's wife, Josie, often traveled under the name Nadia.[6] As a representative of the Front de Libération Nationale (FLN), Fanon was issued a Libyan passport by the Tunisian consulate in 1958 in which he was identified as Omar Ibrahim Fanon.[7] Seeking treatment from the leukemia that ravaged him till his death, in desperation he sought treatment in a hospital in Bethesda, Maryland, a trip arranged by the CIA. Under the care of the National Institute of Health in Bethesda the identity of the patient was recorded as "Ibrahim Fanon no. CC 03-86-00."[8] In these official circumstances that were clandestinely arranged, Fanon died under a Muslim name. The nom de guerre, rather than a complete departure from his name or his politics, signals an intention and a deliberate selection of a *Muslim* name that has religious and political implications. Upon his death, Fanon was finally buried according to his wishes in Algeria at the Ain Karma Shuhada, or martyrs, cemetery on the border with

Tunisia. This was the pinnacle of Fanon's political commitment—a state burial under the auspices of the newly decolonized country of Algeria that represented his shared struggle against French colonialism. The meaning of Fanon's legacy as one of the great theorists of decolonization raises a question of his afterlife and how to understand Fanon through Arab eyes, or even Muslim ones. In death, was Fanon now one of them— Algerian, Tunisian, Libyan—in the struggle for national liberation and decolonization? Was he Arab, Muslim, Black? What did the engagement with decolonial politics mean for his secular commitments?

As Fouzi Slisli argues, the discussion of Fanon's magnum opus *The Wretched of the Earth* (1965) has often subsumed an unacknowledged Islam as a part of his political theory. For Slisli, this gap in Fanonian theory begins with Fanon himself, who failed to recognize the political history of the Islamic traditions of Sufi political collectivities.[9] At the center of this gap is what many have taken as one of Fanon's key contributions to the theory of social movements and decolonization. Namely, Fanon's ideas of peasant "spontaneity" makes no mention of the political traditions of Sufi Islam deeply embedded in Algerian social structure—particularly in the nonurban countryside—while being deeply indebted to them. The notion of spontaneity that Fanon describes as a precursor to decolonization is not simply an improvisation as he describes it. Rather, these tactics were rooted in centuries-old political traditions that were firmly Islamic, and in Algeria, part of a Sufi religious network and social order. Fanon's acknowledgement of this detail appears in his loose reports in *A Dying Colonialism*. In a memorable scene, he describes a debate on the legitimate use of violence: "We diverged on the question of 'rebellion.' For my part, I considered it understandable, like an excess made possible by the excess of colonialism, but I refused to accept the validity of violence. My Muslim comrades did not agree on this point, and we had a long discussion on the subject." As a decolonial tactic, these shifting views on rebellion and violence for Fanon complicates the later endorsement in *The Wretched of the Earth*. Fanon's distinction of "Muslim comrades" is notable for its political and social meanings. As an act of solidarity even in debate, he acknowledges religious difference and a certain imperative to struggle. After describing the influence of another colleague in the debate he closes: "I still had too much unconscious anti-Arab feeling in me to be convinced by a Moslem Arab. It took the speech by that Algerian Jew to shake me."[10] This important gesture that Fanon presents in terms of thinking of his own praxis in relationship to unconscious sentiments describes his comradely deconstruction of his assumptions in the differences between Muslim, Jew, and Arab as political positions. Unraveling such sentiments is pivotal to the unacknowledged slights of epistemological and ontological possibility of the Muslim in relationship to a secularized nationalism that would combine religious difference into a single model of the nation—in this case, the struggle toward Algerian decolonization. Indeed, embedded in Fanon's writing is a decolonial praxis of unraveling anti-Arab and anti-Muslim colonial rhetoric.

In looking toward the denouement in his final book, *The Wretched of the Earth*, Fanon's embrace of the possibility of a "new humanity" is often understood as addressing the contradictions of Blackness and the duality of a colonialism that places settler in opposition to native. This articulation in Fanon's writings of terms such as *indigeneity, settler colonialism,* and *decolonization* often focuses on critiques centering on the production of Blackness. Even as the dialectic for Fanon in *Wretched* is that of Black and Arab, and Blackness and Islam, his notion of a decolonized future constructs these categories through a sense of cultural possibility—the start of a new humanity. Going beyond an essentialist understanding of these terms—Black, Indigenous, Arab, and Islam—Fanon gestures toward a framework of decolonizing praxis in which identity is the beginning of struggle. Nonetheless, the scholarly discussion, and even the inspiration of Fanon's writings, are seemingly one-sided.

While Fanon's classic text *The Wretched of the Earth* has often been read as a source of inspiration for global movements of Black liberation and decolonization, there is a disconnect that involves the social economy of how he deploys the terms Arab, Native/Indigenous, and Black. In the original French text Fanon uses the word *indigenes* that has been translated into the English as *Native* and *Indigenous*. In the language of French colonialism, *indigènes* referred to all colonial subjects as opposed to the settler. In Fanon's complex use of the terms *Arab* and *Black*, similarly indigeneity presents itself as a capacious category. Ronald Judy suggests Fanon uses a dialectical understanding of Blackness in his use of *negre* and *noir* in the original French that corresponds to Black and being Black, as subject and predicate, or becoming and consciousness, in-itself and for-itself.[11] Parallel to this are *Arab, Muslim,* and *Indigenous* as terms politicized as being and consciousness. In, for example, the presence of decolonial struggle in the Sufi traditions of Algerian Berbers, what might a more intricate relationship be to the categories of Native and Indigenous that refers not only to land-based national claims of decolonization but also to an understanding of the peoples and of modern colonized metropole? How does this understanding in contrast with the rural countryside symbolize third world histories and decolonization struggles? Although these questions are placeholders for re-thinking conversations of indigeneity and political theory through Fanon's Native-Black dialectic, I argue for a further reading of Arab/Islam and the Native/Indigenous/Black that gestures toward the formation of Muslim ra-cialization and notions of resistance and anticolonialism in relationship to Muslims and Islam.[12] In this sense, I am offering a discursive reading that imagines power working through racial subordination and the possibility of antiracist and anticolonial radicalism.

El-Hajj Malik El-Shabazz

Malcolm X is undoubtedly one of the most significant twentieth-century figures of Islam in North America. As a historical icon, his memory and writing continue to have a global impact. He is often remembered as a key critic of white supremacy and an inspiration to the Black liberation and revolutionary movements such as the Black Panthers and the power move-ments. Similarly, in ethnic studies, Malcolm X is studied as a political theoretician and critic of the U.S. racial state. But what if we read his po-litical critique as an indictment of white supremacy and read him as a theo-logian of Islam calling for the rejection of white supremacy in the tradition of Black protest religions? How might Islam be a force to combat the moral and ethical corruption of white supremacy, racial capitalism, and settler colonialism? Malcolm's teaching, whether through his writings and speeches or the continued significance of *The Autobiography of Malcolm X*, are a significant body of work that offer vast insights. In particular, the period referred to as Malcolm X's post-hajj years for his break with the Nation of Islam and shift to orthodox Islam offers a complexity of a multira-cial coalition and the need for an intricate retrenchment in revolutionary theory we now call insurgent thought.

In an instructive essay, Edward Curtis argues that Malcolm's theologi-cal intervention and approach is one that depends on an ethical program that demanded Muslims fight for third world liberation and *all* people of color.[13] In this explanation, Islam for Malcolm X is not just a spiritual sys-tem relegated to religious practice but an ethical system from which to engage in political relationships. Here, Curtis expands the philosophical approach to the study of Malcolm X to connect it to the protest tradition of Black religions, on the one hand, and the prophetic tradition of the Abra-hamic religions that speaks to a contestation of the unjust on the other. In reassessing the "holy protest" of Malcolm X's theological and political philosophy, justice as a counter to the evil of white supremacy, suffering, and the colonial structure of power recall the constant invocations of Malcolm to the "teachings of Elijah Muhammad" and the omnipresence of Allah.

In this turn to what might be argued is a liberation theology of Islam, a reassessment of Malcolm X as a social critic and theoretician opens up new forms of thought that have been thus far ignored.[14] Malcolm X is often subsumed under the politically left articulations of liberation politics, even as his political practices showed an ambiguous allegiance to such a political position that often included conservative and reactionary stances. While not programmatic, Malcolm was not clearly aligned with a left or right but was interested in a radical critique of social relations based in the exploitation and exacerbation of Black suffering through racial capitalism and a white supremacist social structure. In this way, Malcolm X and Fanon have a shared connection in terms of their anticolonial analysis and the psychology of the racially oppressed.

In one of his last recorded speeches, "Not Just an American Problem, But a World Problem," delivered at Rochester, New York, on February 16, 1965, Malcolm X refers to a religious and political hybrid from which Black Muslims emerged in relationship to describe the formation of the Muslim Mosque and the Organization of Afro-American Unity (OAAU) to challenge anti-Black racism and white supremacy.[15] This hybrid of political and religious reasoning is what I refer to in this amalgamation of liberation and insurgent thought in which Malcolm was referring to both people of faith and those with sensibilities of the secular left. This late gesture in the life of Malcolm to building alliances between religious and political affiliations was to overcome what was obvious in the rise of Malcolm's organizational ability and charismatic leadership. And while religion and politics were certainly inseparable for Malcolm's visions of Blackness and Islam, he also sought to overcome the narrowness of a separationist argument toward broad-based organization building.

Was Malik El-Shabazz a perfect Muslim? Even if there was such a thing, can a Muslim be anything but a striver, someone caught in the act of becoming, pivoting against white supremacy? If anything, Malcolm was constantly changing, adjusting to the times and the context he lived in. The deification into Saint Malcolm, now at the center of the many hagiographies that posit his secular life as opposed to the sacred, from the outset have ignored his religious life and his contribution to Islamic liberation theology.[16] And yet such debates, because they often depend on a theorization of the political as secular nationalist activity, have often foreclosed theological discussions of thinking through the example of

Malcolm X's critical thought. Even further, the implications for theodicy and the accounts of justice as a divine articulation have been missing. In this way, political traditions of protest that draw on religion have often been pushed to the side in a theologically Christian United States that would equivocate all religion as religion. But what happens when Islam is accepted as religion but is also political opposition and a tradition from which to draw on moral principles of dissent?

Sister Yuri

From 1971 to 1975, Yuri Kochiyama converted to Islam at the behest of Rasul Suleiman, a former bodyguard of Malcolm X. As a key figure in the Asian American movement, this episode has been little remarked in Kochiyama's life. The prison solidarity work that Kochiyama devoted much of her activism toward the end of her life led her on this path in which she joined the mosque at the Green Haven prison as part of a complex solidarity. In describing this process of conversion and joining the prison mosque, Kochiyama refers to the "chauvinism" of organized religion that results in the unequal treatment of women, while conceding that the men of the mosque needed space to undo the oppression that had been wielded upon them.[17] Reflecting Yuri Kochiyama's long-standing practice of what she referred to as revolutionary nationalism, the turn to Islam expressed a commitment to Malcolm X's organizing legacy that was based in a critique of white supremacy and the practice of multiracial Islam. Yuri worked closely with Malcolm to build the OAAU, welcomed Malcolm to the Kochiyama home, and worked to continue his legacy after his death. This subtle move of solidarity, of conversion in the close proximity of working with the imprisoned, speaks to the layers of affective and ethical modalities that are part of her revolutionary practice. As is evident in much of the social movement history that chronicles Black liberation movements, the complex role of Islam as a religious, social, and cultural practice is often not recognized or is only briefly mentioned in passing. Forms of Islam as a parallel tradition of liberation theology more readily associated with Latin American Catholicism[18] have yet to be comprehensively examined as complex and variegated political practices.[19] As Kochiyama describes this gap: "Each time I'd go to the mosque, there was no one I could talk to about my experiences as a Muslim woman, at least not to any Asian."[20] Participating in a new faith tradition was far from simple. For Kochiyama it was embodied and intense. As she explains, "my Muslim life was deep inside me."[21] And while Kochiyama's turn to Islam represents solidarity and the ever-present thinking of collectivity, this sense of finding a moral universe from which to ground political practice is not unique. For example, countless former Black Panthers turned to Islam as a continuation of the philosophical imperative of Malcolm's teachings and the lesson and praxis of anticolonial critique.

Similarly, as I have written with Diane Fujino, Kochiyama participated in acts of solidarity that extend the terms of a politics of third world radicalism to organize around issues such as Palestinian liberation and a critique of U.S. empire in the Philippines, Okinawa, and Hawaii.[22] In her own memoir, a photograph taken in 2001 shows Yuri Kochiyama in San Francisco draped in a Palestinian kaffiyeh during a Free Mumia event.[23] Then, it must be asked, why is it so hard to imagine solidarity beyond the purported realm of the secular left, and why is Islam consistently treated with uncertainty? A quick response is that this is the politics of suspicion that would only view Marx's dictum as "religion is the opium of the masses" and not view religion as the "sigh of the oppressed." That there might be a decolonial approach within Islam is more readily dismissed by a secular left that would rather imagine a future without organized religion and the assumptions of an uncritical believer, apropos of Fanon's admissions in Algeria that I discussed earlier. More pointedly, such a slight of Islam and Muslims is the participation in a political praxis that views religion as ideological rather than cosmological and as a lifeway. Such deep-seated views are far more complex and require a variety of research approaches to understand them, in addition to the depth that Yuri Kochiyama describes only briefly as part of her practice of Islam.

Kochiyama's example offers a segue into activist and intellectual commitments that, following Gramsci, might be called the organic intellectual. To commit to Islam and the process of conversion is no small feat. It is also not without critique and a fundamental interest in politicizing the concept of faith and religion. Was Kochiyama a Muslim? Was she a practicing Muslim in those years? What matters is that there as an example of solidarity that goes beyond the secular and into a politics of revolutionary nationalism that Yuri Kochiyama often adhered to with the notion of religious practice—in other words, a tradition. Such a tradition as a discursive practice lies in a religious faith and is also a political and organizing tradition. Here some interesting parallels emerge in which political action, for example organizing or direct action, can be seen in a relation to religious practice. In other words, how might conversion be a political act of solidarity? What emotions, beliefs, values would be at the center of such action? And how might faith actually be a position of critical engagement?

The Wilds of Islamoleftists and Muslim Communists

There is a need to reclaim political insurgency and insurrectionary thought that allows for the possibility of a radical left from the perspective of Islam and Muslims. The default position under the rubrics of global white supremacy and imperial state terror is that Islam is othered as a patriarchal remnant of a premodern past. Yet such a teleology of liberal modernity would foreclose the possibility of a political tradition of insurgency of Arab, Muslim, and Indigenous peoples. What, in this context, would it mean to talk of Indigenous insurgency and critical thought from the margins of history, from the edges of comprehension?

In France after the Paris attacks of 2015, the pejorative terms Islamoleftist and Muslim Communists appeared as a way to discount liberal left sympathies for immigrants and people of color. The surprising language of the new liberalism of Europe embraces racist sympathies with the rhetoric of antiterror, secularism, and feminism, while unabashedly indulging in anti-Muslim racism. It is as if anti-Arab racism of the 1970s and 1980s has been supplanted by an ever-expanding rhetoric of security, prevention, and antiterror. In this logic, the anti-Muslim liberalism of Europe is conjoined with a shared neoconservatism found across the Atlantic in the racist rhetoric of the United States. Global white supremacy is complicated in the range of political publics that are state sanctioned and often uncritically normalized through the equation of antiterror as anti-Muslim. What this signals is not only the dangerous homogenization of all Muslims but also a foil that dismantles the gains of a politics that opposes white supremacy, settler colonialism, and racial capitalism. In short, anti-Muslim racism is an attack on the global Left.

In contrast, the possibility of what I am calling a Muslim left is what Stefano Harney and Fred Moten have called an undercommon, a place of fugitivity in which dissent and opposition is in formation.[24] The revamped language of white supremacy is one that makes a mockery of antiracism in an age of neoliberal multiculturalism and allows for the category of the "Muslim" to be universalized as a common enemy. There is a wildness to this position of an emerging Muslim that has a being that can only be comprehended as *against*. Yet, as I have described in my rereading of Fanon/Malcolm/Yuri, there is an emergent politics that has more importantly always been *for*. A moral and ethical position is not just one that flatly draws on a politics of decolonization but one that must imagine how this is practiced echoing the warnings of Fanon in *The Wretched of the Earth*.

In two of James Baldwin's great books in the form of a long essay, *The Fire Next Time* (1963) and *No Name in the Street* (1972), he chronicles a range of observations from the ravages of racism in the Jim Crow South and across the United States to the streets of Paris and the racist gaze that disparages the Arab.[25] Baldwin, ever the astute observer of planetary racism, was dismayed by French racism and the continuity of the colonial relationship with North African Muslims. Similarly, in the United States he was drawn to Malcolm X and the Nation of Islam as a counterpoint to his own avowed agnosticism in religion and in politics. For Baldwin, Malcolm was a powerful icon from which he could imagine a sort of pivot from which to understand how his Blackness had been created for him and how he might create himself anew in the admiration of others. Baldwin through Malcolm proved a kind of instance of what I am describing as a critical stance in the world that melded into an otherworldly notion of politics and religion. In what Elijah Muhammad calls this "wilderness of North America," referring to the conditions of wretchedness that would enslave Black people under racial capitalism, lies an apt metaphor that, rather than simply referring to uncultivated land, describes a social relationship of domination and exploitation.[26] As a place of severe social death, this idea of wilderness possesses the possibility of restoring political life. Even further, the wilds that this place of North America stood for is a description replete with meaning, a vast opening in which a response to the evils of society can be found. Such critical assessments have much to provide as critical ethnic studies scholars think through radical epistemologies and the collective work yet to be done to build a new humanity that I have traced in the connection of Fanon, Malcolm, and Kochiyama. And while this recovery of a politics of dissent and protest are central to these figures, it is a way that the structures of the world are imagined in a future tense, in a world yet to be made: a horizon of possibility.

NOTES

1. Sylvia Wynter, "'No Humans Involved:' An Open Letter to My Colleagues," *Forum NHI* 1, no. 1 (1994): 42. Wynter's essay launched a newly inaugurated journal by the NHI Institute in which the first issue was dedicated to the celebration of her work alongside that of Harold Cruse. The table of contents included a "Mission Statement" and "A Black Studies Manifesto," the latter of which was authored by Wynter.

2. Ibid., 70.

3. Alice Cherki, *Frantz Fanon: A Portrait* (Ithaca, N.Y.: Cornell University Press, 2006), 129–30.

4. Ibid., 130; David Macey, *Frantz Fanon: A Biography*, 2nd ed. (New York: Verso Books, 2012), 390.

5. Macey, *Frantz Fanon*, 389–90.

6. Ibid., 6.

7. Ibid., 355.

8. Ibid., 484.

9. Fouzi Slisli, "Islam: The Elephant in Fanon's *The Wretched of the Earth*," *Critique: Critical Middle Eastern Studies* 17, no. 1 (2008): 97–108; and Fouzi Slisli, "'The Idea That One Could Come to Terms with the Arabs': How Frantz Fanon Found Common Ground with Islam in Algeria," *Black Scholar* 42, no. 3–4 (2012): 21–26.

10. Frantz Fanon, *A Dying Colonialism* (New York: Grove Press, 1980), 165.

11. Ronald T. Judy, "Fanon's Body of Black Experience," In *Fanon: A Critical Reader*, ed. Lewis R. Gordon, T. Denean Sharpley-Whiting, and Renée T. White (Cambridge, Mass.: Blackwell Publishers, 1996).

12. Glen Coulthard's recent engagement with Fanon in *Red Skin, White Masks* makes a significant critique of the politics of recognition in multicultural Canada and an argument for autonomous notions of Native sovereignty. Glen Sean Coulthard, *Red Skin, White Masks: Rejecting the Colonial Politics of Recognition* (Minneapolis: University of Minnesota Press, 2014).

13. Edward E. Curtis IV, "'My Heart Is in Cairo': Malcolm X, the Arab Cold War, and the Making of Islamic Liberation Ethics," *Journal of American History* 102, no. 3 (2015): 776.

14. For an early interpretation of Malcolm's religious life see, Abdelwahab M. Elmessiri, "Islam As a Pastoral in the Life of Malcolm X," in *Malcolm X: The Man and His Times*, ed. John Henrik Clarke (New York, Macmillan, 1990), 69–78; and Louis A. DeCaro, *On the Side of My People: A Religious Life of Malcolm X* (New York: New York University Press, 1996).

15. Malcolm X, "Not Just an American Problem, But a World Problem," in *Malcolm X: Collected Speeches, Debates & Interviews (1960–1965)*, ed. Sandeep S. Atwal, http://www.malcolmxfiles.blogspot.com, 2015), 1152–53.

16. Manning Marable's important biography of Malcolm X is a clear example of a Black secular left perspective. Manning Marable, *Malcolm X: A Life of Reinvention* (New York: Viking, 2011).

17. Diane C. Fujino, *Heartbeat of Struggle: The Revolutionary Life of Yuri Kochiyama* (Minneapolis: University of Minnesota Press, 2005), 211.

18. For example, see James H. Cone, *A Black Theology of Liberation*, 1st ed. (Philadelphia, Penn.: Lippincott, 1970); Enrique D. Dussel *Ethics of Liberation in the Age of Globalization and Exclusion*, ed. Alejandro A. Vallega (Durham, N.C.: Duke University Press, 2013); and Gustavo Gutiérrez, *A Theology of Liberation: History, Politics, and Salvation* (Maryknoll, N.Y.: Orbis Books, 1973).

19. An example of this is Sohail Daulatzai's idea of the Muslim International. See, Sohail Daulatzai, *Black Star, Crescent Moon: The Muslim International and Black Freedom beyond America* (Minneapolis: University of Minnesota Press, 2012).

20. Fujino, *Heartbeat of Struggle*, 212.

21. Ibid.

22. Junaid Rana and Diane C. Fujino, "Taking Risks, or The Question of Palestine Solidarity and Asian American Studies," *American Quarterly* 67, no. 4 (2015): 1033.

23. Yuri Kochiyama, Marjorie Lee, Akemi Kochiyama-Sardinha, and Audee Kochiyama-Holman, *Passing It On: A Memoir* (Los Angeles: UCLA Asian American Studies Center Press, 2004), 129.

24. Stefano Harney and Fred Moten, *The Undercommons: Fugitive Planning and Black Study* (New York: Minor Compositions, 2013).

25. James Baldwin, *The Fire Next Time* (London: Hutchinson, 1967), and *No Name in the Street* (New York: Dial Press, 1972).

26. Malcolm X and Alex Haley, *The Autobiography of Malcolm X* (New York: Grove Press, 1965).

CHAPTER 7

Outsourcing, Terror, and Transnational South Asia

Asha Nadkarni

When Chris Jobin's computer programming job was outsourced to India in 2006, he traveled to Bangalore as part of Morgan Spurlock's television series *30 Days* to ask, "Dude, where's my job?" The series, in which a person spends thirty days immersing themselves in another person's lifestyle, documents Jobin's time in India: He lives with a local family; he finds work in a call center; and he has various revelations about himself, India, and the changing global economy. Originally irate over losing his job, at the end of his thirty days he proclaims, "knowing that . . . probably sixteen people are surviving off of my one job in this horrible, horrible country—it's almost . . . charitable." The "charity" that Jobin describes is not just economic, though the episode does show Jobin's shock over poverty in India as well as his dismay at the riots after the death of Kannada actor Rajkumar. But more narrative weight is given to the decision made by Soni (the wife of the family with whom Jobin is living) to work outside the home in a call center. This decision is framed within general statements about Indian tradition versus U.S. modernity, with Jobin observing, "Indians right now are totally 1950s Americans." This statement disarms the challenge posed by outsourcing by placing it within a developmental trajectory in which India is decades behind the United States, both economically and socially. Nonetheless, because Jobin remains the protagonist of this story, the drama of outsourcing to India is framed as a threat to the upward mobility of the white, heteropatriarchal family.[1]

A threat of a different sort was unleashed on December 2, 2015, when married couple Syed Rizwan Farook and Tashfeen Malik opened fire at a holiday party at the Inland Regional Center in San Bernardino, California, killing fourteen people. The couple died hours later in a confrontation with police. Labeled as having carried out "an act of terrorism" by the FBI, the shooters appear to have been supportive of the Islamic State but acting on their own devices. Much has been made of the fact that Farook was born in the United States to parents of Pakistani origin and that Malik (also originally from Pakistan, though she spent time in Saudi Arabia) came to the country legally on a K-1 visa. Indeed, that they both were legally in the country prompted then–presidential candidate Donald Trump to propose a ban on all Muslims from entering the United States.[2] This tragic incident thus both brings up and confuses many of the stereotypes around terrorists. In the first place, Farook and Malik reference multiple nodes of the Pakistani diaspora, allowing us to unpack how, as Junaid Rana argues in *Terrifying Muslims*, "the figures of the terrorist and the migrant are woven together in the figure of 'the Muslim' as a racial type."[3] At the same time, the fact that they were a married couple with a young baby confounds stereotypes of terrorists as male, single, and as rendered outside of the heteropatriarchal family.[4] But to the extent that the San Bernardino case disrupts these figurations, it is immediately folded back into another narrative—one of an Islamic patriarchy that is itself a sign of extremism. As the title of a *Huffington Post* blog post would have it, "Patriarchy Pulled the Trigger."[5]

I begin this essay with these disparate examples to examine outsourcing and terror as two forms transnational circuits between the United States and South Asia take. I trace these phenomena in relation to longer histories of British imperialism, postcolonial nationalisms, and U.S. neoimperialism in the form of development, arguing that they are key to understanding contemporary relationships between, and representations of, outsourcing and terror in the United States. In taking up outsourcing and terror as flashpoints within Asian American studies, I argue that if much of the rhetoric surrounding outsourcing relies on techno-Orientalist tropes (as I will examine in a 2004 *Wired* feature story on outsourcing to India), those surrounding terrorism rely on Orientalist ones (as I will examine in a 2016 *New Yorker* story on the San Bernardino shooters). On one side, we have the new "Asian peril" in the specter of jobs lost to Asians better suited to the current needs of global modernity. On the other side, we have terror as modernity's opposite, a notion popularly expressed in the polarized formulation of *Jihad vs. McWorld*.[6] Examining the gendered implications of these constructions, and asserting that outsourcing and terror are linked through the discourse of development, I suggest they are two sides of the same coin of capitalist modernity gone awry.

In launching this investigation, I also point to the different places occupied by India and Pakistan within the U.S. imaginary and within South Asian American studies. Specifically, thinking through the discursive and material relationship between outsourcing and terror forces us to confront the commonplace perception that associates India with technology and Pakistan with terrorism.[7] This division, as the editors of *The Sun Never Sets* note, is not a new one but is too often obscured within a South Asian American studies wherein India is hegemonic. By tracing the longer histories of outsourcing and terror in relation to imperial, national, and developmental regimes in the subcontinent and the United States, I draw attention to how these stereotypes are linked rather than simply opposed. At the same time, the necessarily mixed approach that such an inquiry requires asks us to think differently about the transnational by drawing attention to the continued place of nationalism and state power in various sites and iterations. Instead of a transnationally inflected Asian American studies, I argue for a transnational, postcolonial approach that provides a truly global framework for tracing circuits of nationalism, immigration, labor, and state power, and that crucially centers development as a way of thinking through these convergences.

"Terrorism from Without" and "Economic Terrorism from Within": Outsourcing, Terror, and Development

> What's going on with this offshoring of American jobs to India and China is nothing but . . . economic terrorism. The job of government is to protect citizens, and that means protect them from terrorism from without, such as foreign terrorists flying airplanes into buildings, or economic terrorism from within, which is exactly what some CEOs of companies engaged in outsourcing are doing.
>
> *Frank LaGrotta, former member of the*
> *Pennsylvania House of Representatives*[8]

The concern articulated by former Pennsylvania representative Frank LaGrotta—that the outsourcing of jobs to Asia represents a threat equal to that posed by the terrorist attacks of 2001—references two different ways in which U.S. futures are in jeopardy. Even as the "economic terrorists" he refers to are the CEOs who move jobs to "India and China," the rhetorical force of the comparison derives from the discursive relationship between brownness and terrorism. Conflating the perpetrators of the 9/11 attacks with U.S. CEOs at first glance seems a stunning indictment of U.S. corporate practices. But what gives this comparison rhetorical weight is the sense that both of the threats are emanating from brown people "over there."

In *In Stereotype: South Asia in the Global Literary Imaginary*, Mrinalini Chakravorty explores the relationship between outsourcing and terror, asking whether they represent "good and bad transnationalisms." Certainly they are connected via the dialectical relationship between work and terror, wherein the antidote to terrorism is development and job creation in the Global South. As two of the most predominant stereotypes of transnational South Asia and South Asians, however, outsourcing and terror rehearse related but opposing concerns: Whereas terror attacks global capital, outsourcing serves it. As such, Chakravorty contends, they "present competing accounts of how we relate to the extension of transnationalism as a cultural and economic phenomenon. They steady very different narratives about the global reaches of certain types of coercion as the exercise of free will."[9] Is development freedom, to paraphrase Amartya Sen, or is freedom signified by attacking the basic premises of development: modernization and global capitalism?[10]

Extending Chakravorty's argument, I argue that both outsourcing and terror are understood as "bad," if distinctive, aspects of transnational South Asia in the United States.[11] Within mainstream U.S. discourse, outsourcing and terror represent different kinds of transnational attacks on the so-called American dream. If terrorism threatens, in the language of Franklin Delano Roosevelt's "Four Freedoms," "freedom from fear," then outsourcing threatens "freedom from want." My framing of the twin dilemmas of terror and outsourcing in these terms deliberately references their imbrication within a longer history of U.S. developmentalism. Roosevelt's Four Freedoms are part of a global discourse of modernization that has roots in Woodrow Wilson's "Fourteen Points" and culminates in Truman's "Point Four" speech, which is commonly understood as inaugurating the age of development. I thus situate this latest moment of transnationalism within the context of a discursive shift beginning around World War I, whereby the globe came to be viewed as a conceptual whole connected through new technologies and posing new threats. The key to containing these threats was not only by securing U.S. territories and strategic interests but also by spreading U.S. values and institutions (especially those related to gender, sexuality, and family) to the globe at large via the apparatus of development.[12] As such, the discourse of modernization necessarily depends on the United States as both the model to be followed and the nation to lead the way.

Thinking through the links between outsourcing and terror, moreover, speaks to longer imperial connections between the United States and India and to longer colonial histories of the extraction of labor from the Global South. As Kalindi Vora argues in *Life Support*, contemporary practices of outsourcing must be placed in relation to colonial allocations of labor and the resultant international division of labor. Focusing on "biocapital as a system of capitalist production, accumulation, and speculation that relies directly on reproductivity as its primary motor," Vora posits outsourcing as a form of affective reproductive labor done in the Global South for the benefit of those in the Global North.[13] This attention to how outsourcing is an extension of colonial divisions of labor and to how the service work of outsourcing is accordingly gendered and racialized is fundamental to historicizing the phenomenon of outsourcing.

Nonetheless, the specificity of British colonial and U.S. imperial regimes in India is not fully accounted for in Vora's discussion. Vora rightly cites the way that British colonialism set up infrastructures that integrated India into the global economy, not least of which was the creation of an English-speaking liberal bourgeoisie who would determine the course of the postcolonial nation's development. Similarly, the colonial allocations of labor that are a legacy of British colonialism pertain to current extractions of labor from India, as Vora demonstrates. Nonetheless, the United States had a specific set of concerns and tactics within the subcontinent as, in the words of the editors of *The Sun Never Sets*, "the territorial empire of the British gave way to the spread of U.S.-led globalization."[14] At issue here is how the United States, as both an ally of and competitor with British colonialism in India, set itself as the modernizing agent in India in the years leading up to Indian independence and then continued to operate as a modernizing force in the region through the guise of development. As Sujani Reddy, Mrinalini Sinha, and others argue, it is precisely because the United States got involved in India through the realm of public health and medicine that it became the agent of modernity in the region as opposed to Britain, which was largely understood as having abdicated this role.[15] This relationship between U.S. imperialism and modernity also paved the way for U.S. developmental regimes in the subcontinent. This is crucial because developmentalism's progressivist creed at once recapitulated many of the commonplaces of colonialism and became a key articulation of postcolonial nationalisms.[16]

From the point of view of the United States, development (both in the form of direct aid and of the transfer of technical knowledge) served a number of purposes. Development was intended to promote U.S. values and institutions, open up new markets for U.S. capital, and serve as part of a Cold War containment strategy. In South Asia, this meant that development aid to the region was supplemented by a military alliance with Pakistan to counter the threat of Indian nonalignment.[17] Additionally, the United States was involved in the Afghan-Pakistan region through supporting (via provisions of money and weapons) proxies fighting the Soviet Union, such as the Taliban and Al-Qaeda, groups that are now prime targets of the U.S.-led "War on Terror."

At the same time, modernization—a doctrine largely conceived in and advanced by the United States—was critical to both the Indian and Pakistani postcolonial states.[18] Indeed, the direction state-led development planning in India took is an important part of the story of outsourcing. Jawaharlal Nehru instituted much of the existing infrastructure for technology in the postindependence era of nation building through the expansion of technical institutes. This of course created the labor pool for the "brain drain," as countries in the Global North recruited a skilled labor pool that had been supported and trained by infrastructure in India. This state-sponsored emphasis on science and technology also created the infrastructure for the contemporary phenomenon of the outsourcing of information technology (IT) labor to India, a phenomenon further made possible by the liberalization of the Indian economy beginning in 1991.[19]

In the case of Pakistan, as Junaid Rana details in *Terrifying Muslims*, the emphasis on modernization and industrialization had several consequences. In the first place, labor-union busting policies from the 1950s on (which were effectively completed by the time of the Zulfikar Ali Bhutto regime of the 1970s) "exacerbated class differences by decreasing the resources available for agriculture and increasing poverty, all the while generating data that perpetuated the dependence model for development aid."[20] This also led to the liberalization of the Pakistani economy through the 1980s and 1990s. One further consequence of this, as Rana traces, is that the impoverishment of already struggling populations led to labor migrations by Pakistanis to points all over the globe.

Although modernization theory fell out of favor by the 1970s (for a variety of reasons, not least of which was that it did not work as predicted), the rise of neoliberalism in the 1980s replaced the global vision of modernization theory with one that was remarkably similar, even if achieved by different ends. The key difference between modernization theory and neoliberalism is the role of the state—instead of the state manipulating development, all that was necessary was to let capitalism run its course.[21] Nonetheless, even if the neoliberal stance toward the state considers it most useful for getting out of the way, there are various state structures, like tax exemptions, that support the outsourcing industry in India. Thus one of the contradictions of the current moment is that neoliberal appraisals of the state as effective only through its absence "[fail] to consider that the current situation [of outsourcing] is the direct result of at least two generations of state-sponsored investment in scientific and technical education."[22] Similarly, U.S. military campaigns in Iraq, Afghanistan, and elsewhere certainly advance through state power—even if much of the labor for them has been outsourced to private companies.

Migrating Jobs, Migrating People: Outsourcing and Terror in the United States

Before the so-termed transnational turn in Asian Americanist scholarship beginning in the 1990s, Asian American studies largely took migration to the United States as a point of departure, thereby reinstantiating a U.S. nationalist frame. South Asian American studies always had a slightly different relationship to this, in that South Asian American studies has had to reckon with the histories of British imperialism, U.S. imperialism, and the condition of diaspora. In this sense, one of the strengths brought by South Asian American studies to Asian American studies more generally was this consideration of the postcolonial within and alongside the diasporic.[23] Nonetheless, many works within South Asian American studies focus predominantly on the post-1965 period, when the Hart-Celler Act brought the first major wave of migration from the subcontinent. This focus has had several consequences. The first is that South Asian migration to the west coast of North America in the late nineteenth and early twentieth centuries has received comparatively less attention. The second is that focusing on post-1965 immigration from the subcontinent naturalizes South Asian Americans as "model minority" subjects skilled in science and math, ignoring the specific history of how Hart-Celler and Nehruvian development in India dovetailed to produce privileged migrants.[24] Finally, it obscures both less privileged migrations and the role of U.S. imperial and developmental policies in South Asian migrations in general.

As Sujani Reddy argues in *Nursing & Empire*, histories of South Asian immigration to the United States that fail to take into account postcolonial conditions in the subcontinent are flawed in that they ignore how U.S. "immigration law was but one tool in the expansion of the imperial nation."[25] To view immigration laws in isolation of U.S. overseas policies, she argues, is to enforce a form of what she calls "model minority exceptionalism," in which immigration to the United States becomes the only possible end point of decolonization. Instead, Reddy coins the term "diaspora of decolonization" to "[reference] the ways in which . . . neocolonialism . . . produced a forced exile from the full promise of a definition of decolonization (understood as the end to the inequities of colonial extraction and expropriation)."[26] In other words, we must read South Asian diasporas in relation to the continued forms of imperialism that deny full decolonization in the subcontinent.

We also must read these diasporas in relation to the longer histories of the abstraction of Asian labor in the U.S. context. As Colleen Lye demonstrates in *America's Asia*, Asia and Asian Americans have always been linked with the economic. Extending Lye's insights, Iyko Day argues in *Alien Capital* that Asian labor's association with abstract capital undergirds settler colonialism. Within what she terms "romantic anticapitalism," "an ideology that anthropomorphizes capitalism's abstract dimension as alien Asian labor," the association between Asian Americans and abstract labor sanctions anti-Asian sentiment as the foundation of the settler-colonial nation.[27] This abstraction is associated with both model minority subjects and with poor migrants (a distinction she glosses by labeling the former "techno coolies" and the latter "retro coolies") as the two faces of abstract labor. In the case of Muslim migrants, as Rana explores in relation to Pakistani labor migrations, "transnational labor migration has created a contingent class subjected to the selective enforcement of policing, deportation, and criminality."[28] Situating outsourcing and terror within this framework, the idea of exporting jobs, rather than importing people, becomes an extension of anti-immigrant politics as a negotiation between white settler colonialism and business needs. Why control racialized labor at the border when you can exploit that labor in their own countries? The logic of this statement is undergirded by the connection between terror and migration in the U.S. racial formation of the Muslim.[29] If one stereotype of Asians is that they are unusually attuned to capitalist modernity, the other stereotype is that they are unfit for that modernity. In either case, Asians and Asian Americans are dehumanized; they are either machines or animals.

Perhaps unsurprisingly, the metaphor of the worker as a machine is brandished time and again in the 2004 issue of *Wired* magazine to which I now turn. Titled "The New Face of the Silicon Age: How India Became the Capital of the Computing Revolution," the magazine cover features the face of a beautiful brown woman staring into the camera.[30] Her hand is covering her mouth, and her turned-out palm is decorated with computer code in the style of a mehendi design. Adding to the innuendo of the image is the text written at the top of the image: "Kiss your cubicle good-bye." This feminine, sexualized image evokes and reinforces outsourced labor as reproductive, as does its allusions to marriage through the gold jewelry the model is wearing and the mehendi pattern on her hands.

Despite putting this attractive face on outsourcing, however, one of the predominant metaphors for the outsourcing worker is that of a machine. In an article in the special issue appropriately titled "The Indian Machine," the Indian labor force as described as "an artificial intelligence, the superbrain that never arrived *in silico*. No wonder [U.S.] workers tremble."[31] This picture of Indian workers as "machines" trades in long-standing discourses of "techno-Orientalism"—what David S. Roh, Betsy Huang, and Greta A. Niu define as "the phenomenon of imagining Asia and Asians in hypo- or hypertechnological terms in cultural productions and political discourse."[32] Whereas Orientalism, in Edward Said's formulation, relies on atavistic visions of Asia as locked in an enervated traditional past and thus out of step with modernity, techno-Orientalist visions take Asia and Asians as representing a dystopic future to be guarded against. In this, argue the editors of *Techno-Orientalism*, both forms of Orientalism are strategies of asserting the United States (or the West more generally) as the normative center. Rendering Asians as examples of "an artificial intelligence" makes them both threatening and containable. In the case of outsourcing to India, this techno-Orientalist view is married to longer-standing Orientalist tropes of India as feminized and sexualized, as the magazine cover implies.

That the United States, as technological leader, has nothing to fear from "the Indian Machine" is affirmed by a second article that claims that rather than "tremble," U.S. workers should simply realize that real innovation remains with the United States. Like computers, "Indian machines" will free up U.S. innovation to focus on more important tasks: "After all, before these Indian programmers have something to fabricate, maintain, test, or upgrade, that something first must be imagined and invented. . . . All of which require aptitudes that are more difficult to outsource—imagination, empathy, and the ability to forge relationships."[33] Returning to *30 Days*,

Chris Jobin has a similar realization, repeatedly remarking in reference to call center work that "there are certain jobs we don't aspire to in America. But Indians aspire to these jobs." The episode ends with Jobin's epiphany that in the United States people can refashion themselves without restrictions; indeed, after *30 Days* Jobin has found work as an actor.[34]

But even as outsourced labor is denigrated as reproductive, the reproductive aspect is also rendered as a threat. The *Wired* feature story begins, "meet the pissed-off programmer. . . . He's the guy—and yeah, he's usually a guy—launching Web sites like yourjobisgoingtoindia.com and no-jobsforindia.com."[35] In this article, as in *30 Days* and the 2006 film and 2010 television series *Outsourced*, outsourcing is dramatized through the dilemma of the white male protagonist who has been displaced. In the article, outsourcing is brandished as a threat to U.S. masculinity and then soothed through the figuration of outsourced labor as reproductive (in this light, the metaphor of marriage that the *Wired* cover evokes comes into stunning focus). But of course it does not really soothe, because instead it goes back to earlier notions of the yellow peril as a racialized economic threat that is also reproductive. Such figurations of outsourced labor thus evoke "race suicide" arguments from the turn of the twentieth century that because Asians had a lower standard of living, would work for lower wages, and were more fecund, they would swamp white America. Such fears are furthermore bolstered by longstanding stereotypes of India as overpopulated, thereby referencing histories of U.S. interventions into reproduction in India through regimes of population control. If there the concern with Indian reproduction was that it would halt development, here the fear is that U.S. workers will be swamped by a workforce who can perform white-collar jobs for "the wages of a Taco Bell counter jockey."[36]

If such techno-Orientalist fantasies are problematic in that they suggest Asians are dangerously attuned to capitalist modernity, discourses of terrorism understand them as opposed to modernity. As Sunaina Maira asserts, "terror is an 'epistemological object' defined by modernity and attributed to the 'nonmodern' and 'nonliberal.'"[37] In current constructions of terrorism as Islamic terrorism, the terrorist as "nonmodern" dovetails with Orientalist figurations of Islam. This is what Rana theorizes as an "Islamic peril," in which the War on Terror links immigration to terror and racializes Muslims in the United States as terrorists, using language that borrows on U.S. Orientalist constructions of Muslims as modernity's atavistic others. As he explains, "constructions of Muslims as a racial group are drawn from a historical genealogy that comprehends Islam as the antithesis of Western modernity and that further perceives Islam as a threat to modernity and democracy and the freedom that they bring."[38] These Orientalist renderings of Islam and Muslims rely on a civilizational ideology embedded in the developmentalism I traced in the last section.

I now return to the San Bernardino shootings, discussing them in relation to a February 22, 2016, *New Yorker* article by William Finnegan titled "Last Days: Preparing for the Apocalypse in San Bernardino." The article details the radicalization of Syed Rizwan Farook and attempts to fill in Tashfeen Malik's backstory, but the key puzzle that Finnegan is trying to work out is "Why did the attack happen?" As quickly as the question is posed it is answered: "There had been no displays of anger, no indication. Only growing piety." The logic is clear; piety itself seems to be the key to the radicalization of the couple into so-called Jihadi culture. This statement about piety, coming at the beginning of the article, is counterpoised throughout with descriptions of an Islam more easily assimilable to U.S. multiculturalism. An interview with Mustafa Kuko, director of the Islamic Center of Riverside (where Farook once prayed and where he married Malik), describes the community he serves as "moderate, passive," saying that its members are simply "looking for the American Dream."[39] Within this context, "growing piety" is a threatening break from a moderate norm and thus becomes in itself a sign for concern.

The piety of Tashfeen Malik is focused on most throughout the article. As a married woman with a six-month-old baby, Malik presents a rather anomalous terrorist figure. But the signs of her radicalization were visible, the article suggests, in the gendered signs of her observance. In contrast to Farook's "blond and attractive" Russian beautician sister-in-law, who was comfortable posing for photos "in a bikini," Malik's conservative dress is referenced time and again. Because Malik "normally wore a niqab—the face veil, leaving only the eyes visible," her husband's male relatives "had never seen her face or heard her voice." The article also mentions that she "declined to drive a car" and "didn't speak to neighbors," calling her a "postpartum shut-in." In painting this picture, Finnegan uncritically reproduces the point of view of the couples' landlord, who says that Malik "did not like to be seen. She did not seem to like people around her. [Farook] seemed ordinary, no worries for me at all. I'm only now thinking that maybe she wore the pants. It could be that she was behind it all."[40]

The focus on the gendered aspects of Malik's observance—her wearing the niqab, her segregation from the men in the family—are translated into an inability and unwillingness to assimilate to "modern" U.S. gender norms. This is what makes Malik suspicious. If U.S.-born Farook appeared "ordinary," then Malik must have, in an ironic turn of phrase, been "[wearing] the pants," and masterminding the attack. In some ways, this presents a contradiction; within a liberal feminist framework, Malik's veiling and preference for gender segregation could be understood as an index of her patriarchal oppression, resonating with long-standing Orientalist ideas about repressive patriarchal countries in which women need saving. But instead, the outward signs of Malik's observance function as a sign of terrifying agency. Whereas the language of saving Muslim women has bolstered the War on Terror, here it is brandished as a pathology of gender roles that itself translates into terror. Thus, in critiquing this article my point is that the conceptual language through which the horror of the shootings is apprehended is impoverished for how it draws on stereotypes as well as for how it impedes any real understanding of what it would mean to prevent such tragedies.

Conclusion: Modi in Silicon Valley

In September 2015, Indian Prime Minister Narendra Modi visited California's Silicon Valley to much fanfare. Modi's itinerary included meetings with major technology companies (three of which—Google, Microsoft, and Adobe—have Indian-born chief executives) and culminated in a town hall–style meeting with Facebook founder Mark Zuckerberg. The enthusiasm with which Modi's overtures to Silicon Valley were met—by the considerable population of Indian diasporics in the region as well as by the U.S. press—glossed over the significantly less savory aspects of Modi's Bharatiya Janata Party (BJP) government and of his political career, particularly his role in the 2002 anti-Muslim pogrom in Gujarat.[41] In other words, those who laud Modi's embrace of neoliberal policies do so at the peril of ignoring the ways in which Modi's neoliberalism goes hand in hand with Hindu fundamentalism and sectarian violence. Prominent U.S. academics of South Asian studies issued an open letter of protest, and over three thousand protesters formed an "unwelcoming party," but for the most part Modi's visit was received as an important attempt to solidify, as he put it, the "India-U.S. partnership as a defining partnership of this century."[42] Key to this enterprise is capitalizing on the links between diasporic Indians and the "homeland," turning the so-called brain drain into a "brain gain."[43] In this sense, Modi's visit to the Silicon Valley engaged with histories of South Asian migration to the United States: not just that of post-1965 skilled workers, which was the population most directly targeted by his whirlwind tour, but also late nineteenth- and early twentieth–century migrations of South Asians to the U.S. West

Coast (a Ghadar legacy more properly embodied by the protests against Modi). The enthusiasm with which many in the Indian diaspora received him furthermore implicates diasporic Indians in the United States for what Vijay Prashad has named "Yankee Hindutva"—the ideological and material ways Indians in the diaspora have supported Hindu fundamentalism in the subcontinent.[44]

I end with Modi's visit for several key reasons. First, the way that Modi links neoliberal economic policies with religious fundamentalism is telling in how it confounds a divide between outsourcing and terrorism—rather than understanding them as confronting each other as unrelated phenomena, Modi's mix of neoliberalism and fundamentalism demonstrates how they are interrelated. Second, Modi's visit raises the issue of the different kind of visibility of South Asian American communities, with India as technology and Pakistan as terror. But even within this bifurcation, it also reminds us that if in the late nineteenth and early twentieth centuries all South Asians were misnamed "Hindoo," now they are all misread as potential "terrorists." Modi's "tough on terror" stance, which was in full display during his speech at San Jose's SAP center, seeks to undo this connection, even though (or, perhaps, precisely because) it is also disturbingly linked to violence against Muslims on the subcontinent.

Finally, Modi's visit to Silicon Valley indexes longer histories of imperialism and neoimperialism. This last point was brought into focus through the controversy surrounding the government of India's February 2016 decision to end Facebook's internet.org and Free Basics—projects that would provide free mobile internet in India but that also raised concerns about net neutrality. In response to the government's decision, Facebook board member Marc Andreessen tweeted: "anti-colonialism has been economically catastrophic for the Indian people for decades. Why stop now?"[45] This (presumably unintentionally) perceptive remark, which names Facebook's digital penetration of India via infrastructure creation as "colonialism," sparked a firestorm of controversy and necessitated apologies on Andreessen's (and Zuckerberg's) behalf. But it is important for how it scrapes away the triumphal language of partnership leveraged by Modi during his visit and reveals much more fraught power relations and imperial histories that persist in both South Asia and the diaspora.

In concluding with Andreessen's comments, I suggest that in order to understand outsourcing and terror as two linked faces of transnational South Asia in the United States, we require a truly global frame; one that uncovers the workings of U.S. power at home and abroad and that seriously interrogates the aspirations and machinations of postcolonial nationalisms as they are in confrontation and collusion with the United States. The problem in this sense is a transnationalism that, in being critical of nationalisms in general, nonetheless reinstantiates U.S. nationalism. Insofar as Asian American studies (even a transnationally inflected Asian American studies) retains a primarily U.S. domestic optic, it cannot (as Kavita Daiya argues following Dipesh Chakrabarty) adequately "provincialize America."[46] Instead as Andreessen's comments suggest, the horizon of decolonization remains ever in the future.

NOTES

1. Morgan Spurlock, "Outsourcing," *30 Days*, FX, aired August 2, 2006.

2. After winning the presidency on November 8, 2016, Donald Trump's statement advocating "a total and complete shutdown of Muslims entering the United States" was temporarily removed from his website, although it later reappeared. Trump subsequently changed his policy to apply to Muslim immigration from countries "compromised by terrorism." After the December 19, 2016, attack in Berlin, Germany, however, Trump reaffirmed his commitment to both banning Muslim immigration to the United States and creating a Muslim registry.

3. Junaid Rana, *Terrifying Muslims: Race and Labor in the South Asian Diaspora* (Durham, N.C.: Duke University Press, 2011), 5.

4. See Jasbir Puar, *Terrorist Assemblages: Homonationalism in Queer Times* (Durham, N.C.: Duke University Press, 2007).

5. James Marshal Crotty, "In San Bernardino Shooting, Patriarchy Pulled the Trigger," *Huffington Post: The Blog*, December 8, 2015, http://www.huffingtonpost.com/james-marshall-crotty/san-bernardino-shooters-c_b_8729896.html.

6. Benjamin Barber, *Jihad vs. McWorld: Terrorism's Challenge to Democracy* (New York: Ballantine, 1995).

7. Rana, *Terrifying Muslims*, 6. See also Gayatri Gopinath, "Bollywood Spectacles: Queer Diasporic Critique in the Aftermath of 9/11," *Social Text* 84–85, nos. 3–4 (2005); and also Vivek Bald, Miabi Chatterji, Sujani Reddy, and Manu Vimalassery, eds., introduction to *The Sun Never Sets: South Asian Migrants in an Age of U.S. Power* (New York: NYU Press, 2013).

8. Quoted in Bob Evans, "Business Technology: The Silos of Protectionism: Time to Raise Them, Or Raze Them?," *InformationWeek*, March 12, 2004, http://www.informationweek.com/business-technology-the-silos-of-protectionism-time-to-raise-them-or-raze-them/d/d-id/1023769?.

9. Mrinalini Chakravorty, *In Stereotype: South Asia in the Global Literary Imaginary* (New York: Columbia University Press, 2014), 190.

10. Amartya Sen, *Development as Freedom* (New York: Knopf, 1999).

11. In making this claim I also acknowledge the slippage between South Asian and Arab but suggest that the slippage is very much to point, as all "brown" people come to been seen as suspect. In addition to Rana, *Terrifying Muslims*, see Nitasha Sharma, "Brown," in *Keywords for Asian American Studies*, ed. K. Scott Wong, Cathy J. Schlund-Vials, and Linda Trinh Võ (New York: NYU Press, 2015). See also Sunaina Maira and Magid Shihade, "Meeting Asian/Arab American Studies: Thinking Race, Empire, and Zionism in the U.S.," *Journal of Asian American Studies* 9, no. 2 (2006): 117–40.

12. See Michael Latham, *The Right Kind of Revolution: Modernization, Development, and U.S. Foreign Policy from the Cold War to the Present* (Ithaca, N.Y.: Cornell University Press, 2010); and Gilbert Rist, *The History of Development: From Western Origins to Global Faith* (New York: Zed, 1997).

13. Kalindi Vora, *Life Support: Biocapital and the New History of Outsourced Labor* (Minneapolis: University of Minnesota Press, 2015), 7.

14. Bald et al., introduction, *The Sun Never Sets*, 8.

15. As Mrinalini Sinha, Sujani Reddy, and Asha Nadkarni show, the debates around Katherine Mayo's 1927 muckraking volume, *Mother India*, were crucial to this. See Mrinalini Sinha, *Specters of Mother India: The Global Restructuring of an Empire* (Durham, N.C.: Duke University Press, 2006); Sujani Reddy, *Nursing & Empire: Gendered Labor and Migration from India to the United States* (Chapel Hill: University of North Carolina Press, 2015); Asha Nadkarni, *Eugenic Feminism: National Reproduction in the United States and India* (Minneapolis: University of Minnesota Press, 2014).

16. In this sense, as María Josefina Saldaña-Portillo argues, "it is precisely the marriage of development and decolonization that discursively legitimates the extraction of resources and productive capacity in a way that the civilizing mission of colonialism never could." María Josefina Saldaña-Portillo, *The Revolutionary Imagination in the Americas and the Age of Development* (Durham, N.C.: Duke University Press, 2003), 22.

17. Latham, *The Right Kind of Revolution*, 69–70.

18. Nadkarni, *Eugenic Feminism*, 136–39.

19. See Vijay Prashad, *The Karma of Brown Folk* (Minneapolis: University of Minnesota Press, 2001); and Reddy, *Nursing & Empire*, 129–31.

20. Rana, *Terrifying Muslims*, 13.

21. Latham, *The Right Kind of Revolution*, 58.

22. Aradhana Sharma and Akhil Gupta, *The Anthropology of the State: A Reader* (New York: Blackwell, 2006), 4.

23. For just two examples of this work see Rajini Srikanth, *The World Next Door: South Asian American Literature and the Idea of America* (Philadelphia, Penn.: Temple University Press, 2004); and Bakirathi Mani, *Aspiring*

to Home: South Asians in America (Stanford, Calif.: Stanford University Press, 2012).

24. Prashad, *Karma,* and *Uncle Swami: South Asians in America Today* (New York: New Press, 2012).

25. Reddy, *Nursing & Empire,* 7.

26. Ibid., 11.

27. Iyko Day, *Alien Capital: Racialization and the Logic of Settler Colonial Capitalism* (Durham, N.C.: Duke University Press, 2016), 154.

28. Rana, *Terrifying Muslims,* 132–33.

29. Ibid., 73.

30. Daniel Pink, "The New Face of the Silicon Age," *Wired,* February 1, 2004, http://www.wired.com/2004/02/india/.

31. Chris Anderson, "The Indian Machine," *Wired,* February 1, 2004, http://www.wired.com/2004/02/india/.

32. David S. Roh, Betsy Huang, and Greta A. Niu, *Techno-Orientalism: Imagining Asia in Speculative Fiction, History, and Media* (New Brunswick, N.J.: Rutgers University Press, 2015), 2.

33. In her discussion of this same issue of *Wired,* Vora rightly contests this vision, arguing instead for "the centrality of creativity, innovation, and imagination in the social lives and experiences of transnational IT workers." Vora, *Life Support,* 69.

34. "Chris Jobin," Internet Movie Database, http://www.imdb.com/name /nm2144875/?ref_=nmmd_md_nm.

35. Pink, "The New Face of the Silicon Age."

36. Ibid.

37. Sunaina Maira, "'Good' and 'Bad' Muslim Citizens: Feminists, Terrorists, and U.S. Orientalisms," *Feminist Studies* 35, no. 3 (Fall 2009): 631–56.

38. Rana, *Terrifying Muslims,* 67.

39. William Finnegan, "Last Days: Preparing for the Apocalypse in San Bernardino," *New Yorker,* February 22, 2016, http://www.newyorker.com /magazine/2016/02/22/preparing-for-apocalypse-in-san-bernardino.

40. Ibid.

41. Because of his part in the 2002 pogrom, Modi was denied a U.S. diplomatic visa in 2005 (his tourist/business visa was also revoked). This prohibition was based on a 1998 law that bars entry into the United States by foreign officials responsible for "severe violations of religious freedom."

42. For the full text of Modi's speech see "Full Text of Narendra Modi's Speech at San Jose," *The Hindu,* September 27, 2015, http://www.thehindu .com/news/resources/full-text-of-narendra-modis-speech-at-san-jose /article7694680.ece. The issues raised in the letter include concerns about

privacy violations with Modi's "Digital India" plan, concerns about his human rights violations, and concerns about academic freedom and the suppression of free speech. "Faculty Statement on Narendra Modi Visit to Silicon Valley," *Academe Blog*, August 27, 2015, https://academeblog.org/2015/08/27/faculty-statement-on-modi-visit-to-silicon-valley/. See also #modifail.

43. "PM Narendra Modi's top quotes from Silicon Valley visit," *The Financial Express*, September 28, 2015, http://www.financialexpress.com/article/economy/modis-silicon-valley-visit-pm-narendra-modis-top-quotes-highlights/142607/.

44. Prashad, *Karma* and *Uncle Swami*.

45. Marc Andreessen, Twitter post, February 9, 2016, 7:29 pm, https://twitter.com/pmarca.

46. Kavita Daiya, "Provincializing America: Engaging Postcolonial Critique and Asian American Studies in a Transnational Mode," *South Asian Review* 26, no. 2 (2005): 2–11.

CHAPTER 8

Asian American Studies and Palestine: The Accidental and Reluctant Pioneer

Rajini Srikanth

Asian Americanists have been interested in Palestine for quite some time, and they have recognized the intersections among the violation of Palestinian rights, U.S. Cold War interventions and military occupations in Asia, Japanese American internment, and settler colonialism in Hawai'i (however, in the context of Hawai'i, it is important not to minimize the complexities of Hawaiian identity and the difficulty of folding in Hawaiian and non-Hawaiian Pacific Islander issues into Asian American studies).[1] Asian Americanists also have a deep understanding of what Lisa Lowe calls "intensified forms of homelessness and displacement."[2] Junaid Rana and Diane Fujino provide a rich recapitulation of 1960s and 1970s solidarity with Palestine of Asian American activists like Yuri Kochiyama and members of Asian Americans for Action ("founded by middle-aged Japanese American women").[3] Several conferences (in 2003, 2005, and 2007) of the Association for Asian American Studies (AAAS) have addressed the question of Palestine. In 2005, *Amerasia Journal* published a special issue on Orientalism and the legacy of the renowned Palestinian American scholar Edward Said, who died in 2003 after a long battle with leukemia. Said's legacy prominently includes his championing of the Palestinian cause. Palestinian rights began to loom large in the consciousness of Asian Americanists following the declaration by the Bush administration of the War on Terror.

The connections between the priorities of Asian American studies and the urgencies of the Palestinian situation came to a climax in April 2013 with the Association for Asian American Studies' adoption of the resolution supporting the academic boycott of Israel. The AAAS was the first academic organization in the United States to adopt the academic boycott resolution. However, despite this pioneering role, AAAS has been slow to claim for itself the distinction of being the "first."

Those who were officers of the AAAS board in April 2013 were relatively taciturn about the association's "courageous" action, neglecting to post on the website the messages of thanks and support that came right after the passage of the resolution from many academic organizations in Palestine and within the United States.[4] Decidedly, the passage of the resolution was a significant stand for Asian Americanists to take. The "adversary" (the pro-Israel antiboycott universe) was formidable—and, indeed, immediately following the passage of the resolution the intimidations and hostilities from this adversarial group began. Amid these onslaughts, the silence from the official body of the AAAS was noticeable and unfortunate. Later in the essay, I address the question of what the board could have done, given that the passage of the resolution set in motion forces that the AAAS board was not prepared to engage.[5]

While the twenty-nine signatories who proposed the resolution were surprised at the silence of the board in embracing the association's pioneer status and its hesitation in proudly proclaiming the accolades as well as the hostile responses it was receiving, others—primarily those outside the AAAS—were surprised that the rank and file of the membership had not spoken out to question and dissent from the vote. Given that approximately 10 percent of the membership had attended the business meeting at which the resolution had been adopted by unanimous vote, many non-Asian Americanists speculated that it was only a matter of time before someone within the association would question the wisdom of the vote and criticize the resolution's passage. But three weeks after April 20, 2013, when the resolution passed, there was no critical voice from within the membership. This led political science professor Jonathan Marks to post a patronizing letter calling for the association to retract its resolution. Perhaps the membership had not understood what it was doing, he suggested. Perhaps the dimensions of the situation were too complex for Asian American scholars to fully comprehend, he averred.

In his letter about the boycott to professors of Asian American studies, Marks expresses surprise that the vote was unanimous and he finds "eerie" the "complete lack of opposition to it."[6] Then he goes on to give the AAAS membership a tutorial on what Boycott, Divestment, Sanctions (BDS) means. Supporting BDS and the academic boycott resolution is akin to calling for the destruction of the state of Israel, he says, and cites other Israel critics and Palestine supporters like Eric Alterman, Norman Finkelstein, and Noam Chomsky who have decried boycott measures despite their grave disagreements with Israel. He then delivers a pointed rebuke to Asian Americanists: "Even if you do not agree with Alterman, Finkelstein, or Chomsky, don't you think that unanimous agreement on a matter about which even Israel critics disagree vociferously is a sign of your field's ill health?" He asks rhetorically, "Are you at all embarrassed?" He draws on the opinion of Asian American blogger Byron Wong, who suggests that perhaps one reason that no Asian American "intellectual" has come forward to repudiate the resolution is that the scholars and activists of the Asian American experience consider the AAAS to be irrelevant to their work, as does Wong, who calls himself a blogger on "'Asian American intellectualism, activism, and literature.'" This is an indictment by an ethnic "insider" that Marks appears to take great pleasure in delivering.[7]

In a spirited response to Marks's condescending post, David Palumbo-Liu asks, "Can't people unanimously feel passionate and committed to one point of view? If it were a resolution in favor of stricter background checks for gun purchases would you be as moralistic and publicly so?"[8] He chastises Marks for belittling the scholarship of Asian Americanists and for suggesting that they had not done their homework when they voted for the resolution: "Your letter moves out from a critique of a single vote to a broad indictment of many fine scholars and teachers, indeed all of those in the field, impugning their moral character simply because their judgment did not coincide with your own."[9]

As I have indicated above, and as Rana and Fujino establish in their essay, the rights of Palestinians is not a new consideration with Asian Americanists. Though Rana and Fujino's recapitulation of the early solidarity of Asian American activists with Palestine is focused on a few individual figures who are known for their cross-ethnic and cross-racial activism, these roots are crucial in illuminating the shared concerns of African Americans, Asian Americans, and Arab Americans.

That Arab American issues could and should enter formally into Asian American research and scholarship was first proposed in 1994 (at the AAAS national conference in Ann Arbor, Michigan) by Moustafa Bayoumi. He raised the question "Is there an 'A' for Arab in Asian American Studies?" Bayoumi presumably posed this question not just to underscore the shared experience of racial profiling of Asian Americans and Arab Americans but also to point out that the politics of U.S. imperialism abroad necessarily reflects back on the ways in which Asian Americans and Arab Americans are constructed as dangerous subjects at home.[10]

Bayoumi has been relentless in his challenge to Asian American studies to move beyond a focus on racial subjectivity and the desire to secure voice and space within the U.S. sociopolitical fabric. He has urged the field to consider how the geopolitical landscape outside the United States and the United States' interventions in places in Asia and Africa have significant implications for Asian Americans' responsibility for ethical citizenship. He has exhorted the field to abandon its preoccupation with questions of identity and focus instead on the politics of solidarity against surveillance, regulation of activism (such as antiwar activism), and punishment for critique of the state.

Two essays by Bayoumi in particular thrust Palestine into the consciousness of Asian American studies. In 2003, Bayoumi linked Asian American studies with "aboriginal rights" and the "question of Palestine." In this essay, Bayoumi provides a fascinating glimpse into the history of the UN Partition Plan of 1947 (the plan for apportioning the land under the British Mandate between the Palestinians and a proposed state of Israel), specifically the Philippines' position on it, and helps us understand the strong intertwinings between Filipino American studies and Palestine. President Manuel Roxas of the Philippines was initially morally opposed to the UN Partition Plan, explains Bayoumi, but he was pressured by the United States to reverse his opposition. The initial opposition and subsequent reversal are recounted by the Philippines' delegate to the United Nations, General Carlos Romulo, in his memoir. The Partition Plan is a moral issue, Romulo writes, and it is "clearly repugnant to the valid nationalist aspirations of the people of Palestine."[11] Romulo was to have delivered his opposition speech to the Partition Plan to the UN General Assembly, but at the very last minute his president instructed him that the Philippines would be voting in favor of partition. Bayoumi describes this "forgotten little drama of quiet diplomacy" as an indication of the "triangulat[ion]" of the "question of Palestine with the Philippines and the U.S."[12] We learn in Bayoumi's essay of the conversations between Roxas and Romulo about how they saw a parallel between the Partition Plan and the U.S. pressure the Philippines faced in 1926 to "segregate the island of Mindanao from the rest of the population of the Philippines" because of the mistaken notion that the indigenous Moros (of Muslim faith) of Mindanao were opposed to the independence of the Philippines.[13] This attempt by the United States to interfere in the territorial integrity of the Philippines and to arbitrarily impose an outcome on its Muslim population in Mindanao without any participation by them leads Bayoumi to make the following argument: "The U.S. was a key player in the founding of the state of Israel and continues to this day to be its most important and ardent supporter at the expense of Palestinian rights. In one very direct way, the Philippines' intimate, neocolonial arrangement with the U.S., however, also carried an impact on the future of the Palestinians as a dispossessed people. . . . The question of the relationship of Islam to identity and of Muslim populations to land is invoked, in both the Mindanao situation and the tragedy of Palestine."[14] The U.S.-coerced reversal of the Philippines' opposition to the Partition Plan almost led to General Romulo announcing his resignation. This revealing episode adds one more detail to the deep historical experience of U.S. imperial pressure on the Philippines. It is not surprising, therefore, that a critique of occupation and colonialism has long characterized Filipino/a American studies. Its scholars and researchers are particularly attuned to these issues and see the strong connection between these coercions, the Palestinian experience following the founding of the state of Israel, and Asian American studies' own founding principles of antiracism, anticolonialism, and anti-imperialism.

In the essay "Our Work Is of This World," which appears in the Edward Said legacy issue of *Amerasia*, Bayoumi asks what are the "politics of knowledge in Asian American Studies" and what is "the heart of its enterprise."[15] Evoking the "revolutionary" epistemological analyses of Edward Said with respect to Palestine, and noting that Asian Americanists' superficial appropriation of Said's critique of "Orientalism" elides completely the oppositional politics of Said in regard to the U.S. position on Palestine, Bayoumi asserts: "The challenge facing Asian American Studies is to learn new histories (Arab and Arab American), particularly in their affinities with other Asian American histories, to consider the role of religion with more complexity . . . , and to involve itself more directly in international struggles for justice, particularly those that the United States continually thwarts. The national/international divide that traditionally separates Ethnic Studies from Area Studies work can no longer hold, and Palestine and Iraq ought now to be seen as Asian American issues."[16]

Similarly, Robert Ji-Song Ku criticizes the problematically selective use by Asian Americanists of Edward Said's critique of Orientalism's foundational impetus to colonialism and the "civilizing" missions of the West:

He notes that Asian Americanists are quick to decry Orientalist framings of the peoples of Asia and of Asian Americans; but very few Asian Americanists have considered that Said first called out Orientalism as a practice of the West in its colonial and bellicose engagement with the peoples of the Middle East. To talk about Orientalism without speaking of Zionism and Palestine, said Ku, is akin to excising the word *immigrant* from Lisa Lowe's *Immigrant Acts*. He writes, "This typically Asian Americanist practice of excising and detaching the question of Palestine from the discourse of Orientalism—and this practice's relationship to the general absence of Arabs and Muslims in Asian American Studies (until, poof, after September 11)—is something that requires closer interrogation."[17]

In 2004, in my book *The World Next Door: South Asian American Literature and the Idea of America*, I discuss two small but significant texts—a short story by Pakistani American writer Tahira Naqvi, "Thank God for the Jews" and the play by Bangladeshi American Sharbari Ahmed "Raisins Not Virgins"—to show their engagement with Palestine and its hold on the imagination of some South Asian Americans.[18] Subsequently, in 2009, I published an essay titled "Why the Solidarity?: South Asian Activism for Palestine." Part of this solidarity comes from the parallel (not exact, I caution) between the colonial and neocolonial experiences of India, Pakistan, and Bangladesh and the evisceration of Palestinians from their lands and the ensuing occupation by Israel of these lands.[19] However, let me quickly dispel the notion of a monolithic South Asian block in solidarity with Palestinians. Both Vijay Prashad and Amitava Kumar have written about South Asian alliance with Israel as part of a growing anti-Muslim sentiment in India following the rise of Hindu fundamentalism.[20]

AAAS Conferences and Palestine

Three of the many conferences of the AAAS have raised the issue of Palestine, and one additional conference took the broader view of the relationship between Asian American and Arab American studies. The 2003 conference in San Francisco was noteworthy for the passage of an important resolution that presaged the passage of the 2013 resolution in support of the academic boycott. The Critical Filipino and Filipina Studies Collective (CFFSC) brought forward an antiwar resolution (to protest the U.S. invasion of Iraq, which took place in March 2003) and, as part of that resolution, included a critique of Zionism and the occupation of Palestinian lands and oppression of Palestinians. Here is an excerpt from the full resolution:

The U.S. invasion and occupation of Iraq is a war that affects global and local communities. This war is a manipulation of the American public's grief over the September 11th tragedy, an illegal and undemocratic campaign to further U.S. multinational corporate interests. The historical record convincingly demonstrates that the Bush administration's "War on Terror" is part of a broader history of U.S. imperialism and colonization, and that this global campaign extends throughout the Middle East, to the Philippines, the Korean peninsula, northern Africa and Latin America. We condemn the United States's government's support of the Israeli states' human rights violations against the Palestinian people and its continued occupation of Palestinian land.[21]

Two members of the CFFSC were at the business meeting to present the resolution; one of them recalled that the part of the resolution that generated a fair bit of hostility was the clause condemning U.S. support of Israel's Occupation and its violation of Palestinian rights. The collective was pressured to remove that clause from the resolution, but the two members who were there refused and stood firm. The resolution was adopted without any changes, but there was a vigorous debate about the wisdom of including the clause critiquing Israel.[22]

In attempting to understand the hostility generated by the critique of Israel, I learned from those who had expressed their reservations that even very progressive Asian Americans were leery of taking a public stance against Israel because of the sense that Asian Americans are still a fragile and vulnerable group and it would not be strategic to draw attention to the organization in this very controversial fashion. Self-preservation rather than active support of Israel's policies appears to have contributed to the effort to remove the condemnation of U.S. support of Israel's violations of Palestinian rights. This caution reflects the compulsion to perform the identity of a "good" Asian American so as to ensure that one does not invite scrutiny upon oneself as a "bad" Asian American—an individual requiring surveillance by the state. This dichotomy parallels what Mahmood Mamdani has famously criticized in his essay "Good Muslim, Bad Muslim" and subsequently in the book of the same title, and Evelyn Alsultany has discussed about the promotional ads by the Council on American-Islamic Relations (CAIR) that portray "acceptable" Muslims (high-achieving, successful, contributing to the military) in which particular visible registers of religiosity are mobilized to underscore the idea of a welcoming, plural, and accepting United States.[23]

Meanwhile, the War on Terror and its aggressive targeting of Muslim Americans (many of whom are South Asian Americans) made abundantly clear that Asian American studies could not ignore the destructive impact of arbitrary detentions and deportations of Muslim Americans, including Arab Americans. Also caught up in the enforcement of the USA Patriot Act were Cambodian Americans—wonderfully captured in the documentary *Sentenced Home*.[24]

However, the solidarity with Arab Americans found expression in Asian American communities, even if not in Asian American studies, even before the formal declaration by the Bush administration of the War on Terror or the bombing of Afghanistan in late 2001. One of the most moving and powerful expressions of solidarity with Arab Americans in the early months after September 11, 2001, came from Japanese Americans; members of the Japanese American Citizens League and other Japanese American organizations came forward to urge Arab Americans not to fall victim to the state's aggression and to resist any erosion of their constitutional rights.[25] Even before the events of September 2001, Japanese Americans declared their concern for Arab Americans. Richard Aoki (Asian American member of the Black Panthers) writes that Japanese Americans were keenly aware of the vulnerable position of Arab Americans during the Gulf War of 1991. He writes that he was approached in 1991 by Japanese American activists to stand in solidarity with Arab Americans in Oakland, California, when the United States intervened in Saddam Hussein's invasion into Kuwait: "I was approached by Jean Yonemura and Yuri Miyagawa, two Japanese American activists, to oppose any possible internment of Arab Americans."[26] After 2001, the intensity of these Japanese American declarations of solidarity with Arab Americans increased.[27] South Asian Americans, who were themselves on the frontlines of the state onslaught on particular communities as part of the War on Terror, necessarily found themselves in solidarity with Arab Americans (organizations like Sikh Coalition and South Asian Americans Leading Together were quick to voice their support).[28]

In 2005, at the annual conference in Los Angeles of the Association for Asian American Studies, a mega-panel organized by Sunaina Maira took up the question of Zionism and its connection to Asian American studies. The participants on this panel were Vijay Prashad, Ibrahim Aoudé, and Magid Shihade. That the program committee had given this issue a mega-panel status was significant; the robust attendance at the panel signaled a keen interest among the conference attendees in the subject of Zionism and why Asian Americanists should care about a critical examination of it. The panel papers were subsequently published in a special issue of the *Journal of Asian American Studies* (JAAS), which was released in 2006. Among the many important terrains of intersectionality that Maira and Shihade's introductory essay to the special issue charts is the significance of 1967 (one year before the Asian American student strikes); this was the year that led to the seizure by Israel of areas of the West Bank, the Sinai Peninsula, and the Golan Heights, when a pan-Arab nationalist force led by Gamel Abdul Nasser was defeated by Israeli forces. Within the United States, pan-Arab nationalism manifested itself in the form of protests against the Israeli seizure of these areas and further claims on land that belonged to Palestinians. Thus, the historical moment of the development of a pan-Asian American identity was also the moment of the emergence of a pan-Arab American identity.[29]

In 2007, at the New York City conference of the Association for Asian American Studies, there was a plenary on the relationship between Asian America and Arab America—not as a foregone conclusion but as an area to examine and explore. Many of the speakers took care to emphasize that a simplistic gesture of solidarity would run the danger of conflating very specific differences in issues of resistance to a militaristic and carceral state.

Gradual but Sure Buildup to the 2013 Resolution

The resolution that was submitted at the 2013 AAAS conference in Seattle was, therefore, no sudden impulse among Asian American studies scholars. Support for Palestine has a long history in the field, and the 2008 and 2012 offensives by Israel against Gaza only heightened the resolve of Palestinian activists within the association that it would be unconscionable to delay a stand against Israel. By this time, the international Boycott, Divestment, Sanctions (BDS) movement, launched in 2005, was slowly gaining momentum, and there seemed to be good reason to make a bold declaration of support for the academic and human rights of Palestinians and end the silence in the United States surrounding Israel's violations of these rights. A group of AAAS pro-Palestine members drafted the resolution and submitted it to the AAAS board in February/March of 2013, accompanied by twenty-nine signatories. It was passed unanimously by the members present at the business meeting in Seattle on April 20, 2013, in a historic and truly remarkable moment.

The text of the resolution invokes the founding principles of Asian American studies, with the initial "whereas" clauses intoning the priorities held dear by many scholars and practitioners of Asian American studies:

> Whereas the Association for Asian American Studies is an organization dedicated to the preservation and support of academic freedom and of the right to education for students and scholars in the U.S. and globally; and
>
> Whereas Arab (West Asian) and Muslim American communities, students, and scholars have been subjected to profiling, surveillance, and civil rights violations that have circumscribed their freedom of political expression, particularly in relation to the issue of human rights in Palestine-Israel; and
>
> Whereas the Association for Asian American Studies seeks to foster scholarship that engages conditions of migration, displacement, colonialism, and racism, and the lives of people in zones of war and occupation; and
>
> Whereas the Association for Asian American Studies seeks to advance a critique of U.S. empire, opposing U.S. military occupation in the Arab world and U.S. support for occupation and racist practices by the Israeli state

Within such a framework, and given the years of buildup to the resolution that I have outlined above, a unanimous vote in favor of the resolution by the members attending the business meeting should not have been a surprise. Yet it was, even to those proposing the resolution, precisely because criticism of the state of Israel has always been taboo within the academy, with those daring to condemn its practices frequently becoming the target of vicious smear campaigns and intimidation tactics.[30] Prior to the business meeting, copies of the flyer explaining the resolution were prominently displayed at the registration table and distributed at some panels, and the announcement of the resolution was posted on the AAAS Facebook page. There was ample opportunity for members opposed to the resolution to attend the business meeting and voice their position; in fact, the signatories of the resolution fully expected that there would be a vigorous discussion of the resolution at the meeting, with the resolution perhaps passing by a slim margin, perhaps being defeated by a slim margin. There were a few questions that emerged at the business meeting: In practical terms, what would it mean to boycott Israeli academic institutions? How wide is support for Palestinians among academics? There was reference to the antiapartheid movement. A brief discussion took place, largely confined to clarifying the outcomes of passage of the resolution, and then the vote, by secret ballot, occurred.

With no preparation for assuming the role of pioneer in calling for the academic boycott of Israel, the Association for Asian American Studies became one. It is in this sense that the unanimous vote was a surprise. However, Sunaina Maira has argued that the Zionist presence in AAAS is minimal or nonexistent, in comparison to the American Studies Association, where it is strong. That the American Studies Association had to launch a two-year vigorous and visible campaign to educate its membership about the conditions of Palestinian life under Israeli control testifies to the influence of Zionists within ASA, she observes. While living in Ramallah, she and Shihade arranged for a delegation of American studies scholars to visit Israel and the West Bank so that they could see for themselves what life was like under Israeli settler colonialism and Occupation. These scholars returned from their trip determined to energize the ASA membership about Palestinian rights and to support the academic boycott.[31] Asian Americanists and other ethnic and Indigenous studies scholars know about settler colonialism, they know about imperialism, they know about racism, they know about violations of rights. Theirs is a lived education.

Nonetheless, prominent Asian American community leaders wrote to the board to express their concern at the vote and to remind AAAS members of the history of solidarity between Jewish Americans and Asian Americans in antiracist organizing. Here is their letter:

> Dear Dr. Danico [the president of the AAAS board in 2013]:
>
> We write as Asian Americans who have worked for the full and equal participation of Asian Americans in our great democracy, regarding the recent decision of the Association of Asian American Studies (AAAS) to boycott Israeli academic institutions. We write to express our concern and to urge AAAS to consider the effects of its resolution.
>
> Like AAAS, we believe it is vital for Asian Americans to participate actively in discussions of public policy, including issues of foreign policy. We commend AAAS for its leadership in the scholarly study of Asian Americans. You have been guided by the principle that increased knowledge benefits everyone. The AAAS's work, and that of the individuals who make up its membership, has ensured that the growing population of Asian Americans is recognized for our role in a diverse society. AAAS also engages the community through its activism.

The AAAS resolution concerns a situation that is complex as well as contentious. People who are reasonable and act in good faith hold a range of opinions on questions of Israel, Palestine, and the Middle East in general. Accordingly, open exchange of ideas about these subjects and from people of all backgrounds should be welcomed. A boycott of points of view on the basis of their origin is contrary to the spirit of open dialogue.

Through our own work on civil rights issues, we know how much Asian Americans have benefited from bridge building—especially with Jewish Americans. The communities have much in common. Coalitions that bring together Asian Americans and Jewish Americans have been crucial to progress on issues ranging from immigration reform to political representation to fighting bigotry. Jewish groups, for example, stood at the forefront with Japanese Americans seeking redress for the World War II internment. For these reasons, and others, we understand when Jewish American friends share with us that a boycott against Israeli academics alone raises painful memories of other boycotts that targeted Jews alone.

In the interest of Asian Americans, we ask that AAAS respond positively to concerns raised by friends in the Jewish American community. Thank you so much for considering our request.

Sincerely,

Vincent Eng, CEO, VENG Group; Former Dep. Dir., Asian American Justice Center

Ginny Gong

Tom Hayashi, Asian Pacific Islander Community Activist, Researcher, and Educator

Hyepin Im, President/CEO, Korean Churches for Community Development

Ken Lee, Asian American Community Advocate

Michael C. Lin, Former OCA National President

Floyd Mori, JACL National Executive Director Emeritus

Priscilla Ouchida. Executive Director, Japanese American Citizens League

Sharon Wong

Frank H. Wu

(Institutional affiliations shown for identification purposes only.)[32]

A group of Asian American studies scholars (including myself, David Eng, Lisa Lowe, Sunaina Maira, Gary Okihiro, David Palumbo-Liu, Vijay Prashad, and Neferti Tadiar) responded to the community leaders' letter. An excerpt of the response is here presented:

Dear Colleagues,

Mary Danico has shared with us the letter Don Nakanishi posted to the AAAS Facebook site. We understand that you raise these issues due to longstanding connections with Jewish American community activists who have allied with Asian Americans in anti-racist and labor organizing in the past. While it must be said that any simple representation of Jewish American opinion is hard because, like our own, that community is comprised of individuals who sometimes hold very different opinions on any single issue, we feel the need to unpack some of the points that you raise in your letter in order to better explain the reasons that we feel it is important for an Asian American academic organization to voice solidarity with Palestinians. Feel free to share this with anyone with an interest. . . .

We imagine that many believe the boycotts by the Association for Asian American Studies and the American Studies Association [ASA] target individual Israeli scholars. This emphatically is *not* the case. One of the very best articulations of the boycott comes from Rabbi Brant Rosen, entitled "Why I Support the ASA Boycott of Israeli Academic Institutions":

http://rabbibrant.com/2013/12/19/why-i-support-the-asa-boycott -of-israeli-academic-institutions/

His article is especially good at addressing the question as to whether or not the boycott is in any way anti-Semitic: "this accusation [that the boycott is anti-Semitic] is abject misdirection. . . . The ASA did not initiate this boycott—it made a principled, good faith decision to respond to the Palestinian call for support. Thus the real question before us when addressing BDS is not 'what about all of these other countries?' but rather 'will we choose to respond to this call?' To miss this point is to utterly misunderstand the very concept of solidarity."

Others worry about its effect on academic freedom, or in general on the issue of individual rights of association. The resolution in no way impinges upon the right of any individual member of the ASA to do as he or she pleases. Nor does it bar any individual Israeli scholar from any ASA formal collaboration unless they do so as a sponsored representative of an Israeli institution. It certainly makes no judgment based on race or ethnicity. In fact in exempting individuals it is far more accommodating than the anti-apartheid boycotts of South Africa as called for by Nelson Mandela. It is a resolution strongly in favor of equality, civil and human rights, and academic freedom. It is based on the premise that academic freedom is indivisible and that we should not condone the denial of academic freedom to Palestinians, or anyone. . . .

Finally, and most importantly, you rightly cite the fine work both Asian American activists and Jewish American activists have historically been engaged in through the years with regard to civil rights and liberties. We see this boycott as directly in line with that legacy. We believe that as Martin Luther King, Jr. stated so eloquently, *freedom is indivisible*. We take this stand in solidarity with Palestinians living under an occupation that has deprived them of not only academic freedom, but also many human rights—they are without rights of free speech, of assembly, of movement, and live under terrible conditions, often without electricity, scarce water supplies, or even adequate shelter, and with severely restricted abilities of earning a livelihood.

This is an issue that has special resonance for those who study the history of the internment of Japanese Americans during the Second World War, for of course the Palestinians living in the Occupied Territories live in what can only be called an open-air prison (a term used to describe the situation by President Jimmy Carter). Furthermore, for many Asian Americans—some of who are of Muslim faith—the question of Palestine and Islamophobia in a post-911 world is absolutely central to the continuing definition of Asian American activism and social justice.

We understand that this is a controversial boycott, but as those who have been involved in civil rights struggles know, controversy is often the starting point of a new and better world. And in that spirit we would be happy to sit down with anyone and discuss this issue with the seriousness and respect you have shown us in this letter.

Solidarity is not a simple act. It involves labor, it involves pain, it involves the loss of family and friends. Many whom one long considers to be close friends sever ties over the question of Palestine and the academic boycott. Sarah Schulman's eloquent articulation about what it means to be in solidarity with Palestine is worth reading in this context.[33]

Asian American studies scholars have studied the pain and anger of exclusion, discrimination, and rejection. They have illuminated the strength of resistance, and they have recorded the demand by Asian Americans for their full membership as residents of the United States. On the question of Palestine, Asian American studies scholars are in the process of a gradual awakening. Through the boycott resolution, the AAAS has made a public stand of its support for Palestine, but there has been little discussion among our membership to understand what the association's support of the boycott means. Passage of the resolution rests on the foundational assumptions of the work of Asian American studies. Therefore, to be a bystander to our own pioneering role at a historic moment signals a retreat from these core values. Can we move beyond the rhetoric of our aspirational commitments to antiracist, anti-imperialist, antiwar, and anticolonialist struggles, and can we be bold enough to condemn the Apartheid Wall, both at our border with Mexico and in Israel, reject Islamophobia, demand an end to police violence, oppressive settler colonialism, and militarism? The question is not whether we should stand in solidarity with Palestinians as they seek the help of the international community, the question is why we have waited so long to declare proudly that we want to translate into action the stand we took in 2013 in being the first academic organization to support the boycott of Israeli academic institutions.

NOTES

1. The Hawaiian sovereignty movement should not be unthinkingly subsumed into Asian American studies. See Lisa Kahaleole Hall, "Which of These Things Is Not Like the Other: Hawaiians and Other Pacific Islanders Are Not Asian Americans, and All Pacific Islanders Are Not Hawaiian," *American Quarterly* 67, no. 3 (September 2015): 727–49.

2. Lisa Lowe made this remark as part of her presentation at the Modern Language Association conference in January 2016 on a panel titled "Why Teach Literature."

3. See Junaid Rana and Diane Fujino, "Taking Risks, or the Question of Palestine Solidarity and Asian American Studies," *American Quarterly* 67, no. 4 (December 2015): 1033.

4. One reason the board offered at the time was that AAAS is a small organization, not fully equipped to respond to the flurry of activity that ensued following the adoption of the resolution; there was no dedicated staff person to update the website.

5. Mary Yu Danico, the president of the AAAS board in 2013, and I, who were referenced in the *Insider Higher Ed* online article that announced AAAS's passage of the resolution, received many vitriolic e-mails from Zionists. Members of the board were called in to speak with their university administrators to explain the organization's move. The hate campaign would likely have gone on for more time than it did had not the famous physicist Stephen Hawking decided in early May 2013 that he would be pulling out of attending a conference in Israel. His high profile made him a more attractive target for the Zionists.

6. Jonathan Marks, "To Professors of Asian American Studies," *Inside Higher Ed*, May 16, 2013, https://www.insidehighered.com/views/2013/05/16/open-letter-about-israel-boycott-professors-asian-american-studies.

7. Ibid.

8. David Palumbo-Liu, "An Asian American Studies Professor Responds," *Inside Higher Ed*, May 20, 2013, https://www.insidehighered.com /views/2013/05/20/asian-american-studies-professor-responds-israel -boycott.

9. Palumbo-Liu is an active contributor to *Huffington Post*, *TruthOut*, and other news outlets on the subject of Palestinian rights; he is a member of the organization United States Campaign for the Academic and Cultural Boycott of Israel (USACBI).

10. In a recent e-mail exchange with Bayoumi (March 5, 2016), I confirmed with him that it was indeed he who had articulated this now legendary call for an engagement of Asian American studies with the Arab American experience.

11. Moustafa Bayoumi, "Staying Put: Aboriginal Rights, the Question of Palestine, and Asian American Studies," *Amerasia* 29, no. 2 (2003): 222.

12. Ibid., 223.

13. Ibid., 222.

14. Ibid., 223.

15. Moustafa Bayoumi, "Our Work Is of This World," *Amerasia* 31, no. 1 (2005): 8.

16. Ibid., 8.

17. Robert Ji-Song Ku, "September 11: Farewell My Birthday," *Amerasia* 27, no. 3 (2001): 253.

18. See Rajini Srikanth, *The World Next Door: South Asian American Literature and the Idea of America* (Philadelphia, Penn.: Temple University Press, 2004), 159–60, for a discussion of Naqvi's depiction of connection between Pakistani Americans and Palestinians. See page 226 for a brief discussion of the converted Muslim in Ahmed's story who travels to West Asia to fight for the Palestinian cause.

19. Rajini Srikanth, "Why the Solidarity?: South Asian Activism for Palestine," *Human Architecture: Journal of the Sociology of Self-Knowledge* 7, no. 5 (2009): 106, http://scholarworks.umb.edu/cgi/viewcontent.cgi?article =1354&context=humanarchitecture.

20. Amitava Kumar, "Lunch with a Bigot," in *Lunch with a Bigot: The Writer in the World* (Durham, N.C.: Duke University Press, 2015), 170. Vijay Prashad's full-length book *Namaste Sharon: Hindutva and Sharonism under US Hegemony* (New Delhi: Leftword Books, 2003) discusses the bond between the right-wing extremist Hindus and Zionists.

21. I received the full text of the resolution via e-mail on January 6, 2016, from Lucy Burns, a member of the Critical Filipino and Filipina Studies Collective that submitted the resolution. She and Jeffrey Santa Ana were present, as was I, at the business meeting where the resolution was discussed and voted upon.

22. Jeffrey Santa Ana wrote in an e-mail communication to, among others, Junaid Rana on May 30, 2015:

> When CFSC's resolution was presented at the AAAS business meeting, there was a lively debate about it. Lucy and I were at the business meeting and I got up to make a statement about CFSC's support of Palestine as a central part of our anti-imperialist and anti-war activism. The resolution passed at the business meeting, but there were those who were quite hostile to it because of its emphasis on condemning Israel's war crimes against Palestinians. Some wanted us to remove this part of the resolution ("We condemn the United States's government's support of the Israeli states' [*sic*] human rights violations against the Palestinian people and its continued occupation of Palestinian land."); and this prompted Lucy and I [*sic*] to defend this part and make it clear that we would not remove it from the resolution. I got up to say this (that we refused to remove this part about Israel's war crimes against Palestinians) at the business meeting. I also recall that the US had just invaded Iraq and started the Iraq War, and we in CFSC were busy attending anti-war rallies and marching in anti-war protests throughout the Bay Area. I recall that our anti-war resolution for the AAAS was very much produced in the spirit of our protests against the US invasion of Iraq and starting the war.

23. Mahmood Mamdani, "Good Muslim, Bad Muslim: A Political Perspective on Culture and Terrorism," *American Anthropologist* 104, no. 3 (September 2002): 766–77; Evelyn Alsultany, "Selling American Diversity and Muslim American Identity through Nonprofit Advertising Post-9/11," *American Quarterly* 59, no. 3 (September 2007): 593–622.

24. *Sentenced Home* (directed by Nicole Newnham) tells the story of three Cambodian American men who fall afoul of the law as young teenagers and who, in a post-9/11 world several years later, get caught in the enforcement of the USA Patriot Act and become targeted for deportation to Cambodia, a country with which they have no ties other than that of birth. One of the men has to be separated from his wife and child.

25. At a conference hosted at MIT in November 2001, I witnessed this powerful and moving pledge by Japanese Americans of their support for Arab Americans.

26. See Diane Fujino, *Samurai among Panthers: Richard Aoki on Race, Resistance, and a Paradoxical Life* (Minneapolis: University of Minnesota Press, 2012), 261.

27. See, for instance, Nina Bernstein, "Relatives of Interned Japanese Americans Side with Muslims," *New York Times*, April 3, 2007, http://www

.nytimes.com/2007/04/03/nyregion/03detain.html?_r=0. See also Rana and Fujino, "Taking Risks," 1029–30; Reverend Michael Yoshii's Buena Vista United Methodist Church in the Bay Area proclaims strong solidarity with the Palestinian cause. See Alameda County's declaration of Palestine cultural day—June 4, 2013. http://mondoweiss.net/2013/07/japanese -american-and-arab-american-communities-in-bay-area-make-solidarity -over-persecution-histories.

28. See Deepa Iyer, *We, Too, Sing America: South Asian, Arab, Muslim, and Sikh Immigrants Shape Our Multiracial Future* (New York: New Press, 2015), 14, 51. See also the reports of South Asian Americans Leading Together.

29. Sunaina Maira and Magid Shihade, "Meeting Asian/Arab American Studies: Thinking Race, Empire, and Zionism in the U.S.," *Journal of Asian American Studies* 9, no. 2 (June 2006): 119–20.

30. Cynthia Franklin is doing research to gather the experiences of all the scholars in the United States who have been victimized by such hostile campaigns.

31. Sunaina Maira's conversation with C. S. Soong of Pacific Radio provides a comprehensive analysis of BDS and the ASA's efforts to pass the boycott resolution. Twenty minutes into the conversation, the conversation moves to the AAAS boycott. "The Academic Boycott of Isreal," Against the Grain, KPFA Radio, March 14, 2016, https://kpfa.org/episode/against-the -grain-march-14-2016/.

32. My thanks to David Palumbo-Liu for retrieving this letter.

33. Sarah Schulman, "What Does It Mean to Be in Solidarity with Palestine?," in *Extraordinary Rendition: American Writers on Palestine*, ed. Ru Freeman (Ithaca, NY: Olive Branch Press, 2015), 404–10.

CHAPTER 9

Against the Yellowwashing of Israel: The BDS Movement and Liberatory Solidarities across Settler States

Candace Fujikane

On April 20, 2013, the general membership of the Association for Asian American Studies (AAAS) passed a resolution in support of the academic boycott of Israel. In light of the complicity of Israeli academic institutions with Israel's violations of international law and human rights and the denial of Palestinians' right to education, the AAAS resolution foregrounds our commitment to academic freedom and our support for the call from Palestinian civil society for the academic boycott of Israeli institutions. As Rajini Srikanth likewise notes in her piece included in this collection, the AAAS became the first U.S. academic organization to support the boycott, followed by the Native American and Indigenous Studies Association (NAISA), the American Studies Association (ASA), the Critical Ethnic Studies Association (CESA), the African Literature Association (ALA), the National Association of Chicana and Chicano Studies (NACCS), the National Women's Studies Association (NWSA), the Association for Humanist Sociology (AHS), and several other organizations. Yet inasmuch as Asian Americanists see the passing of this resolution as signifying our engagement in a global solidarity movement, we had already become much more intimately implicated in events taking place in Palestine and Israel than we could have imagined. Asian American histories of civil rights struggles, like those of other minority groups in the United States, were being swept into the service of Israeli settler-state violence and crimes against humanity in the operations of what I refer to as the "yellowwashing" of Israel.

Yellowwashing is but one of the more recent washings of the state of Israel in a spectrum of hues—red, black, brown, green, pink, and rainbow— deployed to represent it as a nation fully engaging liberal discourses of diversity in alliance with indigenous, minority, and environmentalist groups, including American Indians, Blacks, Latinxs, Arabs, women, and LGBTQI communities.[1] These washings are part of a 2005 campaign to "rebrand" apartheid Israel as "relevant and modern" in the international imaginary.[2] Such tactics include the staging of news stories and media images that direct international attention to Israel's technological and medical innovations and "partnerships" with indigenous and minority groups for the trade in technological or agricultural expertise. The American Israel Public Affairs Committee (AIPAC), the largest U.S. pro-Israel organization, and other similar organizations recruit students at historically Black colleges and universities (HBCU) and those that have large Latinx student populations and train them to become "citizen lobbyists" for Israel.[3] These color washings pivot on the representation of Israel as the subject of anti-Semitism, sharing with indigenous and minority groups histories of genocide and persecution, yet what is clear is that these campaigns do not advance justice for these groups and instead appropriate their histories to camouflage Israel's own status as an apartheid state.

While the 2005 rebranding tactic is ostensibly about the marketing of Israel in a global economy, color washings as public relations campaigns have sought to redirect international attention away from the brutalities of Israeli occupation, apartheid, and state racism, the Palestinian uprising in the Second Intifada, and the historic 2004 Advisory Opinion of the International Court of Justice that the Israeli Separation Barrier/Apartheid Wall violates international law and Palestinian human rights.[4] Color washings work in the service of normalization to conceal evidence of Israel's apartheid operations, such as its ongoing construction of the Apartheid Wall through which Israel is moving to annex 46 percent of the West Bank, separating Palestinians from water resources, food, farms, jobs, schools, and healthcare, limiting their mobility, and isolating Palestinians from each other.

We can track the yellowwashing of Israel in the ways that the state of Israel and American Zionist lobbyists have produced and circulated a

narrative of Israeli alliances with Asian Americans through the figure of
U.S. Senator Daniel Inouye. At the time of Inouye's death in December
2012, former AIPAC president Robert Asher advised Israeli Prime Minister Benjamin Netanyahu that Israel should act to honor Inouye's memory.[5]
In January of 2014, Israel announced that it would name its missile facility
the Daniel K. Inouye Arrow Anti-Missile Defense Facility after the
Hawai'i-based senator.[6] Much has been made of the fact that this was the
first time that Israel had named a military facility after a non-Israeli, and we
can trace in this act of memorializing Inouye the complex underpinnings
of a story of origins and racial rearticulations that attribute U.S. aid to
Israel to a Japanese American member of Congress. The aforementioned
Asher refers to Inouye as "Israel's greatest supporter in Congress." Such a
characterization is predicated on an exchange Asher witnessed between
Inouye and Israeli prime minister Shimon Peres in the mid-1980s; at that
time, Inouye stressed, "We speak kind[ly] of Israel in Congress and loan
to Israel at high interest rates, but give grants to others[.] That is not right.
Mr. Prime Minister, I have studied the situation—there will be no more
loans to Israel."[7] Inouye thus advocated for giving Israel grants instead of
loans. Asher further elaborates: "Think of how much aid Israel has gotten
all together. Inouye was the guy who started it." He concludes with an even
more dramatic statement by insisting that without Inouye, there would
have been no U.S. aid.

What is remarkable here is the way that the naming of the facility is
narrated along the trajectory of a particular kind of origins story of U.S.
federal aid to Israel. In this grand narrative of $130 billion in U.S. largesse
dating back to 1948, Inouye figures in as the moral and ethical conscience
who ushers in a new era marked by the erasure of Israel's debt to the United
States. It was actually U.S. Senator Alan Cranston who sponsored what is
known as the 1984 Cranston Amendment, which stipulates that the United
States would provide Israel with economic assistance not less than the
amount Israel owed the United States on its outstanding debt. In other
words, this amendment makes clear that Israel would never have to repay
any grants or loans from the United States. It is Inouye, however, who has
been publicly credited with orchestrating the approval of the amendment
by the Appropriations Committee, putting the commitment into law and,
in effect, wiping out Israel's debt to the United States while generating what
is today $3 billion in aid from the United States each year.[8] These narra-
tives provide us with an index of how Inouye's support for the state of
Israel is popularly perceived, narrated, and circulated, and, as I will illustrate

here, how central Inouye's positionality as a Japanese American is to this founding narrative of federal aid to Israel.

In this essay, I trace the circuits of yellowwashing narratives representing U.S. aid to Israel through the historical figure and substance of Inouye. Through a critical analysis of such yellowwashing, I argue that the work that many of us have done concerning the intersection of settler-colonial studies and Indigenous studies in Hawai'i is particularly useful in considering articulations of the U.S. settler state with the Israeli settler state and the ways they are mutually constitutive. I also argue that this yellowwashing of Israel opens up another dimension to these color washings: As Israel circulated the figure of Inouye, the substance of Inouye's actions accentuates the ways that U.S. settler colonialism is constitutive of Inouye's positionality as a Japanese American. I then foreground what has been erased in these displacements: Palestinian political agency under deadly Israeli assault. In contrast to the state-sponsored color washings of Israel, the Boycott, Divestment, Sanctions (BDS) movement has enabled broader alliances in an international movement to end Israeli apartheid.

Multiple Displacements and Synecdochical Substitutions: The Zionizing of U.S. Senator Daniel Inouye

Zionists narrate Inouye's support for the state of Israel as driven by the twinned histories of the internment of Japanese Americans and the internment of Jews.[9] But Zionist narratives go well beyond the resonances between concentration camps in their celebration of Inouye's heroism on the battlefield against anti-Semitism. Douglas Bloomfield, legislative director of AIPAC, tells us that Inouye was named by the people of Israel "Trumpeldor" after a champion of Zionism who fought against Arabs in 1920 over the settlement of Tel Hai, a battle that has since taken on mythic proportions as the event marking the inception of the state of Israel:

> [Inouye's] integrity, his quiet modesty, his firm belief in bipartisan
> cooperation won him the admiration and trust of his Senate colleagues
> and all who knew him. Nowhere more than among the supporters and
> people of Israel, where he was affectionately nicknamed "Trumpeldor"
> for the one-armed early Zionist hero. Joseph Trumpeldor, who died
> in the 1920 battle of Tel Hai in the Upper Galilee, had lost his left
> arm in the Russo-Japanese war in 1904; Inouye lost his right arm
> in Italy in the closing days of World War II. For his heroism, Lt.
> Inouye was awarded the Medal of Honor, but it took 55 years to get

that recognition because Japanese-American Nisei servicemen were denied appropriate recognition for their heroism at the time because of their race.[10]

The fantasmatic equation of Inouye as a Japanese American war hero with a Zionist war hero is made in part through the visual congruities of their bodily sacrifices and a teleological narrative that casts Inouye's sacrifice as his contribution to the founding of the state of Israel. This comparison of Inouye and Trumpeldor, however, is only enabled by a series of temporal and geographical displacements and a suturing over of erasures and absences.

In particular, the historical moment of Inouye's heroism as an American patriot fighting to liberate Jews from the anti-Semitic forces of Nazi Germany is removed from its original context and renarrated in sepia tones against the backdrop of Zionist settlements across Palestinian lands decades earlier. If the Zionist mantra has long been "a land without a people for a people without a land," we can see here that Arabs have been made to disappear from Bloomfield's historical narrative of Tel Hai. As Israeli historian Idith Zertal writes, "Tel-Hai was perceived not simply as a tiny outpost in the north of Palestine; it became the entire Jewish community in the homeland, the very idea of settling and conquering the land, the soul of the new 'Eretz Israel.'"[11] Through this series of displacements, Inouye's opposition to anti-Semitism is transposed onto Palestinians' lands, representing the absent Arabs as an unnamed anti-Semitic threat, or as Zertal explains, "Nazi in essence and scope," rather than the besieged inhabitants protecting the lands they had lived on for over a thousand years.[12]

Looking beyond this incorporation of Japanese American history into a Zionist mythos, I return to Bloomfield's narrative and the way he ends with a particularly barbed historical reminder of U.S. racism. Inouye was fighting in a segregated unit for Japanese Americans, and he was not awarded the Medal of Honor until 2000, fifty-five years after he had fought in San Terenzo, Italy. We can situate Bloomfield's narrative in the context of strained Israeli-U.S. relations of that particular moment. The selection of Inouye for the naming of the facility occurs as part of an assemblage of events that include the U.N. General Assembly's 2012 de facto recognition of East Jerusalem, the West Bank, and Gaza as the Palestinian state, Israel's belligerent expansion of settlements in East Jerusalem and the West Bank, and the U.S. condemnation of all Israeli settlements as "illegitimate."

Throughout 2012, Israel intensified attacks on Gazans, and rockets were fired from the Gaza Strip into southern Israel as a response to these attacks, the Israeli blockade of the Gaza Strip, and the expansion of settlements in the West Bank. On November 14, 2012, Israel launched Operation Pillar of Defense in the Gaza Strip, an eight-day offensive that killed 174 Palestinians and injured hundreds. The United Nations General Assembly condemned the offensive, and on November 29, 2012, the U.N. voted to recognize the West Bank, East Jerusalem, and the Gaza Strip as a "non-Member Observer State." Netanyahu revived plans to construct new housing units in the E-1 area that would cut off East Jerusalem from the West Bank and prevent the formation of a contiguous Palestinian state. These plans materialized in a 70 percent increase in the construction of new settlements in the West Bank, including East Jerusalem, in 2013.[13] In October of that year, Israel announced the construction of five thousand more housing units in Israeli settlements in the West Bank. U.S. Secretary of State John Kerry then issued an unequivocal condemnation of the settlements: "Let me emphasize that the position of the United States is that we consider now, and have always considered, the settlements to be illegitimate."[14] Kerry's statement gained international attention for superseding previous statements by the United States that had not included the established settlements.

To counter Kerry's denunciation of the Israeli settlements, the state of Israel selected Inouye for the naming of the facility precisely because he refused to condemn the Israeli settlements. The *Jerusalem Post* reports that former Israel Defense Minister Moshe Arens stressed that Inouye had visited the Israeli settlements with him and that "he was not overly concerned about the settlements."[15] In these Zionist narratives, Inouye's eventual triumph over racism in the United States as a Japanese American is used to leverage his advocacy for Israel in negotiating continuing aid packages and in defense of the settlements through a public narrative of U.S. hypocrisy.

Here, the synecdochical illogics of yellowwashing necessarily operate through the very rhetorical slippages through which Inouye's singular story also comes to stand in for Asian American collective histories of struggle. Bloomfield syntactically transforms Inouye from a Japanese American subject into the category of "Asian American": He argues that Inouye was "the first Japanese-American in the House and later in the Senate, eventually becoming the highest-ranking Asian American politician in American history." Such elisions reiterate and rely upon model minority representations of Asian Americans, painting in broad strokes what Zionists sought to depict as collective Asian American support for the state of Israel, despite the lack of any material basis for this claim.

Settler Colonialisms across U.S. and Israeli Settler States

If Zionists produced a figure of Inouye that then traveled in global circuits to defend Israeli settlements, I would like to turn to the substance of Inouye's support for Israel and what it tells us about the symmetries of settler states and their interlocking logics of occupation. At the time of Inouye's death, Tom Dine, also former executive director of AIPAC, represented Inouye as fighting against the genocide of American Indians and Jews:

> He was a man who saw two injustices—genocide against Native Americans and against Europe's Jews—and he wanted to make sure the Native Americans got help in their restoration and that Israel had America's support in securing itself against those who did not wish Israel's population well and who wished the nation-state did not exist.[16]

Despite Inouye's seeming support for American Indian sovereignty in his work as Chairman of the Senate Committee on Indian Affairs from 1987 to 1995 and from 2001 to 2003, his support for Israeli occupation and settler colonialism is inextricably tied to his own investments in U.S. occupation and settler colonialism.

From our vantage point in Hawai'i, which has been under U.S. occupation since forced annexation in 1898, we have seen the ways that Inouye's political actions have been historically motivated by his own interests as an Asian settler in an occupied territory where 40 percent of the state legislature is dominated by Japanese settlers who make up only 22 percent of the general population and an overall 75 percent of the legislature is made up of Asian settlers.[17] As Kyle Kajihiro argues, while Inouye has been mythologized in a grand morality play where Japanese Americans overcame racial discrimination through their loyalty to the United States, the convergence of events enabled Japanese settlers to gain power in post–World War II Hawai'i: "In their rise to power, the Democratic leadership in Hawai'i forged a new partnership with the military. Looking to modernize Hawai'i's economy but lacking the capital to do so, the young Democrats 'embraced defense spending as a welcome alternative' to the plantation economy (Lind, 'Ring of Steel'). By the 1940s military spending had overtaken sugar and pineapple to become the largest source of revenue for the islands. Democrats sought to leverage their influence to maximize the benefit from these expenditures and maneuvered themselves into key congressional posts where they would have influence in military appropriations."[18] Accordingly, the rise of Japanese settlers like Inouye to political power was made possible by the militarizing of Hawai'i and the establishment of United States Pacific Command (USPACOM), whose area of responsibility includes half the earth's surface.

Inouye has long been criticized for the ways in which he promoted U.S. federal recognition of a Native Hawaiian governing entity in a manner that has actually obstructed Hawaiians' efforts at restoring Hawai'i's independence. What Inouye supported was federal recognition of Hawai'i as a nation-within-a-nation that would allow Hawaiians sovereignty only insofar as Hawai'i remained a domestic dependency under the U.S. Department of the Interior. As Ida Yoshinaga and Eiko Kosasa point out in their critique of Inouye's support for federal recognition, "Inouye's de facto position does not support the return of lands to Native Hawaiians. In fact, he is interfering in the process for self-determined sovereignty of Native Hawaiians, as Mililani Trask has charged. Inouye states in the same *Pacific Citizen* article, 'I cannot envision any Congress approving an act that would propose the seceding of a segment of the state of Hawaii or the state of Hawaii from the Union.' By defining the process as a domestic policy rather than an international human rights issue, he is determining the outcome."[19] Inouye advocated for a contained form of sovereignty that would not pose any significant challenge to the foundations of the U.S. settler state or its occupation of Hawai'i.

Federal recognition, as American Indian, First Nations, and Kanaka 'Ōiwi scholar activists have argued, is yet another way for the United States to consolidate its settler state power and to further the processes of land accumulation by dispossession.[20] Rather than a process for establishing the independence of Native nations, federal recognition has become an operation that domesticates Native nations under the control of the U.S. Department of the Interior. Kanaka 'Ōiwi refusal of federal recognition in Hawai'i has been clearly articulated at the 2014 Department of the Interior (DOI) hearings in Hawai'i that sought 'Ōiwi community responses to the DOI's offer of "assistance" in the formation of a "Native Hawaiian governing entity." 'Ōiwi responded with an overwhelming "'A'OLE! NO!" to the settler state's efforts to set up such a process for federal recognition. As J. Kēhaulani Kauanui notes, "Most immediately, it seemed federal recognition would set up a process for extinguishing most claims to land title—except for whatever the state of Hawai'i and the U.S. federal government may be willing to relinquish in exchange for that recognition—and even then the U.S. federal government would not hold it in trust, so it could not be considered the sovereign territory of any Native Hawaiian governing entity within the U.S. system."[21] Federal recognition, then, is widely seen as a settler state–backed mechanism to seize even more of the 1.8 million acres of lands known as the "ceded" or seized lands, former Crown and Government lands "ceded" to the U.S. federal government at the time of annexation in 1898 and returned to what illegally became the state of Hawai'i in the 1959 Admission Act (about 373,719.58 acres were withheld by federal government).[22] These lands that are held in trust and administered by the settler state continue to be the national land base for the lāhui, the nation.

Moreover, through his support of military buildup in Hawai'i and Israel, Inouye has sought to secure the precarious settler ground that both the United States and Israel occupy. Inouye served as chairman of the Senate Defense Appropriations Subcommittee for three different terms from 1989 to 2012.[23] From 1998 to 2003, he steered $1.4 billion to military projects in Hawai'i, and during this time, Inouye committed $1.9 billion to support Army Chief of Staff General Eric Shinseki's proposal to upgrade the infantry brigade with the Stryker Brigade Combat Team.[24] The transformation, the army argued, would necessitate 23,000 more acres of land, in addition to the over 220,000 acres of land the U.S. military currently occupies in Hawai'i. The 2004 Environmental Impact Study concluded that there would be significant impact to the environment and Hawaiian cultural resources, yet the army began plans for the buildup, and Earthjustice sued on behalf of Kanaka 'Ōiwi cultural practitioners of the 'Īlio'ulaokalani Coalition, Nā 'Imi Pono, and Kīpuka. By 2015, the 233 Stryker vehicles were forced to leave because of Pentagon budget cuts after Inouye's death.[25]

By advocating for the Stryker Brigade, Inouye was also investing in the global defense corporation that manufactures the Stryker vehicles, General Dynamics Land Systems (GDLS). GDLS was contracted in 2010 by the Israeli Ministry of Defense to manufacture 386 Namer (Leopard) armored personnel carriers. The contract with GDLS promised thousands of jobs for small and mid-sized Israeli contractors and suppliers for the Tank Program Administration, jobs that were later threatened when Namer production was shifted from Israel to a GDLS facility in Ohio.[26] Similarly, other military contractors, including Boeing, Lockheed Martin, and United Technologies, whose production lines have been jeopardized by Pentagon budget cuts, have been "rescued" by Inouye's decisions on military spending bills.[27] These three corporations were Inouye's biggest sources of campaign support, and all three supply the Israeli military with weapons used in the assault on Palestinians in the occupied territories.

That Israel chose to name a defense military facility after Inouye is an attempt to disseminate a narrative of settler innocence as the state of Israel is threatened by an enemy it often refuses to name. This selective focus on defense, however, cannot hide the widespread devastation of Israel's multiple military offensive operations, including, most recently, Operations Cast Lead (2008–2009), Pillar of Defense (2012), and Protective Edge (2014), all made possible by the tremendous military aid that the United States gives to Israel. For seven weeks, in July and August 2014, Israel's brutal Operation Protective Edge assault on Gaza massacred over 2,191 Palestinians, including 527 children, while by contrast, 71 Israelis were killed.[28] Over 11,100 Palestinians were wounded; out of this number, 3,374 were children.[29] Brian Wood, head of Arms Control and Human Rights at Amnesty International, explains that a week into the seven-week assault, 4.3 tons of U.S.-manufactured rocket motors arrived in the Israeli port of Haifa.[30] Two weeks later, it was reported that the Pentagon resupplied Israel with munitions, approving the transfer of grenades and mortar rounds to the Israeli armed forces from a U.S. arms stockpile in Israel. Wood explains that reports concerning this resupply were released on July 30, the same day the U.S. government condemned the shelling of a U.N. school in Gaza that killed at least twenty people, including children and U.N. humanitarian workers. Wood writes, "It is deeply cynical for the White House to condemn the deaths and injuries of Palestinians, including children, and humanitarian workers, when it knows full well that the Israeli military responsible for such attacks are armed to the teeth with weapons and equipment bankrolled by US taxpayers."[31]

As these examples of yellowwashing made Inouye all too visible in public performances of settler-state alliances, Indigenous peoples, too, stand together against and across settler states. In August 2014, Kerry made a visit to the University of Hawai'i's East-West Center at the same time Palestinians were being massacred by Operation Protective Edge in Gaza. At a protest outside of the East-West Center, Terrilee Keko'olani read a statement written by the Hawaiian independence organization MANA: Movement for Aloha Nō ka 'Āina, standing in solidarity with Palestinians and concluding, "We are both outraged and strengthened as we witness the Palestinians' own commitment to struggle to maintain their ancestral connections to land, and we are committed to continue to struggle in Hawai'i to liberate ourselves and our lands—toward the liberation of all victims of US empire."[32] As Palestinians in keffiyeh continue to stand on their lands against the construction crews building the settlements in the West Bank with U.S. Caterpillar D9 armored bulldozers and at Palestinian universities against the Israeli military armed with U.S. weapons, Hawaiian independence activist and MANA organizer Andre Perez has worn keffiyeh in solidarity with Palestinians as he stood on sacred Mauna a Wākea against the construction crews that sought to build the Thirty Meter Telescope. Perez explains, "In the so-called 'war on terrorism,' US Army Special Forces soldiers in the Middle East appropriated the keffiyeh. I had a distinct message with this visual symbol. In Hawai'i, we are very much aware of Palestinian struggles, and I wanted to show solidarity with Palestinians and our shared resistance for our land."[33]

I turn now to the BDS movement and the efforts of Palestinian Campaign for the Academic and Cultural Boycott of Israel (PACBI) scholars to lay bare the violence of Israeli academic institutions that serve the Israeli occupation forces. Repeatedly in public debates, those who support the state of Israel have argued that the academic boycott denies Israelis their academic freedom, but the very brutality of Israeli offensives lead Palestinian students and scholars to fight even more fiercely for their right to education as the most potent weapon against Israeli state violence.

The Boycott, Divestment, Sanctions Movement, and Critiques of Israeli Academic Institutions

The 2004 Advisory Opinion of the International Court of Justice on the illegality of the Separation/Apartheid Wall sparked not only Israel's rebranding campaign but also the Boycott, Divestment, Sanctions movement. The Palestinian Campaign for the Academic and Cultural Boycott of Israel was established in the West Bank city of Ramallah in July 2004, and it utilized the strategies of the antiapartheid BDS movement in South Africa. A year later, on July 9, 2005, the Boycott National Committee sent out a call from over 170 groups representing Palestinian civil society for an international solidarity movement to boycott, divest, and sanction Israel based on its thirty-eight-year occupation of East Jerusalem and the West Bank, the Gaza Strip, and the Syrian Golan Heights and its continued expansion into the West Bank by means of the wall.[34] It also foregrounds the status of a majority of Palestinians as refugees at the same time that Arab-Palestinian citizens of Israel are subjected to racial discrimination.

Based on hundreds of U.N. resolutions condemning the illegality of Israel's colonial and discriminatory policies and the failure of Israel to comply with humanitarian laws, Palestinians appealed to the international community for support: "We, representatives of Palestinian civil society, call upon international civil society organizations and people of conscience all over the world to impose broad boycotts and implement divestment initiatives against Israel similar to those applied to South Africa in the apartheid era. We appeal to you to pressure your respective states to impose embargoes and sanctions against Israel. We also invite conscientious Israelis to support this Call, for the sake of justice and genuine peace."[35] The BDS call articulates three main goals: 1) ending Israel's occupation and colonization of all Arab lands and dismantling the wall; 2) recognizing the fundamental rights of the Arab-Palestinian citizens of Israel to full equality; and 3) respecting, protecting, and promoting the rights of Palestinian refugees to return to their homes and properties as stipulated in U.N. Resolution 194. As editors of *Against Apartheid: The Case for Boycotting Israeli Universities*, Ashley Dawson and Bill V. Mullen argue, "By challenging Israeli apartheid using some of the same strategies as the movement against apartheid in South Africa, the BDS movement has a vital role to play in bringing about a democratic transition in occupied Palestine."[36]

The BDS movement engenders a platform for criticisms of Israeli apartheid as well as representations of Palestinian political agency. As Noura Erakat reminds us, what is erased time and again is the violence that facilitated Israel's original colonization of Palestinian lands, the ongoing forced population transfer of Palestinians from the occupied Palestinian territory and from Israel in the Negev region, and the present attacks on the BDS movement. She writes, "In its short existence, without any central leadership, and barely any funding, the global BDS movement has achieved significant milestones. . . . While none of these victories have changed the reality for Palestinians on the ground, they have changed the decades-long attitude that Israel can act with impunity, and they have helped to put Israel's structural violence on trial. More importantly, the BDS call has restored a sense of political agency for Palestinians."[37]

As opponents of the boycott focus solely on the academic freedom of Israelis, our work has been to foreground the denial of academic freedom to Palestinian students and faculty who must survive the daily violence of Israeli occupation. As the work of many scholars has pointed out, including that of Saree Makdisi and Kristian Davis Bailey, Palestinian universities and schools have been shut down or destroyed by Israeli assault, while Israeli universities expand into Palestinian territories.[38] Students and faculty are fired upon with live ammunition and tear gas canisters by the Israeli military forces. In fall 2015, students and youth were killed, arrested, kidnapped, brutally tortured, and placed in indefinite detention by Israeli soldiers and settlers.[39] In December 2015, Israel arrested 90 students at Birzeit University, and at the Palestine Technical University–Kadoorie in Tulkarem the Israeli military has set up a military base on the campus, injuring 726 Palestinians with live ammunition and rubber-coated metal bullets from October to November of that year.[40]

Israeli universities—such as Tel Aviv University, Technion, the Weizmann Institute, the Hebrew University, and Ben-Gurion University—all work with the arms industry, providing not only technological research and development of weapons systems but also the academic "rationale" for assault operations. PACBI cofounders Lisa Taraki and Omar Barghouti point to one of the most devastating products of Israeli universities: Tel Aviv University's Institute for National Security Studies' development of the Dahiya Doctrine, named after the Dahiya suburb of Beirut that was leveled by Israel's attack on Lebanon in 2006.[41] This doctrine, also known as the "doctrine of disproportionate force," is described by the 2009 U.N. Fact-Finding Mission as the use of "widespread destruction as a means of deterrence" involving "the application of disproportionate force and the causing of great damage and destruction to civilian property and infrastructure, and suffering to civilian populations."[42] The mission concluded that the Israeli offensive Operation Cast Lead "was a deliberately disproportionate attack designed to punish, humiliate and terrorize a civilian population, radically diminish its local economic capacity both to work and to provide for itself, and to force upon it an ever increasing sense of dependency and vulnerability" and that that these acts can be defined as "crimes against humanity."[43]

This "academic" doctrine of disproportionate force has been consistently used by Israel in its military offensives in Gaza. In addition to the academic freedom denied to these children killed in the more recent Operation Protective Edge, Israeli occupation forces destroyed civilian structures necessary for sustaining life, including Gaza's only power plant, water and sewage systems, and medical facilities. As a result of Operation Protective Edge, 252 schools in Gaza remain closed, affecting 248,000 students. In summer 2015, the United Nations Relief and Works Agency announced that it would have to close 700 additional schools to 500,000 students in 2016 because of the continuous Israeli siege on the Gaza Strip.[44] Barghouti points out that Israeli academic institutions publicly supported the massacre in Operation Protective Edge as a matter of national security and have rewarded faculty and students who served in the attack on Gaza. Tel Aviv University awarded 850 scholarships to students who took part in Operation Protective Edge.[45]

Palestinian Political Agency: Bringing Down the Apartheid Wall

Correspondingly, our work in the BDS movement is to foreground Palestinian accounts of the effects of Israeli occupation on their academic freedom. One recent collection that does this is *Life in Occupied Palestine*, coedited by Cynthia Franklin, Morgan Cooper, and Ibrahim Aoudé. Mindful of the way the blockade of books is also a metric of the limits to academic freedom in the occupied Palestinian territories and in Israel, this collection was made open access to bypass the Israeli restriction of books into and out of Palestine.[46] Despite these restrictions, Franklin shares the lesson that it is in small events that radical transformation occurs. At one of the *Life in Occupied Palestine* book launches, she explains: "As I witnessed how Lina's small daughter, perched on her lap as Lina skyped in for the Gaza launch, was welcomed into the proceedings as a treasured participant in the still-unfolding stories of resistance and survival so central to *Life in Occupied Palestine*, I learned how the work of storytelling is carried forward often through the very smallest of exchanges, sometimes in a way even more moving than the largest or most sweeping narratives."[47]

In contrast to the grandiose Zionist narratives of war heroes at Tel Hai, one story in *Life in Occupied Palestine* provides an account of a young girl defying the rule of Israeli shells. Refaat R. Alareer, an instructor at the Islamic University–Gaza, describes how during Israel's 2008–2009 Operation Cast Lead, he told his three children his mother's story, drawing continuities between his own childhood under the first Intifada to his storytelling beneath the booming sounds overhead, in whatever room was least likely to be hit by Israeli "stray" missiles launched according to the academic doctrine of disproportionate force. He writes:

> As children living in the first Intifada, for us the stories of my mother and those of my grandparents were our solace, our escort in a blind world controlled by soldiers and guns and death. One day, Mom told us, she was going to school when a shell exploded a few meters away from her. The following day she woke up and went to school like nothing had happened the day before, like she was rejecting the rule of the shells. (In retrospect, I believe that's why I almost never skipped a class in my life.) But my mother has outlived Israel's brutal invasion, and so have her stories. During the attack, the more bombs Israel detonated, the more stories I told, and the more I read. Telling stories was my way of resisting. It was all I could do.[48]

As we hear the detonation of bombs accelerate, so too do we hear Alareer's voice deepening with urgency, telling the stories that sustain them through this assault. In a 2014 "ceasefire," however, Alareer lost a brother and four other family members, as well as the home in which he was telling his children these stories of survival and resurgence.[49] This continuity of violence does not detract from his account of Palestinian survival but rather extends it: His children will carry the memory of his storytelling as he carries the memory of his mother's, and we, too, bear witness to the stories that enabled them to live through the bombings, to refuse the rule of the shells that sought to silence them.

Against this violence, students at Al-Quds University in Abu Dis have been chipping away at the Apartheid Wall and what they describe as a crumbling "wall of fear." In November 2015, when Israeli violence against Palestinian students had escalated to new heights, students in keffiyehs carrying Palestinian flags marched to the Apartheid Wall that runs the perimeter of the Al-Quds campus and took turns hitting it with a sledgehammer, chipping away a deep hole in it, returning week after week.[50] Schoolchildren join them, throwing stones over the wall. A fourth-year media student at Al-Quds explains that students are fighting back with more than stones: "For me, it's clear why they do it: because education is a stronger weapon than stones. The idea of limiting us—it's not just limiting our movement, it's about limiting our thinking. [The Wall] is not just to separate us from Jerusalem. It's a symbol of power and it works somehow because some people are afraid of saying anything about what they witness."[51]She explains that the "wall of fear" is coming down precisely because the intensification of violence has empowered students to speak back.

On October 13, 2015, thousands of Palestinians took to the streets for a "Day of Rage" in Gaza and the West Bank to protest Israeli settlers burning Palestinians alive, Israel's attempts to "Judaise the city" through storming of the al-Aqsa Mosque, and the daily dehumanizing restrictions on Palestinian lives. At Birzeit University, a student who chose to be identified as "Amir" explains that students have been targeted because they are best able to make visible and mobilize protests and acts of resistance: "[Israeli forces] are specifically targeting students because we are the ones who are able to reach different sections of Palestinian society. The main aim of these tactics is to break us, break our will, and reinforce this internalization that no matter what we do, they will creep up on us and lock us up, because they have the power to do so."[52] Students have been working to expose internationally the on-the-ground destruction of Palestinian life as well as Palestinian resourcefulness and resilience. Such testimonies cannot but render undeniably visible the attacks both on the academic freedom of Palestinians and the obligation of the international community to intervene.

Solidarities across Settler States for Decolonial Futures

Asian American, South Asian, and South Asian American scholars such as Sunaina Maira, David Palumbo-Liu, Rajini Srikanth, Malini Johar Schueller, Tithi Bhattacharya, and Jasbir Puar have been at the forefront of the movement for the academic boycott of Israeli institutions. Their work points to the urgency of an Asian American critique that challenges the erasure of Palestinian narratives. The 2013 AAAS academic boycott of Israel was accomplished largely because of the work of Srikanth, Maira, Lucy Burns, Sarita See, Anna Guevarra, Susette Min, and many others. *American Quarterly*'s December 2015 forum on solidarity movements with Palestine illustrates these cross-racial solidarity efforts, and Junaid Rana and Diane Fujino's essay on Asian Americans standing in solidarity with Palestine cites Srikanth's argument that South Asian solidarity activism for Palestine is driven by a shared colonial experience, continuities that we see in the state targeting of Muslims, Arabs, and South Asian Americans after 9/11, as well as the transnationally linked circuits and geographies from the Philippines to Palestine.[53] Maira and Magid Shihade's work in the special issue of the *Journal of Asian American Studies* on the emergence of a critical ethnic studies articulates Asian American and Arab American studies and the conditions, as Edward Said argues, "of colonial occupation as a global condition."[54]

As I argue in this essay, our work in Asian American studies against settler colonialism in the occupied Palestinian territories must also consider the broader contexts of settler colonialism across settler states and the ways that the United States' own operations of settler colonialism articulate with those of the Israeli settler state. By analyzing the mutually constitutive modalities of settler colonialisms in a global context, we can better trace how a historical figure like Daniel Inouye has been circulated by settler states in the global imaginary and how his material support for settler states reminds us of the ways that settler colonialism is constitutive of our positionalities as Asian Americans. Decolonial and international solidarities, however, are also constitutive of Asian American positionalities. True decolonization is, as Eve Tuck and K. Wayne Yang argue, about the repatriation of Indigenous land and life.[55] Examining the limits of Asian American critique offers us new possibilities for genuine decolonial futures in the United States and in Israel and Palestine.

As PACBI cofounder Barghouti states, "Israel may soon be facing its South African moment."[56] Cofounder Lisa Taraka also writes, "We have hope that the resounding calls from around the world to boycott Israel and its institutions will contribute to the struggle for justice and liberation for the Palestinian people."[57] In standing with the people of Palestine, we reclaim our Asian American histories from Zionist yellowwashing projects to help build an international movement for the end to Israeli occupation and apartheid.

NOTES

I'd like to thank the following people for their careful reading of this essay and their invaluable comments and questions: Elizabeth Colwill, Monisha DasGupta, Kyle Kajihiro, Terrilee Keko'olani, Linda Lierheimer, Laura Lyons, Naoko Shibusawa, and Mari Yoshihara. Cynthia Franklin in particular has commented on multiple drafts of this essay, and her own work has inspired me to sharpen the arguments here. Cathy Schlund-Vials organized the space for the initial presentation of these ideas at the Modern Language Association (MLA) forum on Displaced Subjects: Asian American Studies and Palestine in Austin, Texas, in January 2016. Cathy, Rajini Srikanth, Lisa Lowe, David Lloyd, Bill Mullen, and Sean Kennedy offered insightful comments and questions at that forum and in discussions after it, and Cathy has continued to offer incisive questions and suggestions in the editing process. All errors are my own.

1. Sarah Schulman, *Israel/Palestine and the Queer International* (Durham, N.C.: Duke University Press, 2012); Schulman, "Israel and 'Pinkwashing,'" *New York Times*, November 22, 2011, http://www.nytimes.com/2011/11/23 /opinion/pinkwashing-and-israels-use-of-gays-as-a-messaging-tool.html?_r =0; Gale Courey Toensing, "Redwashing Panel Follows Academic Associations' Boycott of Israel," *Indian Country Today Media Network*, December 31, 2013, http://indiancountrytodaymedianetwork.com/2013/12/31/redwashing -panel-follows-academic-associations-boycott-israel-152930; Linah Alasaafin, "Barefaced Hasbarah: Tufts 'Friends of Israel' Exploit Name of Palestinian Writer to Brownwash the Nakba," *Electronic Intifada*, April 10, 2012, https:// electronicintifada.net/blogs/linah-alsaafin/barefaced-hasbara-tufts-friends -israel-exploit-name-palestinian-writer; Israel Ministry of Environmental Protection, "'Green Israel' Brand Strengthened By International TV Campaign," June 6, 2012, http://www.sviva.gov.il/English/ResourcesandServices /NewsAndEvents/NewsAndMessageDover/Pages/2012/06_June_2012 /GreenIsrael_240612.aspx; Gabriel Shivone, "Countering Israeli Greenwashing at the People's Climate March," *Electronic Intifada*, September 21, 2014, https://electronicintifada.net/blogs/gabriel-schivone/countering-israeli

-greenwashing-peoples-climate-march; David Lef, "IDF Most 'Female Friendly' Army in the World," *Israel National News*, March 7, 2013, http://www .israelnationalnews.com/News/News.aspx/165978#.VsTPRnQrKCQ.

2. Sarah Schulman, "A Documentary Guide to 'Brand Israel' and the Art of Pinkwashing," *Mondoweiss: The War of Ideas in the Middle East*, November 30, 2011, http://mondoweiss.net/2011/11/a-documentary-guide -to-brand-israel-and-the-art-of-pinkwashing/; Nathaniel Popper, "Israel Aims to Improve Its Public Image," *Jewish Daily Forward*, October 14, 2005, http://forward.com/news/2070/israel-aims-to-improve-its-public-image/.

3. "'Blackwashing' and the Israel Lobby," *Aljazeera*, March 5, 2012, http://stream.aljazeera.com/story/201203051909-0022080.

4. Thanks to Cynthia Franklin for pointing out the timing of Israel's rebranding campaign in relation to the International Court's ruling.

5. Ariel Ben Solomon, "Israel to Name Arrow Site after Former U.S. Senator Daniel Inouye," *Jerusalem Post*, January 2, 2014, http://www.jpost .com/Defense/Israel-to-name-Arrow-site-after-former-US-senator-Daniel -Inouye-336825.

6. I thank Cynthia Franklin for calling my attention to the naming of the Israeli defense facility after Inouye.

7. Solomon, "Israel to Name Arrow Site."

8. "Senate Panel Proposes Minimum Aid to Israel," *New York Times*, September 26, 1984, http://www.nytimes.com/1984/09/26/world/senate -panel-supports-minimum-aid-to-israel.html.

9. Ariel Ben Solomon, "Late US Senator Honored for Supporting Israel," *Jerusalem Post*, January 19, 2014, http://www.jpost.com/National -News/Late-US-senator-honored-for-supporting-Israel-338603.

10. Douglas Bloomfield, "Friend of Jews and Israel Dies at 88," *Forward*, December 18, 2012, http://forward.com/news/israel/167882/sen-daniel -inouye-friend-of-jews-and-israel-dies-a/.

11. Idith Zertal, *Israel's Holocaust and the Politics of Nationhood*, trans. Chaya Galai (Cambridge: Cambridge University Press, 2005), 17.

12. Zertal, *Israel's Holocaust*, 114. See also Cynthia Franklin, "Eichmann and His Ghosts: Affective States and the Unstable Status of the Human," *Cultural Critique* 88 (Fall 2014): 91.

13. "Report of the UN Secretary General, Israeli Settlements in the Occupied Palestinian Territory, Including East Jerusalem, and in the Occupied Syrian Golan," A/HRC/25/38, February 12, 2013, http://ohchr.org/EN /Pages/Home.aspx.

14. "Kerry: Israeli Settlements Are Illegitimate," *Aljazeera*, November 6, 2013, http://www.aljazeera.com/news/middleeast/2013/11/kerry-israeli -settlements-are-illegitimate-201311613594909400.html.

15. Solomon, "Late US Senator Honored."

16. Solomon, "Israel to Name Arrow Site."

17. Hawaiians make up 15 percent of the legislature and whites 18 percent. For these legislative figures, see Candace Fujikane, "Asian American Critique and Moana Nui 2011: Securing a Future beyond Empires, Militarized Capitalism and APEC," *Inter-Asia Cultural Studies* (2012): 7. For a discussion of Asian settler colonialism, see Candace Fujikane and Jonathan Y. Okamura, eds, *Asian Settler Colonialism: From Local Governance to the Habits of Everyday Life in Hawai'i* (Honolulu: University of Hawai'i Press, 2008); Dean Saranillio, "Why Asian Settler Colonialism Matters: A Thought Piece on Critiques, Debates and Indigenous Difference," *Settler Colonial Studies* 3, nos. 3–4 (2013): 280–94.

18. Kyle Kajihiro, "The Militarizing of Hawai'i: Occupation, Accommodation, Resistance," in Fujikane and Okamura, *Asian Settler Colonialism*, 174.

19. Ida Yoshinaga and Eiko Kosasa, "Local Japanese Women for Justice (LJWJ) Speak Out against Daniel Inouye and the JACL," in Fujikane and Okamura, *Asian Settler Colonialism*, 299.

20. Glen S. Coulthard, "Subjects of Empire: Indigenous People and the 'Politics of Recognition' in Canada," *Contemporary Political Theory* 6 (2007): 437–60; *Red Skins, White Masks: Rejecting the Colonial Politics of Recognition* (Minneapolis: University of Minnesota Press, 2014); Audra Simpson, *Mohawk Interruptus: Political Life across the Borders of Settler States* (Durham, N.C.: Duke University Press, 2014).

21. J. Kēhaulani Kauanui, "Resisting the Akaka Bill," in *A Nation Rising: Hawaiian Movements for Life, Land, and Sovereignty*, eds. Noelani Goodyear-Ka'ōpua, Ikaika Hussey, and Erin Kahunawaika'ala Wright (Durham, N.C.: Duke University Press, 2015), 326.

22. Melody Kapilialoha MacKenzie, ed., *Native Hawaiian Rights Handbook* (Honolulu: Native Hawaiian Legal Corporation, 1991), 29.

23. Daniel K. Inouye Institute, "Timeline," http://www .danielkinouyeinstitute.org/pages/timeline#25.

24. Daniel Inouye, "Don't Fence Them In," *Honolulu Advertiser*, December 17, 2006, http://www.dmzhawaii.org/dmz-legacy-site-two/?p=702.

25. Audrey McAvoy, "Critics Welcome Departure of Stryker Brigade," *Army Times*, July 11, 2015, http://www.armytimes.com/story/military/2015 /07/11/stryker-hawaii/30010615/.

26. Ran Dagoni, "Israel Halves Namer Order with General Dynamics," *Globes: Israel's Business Arena*, January 14, 2014, http://www.globes.co.il/en /article-1000909206.

27. David D. Kirkpatrick and David M. Herszenhorn, "In Battle to Cut Billions, a Spotlight on One Man," *New York Times*, May 30, 2009, http:// www.nytimes.com/2009/05/31/us/politics/31inouye.html.

28. See comparative figures at "50 Days of Death and Destruction: Israel's Operation Protective Edge," *IMEU: Institute for Middle East Understanding*, September 10, 2014, http://imeu.org/article/50-days-of-death-destruction-israels-operation-protective-edge.

29. The disproportionately high number of wounded here is significant: Jasbir Puar argues that Israel's offensives have evidenced an implicit claim to the "right to maim" and debilitate Palestinian bodies as a form of biopolitical control that is extremely profitable to Israel. She points to BDS strategies as a disruption of capitalist accumulation, "The 'Right' to Maim: Disablement and Inhumanist Biopolitics in Palestine," *borderlands e-journal* 14, no. 1 (2015): 12.

30. Brian Wood, "USA: Stop Arms Transfer to Israel amid Growing Evidence of War Crimes in Gaza," *Amnesty International*, July 31, 2014, https://www.amnesty.org/en/latest/news/2014/07/usa-stop-arms-transfers-israel-amid-growing-evidence-war-crimes-gaza/.

31. Ibid.

32. "Statement of Solidarity with Palestine." I thank Ilima Long for a copy of MANA's statement, which can be found at http://www.manainfo.com/home.html.

33. Andre Perez, in discussion with the author, June 6, 2016.

34. "Palestinian Civil Society Call for BDS," *BDS Movement*, July 9, 2005, http://bdsmovement.net/call.

35. Ibid.

36. Ashley Dawson and Bill V. Mullen, eds., *Against Apartheid: The Case for Boycotting Israeli Universities* (Chicago: Haymarket Books, 2015), 8.

37. Noura Erakat, "Structural Violence on Trial: BDS and the Movement to Resist Erasure," in Dawson and Mullen, *Against Apartheid*, 109.

38. Saree Makdisi, "Op-Ed: Why Israel's Schools Merit a U.S. Boycott," *Los Angeles Times*, January 8, 2016, http://www.latimes.com/opinion/op-ed/la-oe-makdisi-why-support-the-academic-boycott-of-israel-20160108-story.html; Kristian Davis Bailey, "Building Unity and Wrecking Walls: Centering the Palestinian Right to Education," in Dawson and Mullen, *Against Apartheid*.

39. "Israel Arrests 90 Students at West Bank University," *MEMO: Middle-East Monitor*, December 21, 2015, https://www.middleeastmonitor.com/news/middle-east/22952-israel-arrests-90-students-at-west-bank-university.

40. Ben White, "The University Where Israeli Soldiers Train on Campus and Shoot Palestinian Protesters," *Middle East Monitor*, December 15, 2015, https://www.middleeastmonitor.com/20151215-the-university-where-israeli-soldiers-train-on-campus-and-shoot-palestinian-protesters/.

41. Lisa Taraki, "The Complicity of the Israeli Academy in the Structures of Domination and State Violence," in Dawson and Mullen,

Against Apartheid, 24–25; Omar Barghouti, "The Academic Boycott of Israel: Reaching a Tipping Point?," in Dawson and Mullen, *Against Apartheid*, 59.

42. In this report, the UN Fact-Finding Mission investigated the Israeli Operation Cast Lead (December 27, 2008, to January 18, 2009). "Human Rights in Palestine and Other Occupied Arab Territories: Report of the United Nations Fact-Finding Mission on the Gaza Conflict," September 25, 2009, 277, http://www2.ohchr.org/english/bodies/hrcouncil/docs/12session /A-HRC-12-48.pdf.

43. U.N. Human Rights Council, "Human Rights in Palestine and Other Occupied Arab Territories: Report of the UN Fact-Finding Mission on the Gaza Conflict," 407–408, 284, http://www2.ohchr.org/english/bodies /hrcouncil/docs/12session/A-HRC-12-48.pdf.

44. "UNWRA to Close Hundreds of Schools," *IMEMC News: International Middle East Media Center*, June 2, 2015, http://www.imemc.org/article /72134.

45. "Tel Aviv U: 850 Scholarships for Gaza Attack Service," *IMEMC News: International Middle East Media Center*, March 25, 2015, http://imemc .org/article/71014/.

46. Cynthia Franklin, Morgan Cooper, and Ibrahim Aoudé, *Life in Occupied Palestine*, a special issue of *Biography: An Interdisciplinary Quarterly* 37, no. 2 (Spring 2014), https://muse.jhu.edu/journals/biography/toc/bio.37.2 .html.

47. Cynthia Franklin, "State Racisms, Academic Boycott, and the Stakes of Life-Writing in the United States and Israel," *MLA Commons*, February 2016, https://mlaboycott.files.wordpress.com/2016/02/franklin-mla-2016 -comparative-state-racisms.pdf.

48. Refaat R. Alareer, "Gaza Writes Back: Narrating Palestine," *Life in Occupied Palestine*. See also Mohammed Omer, *Shell-Shocked: On the Ground Under Israel's Gaza Assault* (Chicago: Haymarket Books, 2015).

49. Franklin, "State Racisms," 3.

50. Ylenia Gostoli, "Palestinian Campus: 'A Wall of Fear Has Come Down,'" *Aljazeera*, November 22, 2015, http://www.aljazeera.com/news/2015 /11/palestinian-campus-wall-fear-151122063345718.html.

51. Ibid.

52. Mariam Barghouti, "Birzeit University Rises Up against Israel's Arrests," *Aljazeera*, January 11, 2016, http://www.aljazeera.com/news/2016 /01/birzeit-university-rises-israel-arrests-160106083537743.html.

53. Junaid Rana and Diane C Fujino, "Taking Risks, or The Question of Palestine Solidarity and Asian American Studies," *American Quarterly* 67, no. 4 (December 2015): 1027–37.

54. Sunaina Maira and Magid Shihade, "Meeting Asian/Arab American Studies: Thinking Race, Empire and Zionism in the U.S.," *Journal of Asian American Studies* 9, no. 2 (2006): 117–40.

55. Eve Tuck and K. Wayne Yang, "Decolonization Is Not a Metaphor," *Decolonization: Indigeneity, Education & Society* 1, no. 1 (2012).

56. Barghouti, "The Academic Boycott of Israel," 56.

57. Taraki, "The Complicity of the Israeli Academy," 29.

PART III

Remapping Asia, Recalibrating Asian America

CHAPTER 10

Transpacific Entanglements

Yên Lê Espiritu, Lisa Lowe, and Lisa Yoneyama

In our collaborative contribution, we examine the geopolitical, military, and epistemological entanglements between U.S. wars in Asia, U.S. racial capitalism, and U.S. empire and argue that U.S. empire and militarism in Asia and the Pacific Islands have been critical, yet underrecognized, parts of the genealogy of the contemporary condition of U.S. neoliberalism. We emphasize that U.S. neoliberalism mediates itself through the U.S. national security state, which is simultaneously a racial state and a settler state; this is expressed not merely in the racialization of Asian and Pacific Islander peoples but significantly in the erasure of historical and ongoing settler colonialism and, furthermore, in a racial social order that simultaneously pronounces antiblackness and Islamophobia. In our elaboration of "transpacific entanglements," historical and ongoing settler logics of invasion, removal, and seizure continuously articulate with other forms of appropriation and subjugation: This U.S. settler logic intersects with racialized capitalism and overseas empire asserts itself—often through the collaborative networks of the U.S.-backed, patriarchally organized, subimperial Asian "client-states"—in transpacific arrangements such as: export processing zones in the Philippines, U.S. military bases in Okinawa and Guam, nuclear test sites in the Marshall Islands, the exportation of nuclear power plants through-out Asia, the partition of Korea, and the joint military operations that demonstrate and secure the empire's reach. In this way, we conceptualize U.S. empire in Asia and the Pacific Islands as at once a settler-colonial formation, a racial and sexualized capitalist formation, and a military proj-ect that permits overseas dominance, appropriation, and exploitation. Em-pire works simultaneously, yet differentially, to naturalize U.S. presence and possession in Asia and the Pacific Islands through the imperatives of national security and wartime necessity, to racialize the peoples it captures, occupies, kills, and governs, and to disavow the historical and ongoing dispossessions of Indigenous peoples.

In *Immigrant Acts: On Asian American Cultural Politics*, Lisa Lowe situated racialized Asian immigrant labor within the history of U.S. capitalism, expanding its global reach through wars in Asia; she noted that U.S. im-migration exclusion acts and naturalization laws managed and produced Asian American racial formation through both exclusion and inclusion in relation to the history of U.S. wars in Asia. As Yến Lê Espiritu has argued in her recent book *Body Counts: The Vietnam War and Militarized Refuge(es)*, and Lisa Yoneyama makes evident in *Cold War Ruins: Transpacific Critique of American Justice and Japanese War Crimes*, American exceptionalism has rationalized U.S. military and capitalist interventions in Asia and the Pa-cific Islands as necessary for the "national security" of the United States and for the humanitarian "rescue" of Asian peoples. The global portrait of the United States as triumphant and humanitarian liberator of Asia, and to a similar extent the Pacific Islands, has buttressed the military buildup against a broad range of America's "enemies," variously named in twentieth-century history as "fascists" during the Second World War, "underdevel-opment" in the U.S.-modeled modernization projects of postcolonial third world countries, "communists" in the Cold War, and "terrorists" in the War on Terror. These links indicate that U.S. militarism and empire in Asia and the Pacific Islands displaces and racializes Asian and Pacific mi-grants and refugees and that the discourse of the United States as libera-tor of Asia is employed in turn to explain the necessary expansion of militarism in the Philippines, Guam, Hawaii, Okinawa, Korea, and Viet-nam and to justify the current wars in Iraq, Afghanistan, Syria, and else-where. In that process, moreover, the settler logic of U.S. imperial nation and its "military-security-academic" regime simultaneously discipline and regulate the class, race, sexual, and other uneven social relations and iden-tities within and along the national border of the U.S. mainland. It is im-perative, therefore, that any attempts at transforming the American present must take into account the geohistorical ramifications of U.S. settler colonialism and its ties to specific transpacific conditions in Asia and the Pacific Islands.

At this moment of reinvigorated U.S. imperialism and globalized militarization, we suggest it is important to interrogate anew the public recollections of the U.S. war in Vietnam. By most accounts, Vietnam was the site of one of the most brutal and destructive wars between Western imperial powers and the people of Asia, Africa, and Latin America. U.S. military policies cost Vietnam at least three million lives, the maiming of countless bodies, the poisoning of its water, land, and air, the razing of its countryside, and the devastation of most of its infrastructure. Indeed, more explosives were dropped on Vietnam, a country two-thirds the size of California, than in all of World War II. Yet post-1975 public discussions of the Vietnam War in the United States often skip over this devastating history. This "skipping over" of the Vietnam War constitutes an organized and strategic forgetting of a controversial and unsuccessful war, enabling Americans to continue to push military intervention as key in America's self-appointed role as liberators—protectors of democracy, liberty, and equality, both at home and abroad.

As a controversial and unsuccessful war, the Vietnam War has the potential to unsettle the master narratives of "rescue and liberation" and refocus attention on the troubling record of U.S. military aggression. And yet, as demonstrated by the recent wars in West and South Asia, the U.S. loss in Vietnam has not curbed the United States' crusade to remake the world by military force. Instead, the United States appears to have been able to fold the Vietnam War into its list of "good wars." The narrative of the "good refugee," deployed by the larger U.S. society and by Vietnamese Americans themselves, has been crucial in enabling the United States to turn the Vietnam War into a good war. Otherwise absent in U.S. public discussions of Vietnam, Vietnamese refugees become most visible and intelligible to Americans as successful, assimilated, and anticommunist newcomers to the American "melting pot." Represented as the grateful beneficiary of U.S.-style freedom, Vietnamese in the United States become the featured evidence of the appropriateness of the U.S. war in Vietnam: that the war, no matter the cost, was ultimately necessary, just, and successful. Having been deployed to "rescue" the Vietnam War for Americans, Vietnamese refugees thus constitute a solution rather than a problem for the United States, as often argued.

The good war narrative requires the production not only of the good refugee but also of the United States as the good *refuge*. The making of the "good refuge" was launched in April 1975 as U.S. media and officials extolled and sensationalized the U.S. airlifting of approximately 130,000 Vietnamese out of the city in the final days before the Fall of Saigon and subsequently encamping the refugees at military bases throughout the Pacific archipelago. With the Defense Department coordinating transportation and the Joint Chiefs of Staff-Pacific Command in charge of the military moves necessary for the evacuation, Vietnamese were airlifted from Saigon on U.S. military aircrafts, transferred to U.S. military bases on (neo)colonized spaces such as the Philippines, Guam, Wake Island, and Hawaii, and delivered to yet another set of military bases throughout the United States: Camp Pendleton in California, Fort Chaffee in Arkansas, Eglin Air Force Base in Florida, or Fort Indiantown Gap in Pennsylvania. While these efforts have been widely covered by the media and scholars alike as "rescuing missions," we need to expose them instead as colonial and militarized ventures.

Moving from one U.S. military base to another, Vietnamese refugees witnessed firsthand the reach of the U.S. empire in the Asia-Pacific region. Far from confirming U.S. benevolence, the U.S. evacuation of Vietnamese refugees made visible the legacy of U.S. colonial and military expansion into the Asia Pacific region. The fact that the majority of the first-wave refugees were routed through the Philippines and Guam revealed the layering of U.S. past colonial and ongoing militarization practices on these islands. It was the region's (neo)colonial dependence on the United States that turned the Philippines and Guam, U.S. former and current colonial territories respectively, into the "ideal" receiving centers of the U.S. rescuing project; and it was the enormity of the U.S. military buildup in the Pacific that uniquely equipped U.S. bases there to handle the large-scale refugee rescue operation. As such, U.S. evacuation efforts were not a slap-dash response to an emergency situation that arose in Vietnam in 1975 but rather part and parcel of the long-standing militarized histories and circuits that connected Vietnam, the Philippines, and Guam, dating back to 1898.

The U.S. initial designation of Clark Air Force Base as a refugee staging point was intimately linked to, and a direct outcome of, U.S. colonial subordination and militarization of the Philippines. Soon after, when President Ferdinand Marcos refused to accept any more Vietnamese refugees, U.S. officials moved the premier refugee staging area from the Philippines to Guam. As an unincorporated organized territory of the United States under the jurisdiction of the Department of the Interior, Guam— specifically, its U.S. air and naval bases, which took up one-third of the island—became the "logical" transit camps for the processing of evacuees. With total land area of about two hundred square miles, and meager local resources, Guam was hardly an ideal location for the large-scale refugee operation. That it became *the* major refugee staging point in the Pacific had more to do with the U.S. militarization of Guam than with U.S. humanitarianism. The U.S. decision to designate Guam the primary staging ground for refugees, even when the island's resources were severely stretched and its inhabitants adversely affected, repeats the long-standing belief that indigenous land is essentially "empty land"—that is, land empty of its Indigenous population. The refugee situation on Guam thus bespeaks the intertwined histories of U.S. settler colonialism and U.S. military colonialism on Guam and its war in Vietnam: It was the militarization of the colonized island and its Indigenous inhabitants that turned Guam into an "ideal" dumping ground for the unwanted Vietnamese refugees, the discards of U.S. war in Vietnam. At the same time, as Jana Lipman argues, the refugee presence bore witness not only to the tenacity but also to the limits of U.S. empire, critically juxtaposing "the United States' nineteenth-century imperial project with its *failed* Cold War objectives in Southeast Asia."[1]

From Guam, many Vietnamese refugees journeyed to Marine Corps Base Camp Pendleton, a 125,000-acre amphibious training base on the Southern California coast, in San Diego County. It was here, at a military base, that the largest Vietnamese population outside of Vietnam got its start in the United States. Like Clark and Andersen Air Force Bases, Camp Pendleton emerged out of a history of conquest: It is located in the traditional territory of the Juaneño, Luiseño, and Kumeyaay Tribes, which had been "discovered" by Spanish padres and voyagers who traveled to Southern California in the late eighteenth century, "owned" by unscrupulous Anglo-American settlers for about a century as the California state legislature repeatedly blocked federal ratification of treaties with Native communities, and ultimately "acquired" by the U.S. Marine Corps in 1942 in order to establish a West Coast base for combat training of Marines. Camp Pendleton's prized land—its varied topography, which combines a breathtakingly beautiful seventeen-mile shoreline and diverse maneuver areas, making it ideal for combat training environment—is thus what Richard Carrico called "stolen land," an occupied territory like Guam.[2]

The material and ideological conversion of U.S. military bases into a place of *refuge*—a place that *resolves* the refugee crisis, promising peace and protection—discursively transformed the United States from violent aggressors in Vietnam to benevolent rescuers of its people. This "makeover" obscures the violent roles that these military bases—these purported places of refuge—played in the Vietnam War, which spurred the refugee exodus in the first place; the construction of military bases as "refuges" also obscures the historical and ongoing settler-colonial occupation of indigenous land, as well as the dispossession and displacement of Indigenous peoples. In the Philippines, from 1965 to 1975, Clark Air Force Base, as the largest overseas U.S. military base in the world, became the major staging base for U.S. involvement in Southeast Asia, providing crucial logistical support for the Vietnam War. In Guam, Andersen Air Force Base played a "legendary" role in the Vietnam War, launching devastating bombing missions over North and South Vietnam for close to a decade. As Robert Rogers documents, Andersen rapidly became the United States' largest base for B-52 bombers. In 1972, Andersen was the site of the most massive buildup of airpower in history, with more than fifteen thousand crews and over 150 B-52s lining all available flight line space—about five miles long. At its peak, Andersen housed about 165 B-52s.[3] The U.S. air war, launched from Guam, decisively disrupted life on the island, underscoring once again the total disregard for the island's Indigenous inhabitants. Finally, as the Department of Defense's busiest training installation, California's Camp Pendleton, the refugees' first home in the United States, trains more than 40,000 active-duty and 26,000 reserve military personnel each year for combat. Camp Pendleton is also the home base of the illustrious 1st Marine Regiment, whose battalions participated in some of the most ferocious battles of the war. As such, the Pacific military bases, Clark and Andersen Air Force Bases, and California's Marine Corps Base Camp Pendleton, credited and valorized for resettling Vietnamese refugees in 1975, were the very ones responsible for inducing the refugee displacement. The massive tonnage of bombs, along with the ground fighting provided by Marine units like the Camp Pendleton's 1st Marines, displaced some twelve million people in South Vietnam—almost half the country's total population at the time—from their homes.

The transvaluation of U.S. military and colonial violence into a benevolent act of rescue, liberation, and rehabilitation finds even deeper genealogy in the racialized constitution of U.S. modernity, humanism, and liberalism, all of which continue to shore up what Richard H. Immerman called the "empire for liberty," or what Oscar V. Campomanes, following William Appleman Williams, in a similar sense called the "anticolonial empire."[4] Williams famously characterized the United States' Open Door Policy since the nineteenth century as "America's version of the liberal policy of informal empire or free trade imperialism," which was at the same time driven by "the benevolent American desire to reform the world in its own image."[5] In other words, the United States developed as a colonizing empire even as it disavowed its histories of colonialism and military take-over through the liberal tenets of freedom, consensus, private property, and self-determination. After the Second World War, the genealogy of liberal empire culminated in the Cold War ascendancy of the United States as a leader of the free world who claimed to have replaced the nineteenth-century colonial order in Asia and the Pacific Islands.

The American image of itself as the benevolent liberator and reformer of the people and land it subjugates is sustained by the discursive force of liberal humanism and humanitarianism for which the notion of "debt" is the operative term. In tracking the emergence of new relations of subjugation around the idea of freedom in the U.S. post-Reconstruction era, Saidiya V. Hartman argues that the trope of debt was deployed to bind the newly emancipated enslaved peoples to a new system of bondage and in-dentureship. Hartman writes: "Emancipation instituted indebtedness. . . . The emancipated were introduced to the circuits of exchange through the figurative deployment of debt. . . . The transition from slavery to freedom introduced the free agent to the circuits of exchange through this construc-tion of already accrued debt, an abstinent present, and a mortgaged future. In short, to be free was to be a debtor—that is, obliged and duty-bound to others."[6] Though firmly situated in the specific geohistorical con-text of the failure of American Reconstruction, Hartman's observation of the "figurative deployment of debt" lays out the constitutive contradiction of post-Enlightenment humanism, helping us understand how the Ameri-can notions of freedom, emancipation, liberty, and property ownership have developed by producing as well as disciplining modernity's others. This contradiction fundamental to the modern ideals of liberty and freed subjects underpins what we also consider to function as the American myth of rescue, liberation, and rehabilitation, a discursive economy of geopoli-tics that consolidated the racialized and heterosexualized logic of subjuga-tion and bondage in the U.S. relationship to Asia throughout the twentieth century.

The American myth of rescue, liberation, and rehabilitation then leaves the indelible marks on the liberated of inferiority, subordination, and be-latedness (to freedom, democracy, and property) but also of indebtedness. It assigns "the already accrued debt" to the liberated. Once marked as "the liberated" and therefore "the indebted," one cannot easily enter into a re-ciprocal relationship with the liberators. This myth, which presents both violence and liberation as "gifts for the liberated," has serious implications for the redressability of U.S. military violence, as Yoneyama observes of the American aggression in the Iraq War.[7] According to this myth, the losses and damages brought on by U.S. military violence are deemed "pre-paid debts" incurred by those liberated by American intervention. The injured and violated bodies of the liberated do not seem to require redress according to this discourse of indebtedness, for their liberation has already served as the payment/reparation that supposedly precedes the violence inflicted upon them. Furthermore, American myths of rescue, liberation, and rehabilitation have seriously threatened the way that postcolonial sovereignty might be conceived. As Chungmoo Choi notes, the dominant historiography of U.S.-Korea relations posits the post–World War II "liberation as a gift of the allied forces, especially of U.S.A."[8] This delegitimized the agency of Koreans in nation-building in the aftermath of Japanese colonial rule, which was followed immediately by the Korean War—the "forgotten" war that consolidated the military-security-industrial-academic complex—and the ongoing Cold War partition. Mimi Nguyen similarly discusses how the U.S. "gift of freedom" to refugees of the war in Vietnam, imposes indebtedness while binding them to the colonial histories that deemed them "unfree."[9]

The predicament of U.S. bases in Okinawa urgently demonstrates the intersection of the settler logic of invasion, removal, and seizure and the American imperialist myth of rescue, liberation, and rehabilitation. As a number of critics remind us, there is not one piece of land in Okinawa's main island that was willingly offered to the U.S. military for use. And yet, under the U.S.-Japan Security Treaty, 75 percent of the entire U.S. base facilities in Japan is accommodated in Okinawa prefecture, which constitutes less than 1 percent of Japanese soil. Okinawa's subjection to Japan began in the seventeenth century when the Ryukyu kingdom came under the rule of the Shimazu domain, followed by its integration as a prefecture into the modern Meiji state that was then emerging into the nineteenth century international and interimperial order. After the Second World War, the United States "liberated" Okinawa from the many centuries of Japanese rule. At the same time, the United States insisted on the possession of Okinawa in exchange for the heavy American military sacrifice in the Pacific battlefronts. Okinawa thus remained under U.S. military occupation for nearly three decades, until its "reversion" to Japan (1945–1972). During the occupation, the United States formally recognized Japan's "residual sovereignty" over Okinawa, thereby pre-empting any Okinawan Indigenous claim to local sovereignty. It also insisted that the United States would maintain control over Okinawa until its eventual approval as a U.N. trusteeship under U.S. authority. As Toriyama Atsushi points out, the two concepts, "residual sovereignty" and "pending" trusteeship, allowed the United States' exclusive management of Okinawa while at the same time helped to contain the Indigenous demands for self-determination and Okinawa's independence. What is important to our discussion is that the American recognition of Japan's "residual sovereignty" rationalized the United States' de facto control over the Okinawan land, the ocean, and the airspace, without contradicting its claims to be the supreme leader of freedom and liberty in the postcolonial world.[10] The ongoing settler logics of invasion, removal, and seizure thus sustains and is in turn secured by the historically rooted and still powerful exceptionalist discourse of the U.S. liberal empire. Yet, it is equally important to remember that this process is far from complete. As Yoneyama argues in her earlier work on the politics of memory inspired by Walter Benjamin, what we hope to offer below is a method of unlearning the "universal history"— Marxist, liberal, or otherwise—in such a way that would enable us to discern and connect the "missed opportunities and unfulfilled promises in history, as well as unrealized events that might have led to a different present."[11] Such a method calls upon us to link apparently separate subjects, contexts, and issues whose connections have been rendered unavailable by existing geographical, political, and disciplinary boundaries.

Although American exceptionalism, humanitarianism, and national security with respect to Asia are more often understood as discourses that address international relations, we wish to emphasize that they are critical parts of a neoliberal racial social ordering within the United States as well, which naturalizes white settlement and perpetuates assaults on Black, Muslim, and poor communities of color. In the nineteenth century until World War II, Chinese, Japanese, Filipino, and South Asians were recruited as racialized noncitizen labor and barred from the political and cultural spheres in the development of the national economy; today, the racialization of Asian immigrants within the United States is no longer exclusively that of noncitizen immigrant labor. The U.S. state responded to challenges by radical social movements of the 1960s and decolonization movements worldwide with aggressive incorporative measures, from the 1964 Civil Rights Acts and the 1965 Immigration and Nationality Act, to the large-scale capital investment in the development and rapid "integration" of Asia into global capitalism. Within these conditions, the racialization of Asian Americans as the model minority has been crucial to the pernicious fictions of multiculturalism and "postracial" inclusion, just as modernization discourse has in an analogous fashion "racialized" the newly industrialized Asian nations to be what Takashi Fujitani calls "model" *modernity* nations.[12] Sociologist Hijin Park discusses this neoliberal positioning of the "East Asian miracle" as the discourse of "rising Asia."[13] The "rising Asia" discourse opposes newly industrialized Asia to less "developed" countries in Africa, Latin America, Central Asia; it is complemented by the fiction of Asian "culture" as traditionally patriarchal and heteronormative, a fiction employed, as Chandan Reddy argues, to discipline black, brown, and queer of color communities, as "backward" and threatening.[14]

These new racial formations signal forms of governance that represent "Asians" as included in both the U.S. nation and in global capitalism, even as Asian and Pacific Islander peoples are forcibly dislocated from sites in which the United States has occupied, interned, and conducted imperial war. In other words, violent exclusion from national belonging has characterized the historical emergence of the United States from its beginnings: justifying the dispossession of Indigenous peoples, the enslavement of Africans and Jim Crow segregation, the stolen labors of indentured and immigrant workers, and the losses of life as the United States waged wars in Latin America, East, Northeast, and Southeast Asia, Central Asia, and West Asia. Yet within the formation we call "neoliberalism," violence accompanies not only exclusion from the nation but also inclusion into it: as "emancipated" slave, indebted poor, grateful immigrant, or rehabilitated inmate. The violence of inclusion, an operation that proposes to convert subjugated others into normative humanity and multicultural citizenship, is clearly also a process of racial governance. Yên Espiritu elaborates this concept as "differential inclusion," to counter the myth of "voluntary" immigration and to emphasize the processes through which different groups are "included" yet simultaneously legally subordinated, economically exploited, or culturally degraded, often in relation to one another.[15] The relative inclusions of Asians and Pacific Islander peoples by postwar racial liberalism, which appeared to legitimize an official antiracism, provided the United States moral legitimacy as it sought to gain Cold War hegemony against the Soviet Union.[16] It built upon the fiction of the U.S. state as the guarantor of civil rights and suppressed radical challenges—from Black Power to third world decolonization movements—even as it extended U.S. militarism and neoliberal capitalism globally.

Contemporary neoliberalism naturalizes the market, buttresses the primacy of the deserving individual, and instantiates the superiority of the private over the public; it moreover affirms "colorblindness" that disavows the persistence of antiblackness, promotes a discourse of "rising Asia" that masks the longer history of North Atlantic empires, and it denies ongoing settler colonialism while justifying imperial war and military basing that occupies, dispossesses, and displaces Indigenous communities. Neoliberalism erases the longer history in which "emancipation," "free wage labor," and "free trade" have enabled the development of what Cedric Robinson calls "racial capitalism"—built upon settler colonialism, slavery, indenture, and unfree immigrant labor.[17] Grace Hong characterizes the current moment of neoliberal restructuring as an epistemological structure of disavowal, a means of claiming that racial and gendered violence has been overcome, while disavowing the continuing assaults on inassimilable poor communities of color.[18] We suggest that where many theorists of neoliberalism, whether inspired by Marx, Weber, or Foucault, observe the defining feature of neoliberalism to be the generalization of the market logic of exchange to all spheres of human life, this definition of neoliberalism often leaves unchallenged such disavowal, and we argue that the critique of neoliberalism must be nuanced in relation to the much longer histories of racial capitalism, colonialism, and militarism.[19] In light of the commodification of human life within slavery, colonialism, as well as in contemporary global capitalism, we insist that what is currently theorized as a "new" financialization of human life under neoliberalism occurred brutally and routinely and continues to occur throughout the course of modern empires. Indeed, what Lowe discusses elsewhere as the "colonial division of humanity" is a signature feature of long-standing liberal modes of distinction that privilege particular lives as "human" and treat other lives as the laboring, replaceable, or disposable contexts that constitute that "humanity."[20] In their recent work on neoliberal forms of "surrogate humanity"— whether gestational surrogacy in India, life extension through medical technologies, or the advanced automation of labor by Amazon robotics— Neda Atanasoski and Kalindi Vora argue that even "post-human" concepts and practices continue to reproduce racial, gender, and geopolitical hierarchies of social difference.[21]

The national security imperatives developed during the Cold War have been critical to the neoliberal reorganization of the state and economy, with consequences for the domestic racial order, which involves the withdrawal of the state from its traditional purpose of social welfare to investment in the repressive arms of the U.S. state: policing, drug enforcement, immigration and border patrol, and prisons—all of which racialize and divide in the distribution of punishments. The privatization of traditional public "goods," such as schooling, health care, and social securities further contributes to the precarity of poor communities of color, while the buildup of policing, detention, and prisons targets and suppresses U.S. black, brown, and Muslim communities. The links between U.S. militarism abroad and policing at home is nowhere more evident than in the Israeli training of police serving in Ferguson, Missouri, who suppressed the community protesting Michael Brown's death with military surplus equipment such as aircraft, armored vehicles, assault rifles, grenades, vests, and tear gas.[22] Rebecca Bohrman and Naomi Murakawa ironically term this refortification of the repressive arms of the state the "remaking big government," while Ruth Wilson Gilmore calls this a transformation from the "welfare state" to the "warfare state."[23] The national security discourse exonerates the neoliberal state for its violent antiblackness and Islamophobia.

The "Asian American" has often been made to serve as the sign that mediates this disavowal of the racial ordering called "postraciality" or "colorblindness," the deployment of which governs this neoliberal restructuring of culture, society, economy, and politics. Whether expressed through Asian immigrant exclusion or inclusion, the U.S. state has produced itself as a global power through the formation of the "Asian American" as a means to resolve the contradictions of the U.S. racial capitalism and its imperial military project. Yet we wish to emphasize that for this reason, now, as before, the "Asian American" is a critical mediating figure for diagnosing racial power and geopolitical ordering. Rather than stabilizing binary categories of white/nonwhite, settler/native, or developed/underdeveloped, the "Asian American" continues still to mediate racial relationality or to triangulate these terms. Asian racial formation continues to shed light on how race is not fixed or essential but a shifting designation within what Stuart Hall terms society "structured-in-dominance."[24] Asian racial formations—as noncitizen labor, as model minority, as threatening capitalist rival—devalue Asians and measure and mediate geopolitical and national transformations. In our current moment, Asianness as "model minority/model modernity" is an index of the present U.S. settler racial order that reduces and dehumanizes blackness as surplus population, constructs Indigenous peoples as extinct or vanishing, and frames Muslims as threatening violence.

In conclusion, we conceive U.S. racial empire as an open process, an unfolding of dynamic, multiple relations of rule and resistance. Alyosha Goldstein discusses U.S. colonialism as "a continuously failing, perpetually incomplete, project that labors to find a workable means of resolution to sustain its logic of possession by disavowing ongoing contestation."[25] Like Goldstein, we understand U.S. racial empire to be continuously failing and incomplete, which suggests that its destruction, exploitation, and administration is never total, that its cruelty and cunning produces contingency and excess that we cannot entirely know or anticipate. In *Body Counts*, Espiritu frames the possibility of anti-imperial collaborations through critical juxtaposition, which she elaborates by interpreting the geography of Vietnamese refugee flight in 1975: The refugees were taken by military aircraft and routed through U.S. bases, from Vietnam to the Philippines to Guam and then to California. This itinerary connects Vietnamese postwar displacement to that of settler colonialism and militarism that has dispossessed Filipino, Chamorro, and Native American peoples and gives rise to an antimilitarist association of incommensurable yet linked groups. This is what Yoneyama describes, in *Cold War Ruins*, as transpacific cultures of reckoning and redress in the face of unredressable war and violence. The related, yet often illegible, struggles against these interlocking formations are the possible political itineraries that Lowe evokes in *Intimacies* as "connections that could have been, but were lost, and are thus, not yet."[26] Thus, in our piece, we take a comparative relational approach and employ the method of critical juxtaposition—the deliberate bringing together of seemingly different historical events in an effort to reveal what would otherwise remain invisible—in this case, to examine the contours, contents, and limits of U.S. imperialism, wars, and genocide in the Asia-Pacific region and racialization on the U.S. mainland. We gesture toward, and call into being, what Yoneyama calls the competing "yearnings" for "justice beyond judicialization" across unlike, asymmetrical, yet linked terrains.[27] We can and must always make "Asia" and "Asian American" signify more than American exceptionalism.

NOTES

1. Jana K. Lipman, "'Give Us a Ship': The Vietnamese Repatriate Movement on Guam, 1975," *American Quarterly* 64 (2012): 3–4 (emphasis added).

2. Richard Carrico, *Strangers in a Stolen Land: Indians of San Diego County from Prehistory to the New Deal* (Newcastle, Calif.: Sierra Oaks, 1987).

3. Robert F. Rogers, *Destiny's Landfall: A History of Guam* (Honolulu: University of Hawaii Press, 1995).

4. Oscar V. Campomanes, "1898 and the Nature of the New Empire," *Radical History Review* 73 (Winter 1999): 130–46. See also Richard H. Immerman, *Empire for Liberty: A History of American Imperialism from Benjamin Franklin to Paul Wolfowitz* (Princeton, N.J.: Princeton University Press, 2010).

5. William Appleman Williams, *The Tragedy of American Diplomacy* (Cleveland, Ohio: World Publishing, 1959), 67, 47.

6. Saidiya V. Hartman, *Scenes of Subjection: Terror, Slavery, and Self-Making in Nineteenth-Century America* (Oxford: Oxford University Press, 1997), 131.

7. Lisa Yoneyama, "Traveling Memories, Contagious Justice: Americanization of Japanese War Crimes at the End of the Post-Cold War," *Journal of Asian American Studies* (February 2003): 57–63.

8. Chungmoo Choi, "The Discourse of Decolonization and Popular Memory: South Korea," *Positions: East Asia Cultures Critique* 1, no. 1 (1993): 80.

9. Mimi Nguyen, *The Gift of Freedom: War, Debt, and Other Refugee Passages* (Durham, N.C.: Duke University Press, 2014).

10. Atsushi Toriyama, "Okinawa's 'Postwar': Some Observations on the Formation of American Military Bases in the Aftermath of Terrestrial Warfare," trans. David Buist, in *The Inter-Asia Cultural Studies Reader*, ed. Kuan Hsing Chen and Beng H. Chua, 267–88 (London: Routledge, 2007), 273.

11. Lisa Yoneyama, *Hiroshima Traces: Time, Space and the Dialectics of Memory* (Berkeley: University of California Press, 1999), 19.

12. Takashi Fujitani, *Race for Empire: Koreans as Japanese and Japanese as Americans during World War II* (Berkeley: University of California Press, 2011).

13. Hijin Park, "Neoliberalizing Differential Racialization: Asian Uplift, Indigenous Death, and Blackness as Surplus," presentation, McMaster University, October 2012.

14. Chandan Reddy, "Asian Diasporas, Neoliberalism, and Family: Reviewing the Case for Homosexual Asylum in the Context of Family Rights," *Social Text* 84–85, vol. 23, nos. 3–4 (Fall–Winter 2005): 101–19.

15. Yên Lê Espiritu, *Home Bound: Filipino Lives across Cultures* (Berkeley: University of California Press, 2003), 47–48.

16. On "racial liberalism" and the postwar incorporation of racialized minorities, see especially Jodi Melamed, *Represent and Destroy: Rationalizing Violence in the New Racial Capitalism* (Minneapolis: University of Minnesota Press, 2011).

17. Cedric Robinson, *Black Marxism: The Making of the Black Radical Tradition* (Chapel Hill: University of North Carolina Press, 1983).

18. Grace Kyungwon Hong, *Death beyond Disavowal: The Impossible Politics of Difference* (Minneapolis: University of Minnesota Press, 2015).

19. See for example, Thomas Lemke ("The Birth of Bio-politics: Michel Foucault's Lectures at the Collège de France on Neo-liberal Governmentality," *Economy and Society* 30, no. 2 [May 2001]: 190–207), who argues that neoliberalism is characterized by the collapse of the distinction between liberal economy and liberal governance and the withdrawal of the state in favor of the apotheosis of the economy such that neoliberal subjects are

controlled precisely through their "freedom." Wendy Brown explains that neoliberalism involves "extending and disseminating market values to all institutions and social action"; "all dimensions of human life are cast in terms of a market rationality"; and the state ceases to be "the Hegelian constitutional state conceived as the universal representation of the people." Wendy Brown, "Neo-liberalism and the End of Liberal Democracy," in *Edgework: Critical Essays on Knowledge and Politics* (Princeton, N.J.: Princeton University Press, 2005), 40–41. See also David Harvey, *A Brief History of Neoliberalism* (Oxford: Oxford University Press, 2005).

20. Lisa Lowe, *The Intimacies of Four Continents* (Durham, N.C.: Duke University Press, 2015), 107.

21. Kalindi Vora and Neda Atanasoski, "Surrogate Humanity: Posthuman Networks and the (Racialized) Obsolescence of Labor," *Catalyst: Feminism, Theory, Technoscience* 1, no. 1 (2015): 1–40.

22. Kristian Davis Bailey, "The Ferguson/Palestine Connection," *Ebony*, August 19, 2014, http://www.ebony.com/news-views/the-fergusonpalestine-connection-403; Tom Giratikanon, Alicia Parlapiano, and Jeremy White, "Mapping the Spread of the Military's Surplus Gear," *New York Times*, August 15, 2014, http://www.nytimes.com/interactive/2014/08/15/us/surplus-military-equipment-map.html.

23. Rebecca Bohrman and Naomi Murakawa, "Remaking Big Government," in *Global Lockdown: Race, Gender, and the Prison-Industrial Complex*, ed. Julia Sudbury (New York: Routledge, 2005); Ruth Wilson Gilmore, "Globalization and U.S. Prison Growth: From Military Keynesianism to Post-Keynesian Militarism," *Race & Class* 40, nos. 2–3 (1998–1999): 171–88.

24. Stuart Hall, "Race, Articulation, and Societies Structured in Dominance," in *Black British Cultural Studies*, ed. Houston A. Baker and Manthia Diawara (Chicago: University of Chicago Press, 1996).

25. Alyosha Goldstein, ed., *Formations of United States Colonialism* (Durham, N.C.: Duke University Press, 2013), 3.

26. Lowe, *Intimacies of Four Continents*, 174.

27. Yoneyama, *Cold War Ruins*, 205.

Tensions, Engagements, Aspirations: The Politics of Knowledge Production in Filipino American Studies

Martin F. Manalansan IV

Filipino American studies is burning! Hot! *"Fil Am* Studies" used to have a marginal presence if not a virtual absence during the early years of Asian American studies. In addition to its California provenance, Asian American studies in its first decades traditionally concentrated on Chinese and Japanese American experiences. However, for the past fifteen years, there has been what has been touted as the "Filipino turn" in Asian American studies or a renaissance of sorts in terms of the dramatic emergence and increase in the numbers of scholars and publications that come under the aegis of "Filipino American." One indicator of this trend is the increased and visible presence of Filipino American academics in the annual meetings of the Association for Asian American Studies. The Filipino caucus in the association now includes over one hundred formal members, most of them tenured or tenure-track faculty, postdoctoral scholars, student affairs administrators, and advanced doctoral students actively engaged in every facet of associational life. Filipino American studies scholarly publications encompass immigration, queer studies, race, sexuality, gender, class, colonialism, postcolonialism, empire, and labor studies illustrating the diversity and capacious landscape of this interdisciplinary field. Another proof of this intellectual ascendancy is a long list of notable works that have become widely read in North America and Europe as well as in the Philippines, where many of these works have been republished in local university and private presses. This paper maps out the roots and routes of Filipino American studies as an institutionalized field and as an affective site of professional and personal aspirations and emotional investments. It maps the general paths practitioners have taken to explore the tenability and plasticity of ideas and concepts as well as in the forging strategies to calibrate, encounter, and resolve the dangers, pleasures, and possibilities of cutting across borders of knowledge formations and traditions to set them with and against the geographic expanse of Filipinos scattered all over the world.

In particular, this essay engages with the various manifestations and issues around this shift or turn. Such an engagement is not a celebration per se but a close interrogation of the smoldering tensions and issues. In other words, this so-called renaissance comes with a heightening of social and intellectual fissures and hierarchies in the field, many of which have existed all along. Therefore, the discussion below aims to briefly map and track the sites, symptoms, maladies, and entanglements of Filipino American studies. I will briefly trace the paths of development by giving attention to the ways in which issues of orientations, institutions, and sites produce flashpoints, tensions, or "flare-ups" including the infamous *Blu's Hanging* controversy and the fraught relationship between ethnic studies and area studies (specifically between Philippine studies and Filipino American studies) as well as the troubling inequalities between North American—and Philippine-based scholars. At the same time, I also offer an analysis and a personal account of various ongoing efforts and dialogue that are fueling recent intellectual projects and activities as a way not to paint a catalog of issues but to limn the various political energies that animate such projects. In particular, I am interested in the question of travel and Filipino American studies or when the readers, researchers, and critics are located not in North America or the Global North but in Asia, specifically the Philippines. I interrogate the various scalar and interscalar connections and disjunctures between what has been circumscribed by some as the field of Filipino American studies and the border crossing or "interloping" across academic fields and geographic borders. By looking at specific sites and texts, such as the recently published anthology *Filipino Studies*, and several conferences, I investigate the conceptual, methodological, and theoretical divergences and debates and probe the political economic grounds and the affective orientations undergirding these activities. The main goal is not to territorialize and ghettoize the field but to unpack the many hopes, dreams, and desires of its practitioners and critics. Therefore, this essay is not strictly an assessment but is more of a generative critique and an aspirational, even personalized, reflection on the possibilities and futures of the field.

I attended my first Association for Asian American Studies conference in Ithaca in 1993, where I witnessed the rather nascent crew of Filipino American studies scholars. At the same conference, I attended a workshop on social science research methods for graduate students and was facilitated by two prominent Asian American studies professors. Among those in attendance were Rick Bonus, Karin Aguilar-San Juan, and myself. During the workshops, one of the facilitators (a senior Chinese American ethnic studies professor who is now retired) blurted out that Filipinos have three kinds of phenotypes—they either look Chinese, Malay, or Indonesian. The Filipinos in attendance just looked at each other. Shocked in disbelief, we remained silent for many reasons, including being junior academics and the impossibility of countering the ridiculousness of the eugenics-tinged statement. From that day on, my cohort of Filipino Americanists (some, like me, who were trained in area studies and in various disciplines) were determined to succeed in our graduate studies and to create a powerful intellectual imprint in the field, which at that time deemed Filipinos to be insignificant facsimiles, doppelgangers, or genetic copies of other Asians without any distinctive "features" or value.

The trajectory of the "Filipino Turn" in Asian American studies can be traced to the early to mid-90s when a group of scholars, some of whom were trained in Southeast Asian area studies, found their way to American and Asian American studies and began to make their presence felt in this space in American academia. The works of E. San Juan, Vicente Rafael, and Oscar Campomanes paved the way for a robust and vibrant field. The nineties decade culminated in a major historical commemoration of the Philippine-American War of 1898. This pivotal event of American imperial rule opened up a space for Filipino American—and Philippine-oriented research that has been long seen as peripheral to the study of the United States and Southeast Asia. This emergence also coincided with the scholarly interests around the heightened global interconnections caused by late capitalism. As such, recent Filipino American studies publications reflect and animate both the "imperial" and "transnational" turns in U.S. humanities and social sciences.

Another important event in during this period was the aforementioned *Blu's Hanging* controversy where the tensions between Filipino American studies and the larger field of Asian American studies reached a major flashpoint. Briefly, in 1998 the literary book award committee of the Association for Asian American Studies awarded a prize to *Blu's Hanging*, a coming-of-age novel published in 1997 by Lois-Ann Yamanaka. After several members and other constituencies protested about the dismal and racist depictions of Filipinos in Hawai'i, the association board rescinded the award. It became a whirlwind of events and the exchange of sharp rhetoric that led to the resignation of almost all of the board members. It created a flashpoint for the entire field of Asian American studies. Many Filipino American faculty, students, and activists were quick to point out the novel is a mere symptom of the longer history of Filipinos being either an afterthought, if not marginal constituents, of the field of Asian American studies. There were also several Filipino American writers and scholars, including Jessica Hagedorn, who adopted an alternative view by highlighting and recognizing the complexities of artistic production and creative freedom. This event highlights the frictive relationship between artistic productions, academic rigor, and the political need for positive nonracist representations much like the phenotypic classification of Filipinos.

Several works have written about this controversy more capaciously, but the purpose of bringing it up here is to highlight this event's repercussions within Filipino American studies.[1] What came out of this controversy in more practical terms is a strong consciousness of the position of Filipino Americans within the American academy in general and within Asian American studies in particular. The group of Filipino American protestors became the core of what is now the Filipino American caucus in the Association for Asian American Studies. In other words, the *Blu's Hanging* controversy highlighted the predicament of Filipinos and, in fact, became one of the animating historical and coalitional forces for the "Filipino turn." While this is a traceable path, it does not mean that the caucus practitioners have become a kind of policing force aimed at ferreting and dismantling "negative" representations and views of Filipino Americans. The strong institutional presence of Filipinos, both in the association and in academia, made possible the capacity to be open to critique (even to what some might call negative viewpoints) without losing the political passion and intragroup empathy or ethnic solidarity. In other words, even during the controversy itself, Filipinos took to either side, but at the end of the day, the event opened the door to a critical field that is both politically and intellectually attuned to shifting events or situations.

Having laid out the historical and structural antecedents to Filipino American studies today, albeit in a provisional and abbreviated manner, we need to get to the heart of the matter, which is the constitutive elements of the field. To jump-start the discussion, let us turn to the problem of nomenclature. *What's in a name?* Philippine studies, Filipino studies, and Filipino American studies are used in various contexts, sites, and for various interests and functions—often, much like in this essay, they are used together. While it is instructive to attend to the various, oftentimes erratic, ways in which these categories are used—Philippine studies is popularly seen as the area studies–based concentration on the nation and the state, Filipino studies involves the global diaspora and American empire, and lastly, Filipino American studies focuses on the Filipino experiences in the United States—it is crucial to see how scholars often refuse, crisscross, circumvent, or rearticulate these seemingly static monolithic notions and fields.

I use "Filipino American studies" provisionally as a way to signal my own institutional positionality but also to emphasize a category in flux, open to rearticulations. I also use it not in the strictures of the American academy as being only about the study of minorities in the United States of America that operate under the rubric of ethnic studies. I find my ambivalent and tentative use of "Filipino American studies" betrays my affinity with the idea of "Filipino Studies." Oscar Campomanes's canonical essay utilizes the term "Filipino Studies" where "Filipino" is a vernacularizing nexus or part of a mediating process that involves contestations and reformulations subject to the maneuvers and agency of Filipinos as well as the decentering of calcified notions of the nation and nationalism by acknowledging the diaspora and its "heteroglot/heterogenous composition."[2] He is the pioneering scholar who retraced the boundaries of the study of the Philippines and Filipinos within and across Asian (area) studies and transnational/postnational American studies. As such, he then locates Filipino studies within local, national, and transnational contexts as a way to capture and localize the multiscalar and multisited contexts of Filipino experiences.

His conception is attentive to the transnational contexts of Filipino experiences and the circulation of Filipino American studies intellectual projects. As stated above, the production and dissemination of ideas and the scope and breadth of research topics in the field has been transnational and has lead to two major sets of frictive dilemmas. The first is the question of the travel of Asian American/Filipino American studies or what happens when ideas and theories move across political and disciplinary borders. The second, which is very related to the first, entails the question of material and economic conditions of intellectual production.

The dilemma and reality of Filipino American studies' mobility has led to fraught and problematic encounters. Because of its transnational circulation and research stance, it has been accused of uncritically applying U.S. ethnic studies' ideas on race, experiences around multiculturalism, and other so-called American theories to the Philippine context. As such, Filipino American studies is necessarily negotiating the treacherous borders of area studies, American studies, diaspora studies, and ethnic studies. These border-crossings typically involved questions around methodology, archives, and pedagogy. The problem of borders points to the issues around understanding the traffic and travel of intellectual productions, especially around directionality and orientation.

Various Asian American scholars have interrogated these specific quandaries between ethnic studies and area studies. Lisa Yoneyama argues that such tensions, particularly around area studies and ethnic studies or more specifically between Asian and Asian American studies, can be generative of "new questions and objects of inquiry."[3] Despite the limitations of Title VI funding that enables U.S.-based area studies centers where such funds specifically mandate against the study of migration to the United States and national diasporas, Asian American studies scholars have been adamant about the need for dialogue and conversation. Echoing Campomanes, Yoneyama illustrates how travel of institutionalized fields of inquiry can reveal the limitations and instability of such disciplinary boundaries, while at the same time warns about the possibility of U.S.–based Asian American studies being able to create "new matrices of power to produce and assign certain subjectivity with voice and visibility, while determining the discursive parameters of what can and cannot be articulated."[4] She argues that while there is a call for more mobility and conversation between intellectual fields and geographic areas, there is a wise caution about the colonizing tendencies of Western-based ideas and institutional presence in the Global South.

To address these possibilities and pitfalls, Colleen Lye and Rika Nakamura provide alternative frameworks and strategies. Lye recalls and recuperates the "Third Worldism" spirit or ethos that fueled the Asian American movement thereby creating the field of Asian American studies. Such Third Worldism focused on the various political and social agendas and political tactics that animated the Bandung Conference and propagated, at least for a moment, a possibility of existence and survival for Asia and its other allies in the Third World without the superpower such as the United States. Lye admonishes Asian American studies scholars not to indulge in a nostalgic yearning for Bandung and other past events but to incorporate Asian studies scholars' critical fuselage and tools to bear upon a forging of critical links between the lessons of the Bandung era particularly around the needs and limitations of nationalist self-determination while applying the "strategic demands of the 'logic of the situation'" to present-day predicaments of neoliberal globalization, including those in U.S. contexts.[5] In short, Lye offers a particular, yet powerful example of linkage and possible points of collaboration. Following Lye, Nakamura offers another possibility of Asian studies and Asian American studies productive encounters, which is the possibility for a "comparative minority studies" where Asian American studies scholars can "decentralize their work and perspectives" through what she calls "Asian based Asian American Studies" (where Asia, not America, is the reference point) that deploy a transpacific framework and critical comparisons that enable an expansion of notions of majority/minority dynamics, particularly in dislodging the idea of Asian Americans as always already abject or marginal.[6]

In the specific case of Filipino American studies, Oscar Campomanes offers a trenchant model of what Yoneyama, Lye, and Nakamura have advocated specifically for the study of the Philippines and its diaspora. His prescient and astutely crafted essays revolve around what he has called "Filipino Studies" that was briefly discussed above.[7] Campomanes traces the fraught and multivalent constitution of *Filipino* particularly in terms of its colonial history and present-day entanglements with global capital. Instead of maintaining static notion of Filipino as always already framed with its contingent link to the nation, he argues for a more vernacular notion of Filipino and Filipinoness that does not depend on the national scale but rather flits around and can be variously embedded in or contextualized by other alternative levels of geographic, political, and historical levels of complexity. He advocates for "vernacularization" or a creative, critical, if not "radical epistemology" where empire and capital become integral to the critical analysis of subjects and collectivities that moves away from the nation-centered roots of intellectual productions of area and ethnic studies.

However, the problems of borders are not just semantic or intellectual but also material and economic, specifically around the unequal power distribution in intellectual production between Philippine-based and mostly U.S.-based scholars. Reynaldo Ileto, Carol Hau, and Francisco Benitez and Laurie Sears have vigorously presented and skillfully mapped the tensions and issues that are at the heart of numerous debates and polemics around the study of the Philippines and its diaspora.[8] The issues of collaboration and the politics of citationality are just two of the numerous pressing concerns that pervade projects at the interface of Philippine and Filipino American studies. The problem of authority and authenticity—who speaks for whom—calls to mind what Hau terms "epistemic privilege," which points to the unequal and situated distribution of intellectual reach, valuation, and prominence, or to put it another way, the politics of intellectual location.[9] The evaluation of one's scholarship and its mode of circulation depend on one's distance from the center of power. In this case, scholarship on the Philippines and its diaspora are subjected to divergent standards, nativist impulses, eruptions of "Western" guilt, accusations of elitist language, and various modes of academic chauvinisms and exclusions. But what is to be done? What is being done?

The typical explanation for the perceived "rift" between Philippine studies and Filipino American studies is the facile notion that scholars in Filipino American studies do not read works from Philippine-based scholars. The trouble is not merely about what people are reading and quoting but rather addressing the basic structural inequalities that make scholarly exchanges difficult, if not tenuous. To confront and attempt to resolve the predicaments of Filipino American studies in the U.S. academy and its interface with scholarship from and about the Philippines, it is necessary to contextualize inequalities and the attempts to address them within and against the realities of North-South imperial relations, neoliberal university policies, and disciplinary formations. "Collaboration" has become a buzzword for many of these attempts at resolving the issues. What follows is a description of various attempts on the ground to address the various tensions and issues. The description is not an audit but rather a more personal contemplation of the ebullient surging of collective energies and emotions, the shortcomings of goals and mission, the structural and material limits, and the overall incompleteness of various attempts, many of which are still in motion.

One of the major activities I have been involved in is in the creation of a strong network of scholars. At the AAAS conference, I was part of the group of Fil Am members who set up the Filipino American caucus that became infamous for their riotous, loud, and lively meetings. But despite the encouraging number, the opportunities for networking and mentoring, and the creation of conviviality, there are still pressing problems that need to be addressed. The caucus is a loose group of mostly graduate students, faculty, and staff from American universities. Suggestions have been made to extend or conduct outreach to those outside academia and to undergraduates. In addition, the very mission of the caucus needs to confront the realities of inequality within the United States and between the United

States and Asia, specifically the Philippines. While there have been rare occasions where Philippine-based scholars have attended the AAAS conference, the caucus needs to address in some manner the limits and possibilities of widening the extent of membership and communication links outside the usual institutional sites.

In 2008, I co-organized the Philippine Palimpsests conference at the University of Illinois where around thirty Filipino American scholars converged to discuss research themes and to forge stronger ties. The name, as the metaphoric use of "palimpsest" suggests, was conceptualized around the layering, erasures, and reinscriptions of histories, spaces, and cultures, or a deep engagement with the "porousness" and permeability of intellectual and political borders. As an invitation-only conference, Palimpsests was beset by issues of representation and scope. Ironically, the keynote speaker, Reynaldo Ileto, who was then based at the National University of Singapore, was the only non-U.S.–based scholar who attended. Scholars who attended were not necessarily people who were clearly Filipino Americanist at least in their training, research institutional formation, and affiliation. The framing of the conference was based on who we knew, and therefore was seen (rightly) by many as not very inclusive. It became clear that the next iteration should be more expansive. But the lessons learned from this conference were not just about the limitations of funding, the need for geographic and disciplinary capaciousness, and the necessary function of outreach and the critical questioning of community. They are clearly about creating more ambitious intellectual projects that could potentially resolve the aforementioned problems head-on.

Filipino Studies: Palimpsests of Nation and Diaspora is the anthology of essays inspired by the conference and written by many of its participants.[10] It is related to and, at the same time, departs from several related anthologies in significant ways. Numerous interdisciplinary anthologies about the Philippines and its diaspora have been published before. The 2006 collection by Tiongson et al. and the 2012 collection by Coloma et al. deal with Filipinos in the United States and Canada, respectively. They are focused on issues of invisibility and representation and are projects that seek to put forward archives of experiences of Filipinos in both countries.[11] Tolentino's edited volume of *positions: east asia cultures critique* provides critical perspectives on late twentieth- and early twenty-first-century cultural productions marked by the end of martial law and shaped by the oeuvre of one of the foremost film directors, the late Lino Brocka. Rafael's 1999 collection of mostly previously published works of U.S.-, Philippine-, and

Australian-based scholars aims to "call attention to the frayed and porous passages between what is inside and outside not only of the Philippines but also that which is commonly thought of as the 'West.'"[12] Patajo-Legasto's 2011 voluminous collection has a sizeable section on Filipino American experiences but depends on an eclectic telos and genealogy of Philippine studies.[13] What is clear in these body of works is the shifting and multivalent conception of Philippine and Filipino as well as the various ways in which publications, whether published in the Philippines or in the United States, have specific audiences as well as particular notions of interdisciplinarity. At the heart of the Filipino studies anthology is an attempt to engage with other sites and texts that might at the outset seem similar or connected but do not easily cohere. Enumerating the various efforts at "dialogue," there is an admission such efforts are not enough:

> We look towards possible links and strategies to overcome the difficulties.
> Many of the contributors are typically the only "Philippine experts"
> on their campuses. While this virtual isolation places an extraordinary
> burden on pedagogy, research and institutional visibility and survival,
> the meeting of various scholars through conferences may be one way
> to assuage this onus. The Palimpsests conference together with those
> at the University of Hawai'i Center for Philippines Studies and the
> biannual ICOPHIL (International Conference on Philippine Studies)
> are just among a few attempts to link and connect scholars into
> a communal hub and network of collaboration, conversation and
> debate.[14]

At the same time, the anthology was upfront about its aspirational trajectory, despite its acknowledgement of the limitations of the collection. Such awareness belies the kind of work that still needs to be done and the kinds of conversations that still need to happen:

> Clearly, these are not enough. More creative and effective strategies
> and activities need to be forged to address the various issues discussed
> briefly mentioned above. However, because of the Global North site of
> this anthology's publication, distribution/dissemination and the
> institutional affiliations of most of its contributors, we are aware of the
> limits and possibilities of reaching various reading communities across
> regions and borders. Nevertheless, we offer these essays as a contribution
> towards expansive dialogue between and among scholars and other
> audiences in various sites. We recognize the difficulties and hurdles,
> but as a collective effort, Philippine Palimpsests, true to the core
> denotation of the word palimpsest, are open to the revisionary and

trace-like qualities of knowledge formations. We reject the static
hierarchical formations of native versus stranger, nation versus
diaspora, and of the here and there. However, we also appreciate and
concede the multi-directional, striated and inter/intra scalar power
arrangements in the production of academic knowledges about the
Philippines. We are open to more hopeful and sometimes ambivalent
thoughts and longings for a viable future or set of futures. We remain
committed to exploring other processes of building alternative
strategies for collaborative knowledge formations. the final analysis,
we go by what Carolyn Hau has wisely admonished scholars on the
Philippines which is to interrogate our own positionings, to think of
our works not as final statements that excludes other scholarship but
are open gestures and attempts towards new conversations and
collaborations, to think more broadly and aspirationally about
emancipatory politics and futures, and to open up capacious vistas of
"what it means to live as, and call oneself, Filipino.[15]

One of the ways the Filipino studies anthology attempted to situate itself
is through an explicit mapping of its location within the constellation of
previously published works and events that have attempted to address the
theoretical, methodological, and political divide. My coeditor and I emphasized that the contributors speak from specific transnational locations, the
American academic landscape, and other social locations. We also humbly[16]
acknowledged that the anthology did not speak for all Filipinos and Filipino scholars everywhere and at all times but instead the contributors
speak "from" the structurally, historically, and politically positioned viewpoints and perspectives. The essays went beyond identity and invisibility
questions and attempted to capaciously think about cultural production,
social justice and transformation, structural politics, historical passages,
and collective actions. It is equally important to note that this collection is
not solely a product of ethnic studies scholars, as can be gleaned from the
biographies of the contributors. Contributors included scholars trained in
area studies and other disciplines. As such, *Filipino Studies* attempts to bring
together conversations between fields such as critical ethnic studies, cultural studies, area studies, and the traditional disciplines (e.g., literature
and anthropology), thereby circumventing the calcified notion of field and
discipline. At the same time, even with such variegated interdisciplinary
contexts, there were several strong intellectual traditions and angles that
permeated most of the essays, one of which is Filipino American studies.
We recognized the undercurrents and histories around the establishment
and survival of Filipino American studies that opened up new viable spaces

for the study of the Philippines in the American academy where it previously occupied a marginal and lowly status in area studies, more specifically, Southeast Asian studies.[17]

While acknowledging the importance of Filipino American studies' presence and emergent status in the American academy and in bringing area studies and ethnic studies in conversation with each other, the contributors in this collection did not consider themselves and their works as uncritically applying ethnic studies ideas on race and other so-called American theories to the Philippine context. Rather, they were involved in an exploration of the tenability and plasticity of ideas and concepts. Instead of focusing on the exceptional character of the Philippines, the essays were seeking capacious ways to calibrate the dangers, pleasures, and possibilities of cutting across knowledge formations and traditions to then set them against the geographic reach of Filipinos scattered all over the world.

In the end, *Filipino Studies*, as I have asserted above, is still not enough to even begin to unravel the tangled web of "roots and routes" of the intellectual productions around the Philippines and its diaspora. The dialogue should continue. As I am writing this piece, the organizing of Palimpsest 2 at University of California, San Diego, is underway. Utilizing the lessons learned from the first Palimpsest conference, the University of California organizers are opening up the call to advanced graduate students and junior faculty in the United States and Canada. Even with this renewed and expanded activity, several things remain unresolved. While Palimpsest 2 organizers are trying to find a way to fund a Philippine-based scholar to participate in the conference, what remains unexplored and untouched is the structural inequality that foments distrust and dismissal and the need to find ways in which other forms of interfield dialogue beyond face-to-face conversations in conferences and meetings. Several Philippine-based scholars have expressed the sentiment in terms of how their American counterparts get to publish so much while they toil under horrible teaching loads and dismal salaries (anywhere in the range of five to ten courses a semester and two hundred to five hundred dollars per month). So while the "Filipino turn" in U.S. academic publishing may be a source of celebration for U.S.-based scholars, it can also be a source of discomfort, anger, jealousy, and antipathy for colleagues back in the Philippines.

Through various conversations with academics in both the United States and in the Philippines, I have gathered a list of suggested strategies, a few of which I will enumerate here briefly as a way to assess them sometime in the future and as a way to end this essay on a hopeful note. One of the more popular suggestions is the use of the Internet as a way to systematically include scholars from the Philippines in conferences and meetings in the West. This is not a novel idea by any means, but it has not been used in an extensive and regular manner, particularly in conversations around Filipino American and Philippine studies. A book exchange program can be launched to enable Philippine-based scholars access to more expensive books published in North America. Another is the establishment of a scholar exchange involving the recruitment of postdoctoral scholars into Asian American studies departments in the United States possibly tapping into but not necessarily depending on established programs such as the Fulbright. However, one of the more notable and pressing suggested strategies is the opening up of curricula, pedagogy, and research agendas to various theories and methodologies in both fields. As I have discussed above, Asian American studies scholars such as Campomanes, Lye, and Nakamura have advocated this idea for years and some university programs have implemented this, but such strategy also needs to go beyond local academic settings. It is important to maintain the conversation between the fields beyond conference papers but to crystallize these productive conversations in the formation of scholars and experts about the Philippines. The problem is that the idea of a transnational and expansive implementation strategy encounters the realities of funding and structural limitations. It might be possible to combine a combination of fundraising from public and private sources in the Philippines and the United States to come up with a structured set of activities and projects that will transform these aspirations, strategies, and ideals into realities. But in the meantime, the work goes on and the debates, tensions, and entanglements continue to be fueled by an excitement toward future possibilities. Filipino American studies or, to be more appropriate, Filipino studies is poised to confront these various inequalities and conversations specifically, as Oscar Campomanes has wisely offered, the field and its scholars are equipped to handle such challenges because a vibrant and radical study of the Philippines and its diaspora, including those in the United States, has emerged from and is fueled by persistent history of anti-imperial and anticolonial practices. The intellectual fire continues to burn.

NOTES

1. For journalistic accounts see Mindy Pennybacker, "What Boodah You? The Authenticity Debate," *Nation*, March 1, 1999, http://www .thenation.com/article/what-boddah-you-authenticity-debate/; Donna Foote, "Trouble in Paradise: A Hawaiian Novelist Sparks a P.C. Protest,"

Newsweek 132 (7): 63; and Somini Sengupta, "An Author Who Gathers Prizes and Protests," *New York Times*, February 8, 1999. For scholarly assessments, see Darlene Rodrigues, "Imagining Ourselves: Reflections on the Controversy over Lois-Ann Yamanaka's Blu's Hanging," *Amerasia Journal* 26, no. 2 (2000): 195–207; Mark Chiang, "Autonomy and Representation: Aesthetics and the Crisis of Asian American Cultural Politics in the Controversy over Blu's Hanging," in *Literary Gestures: The Aesthetic in Asian American Writing*, ed. Rocío G. Davis and Sue-Im Lee (Philadelphia, Penn.: Temple University Press, 2006), 17–34; Candace Fujikane, "Sweeping Racism under the Rug of 'Censorship': The Controversy over Lois-Ann Yamanaka's Blu's Hanging," *Amerasia Journal* 26, no. 2 (2000): 159–94; Cynthia Wu, "Revisiting Blu's Hanging: A Critique of Queer Transgression in the Lois-Ann Yamanaka Controversy," *Meridians: Feminism, Race, Transnationalism* 10, no. 1 (2009): 32–53; and Elda E. Tsou, "Catachresis: Blu's Hanging and the Epistemology of the Given," *Journal of Asian American Studies* 14, no. 2 (2011): 283–303.

2. Oscar Campomanes, "The Vernacular/Local, the National, and the Global in Filipino Studies," *Kritika Kultura* 3 (July 2003), http://journals.ateneo.edu/ojs/index.php/kk/article/view/1566.

3. Lisa Yoneyama, "Asian American Studies in Travel," *Inter-Asia Cultural Studies* 13, no. 2 (2012): 294.

4. Ibid., 296.

5. Colleen Lye, "U.S. Ethnic Studies and Third Worldism, 40 Years Later," *Inter-Asia Cultural Studies* 13, no. 2(2012): 192.

6. Rika Nakamura, "What Asian American Studies Can Learn from Asia? Towards a Project of Comparative Minority Studies," *Inter-Asia Cultural Studies* 13, no. 2 (2012): 251.

7. Oscar Campomanes, 1997. "New Formations of Asian American Studies and the Question of U.S. Imperialism," *positions* 5, no. 2 (1997): 523–50.

8. See Reynaldo C. Ileto, "Nation and Empire in the Intellectual Biographies of Southeast Asian Scholars," *Asian Studies* 59, no. 3–4 (2014): 9–17; Caroline Hau, "Privileging Roots and Routes: Filipino Intellectual and the Contest over Epistemic Power and Authority," *Philippine Studies: Historical and Ethnographic Viewpoints* 62, no. 1 (2014): 29–65; and J. Francisco Benitez and Laurie J. Sears, "Passionate Attachments: Subjectivity and Diaspora in the Transpacific," in *Transpacific Studies: Interventions and Intersections*, ed. Janet Hoskins and Viet Nguyen (Honolulu: University of Hawai'i Press, 2014).

9. Hau, "Privileging Roots and Routes."

10. Martin F. Manalansan, IV and Augusto Espiritu, *Filipino Studies: Palimpsests of Nation and Diaspora* (New York: New York University Press, 2016).

11. See Antonio T. Tiongson Jr., Edgardo Gutierrez, and Ricardo V. Gutierrez, eds., *Positively No Filipinos Allowed: Building Communities and Discourse* (Philadelphia, Penn.: Temple University Press, 2006); and Rolando Tolentino, ed., "Vaginal Economy: Cinema and Sexuality in the Post-Marcos, Post-Brocka Philippines," ed. Rolando Tolentino, special issue, *positions: east asia cultures critique* 19, no. 2 (2011).

12. Vicente Rafael, ed., *Discrepant Histories: Translocal Essays on Filipino Cultures* (Manila: Anvil Publications, 1995), xv.

13. Priscelina Patajo-Legasto, ed., *Philippine Studies: Have We Gone beyond St. Louis?* (Diliman: University of the Philippines Press, 2008).

14. Martin F. Manalansan, IV and Augusto Espiritu, *Filipino Studies: Palimpsests of Nation and Diaspora* (New York: New York University Press, 2016), 9–10.

15. Ibid., 9.

16. Humility is an important component of the conversation and the attempt to bridge the two fields. My personal observation is that in many of the conferences I attended with Philippine- and American-based scholars in attendance, there are several performances of academic expertise, either a masculinist (heterosexist) tendency of cutting everybody down or a reticence to critique anyone for fear of personal vendettas thereby overemphasizing consensus. Humility is not about emphasizing consensus over critique but rather to be generous and open in a moment of critically assessing other scholars' work. What of the things I am saying here is that while we need to face and tackle the material and structural issues head on, there needs to be a stronger acknowledgment of the kinds of affective and emotive structures that need to be emplaced together with the remedies or solutions that are either ongoing or are being proposed.

17. In various Title VI Asian studies centers in U.S. universities and colleges and in conferences such as the Asian Studies Association, Southeast Asian studies is a woefully represented field. Philippine studies is in an even rarer presence, if not totally absent in such sites and events.

CHAPTER 12

Asian International Students at U.S. Universities in the Post-2008 Collapse Era

Cynthia Wu

Conduct a search in either the mainstream press or specialized higher education periodicals about international enrollment and countless hits will appear on the recent influx of students from Asian countries. This essay fills a gap in Asian Americanist scholarship, which has just begun to make sense of international student enrollment in the present day. Some research has already been published on students from Asia who have studied at U.S. universities in earlier times.[1] However, the contemporary versions of this transhistorical occurrence require more examination. Part of the reason why Asian American studies may shy away from participating in these discussions is its primordial commitment to recovering a usable past defined by domestic, working-class interests. The more difficult issue of capitalist accommodation has only recently begun to find a foothold in the field. These early Asian Americanist works have also invested themselves in debunking the discourses that have cast Asian-raced subjects in the United States as perpetual foreigners incapable of or uninterested in becoming part of the nation. For the above reasons, modern-day sojourners in the form of middle- and upper-class students are anathema. Despite the field's transnational turn and its concurrent laying of claim to a "subjectless discourse"

unfettered by limits on our referents, casting attention on the phenomenon of Asian international students in the early twenty-first century causes
friction because of this intellectual past.[2]

This essay examines articles in periodicals geared toward higher education professionals such as the *Chronicle of Higher Education* and *Insider
Higher Ed*. The pieces in these industry-specific journals are accompanied
on occasion by references from other media sources where relevant.
As such, I focus not on the perspectives of Asian international students
themselves but on how the general American public, of which academic
professionals are a part, has held forth on questions that enrolling these
students in large numbers have raised.[3] Additionally, I locate these discussions within a transhistorical view of Asian bodies more generally—
as aggressively recruited entities shoring up the United States' economic
interests and unfortunate reminders of the nation-state's failure to meet its
capitalist-expansionist needs. I show how the paradox that accompanies
the perception of Asian people by the Anglo-American imagination is a
projection of the United States' own displeasure about its higher education industry. In recent generations, the academy has transformed into a
supplier of a consumer item—that is, a degree—rather than a service for
the common good. By extension, institutions have begun to regard students as customers as opposed to learners. In the midst of these shifts,
larger concerns about the high-stakes standardized testing of domestic
students, which has resulted in a lack of preparation for college, are displaced
onto another population. Concurrently, academia's frustration with how
domestic students have attempted to leverage their position in higher
education—through acts of deception, increased reliance on parental involvement, and a preoccupation with operationalizing the college experience in lieu of intellectual pursuit—are projected elsewhere. The grievances
in higher education about Asian international students have become light-
ning rods that channel the frustrations surrounding early twenty-first-
century U.S. higher education in general.

Asian Fraud

News reports on international students invoke a series of recurring topics
to explain the cause of their presence in the United States. The first concerns the growing consumer classes in Asian countries, particularly China.
Chinese nationals have started seeking new ways to increase their standing
in the global economy. For these largely middle- and upper-class subjects,
a U.S. college degree is one step in this process. Another frequently raised

issue in these articles is the level of preparation among international students. Instructional staff express bewilderment, disdain, resignation, or well-meaning concern about students' poor facility with written and spoken English and lack of acculturation into U.S. norms of classroom conduct. Accounts of cheating, plagiarism, and other types of academic dishonesty are common. Reporters tend not to shy away from addressing U.S. universities' recent interest in international tuition dollars. The financial strain on higher education is undeniable. The 2008 economic collapse, which exacerbated years of declining support for public universities, created conditions of precarity for many industries, academia included. Coupled with the rising numbers of administrators (and their salaries) and a marketing sensibility more attuned to amenities over instruction, colleges and universities were left scrambling to make up the difference.[4] For universities, the seeking of additional forms of revenue and the cutting of costs took various forms: a surge in corporate and private donor courtship; the replacement of in-rank faculty members with adjuncts; a growth in class sizes; an increase in online curricula; and the ballooning of tuition and other fees. Institutions' appeals to international and (for public universities) out-of-state students took place alongside these other changes.

The conditions of the present day depart in significant ways from the advent of large-scale migration to the United States from Asia in the mid-nineteenth century. There are economic differences between the laborers of the past and the largely middle-class students of today.[5] For these reasons, we must not conflate the two populations across this chasm, subsuming them simplistically and ahistorically under the banner of racial or ethnic similarity. We must also not conflate the conditions under which they were encouraged to come to the United States—as indentured workers versus degree seekers. However, the stubbornness with which racialized patterns of perception cling to Chinese bodies indicates a degree to which the Asian-raced figure persists as a troubling disturbance at times of economic and structural change.

One of the most extensive articles on international student enrollment was published in 2011, before more recent projections and confirmations of the trend's downturn. "The China Conundrum," appearing in the *Chronicle of Higher Education*, focuses specifically on the challenges that fraud, academic dishonesty, and other acts of deception among Chinese international students pose for educators. The authors report on "widespread fabrication on applications, whether that means a personal essay written by an agent or an English-proficiency score that doesn't jibe with a student's speaking ability." Hence, admissions officers at U.S. universities are left to "struggle to distinguish between good applicants and those who are too good to be true."[6] Causes of frustration for university professionals once students are enrolled include their lack of engagement with extracurricular life, tendency toward clannishness, and reluctance to speak in the classroom. This landmark article is hardly the only account that addresses U.S. university professionals' difficulties with Asian international students. Many others attest to similar worries.

A first-person narrative by an American educator hired on an annual contract by a college-preparatory school in China geared toward U.S. admissions reports on a litany of acts—performed through predatory agents—that would ordinarily be considered cheating. The fabrication of transcripts, essays, and letters of recommendation were simply standard procedure, this educator claimed. Given the commonness of these practices, the author measuredly states that "the SAT [Scholastic Achievement Test] tends to be the only thing in a Chinese student's file that American admissions offices can count on."[7] However, he also dismisses its usefulness because scores tend to be more indicative of test-taking skills. Although I do not disagree with this claim, I observe that he fails to mention the extent to which rote test mastery also benefits U.S. applicants. Many, likewise, do not enter college with the writing and critical thinking skills commensurate with test scores, especially if they have enrolled in a test preparatory class.

The SAT and other standardized exams such as the Test of English as a Foreign Language (TOEFL) and Graduate Record Examination (GRE) have become beleaguered institutions in the context of international admissions from Asia. Multiple accounts circulate about enterprising individuals who acquire test questions in advance to release in East Asia and test takers employing others to sit for the exam in their place using false passports as identification. In one case, thousands of students in China and South Korea had their scores temporarily held while officials investigated one of the affected test dates, leaving them in limbo only days before an application deadline.[8] Because student visas need to be obtained by proving admission to a U.S. college or university, federal authorities regard cheating on standardized tests as immigration violations. As one homeland security agent puts it: "These students were not only cheating their way into the university, they were also cheating their way through our nation's immigration system."[9]

On the other side are institutions that allegedly admit applicants who exist as students only on paper while staying in the country for other purposes. In early 2015, an owner of four vocational schools in Los Angeles's

Koreatown was indicted in what is known colloquially as a "pay-to-stay" operation for "admitting foreign nationals who were not bona fide students and never had any intention of taking classes."[10] The charges included immigration fraud, document fraud, and money laundering.

All told, the accumulation of reporting on Asian practices of gaining admission to U.S. universities—and, therefore, the country—sounds eerily similar to an earlier discourse of Asian duplicity at the time of Chinese exclusion. Readers of this volume will not need an extensive explanation of the limited terms on which migrants of Chinese origin could enter the United States back then or an explication of the practices of interrogation at the Angel Island Immigration Station to determine their legitimacy. The lengthy, convoluted, and often bad-faith interviews that prospective immigrants underwent are standard knowledge in Asian American studies. Less commonly discussed is the photographic technology that was used to document and surveil them in tandem with interrogation. Anna Pegler-Gordon's findings on immigration restrictions and photography show a mutually constitutive relationship in their development. The Chinese were the first ethnic group required to procure identity certificates with photographs for entry into the United States. In fact, the certificates that Chinese women needed to carry after the Page Law of 1875 "were the first U.S.-issued photographic identity documents" ever.[11] Present-day calls for better photographic and video confirmation of Asian university applicants' identity—such as suggestions that they be interviewed via video chat technology—echo previous regimes of questioning and visual inspection from the nineteenth and early twentieth centuries.

That Asian-raced people are inherently unreliable until proven otherwise or that fraud tends to accompany any dealings with Asia is not a new concept. However, I am not making a case that any of the practices alleged by these pieces of journalism—doctoring transcripts, hiring professional test takers, submitting essays one did not write—are baseless. What I am claiming is that reports of these actions, when perpetrated by Asian students, feed into a historical racialization of Asian bodies as essentially criminal, dubious, or questionable.

Contrast the numerous accounts of cheating and illegality among Asian international students with the same enacted by Americans described in racially neutral ways, and the racial specificity of fraud will come into better focus. In 2013, a fraternity member at the University of Georgia was arrested and convicted of masterminding a fake identification card ring, spending ten weeks in jail, a sentence that, as the *Chronicle of Higher Education*'s reporter sympathetically points out, caused him to miss both

Thanksgiving and Christmas. Portrayed as an astute entrepreneur, he is quoted as declaring himself "a pretty good businessman" who knew how to sell "a good product."[12] When questioned about whether or not he was remorseful, he matter-of-factly stated that both the university culture and the local bar industries in Athens thrive on underage drinking and that underage students will get their alcohol one way or another. It bears mentioning, lest anyone assume that differences in representation between this counterfeit artist and Chinese falsifiers of passports can be explained by individual journalistic style, that one of the reporters for this article also coauthored the aforementioned "The China Conundrum."

The Educational Testing Service's woes with the security breaches in their standardized tests taken in Asia might be salacious news. However, homegrown test takers for hire have a decidedly different cast. A graduate of a highly regarded high school in New York's Long Island launched a lucrative business taking the SAT and the American College Testing (ACT) tests for others. Described as having been "a top student, vice president of the business club and a varsity athlete"—in short, all of those factors that seem to predict normative standards of success in college and beyond—his other attribute, "his ability to ace standardized tests," was what eventually got him into legal trouble.[13] At one point, the correspondent interviewing the perpetrator feigned ignorance about the demographics of his affluent hometown, asking how the students paid the $2,500 fee he collected. His response incriminated their parents, which—up until that point in the conversation—were not assumed to be involved. Still, that figure is lower than the $6,000 specified for test taking services in stories about cheating busts among East Asian applicants to U.S. colleges.[14]

Much media coverage, be it sympathetic or not, on concerns raised by accounts of fraud among East Asians implicates parents more forcefully than in other contexts. Particularly in stories about China, the references to the stakes presented by the one child policy are meant to explain deterministically what would be called "helicopter parenting" when practiced by the middle and upper classes in the United States (who are, of course, under no such government restriction). This is not to say that parental over-involvement is tolerated when issuing from American families; ask any higher education professional for anecdotes and the responses will be eye opening. However, there are always exceptions. A 2010 article written by an editor at *Harvard Magazine* mourns the demise of adult-level independence among today's undergraduates. Parents tend to be so ready with support throughout the K-12 years that it can be hard to let go: "Home life has changed in ways that would seem to undercut children's development of autonomy. There was a time when children did their own homework. Now parents routinely 'help' them with assignments, making teachers wonder whose work they are really grading."[15] The author also raises the question of to what extent these students' application materials granting them admission to Harvard were their own: "Once, college applicants typically wrote their own applications, including the essays; today, an army of high-paid consultants, coaches, and editors is available to orchestrate and massage the admissions effort." Yet, the author also cites the dean of admissions who does not see this as a problem. This university administrator is on record claiming that "for the most part, the helicoptering has *worked*, and is perceived as a positive thing by students."

What this admissions dean means by *"worked"* is unstated. His definition of success may tautologically make recourse to the very presence of these students at the most handsomely resourced university in the world. The fact that they have emerged through the gauntlet of Harvard's notoriously difficult selection process is itself regarded as evidence of this parenting style's success. To be sure, positive assessments about the results of very close parental involvement are rare among higher education professionals. However, I have yet to see *any* account that buffers the pathologization of this phenomenon when referencing East Asian applicants to U.S. universities. There, the over-structuring of time and the instrumentalizing of activities, as initiated by parents, take a more sinister register. The speculation of what is or is not legitimately a student's writing also arises differently in these two contexts. Among U.S. admittees to Harvard, where does extensive parental editing end and where does parental authorship begin? This question is posed with exasperation, yet shrugged off with a sense of futility. Yet, stories about Chinese parents with limited English proficiency outsourcing the labor of writing essays to profiteering agents are met with uncomplicated condemnation. A subtler but no less significant contrast exists in *Harvard Magazine*'s depiction of present-day U.S. students' stunted "autonomy." One of the structuralist fallacies pertaining to the values of the West versus those of the rest relies on Enlightenment-era notions of autonomy and self-possession. Articles that attempt to make sense of the social segregation on campus between international and domestic students index the culture clash between so-called individualistic American and collectivist Chinese cultures. Yet, this very lack of independence and self-starting on the part of American students is a perennial complaint among university professionals—faculty and staff alike. We also need to consider these declarations of exceptionalist American individualism in the context of the fact that children of alumni are routinely admitted to elite universities with lower grade point averages and test scores than what is typical. The fiction that in the United States, one always and necessarily is a product of the sum of his or her individual choices, borne of free will, looks even more suspect when we take legacy advantages into account.

I am not condoning the reported acts of duplicity that, if real, put a damper on the learning experience for everyone involved. Cheating on tests and other forms of academic dishonesty are the bane of every educator. They lower morale for students who do not engage in those behaviors. However, the discrepancies in how the same or similar actions are portrayed among U.S. versus East Asian students show how differently the two groups are perceived among higher education professionals in discussions about academic integrity.

The Diversity Deceit

University administrators are quick to defend their enrollment of international students, pointing out that nurturing a global perspective is absolutely crucial. For domestic students, interacting with people from abroad will provide an edge in a world that demands knowledge of topics beyond their national borders. However eager universities are to sing the benefits of international students on their campuses, they are less likely to invest resources to encourage interaction among the different populations. There are numerous news stories of East Asian and U.S. students experiencing parallel lives without having much contact, a result often attributed to the aforementioned dissimilarities in worldview. According to one study, over half of all East Asian international students have no domestic friends.[16] There is an overwhelming impression that East Asians lack interest in engaging with Americans. These reports hearken back to earlier concepts of Asian people as those who actively resist integration, which gave rise to early race- and nation-based restrictions on immigration and naturalized citizenship and the failure of oft-cited Supreme Court cases filed by Takao Ozawa (1922) and Bhagat Singh Thind (1923) to challenge those laws. Contemporary discussions about international student life on U.S. campuses resonate eerily with these perceptions of Asian people from the past.

Several articles do attempt to debunk the image of inherently recalcitrant racialized subjects who are resistant to integration and who huddle defensively among themselves. If international students seem unwilling to initiate contact with domestic students, the reason may be that they sense others' indifference or, in certain cases, outright hostility. Overt racial prej-

udice in the form of vandalism and online or face-to-face hate speech occurs along with subtler microaggressions.[17] Nevertheless, there have been
some institutional measures taken to address these problems. One exception to the relative inattention other schools pay to fostering meaningful
interaction between East Asian and U.S. students lies in an initiative at the
University of Illinois at Urbana-Champaign (UIUC). The flagship campus of the public university system in Illinois is among those with the highest numbers of students from China in the United States. It has launched
a multifaceted effort headed by student affairs staff, administrators, and
students—both international and domestic—to improve the college experience for everyone involved.

The Director of International Student Integration at UIUC, Nicole
Tami, is skeptical of the name of her title, preferring more neutral terminology without the baggage that "integration" presents. About integration,
she states that it "is a very personal choice and I see it as part of a very vast
spectrum. . . . On one end is certainly assimilation and I think some people
definitely mean that when they say integration. The other end of that, I
might use a word like inclusion or engagement."[18] She dispels the notion
that self-segregation is specifically Chinese, indicating that when debrief-
ing with American students who return from studying abroad, she finds
that they, too, express regret for not speaking the language and interacting with locals more. One of the student leaders attempting to foster more
international-domestic interaction self-identifies as Asian American. Amy
Lin started a conversational English group to bring both constituencies
together. The idea was birthed after Lin spent terms studying in China
and France, which made her think more carefully about the experiences
of students away from their native countries. During the 2015 football
season, international student sports fans Bruce Lu and David He began
broadcasting Fighting Illini football games in Mandarin. Lu says that
"American football isn't widely recognized in mainland China."[19] He hopes
the broadcasts will engage his fellow compatriots more fully in student life
on a campus where athletics has a high profile.

Despite the optimistic possibility of friendly interaction between international and domestic students, any assumption that the above efforts serve
the honorable cause of diversity—and, with it, inclusion or integration—
is suspect. The spike in international enrollment at UIUC has taken place
with a concurrent decrease in the number of African American students.
Alarmingly, in 2014 the number of African Americans in the entering class
was actually lower than that in 1968.[20] This backsliding is worrisome
and has not gone unnoticed by international students themselves who

understand their place as out-of-state tuition payers edging out disenfranchised U.S. people of color. Wenrui Chen, a seventh-year PhD student from China at the time of her interview with the reporter, made a pointed critique of these demographic shifts since her arrival at UIUC: "'Obviously, it's financial issues; the university is trying to cash in, at least partially, to deal with the financial crisis' she says, noting that the 'diversity' argument for recruiting foreign students seems like mere rhetoric when the number of African-American students has fallen."[21]

The financial bottom line is the one place where a variant of the word *diversity* has been used accurately in these news reports. The heavy skew toward China among international students currently enrolled in U.S. universities today is cause for concern from an investment standpoint. Savvy financial planning in any sector touts the rule of diversification. A portfolio should contain a mix of investments across a range of industries and a balance of growth and risk protection. Universities' heavy dependence on China, as some have acknowledged, is tantamount to putting too many eggs into one financial basket. Changes in social or economic conditions in the countries most heavily relied upon for revenue would have repercussions for the tuition stream. Ronald B. Cushing, the Director of International Services at the University of Cincinnati states: "There's always a concern when the majority of your population comes from one, two, or three locations. . . . You're that many international incidents away from losing a large segment of your student population."[22] At the University of Denver, Marjorie S. Smith, Associate Dean of International Student Admission, chimes in on the insight she gleaned from the Asian economic crisis of 1997, which caused a steep decline in the number of students from Southeast Asia: "From that we learned in order to reduce risk, you really have to keep your international population diverse."[23] Another expert sounds the alarm on what might be the obvious solution to this dilemma, which is to draw students from another country when a formerly reliable origin dries up. This tactic relies only on "shifting, not diversifying the source."[24] There has been important work done on campus diversity initiatives being coopted for neoliberal ends.[25] However, the blatantly market-laced language of diversification used to discuss universities' economic dependence on international students makes this connection overt.

Codes to Decipher

Over the course of reading these articles on U.S. higher education's relationship with Asian international students, I have found myself nodding sympathetically to some of the anecdotes even as I read these accounts critically. As someone employed at a U.S. university, I am closely affected by the increasing corporatization of the academy—a trend that, according to my own observation, has worsened since I began teaching at the college level in 1997. Shifting the referent of this discussion slightly, I want to remind readers that the policies of the No Child Left Behind Act of 2001, which uses standardized test scores to punish so-called underperforming public schools, have prompted a decline in the amount of time K-12 teachers spend on skills not measured by multiple choice tests, such as writing and critical thinking. Many schools have also reduced or eliminated their arts programs in response to this legislation. During the same time, teachers' unions have come under attack by conservative forces. The cloud of precarity and surveillance under which K-12 instructors work has negatively affected the education they can deliver.

Because of the changes of the recent past, a significant proportion of my undergraduates are not reading and writing at the college level. More alarmingly, some have skills below those typical of first-year high school students. It is often difficult for me to encourage them to think past commonly accepted norms. Paper guidelines that explicitly give authors freedom and latitude tend to prompt anxious pleas for help rather than excitement and innovation. Many students think regurgitating material from lectures is all that is required of them. Media reports on Asian international students frequently lament the triad of poor English language proficiency, lack of critical thinking, and habits of rote learning at the expense of creativity.[26] However, these complaints are germane to early-twenty-first-century life in the academy overall. Students in general, be they international or domestic, are poorly prepared for college for reasons that are largely beyond their control.

The flip side to these laments is my contact with plenty of international students who rebel against the homogenizing effects of contemporary global culture's pressures. I have witnessed one student from China take her Asian American peers to task for favoring the discourse of cultural appreciation over that of economic redistribution. A student from Singapore asked for supplemental reading when a course was too easy for her. Another Chinese student—one who was the president of the minority students' association in his major, suggesting a kinship with U.S. people of color—occasionally stayed after class to initiate smart-alecky but friendly debates about the course material with me. These are behaviors more readily attributed to Americans, and to be fair, I have also had my share of similar encounters with students from the United States. In an environment that conditions everyone, regardless of national origin, to treat their college experience as a hurdle to clear rather than a space for contemplation, however, these incidents have gotten more scarce from all quarters as the years go by. In the pool of students I have caught cheating or plagiarizing during my career, both the domestic and the international are represented. Students from both populations, in an increasingly consumer-oriented academy, have complained to a chair (whose role is now more akin to that of a restaurant manager than that of a department's intellectual visionary) about my grading or expectations.

"The China Conundrum," the landmark article I referenced earlier, ends with a gravitas-inducing description of the gulf between international students and those who are charged with teaching them. About an English language instructor's well-intentioned but failed efforts to "reach" and "engage" Chinese undergraduates, which "keeps [him] up at night," the authors declare solemnly that these students "are like a code he's still trying to decipher."[27] This pronouncement about Asian students' reticence or recalcitrance (depending on how one sees it) reprises historical concepts about the inscrutability of Asian people. Combined with the authors' earlier claims about "deepening concern that American colleges have entered China without truly understanding it," the solution to the problems elucidated, it is implied, will be found by appealing to the ethnographic—a venture presumed to be difficult, if not impossible, because of informants who are frustratingly resistant to reading.

To those of us more attuned to thinking critically about the spread of academic capitalism, however, the problem is not the oft-referenced culture clash between U.S. conventions of schooling and the mores of the Asian international students we now rely heavily upon. The problem is that we, as university staff, have not acknowledged our own complex, ambivalent, and downright stressful entanglements in a flawed industry bent on sustaining itself at all costs. We have become comfortable thinking about the interests and subjectivities of faculty as being profoundly dissimilar from those of our students, no matter from where they hail. Although the bureaucracy of institutions may organize what Margaret Price calls "kairotic spaces" in ways that unintentionally encourage guarded, adversarial, or perfunctory interactions between students and instructional staff, our mutual participation in a structure defined by corporatization is common ground from which we can work to halt the declension of our places of learning.[28] To these ends, we need to proceed with a critical university studies perspective in the classroom. We need to make transparent the workings of the institution of which we are a part. We need to teach material that provides our students, domestic and international, with a usable past for intervening in disruptive contemporary trends. The code that begs deciphering is not the inscrutable Asian-raced subject. It is ultimately the academy and its economic logics of value and validation.

NOTES

For dialogue and inspiration during the writing of this essay, I thank Kritika Agarwal, Tim Dean, and Keith Otto.

1. Edward J. M. Rhoads discusses the Chinese Educational Mission, an initiative during the late nineteenth century that sent young Chinese men to study at New England universities with the intent of bringing knowledge back to China in order to facilitate its modernization. Edward J. M. Rhoads, *Stepping Forth into the World: The Chinese Educational Mission to the United States, 1872–1881* (Hong Kong: Hong Kong University Press, 2011). Chih-ming Wang examines the literature and journalism that emerged from Chinese students studying in the United States during the early to late twentieth century in *Transpacific Articulations: Student Migration and the Making of Asian America* (Honolulu: University of Hawai'i Press, 2013). Aihwa Ong addresses Asian elites studying in the United States and Great Britain during the late twentieth century in *Neoliberalism as Exception: Mutations in Citizenship and Sovereignty* (Durham, N.C.: Duke University Press, 2006).

2. The term "subjectless discourse" was coined by Kandice Chuh to inaugurate a shift in Asian American studies from a field defined by an object of investigation to one organized around a mode of critique. Kandice Chuh, *Imagine Otherwise: On Asian Americanist Critique* (Durham, N.C.: Duke University Press, 2003).

3. For a qualitative study of international student experiences, see Lisong Liu, "Return Migration and Selective Citizenship: A Study of Returning Chinese Professional Migrants from the United States," *Journal of Asian American Studies* 15, no. 1 (February 2012): 35–68.

4. Although 2008 has functioned as a convenient before-and-after point for thinking about the structural changes of the recent past, the seeking of tuition dollars from abroad has predated it. When my institution interviewed me for the position I hold now, an event that took place in December 2007, a colleague remarked that students from China and South Korea had been keeping the university afloat for years.

5. There is widespread misconception that all international students are wealthy. In fact, most of them are simply middle income, and there are a fair number of first generation college students in that mix. For a report on a study of the economic backgrounds of international students, see Elizabeth

Redden, "Are International Students Satisfied?," *Inside Higher Ed* 20 (August 2014), https://www.insidehighered.com/news/2014/08/20/new -survey-offers-insights-international-student-satisfaction-three-countries.

6. Tom Bartlett and Karin Fischer, "The China Conundrum: American Colleges Find the Chinese-Student Boom a Tricky Fit," *Chronicle of Higher Education*, November 3, 2011, http://www.chronicle.com/article/The-China -Conundrum/129628.

7. Bruce G. Hammond, "The Chinese Are Coming, and They Need Help with the Admissions Process," *Chronicle of Higher Education*, November 15, 2009, http://www.chronicle.com/article/The-Chinese-Are-Coming-and/49126 ?key=Hj0nIV8%2FZHVLMHJgfiFGKyVVbSxwdkh4Oi4TMSQaZ19W.

8. Richard Péréz-Peña, "SAT Cheating Inquiry Delays Scores for South Korea and China," *New York Times*, October 29, 2014, https://www.nytimes .com/2014/10/30/world/asia/sat-cheating-inquiry-delays-scores-for-south -korea-and-china.html?_r=0.

9. Scott Jaschik, "Chinese Nationals Indicted for Elaborate Cheating Scheme on Standardized Admissions Tests," *Inside Higher Ed*, May 29, 2015, https://www.insidehighered.com/news/2015/05/29/chinese-nationals -indicted-elaborate-cheating-scheme-standardized-admissions-tests.

10. Elizabeth Redden, "Three Indicted in Alleged Student Visa Scam," *Inside Higher Ed*, March 13, 2015, https://www.insidehighered.com /quicktakes/2015/03/13/three-indicted-alleged-student-visa-scam.

11. Anna Pegler-Gordon, *In Sight of America: Photography and the Development of U.S. Immigration Policy* (Berkeley: University of California Press, 2009), 29.

12. Karin Fischer and Eric Hoover, "A River of Booze: Inside One College Town's Uneasy Embrace of Drinking," *Chronicle of Higher Education*, December 1, 2014, http://www.chronicle.com/interactives/alcohol_main.

13. Alison Stewart, "The Perfect Score: Cheating on the SAT," *CBS News*, January 1, 2012, http://www.cbsnews.com/news/the-perfect-score -cheating-on-the-sat/.

14. Scott Jaschik, "Chinese Nationals Indicted for Elaborate Cheating Scheme on Standardized Admissions Tests," *Inside Higher Ed*, May 29, 2015, https://www.insidehighered.com/news/2015/05/29/chinese-nationals -indicted-elaborate-cheating-scheme-standardized-admissions-tests.

15. Craig Lambert, "Nonstop: Today's Superhero Undergraduates do '3,000 Things at 150 Percent,'" *Harvard Magazine*, March–April 2010, http://harvardmagazine.com/2010/03/nonstop.

16. Karin Fischer, "Many Foreign Students Are Friendless in the U.S., Study Finds," *Chronicle of Higher Education*, June 14, 2012, http://www .chronicle.com/article/Many-Foreign-Students-Find/132275.

17. Elizabeth Redden, "'I'm Not Racist, But': Recent Incidents Bring to Light the Problem of Discrimination against International Students," *Inside Higher Ed*, October 16, 2012, https://www.insidehighered.com/news/2012/10/16/tensions-simmer-between-american-and-international-students.

18. Elizabeth Redden, "At U. of Illinois, Growth in the Number of Chinese Students Has Been Dramatic," *Inside Higher Ed*, January 7, 2015, https://www.insidehighered.com/news/2015/01/07/u-illinois-growth-number-chinese-students-has-been-dramatic.

19. Julie Wurth, "UI Bringing Chinese Language to Broadcast Booth," *News-Gazette*, August 8, 2015, http://www.news-gazette.com/news/local/2015-08-28/ui-bringing-chinese-language-broadcast-booth.html.

20. Christine Des Garennes, "Prescription for Disaster," *News-Gazette*, October 12, 2014, http://www.news-gazette.com/news/local/2014-10-12/prescription-disaster.html.

21. Redden, "At U. of Illinois."

22. Ian Wilhelm, "U.S. Colleges Seek Greater Diversity in Foreign-Student Enrollment," *Chronicle of Higher Education*, September 25, 2011, http://www.chronicle.com/article/US-Colleges-Seek-Greater/129098.

23. Ibid.

24. Jason Lane and Kevin Kinser, "Is the International-Education 'Bubble' about to Pop?," *Chronicle of Higher Education*, April 15, 2013, http://www.chronicle.com/blogs/worldwise/is-the-international-education-bubble-about-to-pop/32099.

25. Notable examples of this work include Sara Ahmed, *On Being Included: Racism and Diversity in Institutional Life* (Durham, N.C.: Duke University Press, 2012); Roderick A. Ferguson, *The Reorder of Things: The University as Its Pedagogies of Minority Difference* (Minneapolis: University of Minnesota Press, 2012); and Stephanie L. Kerschbaum, *Toward a New Rhetoric of Difference* (Urbana, Ill.: Conference on College Composition and Communication, 2014).

26. An illustrative example of the tendency to characterize Asian international students thusly comes from a faculty member. See Adele Barker, "A Professor's Experience with Unprepared Chinese Students," *Inside Higher Ed*, October 19, 2015, https://www.insidehighered.com/views/2015/10/19/professors-experience-unprepared-chinese-students-essay. To the list of common gripes, Barker would add international students' reluctance to attend office hours, a trait I have also noticed among domestic students.

27. Bartlett and Fischer, "The China Conundrum."

28. Margaret Price, *Mad at School: Rhetorics of Mental Disability and Academic Life* (Ann Arbor: University of Michigan Press, 2011).

CHAPTER 13

Asians Are the New ... What?

Kandice Chuh

On May 15, 2015, a coalition of sixty-four Asian American organizations filed a complaint to the U.S. Departments of Education and Justice.[1] This "Complaint against Harvard University and the President and Fellows of Harvard College for Discriminating against Asian-American Applicants in the College Admissions Process" alleges "unlawful racial discrimination that led to the rejection of admission of highly qualified Asian American applicants."[2] By way of introduction, the complaint explains that "over the last two decades, Asian-American applicants to Harvard University and other Ivy League colleges have increasingly experienced discrimination in the admissions process."[3] It continues: "It has become especially difficult for high-performing male Asian-American students to gain admission to Harvard University and other Ivy League colleges."[4]

The complaint establishes that it is more difficult to gain admission for an Asian American applicant than for those from other racial groups. It notes, for example, that despite an increasingly high record of achievement on the standard quantitative metrics used for admission consideration, and a substantial increase in the population of Asian Americans, Asian American enrollment at Harvard has remained at a steady 17–20 percent. The complaint submits that "Asians have the lowest acceptance rate for each [SAT] score bracket, lower than Whites, Blacks, and Hispanic [*sic*]."[5] Such facts and figures, which serve as the empirical grounds of the complaint, are drawn from a number of published academic studies;[6] the complaint also relies heavily on a 2014 federal lawsuit filed by the Students for Fair Admissions against Harvard University regarding similar issues.[7] Another of the complaint's sources uses similar data to make the qualitative claim that "Asians are the 'new Jews.'"[8] This assertion is echoed in such mainstream media outlets like the *Wall Street Journal*'s coverage of these cases (a case in point is an op-ed titled "The New Jews of Harvard Admissions").[9] The complaint invokes the Fourteenth Amendment equal protection clauses, as well as Title VI of the 1964 Civil Rights Act, as the governing law on these matters.

Asian Americans—or, more commonly, referred to as just Asians—are in other venues touted as the "new whites"—i.e., the group on the verge or in the process of successful assimilation and incorporation into the tacitly reconfirmed whiteness of the U.S. nation. To wit, Asians are supposedly on the "rise": "The Rise of Asian Americans," a report by the Pew Research Center initially released in 2012 and updated in 2013, opens by summarizing that "Asian Americans are the highest income, best-educated, and fastest growing racial group in the United States. They are more satisfied than the general public with their lives, finances, and the direction of the country, and they place more value than other Americans do on marriage, parenthood, hard work and career success."[10]

Narratives like these complement and buttress the notion that the whole of Asia is rising, a phenomenon much thematized in venues like the *Financial Times*. The twenty-first century is, after all, putatively "The Asian Century," or sometimes more inclusively "The Pacific Century."[11] Forecasting the global economic dominance of China at the end of the twentieth century, such views were affirmed by the simultaneous assertion of the waning of "The American Century." As the United States confronted a historic downgrading of the credit rating of the U.S. government at the start of the 2010s, Laura Kang concisely notes, 72 percent, or $1.22 trillion of U.S. Treasury securities, were in Chinese hands, with another $1.1 trillion held by Japan. By the 2010s, China and Japan were in the U.S. and U.K. financial press trading places as the world's "biggest creditor nation"; by 2012, Chinese state- and private-owned companies had together become the single largest investor in fifty-four African nations; there are now more billionaires (in U.S. dollars) in China than there are in the United States.

India, too, is on the rise, with a 7.3 percent rise in GDP and regular characterization as possessing the world's fastest-growing economy.[12] As the dominant story goes, if India sustains its rate of growth, then its potential as a global economic force on par with China and the United States will be realized. Since joining the World Trade Organization in 2001, India has been positioned in the U.S. financial press to become the next China (i.e., with high purchase power that could make the U.S. economy more robust while, of course, presumably having beneficial effects in India). Increasingly deregulated by nation-states and characterized by what David Harvey describes as "the regime of flexible accumulation," which features the expansion and liberalization of finance capital through the later decades of the twentieth century, contemporary capitalism has underwritten both the mobilization of low-wage Asian labor, primarily women, and those of the managerial class bearing "flexible citizenship," in Aihwa Ong's terms.[13]

Of course, these manifold assertions of Asian and Asian American success cover over the sharp unevenness of distribution and the unavailability of even the option of assimilation among Asian and Asian American groups. For example, the rise of China and India is accompanied by a reported two out of three people living in hunger (especially in southern Asia); or, for example, those of Southeast Asian and Pacific Islander descent experience high rates of poverty and incarceration in the United States.[14] In this light, admission to Harvard is strikingly inappropriate as a measure of life chances. Nor does the anti–affirmative action stance held by the complaint accurately reflect the majority view in favor of affirmative action held by the Asian American voting population established by some studies.[15] And, in the nefarious ways that model minority discourse has done since its emergence in the Cold War era, this contemporary iteration effectively pits racially minoritized groups against each other while deftly disavowing indigenous dispossession that is the foundation of the U.S. nation.

While it is vital to continue refusing the empirical accuracy of model minority discourse, in part by disaggregating "Asian American" and detailing the vast heterogeneity it covers over, and by criticizing mainstream media's participation in the occlusion of such heterogeneity and the pernicious effects that ensue, I take a somewhat different tack in this essay. As Laura Kang enjoins us to do, my effort here is to account for the Asian American subjects who are drawn *to* capital—who, in effect, have enthusiastically identified *as* the model minority—to consider the implications of these contemporary forms of Asian racialization to the work and objectives of Asian Americanist critique. I take as axiomatic the constitutive ambivalence that has characterized the production of Asian as a racial category in the U.S. political and cultural imagination—a process I refer to as Asian racialization—such that Asianness is generally conceived of as operating between whiteness and color, as a designation of a "middleman" model minority in business transactions and in the social ontology of the U.S. populace. In what follows, I suggest that apprehending the instrumental role of Asian racialization in securing the continuing dominance of capitalism as the defining feature of the U.S. nation in the era of globalization requires a critical reckoning with the model minority–identified Asian American subject. Doing so elucidates the ways that racial capitalism takes particular interest in Asianness in the current conjuncture.[16] An emergent challenge for us, in brief, is the short-circuiting of Asianness and Asian Americans as functional, active agents of racial capitalism and the U.S. nation.

As important, I am concerned with locating this present consideration in the frame of the contemporary U.S. university. Part of the impetus to reflect anew on the aims of Asian Americanist critique arises from the compelling arguments by Roderick Ferguson and Jodi Melamed (among others) regarding the neoliberal university's cooptation of "minority difference"; this cooptation has largely dissipated the transformative energies accompanying the establishment of ethnic studies.[17] Even while scattered efforts to establish Asian American studies programs continue to punctuate the landscape of higher education, it is patently clear that institutionalization is and never was a guarantee of either institutional or broader social transformation. Insofar as the organizing political project of Asian American studies remains the address of material inequality by means of pursuing lines of inquiry afforded by attending to the specificities of Asian racialization, it is necessary to rearticulate how we go about doing so in relation to the contemporary university. As Viet Thanh Nguyen observed some years ago, the politics of Asian American studies—or, more precisely, the "Asian American intellectual class"—do not align neatly with the politics of people of Asian descent living in the United States.[18] Nguyen describes this intellectual class as capitalizing on the histories, experiences, and cultural forms that attest to the racism underpinning Asian racialization in the nineteenth and twentieth centuries. We might understand this as an overidentification with the subjects of these histories despite our locational difference from them.

If there has been considerable attention paid to the "town and gown" disjuncture that reportedly accompanied the institutionalization of Asian

American studies—a structural factor that precipitated the emergence of such an intellectual class—there needs now to be a dismantling of the assumption that *town* (i.e., "the community") refers only or even primarily to groups living marginal lives. What are the responsibilities of Asian American studies, of Asian American(ist) intellectuals, in the face of the normative Asian American subject—of the subject who identifies as a racial minority in order to further majoritarian ends? The project I am proposing is to continue to attend to the production of group-differentiated vulnerability (paraphrasing Gilmore's cogent definition of racism) while holding in mind the Asianization of institutional and material power.[19] Indigenous and especially Native Hawaiian theorizations of settler colonialism have alerted us to the political and intellectual urgency of attending to the Asianization of power and resources; this essay poses and engages such matters by bringing that critical awareness together with the growing Asian Americanist attention to the majoritarian Asian American subject.[20]

Asia, Rising

As of 2010, the U.S. Census Bureau reports immigrant and U.S.-born people of Asian descent together constitute about 5.8 percent of the total U.S. population, which amounts to roughly 18.2 million people. In 1965, those of Asian descent represented less than 1 percent of the total population. Asian immigrants are now the largest group of new migrants to the United States and are likely the most highly educated group of immigrants in U.S. history. While noting that there are "sizable" differences among different Asian groups, the aforementioned Pew Research Center report explains that Asians in the United States, in comparison with the total U.S. adult population, "exceed not just in the share with a college degree (49% vs. 28%), but also in median annual household income ($66,000 versus $49,800) and median household wealth ($83,500 vs. $68,529)."[21] And, it identifies the Asian population in the United States, and specifically recent immigrants, as distinctive in educational attainment in comparison to those living in their countries of origin. For example, almost 70 percent of recent immigrants from South Korea and Japan have at least a bachelor's degree, in contrast to about one-quarter of those living in those countries. The report summarizes: "A century ago, most Asian Americans were low-skilled, low-wage laborers crowded into ethnic enclaves and targets of official discrimination. Today, they are the most likely of any major racial or ethnic group in America to live in mixed neighborhoods and to marry across racial lines. When newly minted medical school graduate Priscilla Chan married Facebook founder Mark Zuckerberg last month, she joined the 37% of all recent Asian-American brides who wed a non-Asian groom."[22] Despite being largely first-generation immigrant (74 percent of Asian American adults were born outside of the United States), Asian Americans are arguably exemplars of "economic success and social assimilation."[23]

Pew Research Center's "The Rise of Asian Americans" report enjoins critical engagement, which could proceed in any number of ways, among them attention to the identification of heteronormative interracial marriage, as a measure of successful assimilation; the singling out of the Asian American woman as exemplifying assimilative mobility (she is both highly educated and married to a white entrepreneur, rendering sharply evident the sexualization and gendering of success indices); and the substantial percentage of those without college degrees or the numbers of wage-earning people constituting the households that earn above general public average income. I limit my focus here to the amplification of the historical framing invoked by the report.[24]

The report briefly rehearses conditions that precipitate contemporary Asian immigration to the United States:

> Large-scale immigration from Asia did not take off until the passage of the landmark Immigration and Nationality Act of 1965. Over the decades, this modern wave of immigrants from Asia has increasingly become more skilled and educated. Today, recent arrivals from Asia are nearly twice as likely as those who came three decades ago to have a college degree, and many go into high-paying fields such as science, engineering, medicine and finance. This evolution has been spurred by changes in U.S. immigration policies and labor markets; by political liberalization and economic growth in the sending countries; and by the forces of globalization in an ever-more digitally interconnected world.[25]

This passage acknowledges the shifting political economic conditions that precipitate the "rise of Asian America." Indeed, the impact of the 1965 act is familiar territory for Asian American studies. Briefly, we may recall that the act ended the suppression of migration from Asian and Latin American countries and the favoring of migration from Western European countries enacted in 1921 and elaborated in 1924 legislation that established quotas based on national origins. The 1965 act emphasized workforce skills and familial relationships as desirable qualifications for immigration; it is

best understood as a new regime of immigration regulation directed toward
ensuring that educated or skilled prospective migrants able to count on the
resources of family members living in the United States were selected over
others. Those in the United States must accordingly attest to their willingness and ability to offer economic support to new migrants they wish
to sponsor, a policy that correlates with what has now become the familiar
expectation that fundamental needs of those living in the United States
are to be met not by the state (i.e., public resources) but by personal (private) relations. Contrary to the bootstraps narrative that requires (the
model minority as) the exemplary American subject to follow and/or fulfill an arc from poverty to riches, post-1965 Asian migrants were likely as
not to have resources to draw on upon arrival. This group of immigrants
is distinguishable from those whose entry was regulated by the United
States Refugee Act of 1980, which revised existing immigration legislation and facilitated entry of persons displaced and often nearly entirely
dispossessed of private resources as a consequence of the wars in Southeast
Asia. In short, U.S. immigration policy precipitated the contemporary,
if unevenly experienced, rise of Asian America by transforming regulation through exclusion to regulation through selective distribution of
life chances.

We can thicken this understanding of the effects of U.S. immigration
policy changes by recognizing them as part of the course of U.S.-Asian
geopolitics from at least the Second World War forward. The United
States' multivalent investment in the production of certain Asian nations—
Japan in particular—as, in Takashi Fujitani's telling phrase, exemplary of
"model modernity" and thus suitable for participation as a U.S. ally in the
global circuit of capitalist exchange, subtends the upward trajectory of East
Asian Americans. Detailing the history by which Japanese Americans
emerge as model minorities in the U.S. imagination specifically in the
1960s, crystallized as such by sociologist William Petersen's *New York
Times* article, "Success Story: Japanese-American Style," Fujitani observes
that "the prominence of Japanese Americans as the 'almost, but not quite
white' minority coincides in both logic and historical timing with the construction of a discourse on Japan as the honorary white nation".[26]

> As early as the summer or fall of 1942, some civil and military officials as
> well as advisers . . . were beginning to envision Japan as a potential ally
> in the struggle to establish U.S. hegemony in East Asia. Over the
> transwar years, this notion triggered a fundamental transformation of
> popular images about Japan and the Japanese people that clearly

accelerated in the postwar and Cold War years. Dominant images of
Japan underwent a miraculous metamorphosis, from those of a
backward nation peopled by an insectlike or herdlike population to
those of the United States' most reliable, friendly, and democratic
ally. . . . As the democratic, capitalist, and almost, but not quite white
nation, "Japan" came to be deployed as the new model for aspiring
peoples of color throughout the world.[27]

On the domestic scene, this miraculous metamorphosis, from the "enemy
alien" who needed to be interned to the model minority who had overcome
such discrimination and found success in America as Americans, accompanied the postwar political economic rehabilitation of Japan under the rubric
of "modernization." This process, deliberately in contrast to "Westerniza-
tion," which too strongly connoted colonialist imposition, was to dissociate
liberal democracy and capitalism from U.S. influence and instead to establish these as features necessary for the future of the nation in the modern
world. The U.S. project, as Fujitani reports using governmental memo-
randa from the period, was "'to show Asiatics what they can do for themselves, building partly on our experience but mainly on principles and
methods which are a common inheritance of mankind.'"[28] The incorporation of Japan into the U.S. economic sphere of influence under the auspices
of modernization in turn contributed to the obfuscation of the widespread
atrocities and ongoing consequences of Japanese imperialism.

Assurance that the self-determination the U.S. was proposing via its
modernization theory would produce the "right" kind of modernization—
i.e., grounded in industrial capitalism and liberal democratic processes,
as against communist or socialist alternatives—came in the dominating
role that the United States played in crafting the 1944 Bretton Woods
Agreements Act that constructed a unified international monetary system, including the establishment of the World Bank and the International Monetary Fund. As Kang summarizes, "Heavily dominated by
American and U.S.-trained economists, these two international financial
institutions were conjoined in a particular architecture of late capitalism
that would perpetuate older imperialist inequities but with the United
States now at its apex."[29] While excluded from the Marshall Plan's distribution of postwar financial aid, Asian countries nonetheless received just
under $6 billion from the United States, with China and India as foremost
recipients. These Cold War efforts to establish U.S. hegemony in Asia
played out through collaborations between specific Asian entities and
the U.S. government. Asia—or, at least, some specific parts of it, which

came to function as a metonym for the whole—in effect functioned as a U.S. investment in its own future.

The contemporary model minority is, in short, a figure and lived subjectivity that emerges at the conjuncture of the rise of global capitalism and U.S. neoimperialism. Clearly, there is a homology between the modernization of Asia and the domestic figure of the model minority that emerges in and following the Second World War.[30] By contrast, I note that U.S. foreign policy actively refused investment in Africa during the same period, and such sociology as Gunnar Myrdal's work concretized into the architecture of postwar hegemonic U.S. culture and politics the idea of black pathology, factors that contributed to the traction of model minority discourse.[31]

Modernization as a process of incorporation recalls the teleological narrative of progress that organizes the bourgeois liberal philosophy underpinning modernity, and its cathection to the compulsory establishment of capitalism as *the* world economic order through the machinery of imperialism. This is to recall that the production of the East under the sign of "Asia" is a factor and function of the idea of modernity itself. "Asia," we remember, is meaningful only as a name for a relationship to global geopolitics; it is an engineered geography metaphor. In this respect, Asia rises because it is made, linguistically, geopolitically, and economically, to rise, and the location of the origins of contemporary Asianness in the trajectories of modernity—which is to say, the trajectories of slavery and indenture, of colonialism and dispossession—is thrown into relief.

Access and Excess

As Christine So reminds us, participation in the circuits of capitalist exchange is theoretically a marker of equality among the agents. Yet we know that "they are not truly 'equal': the contradiction of capital, however, necessitates that the exchange be based on equality, a presumption that in fact disguises the unequal class relations that exist," as well as the impact of race, gender, indigeneity, and sexuality in the structuring of social relations.[32] The model minority/modernity in this regard experiences "equality" as either aspirational or that which can be achieved only by surpassing it.

This is plainly evident in the above-referenced complaint made to the Departments of Education and Justice. The complainants' robust claim of model minoritarianness for Asian Americans, made in part by recalling the long history of formal anti-Asian discrimination and in part by insisting on the excellence of Asian Americans in all aspects of life, evinces this less than/greater than dynamic. The complainants take pains to detail the superlative achievement of Asian American students by all normative measures of academic achievement and enumerate the Nobel laureates, world-renowned architects, musicians, and technology pioneers who are of Asian descent. This in order to establish decisively the falsity of stereotypes that hold Asians to be uncreative, docile, and so on, and in the process, to secure the value of the Asian American to U.S. society. By this account, Asian Americans have overcome language barriers and the "bamboo ceiling"; they have disallowed discrimination from hindering achievement; they are, the complainants insist, truly the model minority, which is to say the avatar of the promise of America.

Section 3 of the complaint, titled "Harvard University's Discrimination against Asian-Americans and Harm to Asian-American Families," announces in boldface the heart of the complaint: "We believe that a racially based admission process has played a major role in Harvard and other Ivy League colleges' discrimination against Asian-American applicants. Racial discrimination based on racial quotas, stereotypes and prejudices are other important factors because the discrimination Asian-Americans has suffered is more severe than that suffered by white Americans, another racial group not favored by Affirmative Action."[33] In its subsection titled "Creating racial barriers between Asian-Americans and other racial groups," the complaint further explains that "most Asian-Americans want to merge into the American melting pot and to develop pleasant relationship [*sic*] with other racial groups. However, the discrimination by Harvard University and other Ivy League Colleges is creating a racial divide between Asian-Americans and other racial groups."[34] It continues by identifying "Harm to Asian-American Families" in terms of the "pro-education culture" with which Asian Americans are "blessed" and the devotion of Asian American parents to securing a "good future" through educational attainment. These qualities, the complainants explain, make rejection from Harvard and other Ivy League institutions distinctively injurious to Asian Americans and firmly locate the explanation for Asian American success to cultural rather than socioeconomic factors.

The complaint describes Asian Americans as targets of racial discrimination akin to antiblack and antibrown racism and as suffering from being not-white, not-black, and not-brown. While deftly erasing the access that affirmative action policies have afforded Asian Americans and reiterating a strongly heteronormative nuclear family and an abiding attachment to America as the land of opportunity as the irreducible ground of Asian America, it argues against the groups "favored" by affirmative action. This is model minority discourse deployed in ways that benefit white supremacy but also specifically assert Asian superiority. Notably, the complaint does not address "legacy admissions," which, as a study by Michael Hurwitz shows, increases the odds of admission for legacy applicants threefold and clearly favors the white racial dominance of student bodies at "elite" colleges and universities.[35]

In its wholesale embrace of model minorianness, the complaint seems almost a caricature of itself, and yet: sixty-four Asian American organizations drawn from across the country and representing both local groups (e.g., the Millburn Short Hills Chinese Association) and professional associations (e.g., American Society of Engineers of Indian Origin) are signatories, compelling us to take it seriously as a snapshot, however narrowly framed, of Asian America. Moreover, strong resonances between the Asian America captured by this complaint and that of the Pew Center's report evince an enormous gap between the politically radical subject of Asian Americanist critique and "the Asian American community." Here, "the community" decidedly does not refer to those formed as a result of historic and ongoing policies of exclusion, dislocation, disenfranchisement, other forms of state-sanctioned, structured discrimination, or those established through the circuits of capital that recruited "coolies" and migrant labor in the wake of the formal abolition of slavery. Rather, it designates a largely highly educated professional class for whom, in the language of the complaint, "harm" is measured in terms like "additional study pressure" and the "negative impact" of rejection from Harvard on Asian American students' "trust in American institutions" as well as "self-identification and mental health."[36]

My point is not that Asian Americans do not experience discrimination or that the racial makeup of higher education is not a salient index of the continuing mattering of race. Neither is my intent to minimize physical and mental health concerns, which I take to be an indication of precisely the production of group-differentiated vulnerability, nor is it to celebrate affirmative action as the key to producing social justice. I also emphasize again that "the Asian American community" as represented in the complaint is nowhere near an adequate accounting for the circumstances of Asian people in the United States. What I am highlighting is that the decidedly elitist Asian American/model minority of the complaint seeking to capitalize on racial difference is both and simultaneously an active agent of racism in its stance against affirmative action and itself a product of racial capitalism. To put it another way, I think what we are seeing is the potency of model minority discourse and its sustaining political economic structures in both inducing identification with the exceptionalism that is Asian difference and affirming the unquestionable value of majoritarian U.S. culture and politics.

It is precisely coincidental that higher education serves as the field of contestation in this moment. For, as a historical phenomenon, the particular form of capitalism referred to as globalization entails the establishment of the knowledge economy. While modes of production and labor that emerged in earlier eras continue, they have been supplemented and in some respects overwritten by the commodification of innovation and knowledge itself. The university has in this context been both a key site of globalization and one in which criticism of its devastating effects, differentially distributed across the world, has been mounted. Educational policies both within and outside of the United States feature "the global" as both an aspiration and marketing strategy and are explicitly shaped toward the broad goal of enhancing national competitiveness in the global marketplace.[37] In a knowledge economy, higher education gains greater prominence as an apparatus of national competitiveness, and the enormous expansion of state-sponsored universities across the world bespeaks this sensibility.[38] The interests of higher education, capital, and of the state grow increasingly to be one and the same, with resources flowing to potentially patentable research and away from work less easily commodified. It is no wonder, then, that access to Harvard holds such sway as the icon of success.

Asian racialization in this regard turns out to be exemplary of the flexibility of the accumulation of capital characterizing the current conjuncture. Asians are not the new Jews, or the new whites, but that does not negate the availability of majoritarian lifeways as Asian American achievements. While majoritarian subjects come in all colors, we would do well to recognize the thick and robust cultural and political economic apparatus that orients Asian racialization toward model minoritarianism.

Toward Pedagogies of Entanglement

Vijay Prashad poses, as a question to accompany "How does it feel to be a problem?," the prescient and memorable opening of W. E. B. Du Bois's *The Souls of Black Folk* (1903), "How does it feel to be a solution?"[39] Addressing Asians and South Asians in particular, Prashad explains, "this question asks us brown folk how we can live with ourselves as we are pledged and sometimes, in an act of bad faith, pledge ourselves, as a weapon against black folk."[40] How do we refuse, disidentify from, and act to dismantle the systems that transform people into problems and solutions? And how do we do so with critical awareness of the shifting currents of racial capitalism?

In posing such questions, I realize I am but restating some of the key principles that have organized Asian Americanist critique since its inception. In this sense, this essay is merely to acknowledge that the work of such critique remains unfinished. Moreover, it is also to identify as a specific project that might help us address the current conjuncture, the elaboration of Asian American studies as a rubric within and through which we can bring to bear the entangled histories that underlie the emergence and effects of a figure like the model minority. This might mean, for example, illumination of the role of slavery and indigenous dispossession in the founding of an institution like Harvard. Established in 1636, Harvard was instrumental in what Craig Steven Wilder describes as "Christian expansionism" and the "conquest of indigenous peoples," as well as being a major beneficiary of the African slave trade and slavery.[41] Wilder explains, "The birth of slavery in New England was also the dawn of slavery at Harvard," a history of a foundational relationship to slavery recognized by early nineteenth-century efforts to disavow the association.[42] In its earliest moments, too, Harvard dedicated itself to Christianizing Native peoples—a history punctuated in the early twentieth century by Charles Peabody's (of Harvard's Peabody Museum) desecration and robbing of the ceremonial and burial mound of Chickasaw and Choctaw peoples.[43] Of course, this history alone is insufficient to catalyzing disidentification, and/ but conceiving of it as *Asian American* history—as subtending the rise of Asian America—perhaps gums the works such that the presumed object of inquiry ("the Asian American") is rewritten to a radical relationality. We might, for example, thus take up Jodi Byrd's critical recounting of the mobilization of Japanese Americans interned during World War II at the Colorado River Indian Reservation as "an incarcerated work force who could 'improve the land for future Indian, and then white and non-Indian, use.'"[44] Or, in other words, we must continue to pursue the critique of the Asianization of power mounted by Indigenous scholars working in and through the Pacific Islands and the Americas. And/or, for example, we might exemplify the kind of work of Lisa Lowe's *The Intimacies of Four Continents*, which illuminates the inextricable relationality among European liberalism, settler colonialism in the Americas, the transatlantic slave trade, and the East Indies and China trades in the late eighteenth and early nineteenth centuries, and follow its practice of taking up entanglement as object and method of research.[45] These are, Lowe demonstrates, imbricated streams of history and culture that organize the ontoepistemologies and geopolitical economic structures we refer to as "modernity."[46]

What difference can emphasis on the ongoingness of U.S. colonialism at "home" make to the elicitation of Asian American subjects disidentified from aspirations to the achievement of model minority/modernity status? What impact might concerted attention to the shifting terrain of racial capitalism have on our ability to mobilize the critique of Asian racialization as part of the project of apprehending and defunctioning racial, colonial modernity? We cannot know in advance the impact that such pedagogies of entanglement might have, but it is, I believe, clear that we cannot not bring to bear the radical relationality that is the condition of possibility of the Asian American subject.

NOTES

I thank the 2015–2016 participants, and especially Neil Agarwal, Ujju Aggarwal, Mark Drury, Peter Hitchcock, Stefanie Jones, Manissa Maharawal, Jack Norton, Robyn Spencer, and David Stein, of the CUNY Graduate Center's Center for Place, Culture, and Politics' seminar for their incisive responses to an earlier draft of this essay. Special thanks to Ruth Wilson Gilmore, director of the center and a critically generous interlocutor distinctly important to this essay; Laura Hyun Yi Kang, who posed the questions and provided the scholarship and collegiality that gave shape to early unformed curiosity; and Lisa Lowe for astute and timely feedback. Ongoing conversations with Karen Shimakawa underwrite this essay. Cathy Schlund-Vials elicits best efforts to do good work by her example; I'm grateful for her careful engagement and input. I am, of course, wholly accountable for the ideas offered here.

1. See the Asian American Coalition for Education website for more information on this group, http://asianamericanforeducation.org/en/home/.

2. Complaint against Harvard University and the President and Fellows of Harvard College for Discriminating against Asian-American Applicants in the College Admissions Process, 2. The complaint may be accessed through the *Chronicle of Higher Education* website, http://www.chronicle.com/blogs/ticker/asian-american-groups-seek-federal-investigation-of-alleged-bias-at-harvard/99053. The Department of Education dismissed the complaint on July 7, 2015.

3. Ibid.

4. Ibid.

5. Ibid., 12.

6. The complaint cites Thomas J. Espenshade and Alexandra Radford's *No Longer Separate, Not Yet Equal* (Princeton, N.J.: Princeton University Press, 2009) as the authority on these statistics.

7. The complaint filed by the SFFA in the U.S. District Court for the District of Massachusetts may be found here: https:// studentsforfairadmissions.org/wp-content/uploads/2014/11/SFFA-v. -Harvard. Students for Fair Admissions is an organization headed by former investment banker Edward Blum, described by Jeff Yang in an op-ed as a "frustrated Republican congressional candidate who has chosen to make a career out of waging war on laws and policies that give 'special privileges' to minorities." It is questionable whether Asian Americans are the driving force behind this lawsuit, so while I note that the federal case is a source for the complaint made to the DOE and DOJ, I emphasize this uncertainty. Jeff Yang, "Harvard Lawsuit Is Not What It Seems," November 24, 2014, www .cnn.com/2014/11/24/opinion/yang-harvard-lawsuit/. Students for Fair Admissions' website is cryptic as to its membership: https:// studentsforfairadmissions.org/.

8. Daniel Golden, *The Price of Admission: How America's Ruling Class Buys Its Way into Elite Colleges—and Who Gets Left Outside the Gates* (New York: Crown Publishers, 2006).

9. *Wall Street Journal*, May 19, 2015.

10. Paul Taylor, ed., *The Rise of Asian Americans* (Washington, DC: The Pew Center, 2013), 1.

11. From popular publications like *Forbes*, the *Financial Times*, the *Guardian*, and the *New York Times*, to reports by institutions like the World Bank, the nomination of the twenty-first century as the Asian century is both heralded and debated. So established a construct has "the Asian Century" become that it merits a descriptive entry in Wikipedia.

12. These assertions of the rise of India are ubiquitous; exemplary accounts are found in the *Financial Times*, *Fortune*, and *Forbes*.

13. Laura Hyun Yi Kang, "Late (Global) Capital," in *The Routledge Companion to Asian American and Pacific Islander Literature*, ed. Rachel Lee (New York: Routledge, 2014), 301–14; Laura Hyun Yi Kang, "The Uses of Asianization: Figuring Crises, 1997–98 and 2007–?," *American Quarterly* 64, no. 3 (September 2012): 411–36; David Harvey, *The Condition of Postmodernity* (London: Blackwell, 1989); see also David Harvey, *A Brief History of Neoliberalism* (New York: Oxford University Press, 2005); Nana Oishi, *Women in Motion: Globalization, State Policies, and Labor Migration in Asia* (Stanford, Calif.: Stanford University Press, 2005); Aihwa Ong, *Flexible Citizenship: The Cultural Logics of Transnationality* (Durham, N.C.: Duke University Press, 1999).

14. The World Hunger Organization maintains this data. See "World Hunger and Poverty Facts and Statistics," http://www.worldhunger.org/2015 -world-hunger-and-poverty-facts-and-statistics/, accessed May 11, 2017. See "Critical Issues Facing Asian Americans and Pacific Islanders," https://www .whitehouse.gov/administration/eop/aapi/data/critical-issues, accessed February 12, 2016 ; see also "Southeast Asian Americans and the School-to-Prison-to-Deportation Pipeline," a policy report published by the Southeast Asia Resource Action Center (2015), http://www.searac.org/content/searac -publications. It notes that a 2002 study of the California Youth Authority found trial, incarceration, and deportation rates disproportionately high given their respective populations for Cambodian, Laotian, and Vietnamese youth.

15. A report by the National Commission on Asian American and Pacific Islander Research in Education (CARE) cites studies indicating 60– 75 percent of Asian American college students and/or voters support affirmative action policies. "The Attitudes of Asian Americans Toward Affirmative Action," care.gseis.ucla.edu/wp-content/uploads/ . . . /CARE -affirmative_action_polling-1v2.pdf, 1. CARE's report challenges the data cited in *Fisher v. Texas*, which claimed that Asian Americans opposed affirmative action by a factor of 52:1.

16. On contemporary racial capitalism and corollary definition of racism, see Ruth Wilson Gilmore, *Golden Gulag: Prisons, Surplus, Crisis, and Opposition in Globalizing California* (Berkeley: University of California Press, 2007). See also Cedric Robinson, *Black Marxism: The Making of the Black Radical Tradition* (Chapel Hill: University of North Carolina Press, 2000).

17. Roderick A. Ferguson, *The Reorder of Things: The University and Its Pedagogies of Minority Difference* (Minneapolis: University of Minnesota Press, 2012); Jodi Melamed, *Represent and Destroy: Rationalizing Violence in the New Racial Capitalism* (Minneapolis: University of Minnesota Press, 2011).

18. Viet Thanh Nguyen, *Race and Resistance: Literature and Politics in Asian America* (Oxford: Oxford University Press, 2002).

19. Gilmore, *Golden Gulag*, 28.

20. See, in addition to Kang and Nguyen, Victor Bascara, *Model Minority Imperialism* (Minnesota: University of Minnesota Press, 2006), and Christine So's *Economic Citizens* (Philadelphia, Penn.: Temple University Press, 2007), both of which are invoked later in this essay. See also Candace Fujikane and Jonathan Y. Okamura's *Asian Settler Colonialism: From Local Governance to the Habits of Everyday Life in Hawai'i* (Honolulu: University of Hawaii Press, 2008).

21. Bruce Drake, "Asian-Americans Lead All Others in Household Income," Pew Research Center, April 16, 2013, http://www.pewresearch.org

/fact-tank/2013/04/16/asian-americans-lead-all-others-in-household
-income/.

22. Taylor, *Rise of Asian Americans*, 1.

23. Ibid.

24. This essay inaugurates a broader project that will more fully address these other avenues of inquiry.

25. Taylor, *Rise of Asian Americans*, 9.

26. Takashi Fujitani, *Race for Empire: Koreans as Japanese and Japanese as Americans during World War II* (Berkeley: University of California Press, 2011), 230. See also Victor Bascara, *Model-Minority Imperialism* (Minneapolis: University of Minnesota Press, 2006).

27. Fujitani, *Race for Empire*, 230–31.

28. Fujitani, *Race for Empire*, 231–32.

29. Kang, "Late (Global) Capital," 303.

30. This history could be drawn further back, to the late nineteenth century, when congressional and public debates regarding the United States' occupation of the Philippines, Guam, Puerto Rico, and Hawai'i registers the fear of Japan as a competitor imperial power. This competition contributed to the United States' interest in overtaking noncontiguous lands that would be difficult to administer; one of the results of such colonization was the growth of the U.S. Navy.

31. See Peter Schrader, *US Foreign Policy towards Africa: Incrementalism, Crisis and Change* (New York: Cambridge University Press, 1996).

32. Christine So, *Economic Citizens: A Narrative of Asian American Visibility* (Philadelphia, Penn.: Temple University Press, 2007), 4.

33. Complaint against Harvard University, 15.

34. Ibid., 17.

35. Michael Hurwitz, "The Impact of Legacy Status on Undergraduate Admissions at Elite Colleges and Universities," *Economics of Education Review* 30, issue 3 (June 2011): 480–92. The study compares SAT score data sampled from thirty "highly selective" colleges and universities—twelve private liberal arts schools and eighteen private research universities.

36. Complaint against Harvard University, 16.

37. The special issue of *Traces: A Multilingual Series of Cultural Theory and Translation*, "Universities in Translation: The Mental Labor of Globalization," edited by Brett de Bary, provides exceptionally clarifying analyses of the relationship of the knowledge economy to both the contemporary situation of the university on a global scale and the particular forms of "mental labor" elicited within it.

38. See Philip G. Altbach and Toru Umakoshi, eds., *Asian Universities: Historical Perspectives and Contemporary Challenges* (Baltimore, Md.: Johns Hopkins University Press, 2004), on "massification."

39. Vijay Prashad, *The Karma of Brown Folk* (Minneapolis: University of Minnesota Press, 2001), viii.

40. Prashad, *Karma of Brown Folk*, viii.

41. Craig Steven Wilder, *Ebony & Ivy: Race, Slavery, and the Troubled History of America's Universities* (London: Bloomsbury Press, 2013), 17.

42. Ibid., 29, epilogue.

43. Jodi Byrd, *Transit of Empire: Indigenous Critiques of Colonialism* (Minneapolis: University of Minnesota Press, 2011), ch. 4.

44. Byrd, *Transit of Empire*, 185.

45. Lisa Lowe, *The Intimacies of Four Continents* (Durham, N.C.: Duke University Press, 2015).

46. Lowe, *Intimacies of Four Continents*, 21.

PART IV

Toward an Asian American Ethic of Care

CHAPTER 14

Asian Americans, Disability, and the Model Minority Myth

Yoonmee Chang

Most of the characters in Harper Lee's *To Kill a Mockingbird* (1960) are disabled.[1] The text begins with Jem's disfigured arm, which provides the occasion for Scout's story.[2] Of course there is "Boo" Radley, who suffers extreme sociophobia; and the heroic Atticus Finch is developing arthritis and has a bad eye. Disability is the crux of Atticus's defense of Tom Robinson, an African American who is falsely accused of raping a white woman. After establishing that the victim was punched in the right eye and beaten heavily on her right side, Atticus displays Tom's body to the courtroom. He wants everyone to see that Tom's left arm is withered. Based on the common sense that a punch is thrown across the body (the attacker's left hand would hit the victim's right side and vice versa), Atticus argues that Tom, with his impaired left arm, could not have beaten the accuser. But in the end, Atticus fails. Instead of disability overriding race, race trumps disability. A black man, disabled or not, has no chance against a racist jury.

The subordination of disability to race has different valences. For Tom, disability is subordinate to the pejorative racism against African Americans. What if a disabled Asian American were on the stand? What would be the opinion of her race and how would that effect the visibility of her body? *Mockingbird*'s jury might not have taken kindly to an Asian person either, but for a good part of the twentieth and twenty-first centuries, Asians and Asian Americans have been racialized *positively*, their race construed as an individual and social asset. Would favorable racializations clear the view to see disabled Asian American bodies?

It turns out, however, that as with Tom Robinson, Asian Americans' disabilities are obscured by race. For Tom, it is the intransigent racism against blacks, but for Asian Americans it is, counterintuitively, the favorable constructions of their race. These positive constructions are—as has become a first premise in Asian American studies—consolidated in what has come to be known as the "model minority myth." The positive racializations of the model minority myth are central to making disabled Asian American bodies hard to see. They are obscured and invisible, sometimes under claims of super-ability. While contempt for Tom's race discounts his impairment, racial admiration for Asian Americans likewise makes their disabilities illegible.

An Asian American Walks into a Bar . . .

In September 2015, I was having a drink with a friend when, having briefly stepped away from the table, I returned to find my wine glass gone. The restaurant manager approached and explained that she noticed that I was walking clumsily. Deeming me intoxicated, she confiscated my drink. Not wanting to embarrass my companion or myself, I courteously apologized and thanked the manager for her attentiveness.

A few months earlier, I had suffered two Transient Ischemic Attacks (TIAs), commonly referred to as "mini-strokes." TIAs do not usually leave symptoms and if they do, they are minor. I was left with nerve damage in my left leg and foot, which caused perpetual numbness, manifest in the uncomfortable sensation that my limb was always asleep. This injury derailed my sense of proprioception. Proprioception is the ability to gauge how hard the foot should hit the ground on a sandy beach versus a concrete sidewalk. It is the ability to know how to tip-toe or stomp. The brain and body coordinate so that the latter modulates itself to produce a steady gait, whether it is trying to scramble across a rocky terrain or *trying to walk*.

I held my tongue at the restaurant, but I called the manager a few days later. She was defensive and uninformed. She had not given disability a thought. The manager is not alone in her ignorance, but overlooking disability stems from more than a passive failure of perception or innocent misinterpretation. It is the product of desire, of willful denial and obfuscation. Disability is *made* invisible.

For Asian Americans, disability is especially and particularly invisible. Race might or might not have been a factor in the restaurant manager's misreading of my body, but if it were, it would not have helped her recognize that I was disabled. Being Asian American predisposes the disabled body to go unseen. I use "Asian American" because I am referring to the particular construction of the Asian-raced body in American culture. That construction is the designation of Asian Americans as model minorities. I focus on two aspects of the model minority myth vis-à-vis disabled Asian Americans. First, I examine how the historic development of the model minority myth produces, if not relies on, the invisibility of Asian American disability. As a result, Asian Americans have to prove that they are disabled—they have to "cripsplain." Second, I examine an opposite effect—the overrecognition of Asian American disability. For the unseen disabled Asian American model minority, is this welcome attention or ill-boding? What underlies the enthusiasm for seeing Asian American bodies impaired?

Nisei Friend

As a thesis, the model minority myth ascribes normative, if not superior, ability to Asian Americans. As such, it presumes that Asian American bodies are normatively formed. Disability is thereby unintelligible within the discourse of the model minority myth. This unintelligibility is not just the result of passive inattention (as with the trigger-happy, wine-removing restaurant manager). Rather, the model minority myth quite purposefully obscures Asian American disability. The obfuscation of disability is not only caused by the model minority myth but is also fundamental to the myth's creation. Obfuscating disability is the product of the model minority myth, as well as its progenitor.

The origins of the model minority myth are invariably traced to a pair of 1966 articles by Berkeley sociologist William Petersen. They bookend that year: the first article, in January, focuses on Japanese Americans and the second, in December, on Chinese Americans.[3] Neither article coins the phrase "model minority," but the individual words are peppered throughout, and the construction is evident.[4] Both articles, appearing on the heels of the 1964 Civil Rights Act, the 1965 Voting Rights Act, and the 1965 Immigration and Nationality Act (a.k.a. the Hart-Celler Act) shame African Americans. The model minority myth's now-familiar prescription is that African Americans should stop agitating the state and start emulating the self-sufficiency of the docile, industrious Asian Americans. Also familiar is that this invidious juxtaposition turns blacks and Asian Americans into adversaries.

Compliant subjectivity and hard work are the key traits of model minority behavior. Petersen illustrates this in his first article, "Success Story, Japanese-American Style." He makes his case through the Japanese American internment, noting that throughout the upheaval of dislocation and imprisonment, Japanese Americans were, in the majority, commendably acquiescent and accommodating. After their release, Japanese Americans did not exhibit social pathologies, as might be expected because of the trauma, institutionalization, and racism of the internment. Rather, Japanese Americans diligently applied themselves to hard work, thereby quickly re-establishing themselves, so much so, that in some socioeconomic measures they outperformed whites.[5] This remarkable postinternment rebound showed that Japanese Americans were not only succeeding but succeeding even when they were set up to fail.[6] The model minority myth endows Asian Americans with not just ability but also exceptional, even hyper-ability.

The depiction of Asian Americans as highly able/hyper-able assumes that they have normatively abled bodies or better. This is embodied in the figure of the nisei soldier.[7] The nisei soldier is the prototypical model minority (more precisely, he is a proto-model minority). For one, he is a figure of pronounced compliance. Some Japanese Americans considered the draft an outrage, another racist injustice imposed on the internees. Others eagerly yielded, believing that military service was a prime opportunity to prove that they were bona fide Americans. The determination of the latter, grouped to form the 442nd Battalion, the segregated Japanese American unit, is evident in the unit's slogan: "Go for Broke!"[8] This rallying cry espouses an ethic of hard work; in this case, a declaration of life-threatening diligence, in the service of national identity.

The nisei serviceman had to have abled bodies to enlist in the military. To be inducted, they would have had to pass medical exams as well as arduous tests of strength and endurance. The nisei stayed true to their slogan ("Go for Broke!"), persevering through danger and injury to get their job done.[9] The fulfillment of this exceptional military labor is manifest in that the 442nd Battalion stands as the most decorated unit in U.S. military history. Today, aged nisei receive belated national honors and visit the WWII Memorial in wheelchairs, some of the veterans bearing amputations. Their current bodily status is a signifier of their previous one—

the past able-bodiedness that allowed them to toil their way through the war and arrive here, half a century later, to be graced by memorials and garlands. The combination of compliance and hard work make the nisei servicemen an apt example of a proto-model minority. By "proto" I do not mean "in incipient stages of development"; rather, I mean "that which came before and has yet to be codified." It is often suspect to use a current term to explain a historical phenomenon. I do not mean to use the present to shape the past. Rather, I hope to show how the past is rich with conditions that inform what comes after it and thereby shapes the critical lenses of the present.[10]

Given the configuration of compliance and hard work evinced by the nisei soldier, it is not surprising that Petersen uses this figure to advance his model minority thesis. What is surprising is that he invokes John Okada's novel *No-No Boy* (1957) to do so: "In John Okada's novel *No-No Boy*, written by a veteran of the Pacific war about a nisei who refused to accept the draft . . . the hero struggles to find his way to the America that rejected him and that he had rejected. A nisei friend who has returned from the war with a wound that eventually kills him is pictured as relatively well-off. In short, in contrast to the works of James Baldwin, this is a novel of revolt against revolt."[11] This reading is puzzling, to some heretical, since *No-No Boy* has been canonized as a founding work of Asian American protest literature.[12] Petersen's interpretation turns the text into a novel of compliance ("this is a novel of revolt against revolt."). This reversal is based on misrepresentations and distortions. Petersen describes the novel in crude brushstrokes. The novel's "hero" (in the sense that he is the main protagonist) is the "no-no boy," who pays for his recalcitrance by returning to a lifetime of financial struggle and social rejection. His "nisei friend," having obediently served in the army, is "better off"; he and his family are economically stable and he is welcomed into the community of nisei veterans. Petersen puts forth this "nisei friend" as the proper model of being a minority. His behavior (compliant and diligent service in the military) and his outcome (socioeconomic mobility) are characteristic of the model minority identity that Petersen seeks to define.

This reading of *No-No Boy* distorts the structuring theme of the novel. One of its major points is that the relationship between "the hero" and his "nisei friend" is not so tidily mapped. Loyalty is presented as an ambiguity, not a fixture in a binary. Likewise, Petersen's omission of the central characters' names turns them into types: "The hero" is a recalcitrant no-no boy/anti–model minority; and the "nisei friend" is the compliant nisei soldier/model minority. This anonymization is a conspicuous manipulation.

The "nisei friend" is Kenji, a prominent character who has prominently lost his leg during the war. His traumatic amputation saturates Okada's novel and confronts the characters and readers at every turn, figuratively and physically. Anonymizing Kenji as a "nisei friend" is like describing Ahab as a cranky fisherman. This unnaming obstructs the recognition of Kenji as Kenji qua Kenij, a nisei veteran with a traumatic disability.

Petersen does not totally omit reference to Kenji's injury. He breezily notes that Kenji "returned from the war with a wound that eventually kills him." For convenience, I will collapse this to "war wound," a more concise phrase that does not alter Petersen's meaning. Like "nisei friend," "war wound" is anonymizing and atomizing. Petersen admits the severity of the wound, noting that it is fatal, but generalizing it as a "war wound" veils the specific nature of the wound. The anonymization shields the reader from the catastrophic nature of Kenji's injury and the grim consequence of amputation. It withholds from the reader an engagement with an Asian American amputee. It withholds an opportunity to encounter—and see— a disabled Asian American body.

Asian Americanists and others routinely praise *No-No Boy* as ground-breaking for its complex representation of Asian American sensibilities. An-other reason for the novel's high standing is its stark, even confrontational, display of disability, which anchors the text's themes as well as narrative movement. The weight and visibility given to Asian American disability in Okada is evident in that it requires manipulation to diminish its repre-sentation. Petersen's manipulations actually make a provocative sugges-tion. Because he has to obscure disability in order to develop the model minority myth, he shows that the model minority myth and disability are incompatible. The choice of *No-No Boy* thereby suggests a constitutive relationship between the model minority myth and disability. Petersen could have used a different text, but that he chose Okada's makes the sug-gestion that a condition (or at least an accompaniment) of the birth of the model minority myth is the erasure of disability.

Taylor Swift and Cripsplaining

In September of 2015, Ryan Adams released a cover album of Taylor Swift's record-breaking *1989*. If the disjunction is not obvious, Adams, a prolific, critically and popularly received alt-country artist, notes himself that the project was a "weird idea."[13] Intuiting that his moody iconoclasm would be taken as more "serious" than Swift's ear candy, Adams is quick to note that he was not trying to improve Swift's work. Quite the opposite, he makes clear that Swift is already good: "These songs [Swift's] are incredible. . . . They're just super powerful and they can tear you up. They're very vulnerable and brave."[14] Adams was not trying to transform Swift's work. He was not seeking to supplement or reshape *1989* as if it needed those transformations to have aesthetic merit: "There was[n't] anything missing [in Swift's songs]. . . . It wasn't like I wanted to change them because they needed changing."[15] Instead, Adams perceives his cover as "not a reimagining or a reconstruction at all . . . [but] a parallel universe. That's how I think of it. We're creating an alternate universe, like in Marvel Comics."[16]

Adams's vision of an "alternate universe" where his cover does not cross paths with Swift's original is coy. It is simple enough to observe that Adams and Swift's *1989*s are always coupled, and not just to reference the original as source material. Most reviews give Swift due credit as an exceptional artist. But they still claim what Adams clearly stated he was not doing, which is improving her music. For instance, the *Telegraph* is impressed with Swift's "perfect songcraft" but quizzically argues that Adams perfected these already perfect songs.[17] The answer to this riddle is that Swift's "perfect songcraft" is buried under "gleaming surfaces" and it took Adams to scrape the songs clean and "beautifully evoke[] the ghosts in Taylor Swift's pop machine."[18] Adams cleared the tinsel and "followed a straight line to the song's source, diving down into the emotional pits where these words and tunes were first concocted."[19] Likewise, the *New Yorker* recognizes an earnestness in *1989* but suggests that Adams plays Taylor Swift better than Taylor Swift, describing his cover as "more sincere than the original."[20] The *Atlantic*'s review is of the minority that recognizes that Adams's cover is good but the virtuosity is Swift's. Yet the title of the review—"Ryan Adams's *1989* and the Vindication of Taylor Swift"—bespeaks that this more thoughtful assessment remains entrenched in the vocabulary of Adams superseding Swift.[21] The "vindication" refers to Swift's recognition as a serious artist. Yet the title indicates that this vindication is achieved through Adams. Even as the *Atlantic* makes the point that the genius belongs to Swift, it speaks in an Adams-centric language in which Swift's genius needs his intervention.

It is not insignificant that the artist who does Taylor Swift better than Taylor Swift is a man. Adams's "vindication" of Swift is by way of "mansplaining" her music. The subtext of the reviews above is the gender stereotype that when a woman speaks of heartache, especially a young woman (and especially this young woman), she is whining after a boy.[22] In contrast, a man's exploration of emotional loss is brave, real, and admirable. Adams's mansplaining—shifting Swift's red lipstick tunes to the register of masculinist gravitas—legitimates Swift as a serious musician.

What does Taylor Swift have to do with disabled Asian Americans? The differences are obvious and I do not mean to obscure Swift's privilege, even if there are instances in which she is relatively subordinated by gender. The similarity is that Swift and disabled Asian Americans are not seen for who they are or what they do. They need explanations and justifications to be visible as themselves (for Swift, as a talented musician; and for disabled Asian Americans, as being disabled). Swift was justified through another musician, but disabled Asian Americans bear the burden of explaining themselves by themselves. Vis-à-vis the model minority myth's erasure, disabled Asian Americans have to convince others that they are disabled—they have to cripsplain. I use this term not just because it cleverly rhymes with "mansplain" but because both are processes of unveiling that which was not hidden. Cripsplaining and mansplaining make things legitimate and visible (disabled bodies, bona fide talent), even as those things are already legitimate and apparent. Mansplaining exploits the power of gender, but disabled Asian Americans speak for themselves from a marginalized position.

I experienced the need to cripsplain after an accident in the Spring of 2013. I was left with a permanent physical disability that involved the partial amputation of my fingers. Seeking an ADA accommodation was difficult. Floating around was the discourse of "overcoming" my disability. Here was the need for cripsplaining, proving the reality and severity of my disability. I resorted to few strategies: verbal hyperbole, visual hyperbole, and legal action. These strategies are neither solutions nor suggestions; they are indications of failure. Their need bespeaks the strong drive to deny Asian American disability. The definitions of these strategies are self-evident, but I want to say a word about legal action. Insofar as legal action is meant to level the playing ground, I thought it was a good idea. Then I wondered, why should ADA compliance be costly? Why should I outsource the job and foot the bill? Legal action does not produce equity but amplifies inequity, giving access to equity to the economically privileged. I handled the ADA negotiations on my own. For entities that might have lent a hand, my disabled body was not on the docket. It did not exist in their ken.

Race and model minority discourse were not overt in this experience, but that does not mean they were not there. In *Racial Asymmetries*, Stephen Hong Sohn argues that texts by Asian American writers do not have to address Asian American subjects to be categorized as "Asian American." This does not render anything or everything Asian American. The texts

still illuminate Asian American experience but through "relational, refrac-
tive, and comparative formations."[23] For example, Sohn reads Sabina
Murray's *Forgery* as producing a concatenation that does not start with
Asian Americans but ends with them.[24] The novel's setting is 1963 Greece,
which invokes a string of associations: Greece's entanglement in the Cold
War, the Truman Doctrine, the Korean War, and the Vietnam War. 1963
Greece is the only element represented in the novel, but it stands for more
than itself. It is a gateway that shepherds the readers' visions to a wider,
relational field. It is a node that refracts the mind toward topics that are
eminently comparative and linked.

For me, the refractory node was the word *overcome*. This word and its
logic are saturated with race. The refraction is obvious in reference to African Americans, especially as the anthem of the civil rights movement
revolves around this word. For Asian Americans, the racial meanings of
overcome invoke the construction of Asian Americans as model minorities.
Petersen's work is an eminent example: His treatise on the rapid socioeconomic recovery of postinternment Japanese Americans affix *overcome* to the
perception of Asian Americans as model minorities. Likewise, the idea that
I should overcome my disability echoes and amplifies this perception. Racial
discourse structured the situation, even if it was not spoken aloud.

Even as my assignation as a model minority was not spoken, I was certainly treated as one. The discourse of "overcoming" ignores the simple
fact of the body. Depending on the disability, it asks for the impossible.
No-No Boy provides a cogent example. Kenji, the nisei friend/model minority, does not overcome his disability; rather, he is overtaken by it. The
loss of his leg cannot be surmounted; the injury defeats Kenji, ultimately
killing him. It would be inane to advise Kenji to overcome his disability.
That would indicate an ignorance to Kenji's body, the inability or refusal
to see the fact and nature of his disability: the material phenomenon of
missing flesh and the certainty that the flesh will remain missing forever.
Prosthetics might come to mind, but there are several problems. No matter
how advanced, prosthetics will always be an approximation of biological
bodily function. Second, in reference to the model minority, the discourse
of overcoming, including as it relates to disability, is pointedly about self-
reliance; succeeding without external assistance. Last, the nature of some
injuries (like mine), are impossible to fit with a functioning prosthetic.

My injury is not as grave as a severed leg, but it did require amputation.
As with Kenji, this is a highly visible condition that should readily impart
the fact and nature of my disability. Yet it was not. Overcome? I cannot re-
grow my fingers. Neither am I endowed with superlative abilities that are

unaffected by or can supersede the loss of body parts: I am not a model minority. I am not immune to injury. My disabled body is material. It occupies space and has a shape. It is a sight that warrants being seen.

Good Luck

In an episode of the old sitcom *The Jeffersons*, Bentley, the buffoon character, goes to George's apartment in search of a lost lucky coin. It goes something like this: Bentley crawls under a desk and clamorously bumps his head as he re-emerges, lucky coin in hand. Bentley rubs his sore pate and declares, "Thank goodness I had my lucky coin!" Always cantankerous, George points out that Bentley's so-called lucky coin caused him to hurt his head. Bentley concurs but also counters, "But thanks to my lucky coin, I just bumped my head. I could have put out an eye."

I am lucky like that, too. I am told that I have just bumped my head. I severed my fingers, but I could have suffered a much more debilitating spine or head injury. The two TIAs were precisely that—temporary attacks, not full strokes that caused permanent damage. Now as I write, I have a broken foot. I am sure there is a bright side to that, too. Bentley's foolish illogic is obvious and scripted to incite laughter. But with disability, this same ridiculousness is intelligible and intelligent, taken as a good attitude. Megan Devine, author of the blog *Refuge in Grief: Emotionally Intelligent Grief Support*, offers an alternative approach. Rather than dilute the severity of disability and the accompanying grief, why not accept that "some things in life cannot be fixed. They can only be carried."[25]

My second disablement (the TIAs in 2015) was not minimized but, to my surprise, readily noted. Movement was swift to secure medical leave and minimize disruption to my classes. My disability was hypervisible and eagerly attended to, exceeding my own conception of injury. But in an odd turnaround, I was the one who minimized the situation and insisted on finishing the semester. I refused to let this setback mitigate my strength, dedication, determination, and resilience. My attitude smacks of model minority behavior with an important difference. It was not imposed on me; I was electing it myself. Was it me who was obscuring Asian American disability, including my own?

This contradiction is less puzzling in a wider context. My alacrity to remain on the job was not welcome. I was on notice, lest I become disruptively sick again. Thus, even as my disability was hyperrecognized, I ended up at a familiar place—I would have to erase disability from my body. Of course, I was the one who insisted on model minority perseverance, and

I am not cynical enough to think that the shift from my disability's hyper-recognition to its suppression was calculated. But hyperrecognition is a fertile precondition. By inviting push back, it turns the afflicted individual into the perpetrator of her own erasure.

Every time I returned to the classroom, I displayed my body as that of a persevering model minority. In *To Kill A Mockingbird*, Atticus' showcasing of Tom's body is not weighty enough to supersede the hostilities against Tom's race. Likewise, the repeated exhibitions of my body contributed to the lack of nuance and complexity allotted to my race. Even if those gross generalizations look like praise, they have damaging effects. They hinder our ability to see Asian American bodies that cannot simply "overcome."

My initial thinking vis-à-vis the hyperrecognition of my TIA was that it expressed resentment against the model minority, delight that Asian Americans were impaired or otherwise falling behind. I planned to argue that we end where we began, looping this schadenfreude back to the nineteenth century "Yellow Peril," in which the Asiatic figure was a toiling drudge who was not getting far. But this is not my conclusion. We end where we began in a different way. On the one hand, model minority bodies are presumed to be vigorous and hyper-able, a construction that does not admit disability. On the other hand, when that vigor is compromised it is sometimes readily-recognized. But that recognition can supply the conditions to invoke the model minority myth once again, to demand proof (or prove to oneself) that model minority vigor will conquer disability. The hyperrecognition of Asian American disability becomes the basis of its invisibility.

The wine confiscation incident of September 2015 repeated itself later that term. I recovered from my TIA symptoms, but I had broken my right foot. Vanity kept me from wearing the unsightly boot cast, so walking in civilian shoes caused my right leg to buckle. As I was leaving a restaurant, the manager dashed out to advise me not to drive. In any case, he wanted my ID information. This time I disagreed. After twenty minutes of arguing, I conceded. I gave the manager my information. I was exhausted. It was not going to be me, that night, who would teach this person to recognize the difference between being disabled and being drunk. I do not know if my being Asian American informed the manager's actions. I do know that I am an Asian American whose disability was once again not seen. My race is undoubtedly visible, but my disability does not share that conspicuousness.

I hope that for the manager that somewhere, sometime, even for a glimmer, maybe even because of our conversation, the issue of disability will knock about his head. Perhaps it will even surface to inform his behavior and perceptions. I wish this also for others whose sense of sight gives them power. Our chances are small, but it might happen. Who knows? We might get lucky.

NOTES

1. Harper Lee, *To Kill a Mockingbird* (New York: Grand Central, 1976).

2. David Mitchell and Sharon Snyder make the influential argument that disability propels or inaugurates common narratives. This is salient in Lee's novel in that Jem's disabled arm provides Scout the occasion to tell her family's story. David Mitchell and Sharon Snyder, *Narrative Prosthesis: Disability and the Dependencies of Discourse* (Ann Arbor: University of Michigan Press, 2001).

3. William Petersen, "Success Story, Japanese-American Style," *New York Times Magazine,* January 9, 1966, 1–2, 33–43; and "Success of One Minority Group in the U.S," *U.S. News and World Report*, December 26, 1966, 6–9.

4. Petersen speaks of a "racial minority" that has become a "model of self-respect and achievement." Petersen, "Success of One Minority Group in the U.S," 6.

5. Petersen, "Success Story, Japanese-American Style," 38, 4.

6. Petersen is making an obvious comparison to slavery and again shaming African Americans. He argues that both the internment and slavery were forms of massive institutional racism, yet Japanese Americans persevered. Petersen, "Success Story, Japanese-American Style," 1–2.

7. Japanese Americans who served in WWII are frequently referred to as nisei, as it was the nisei generation, American-born and American citizens, who were eligible for military service.

8. The 442nd Battalion is nearly always described as a Japanese American unit, but it included other races. For instance, Young Oak Kim, a Korean American, was a highly decorated colonel in the 442nd Battalion.

9. Bill Yenne provides numerous accounts of nisei bravery and persistence, even as they were carrying severe, and sometimes mortal, injury. Bill Yenne, *Rising Sons* (New York: St. Martin's, 2007).

10. Petersen follows the same methodology in that he uses an event that preceded his theorizations (the internment) to support those theorizations.

11. Petersen, "Success Story, Japanese-American Style," 36; John Okada, *No-No Boy* (Seattle: University of Washington Press, 1994). Note that Petersen constructs the author himself as a model minority, praising Okada for writing a "novel of revolt against revolt."

12. The editors of *Aiiieeeee!* famously branded and brandished *No-No Boy* as exemplary of expressing the proper, antihegemonic Asian American sensibility. *Aiiieeeee! An Anthology of Asian American Writers*, ed. Jeffrey

Chan, Frank Chin, Lawson Inanda, and Shawn Wong (New York: Meridian/Penguin, 1997).

13. David Brown, "Ryan Adams on His Full-Album Taylor Swift Cover: 'You Just Have to Mean It,'" *Rolling Stone*, September 2015, http://www.rollingstone.com/music/news/ryan-adams-on-his-full-albumtaylor-swift-cover-you-just-have-to-mean-it-20150921.

14. Tom Breihan, "Premature Evaluation: Ryan Adams' *1989*," *Stereogum*, September 2015.

15. Brown, "Ryan Adams on His Full-Album Taylor Swift Cover."

16. Ibid.

17. Neil McCormick, "Ryan Adams' 1989 Review: 'Beautifully Evokes the Ghosts in Taylor Swift's Pop Machine,'" *Telegraph*, September 22, 2015, http://www.telegraph.co.uk/music/what-to-listen-to/ryan-adams-1989-review-taylor-swift.

18. Ibid.

19. Ibid.

20. To be fair, Ian Crouch praises both Swift and Adams: Swift for writing good songs and Adams for knowing how to sing a good song well. "Good pop songs sound good when anyone plays them, because they are often just really good songs, whether it's cool to say so or not." Ian Crouch, "Haters Gonna Hate: Listening to Ryan Adams's *1989*," *New Yorker*, September 22, 2015, http://www.newyorker.com/culture/culture-desk/haters-gonna-hate-listening-to-ryan-adams-1989.

21. Spencer Kornhaber, "Ryan Adams's *1989* and the Vindication of Taylor Swift," *Atlantic*, September 22, 2015, http://www.theatlantic.com/entertainment/archive/2015/09/ryan-adams-taylor-swift-1989/406744.

22. The media have delighted in scrutinizing Swift's romantic life vis-à-vis her song lyrics. She is construed as a "serial dater" who "cannot hold onto a man."

23. Stephen Sohn, *Racial Asymmetries: Asian American Fictional Worlds* (New York: NYU Press, 2014), 11. Regarding the author, Sohn selects those who are marked in some way as Asian-raced. This enables him to include mixed race authors, including those who are several generations removed from their Asian ancestry. Making the mark of the Asian race a criterion to be an Asian American writer is not essentialism but the recognition that being marked as such makes the author subject to experiences that are specific to those marked as Asian.

24. Sabina Murray, *Forgery* (New York: Grove Press, 2008).

25. Megan Devine, "Refuge in Grief: Emotionally Intelligent Grief Support," http://www.refugeingrief.com. I thank Mimi Khuc for bringing this website to my attention.

CHAPTER 15

Buddhist Meditation as Strategic Embodiment: An Optative Reflection

Sharon A. Suh

It is perhaps an understatement to say that meditation has held pride of place in American Buddhism since its historical meeting with the Beat generation, Alan Watts, and the rise of the *vipassana* (insight meditation) movement led by teachers such as Jack Kornfield and Sharon Salzberg, who pioneered the development of the Insight Meditation Society.[1] The distillation of Buddhist traditions into mindfulness meditation can be seen throughout corporate culture, popular media, psychotherapy, sports psychology, and even in elementary school classrooms as pedagogical method.[2] Yet, at what point does the distillation of Buddhist traditions into meditation practices become a dilution of the tradition where the ritual elements, devotional richness, and even diversity of practitioners of Buddhism have been somewhat blurred? The development of mindfulness through meditation offers critical skills for honing attention on the present and for stress reduction; however, there has been little theoretical analysis and critique of the subordination of the body to the mind in meditation and virtually no mention of the raced and racialized bodies that are often blurred in the process of distilling Buddhism into a singular practice. This curious silence, I maintain, belies the tacit assumption of a generic white meditating body, a body that because of its very whiteness requires little theorizing or even attention as critics of white privilege and contemplative/meditative practices such as Laurie Cassidy, bell hooks, and Ann Gleig argue.[3]

In a similar practice of omission, there has been relatively little to no discussion of the potential value of exploring mindfulness and meditation in the lives of Asian Americans whose bodies are often rendered invisible in the larger discourses of meditation in the United States and in Asian American studies. The reasons for this general neglect are threefold: First, the focus on religion is a relative newcomer to the discipline itself, despite the fact that Asian Americans have built temples and churches since their first arrival in the Hawaiian Islands and United States. Scholars tend to attribute the paucity of early studies of Asian American religions to the influence of Marxist views of religion that shaped the early Asian American movement.[4] Hence, the relationship of religion to the field of Asian American studies in its nascence was one of discomfort and perhaps suspicion, although since 9/11 there has been increasing attention to the relationship between religion, race, and globalization.[5] Secondly, most studies of Asian Americans and Buddhism have tended to focus on issues related to immigration, acculturation, and the uneasy relationship between religion and race, while specific discussions of meditation have been associated primarily with the monastics and not so much the laity that one finds in larger discourses of mindfulness and insight meditation noted above. A third factor lies in the assumption that since, as the 2012 Pew study on Asian American religiosity indicates, Asian American Buddhists do not seem to meditate very much (14 percent of those surveyed claimed to meditate daily), then meditation must not be a salient area of research.[6]

As a scholar of Asian American Buddhism and self-identifying Buddhist, I agree wholeheartedly that the development of mindfulness through meditation offers much-needed skills for the honing of attention to the present since most of the time our minds are wandering endlessly and often caught up in negative mental states and habits. Yet, I would also say that within contemplative studies, there has been little theoretical analysis and critique of the subordination of body to mind in meditation and virtually no mention of raced and racialized bodies. Thus, in this essay I make the following claims upfront: First, what we know of as mindfulness meditation and insight meditation emerged out of the privileging of white American Buddhisms over and against Asian American forms of practice that have been deemed overly popular, devotional, and, by extension, inauthentic. Therefore, authentic engagement of meditation for the purposes of

dismantling white supremacy should begin with the white privilege that
entangles much of American Buddhist practice. Second, despite the legacy of white supremacy and privilege that shapes much of the contemporary
discourse of meditation, it is possible to render visible the raced bodies that
have been largely ignored in the construction of American Buddhism. And,
finally, meditation can be revisioned and practiced as a skillful means to
heal the bodily alienation and internalized white supremacy that affects
many people of color.

Despite my training and publications in the field of Buddhist studies
and my deep interest in meditation, I have often found myself at odds
both within the scholarly tradition of Buddhist studies, which remains
heavily shaped by textual studies at the expense of lived religiosity, and
in U.S. meditation centers where I often experience minoritization
because of the predominance of white meditation practitioners. That is,
neither my original academic discipline nor the places of practice that I
have visited attend to the very embodied nature of Buddhism that people
of color such as myself crave.[7] While I have explored this sense of mar-
ginalization and minoritization through my previous work on Korean
American Buddhists in Los Angeles, and most recently in my analysis of
racist images of Buddhists and Asian/Asian Americans in film, I take the
occasion of this essay to imagine an embodied Buddhist meditation practice that can constructively respond to racialized experiences of people of
color by emphasizing and prioritizing difference and bringing the body
in all of its corporeal specificity front and center as the locus and focus of
practice.[8]

What follows is my optative take on an Asian American Buddhist praxis
that reimagines meditation as a means of embodiment or bodily presence
in contradistinction to the centuries of erasure that have plagued many an
Asian American Buddhist in the construction of an American Buddhism
for which I still continually ask—Whose America? Whose Buddhism?
Such an optative meditation practice is one that will give due attention to
the very real and lived experiences of racialization and bodily alienation
experienced by Asian Americans and one that encourages practitioners to
settle into the body as it is and not to make attempts to transcend its historically located, socially constructed, and at times antagonizing anxieties
stemming from its perceived difference. The essay thus aims to disrupt the
common Buddhist units of measure and authenticity (meditating monks)
that have their troubled history in Orientalism and Protestantization and
are uncritically reproduced in larger Asian American discourses that continue to overlook the Buddhist laity as appropriate bearers of authentic

religion. In so doing, it also claims a space for lay Buddhist practices as legitimate foci of study in the field of Asian American studies and expands the scope of Asian American studies of Buddhism beyond the narrow bandwidth of monks, nuns, and temples.

Thus, the approach I take in this reflective essay is part of a larger effort to propose alternative ways of understanding Buddhism on the ground—that is, in the complex and often messy lives of Buddhists who do not live on high mountaintops or cloistered in monasteries and nunneries. Such an approach pushes for a more pluralist vision of Buddhism that engages the everyday embodied experiences of men and women whose lay lives are the training ground for liberation. Such a focus on the laity lays bare the imbalanced and skewed perception of the Buddhist world as one populated by monastic virtuosos and theorizes spaces for the nonelites in the Buddhist social economy. This constructive practice thus reveals itself as one inherently committed to revealing power dynamics of privilege and other forms of lack, especially in the intersecting formations and allegiances to racial, sexual, economic, and gender discrimination.

The impetus to reimagine and embody Buddhist meditation emerges as a strategic response to bell hooks's critique of the pervasive white supremacist body aesthetics that continues to assault a person's efforts to think well of his or her self in order to assess the potential liberation involved in reclaiming insight meditation and mindful practice as a means of settling into our very specifically raced Asian American bodies. The construction of an embodied Buddhism thus takes the corporeal specificity of bodies as a starting point and space that is not to be transcended in the pursuit of nirvana or ultimate liberation but rather as a starting and end point—the point of departure and the place of return. In her book, *Writing beyond Race: Living Theory and Practice*, hooks reminds us that "white supremacist thinking informs the consciousness of everyone irrespective of skin color."[9] She further advises:

> If we are to truly address issues of race and racism then our society
> must make the creation of the conditions for optimal well-being a
> central aspect of anti-racist struggle; however, this will require
> everyone to place psychological issues at the forefront. Issues of
> self-esteem will need to be primary; we will need to focus on defining
> and creating the necessary conditions wherein healthy self-esteem can
> be nurtured and can flourish. We will need to fully understand the
> process by which those folks with wounded and damaged self-esteem
> may be able to heal. . . . In this case, healthy self-esteem could serve as

the foundation for a progressive anti-racist politics that could change how we relate in everyday life.[10]

As hooks notes, the pursuit of ideal beauty and the culture of white supremacist body aesthetics corroborates and colludes with the white supremacist notion of the right body as the white body, which has its corollary in many predominantly white Buddhist *sanghas* where it is the white body that is taken as normative from which others cannot but depart. Responding to hooks's clarion call for the development of healthy self-esteem and the ability to think well of oneself, the construction of an embodied Buddhism is a reclamation project of sorts that seeks to reclaim that positive sense of self and subjectivity from the devastating effects of white supremacy through meditation on and through our own bodies.

As many of people of color can attest, there is much psychic damage already done to bodies that do not conform to what is constructed as the right body. For many racialized peoples, the body develops into an unequal battlefield upon which the struggle for identity, wholeness, and selfhood is fought. Old psychic wounds are constantly reopened and new wounds inflicted as people of color are constantly bombarded with messages of their own inadequacies and inability to meet a standard of whiteness perpetuated in our culture. So, what might an embodied Buddhist approach that reconceptualizes meditation as a practice to settle into the body offer people of color whose very bodies are assaulted physically, socially, psychologically on a daily basis? Can Buddhist meditation serve the many warriors defending the self? While a seemingly funny question since Buddhism is usually touted as a religion of nonself, the efficacy of the practice comes in and through its application for rendering everyday life more manageable in the present. While traditional Buddhist studies has often overlooked the potential of Buddhist practice and devotion to center a decentered self, I maintain that it has exciting potential to render new visions of selfhood that are affirming, whole, and created not in an image of lack but in an image of radical acceptance of the self as it is.

Reinhabiting the Racialized Body through Meditation

So, if Buddhism can be liberatory and useful for naming and ultimately deconstructing the ravages of white supremacy, certainly reinhabiting "the body" is a good place to start. I put "body" in quotes because of course there is no ultimate generic (read: white) body, and in Buddhism, the body is seen as a combination of five aggregates of energies—form, sensation, perception, volition, and consciousness. Therefore, there is a fluidity of identity that Buddhism points to and through meditative contemplation on the transformative nature of the body, one can learn to re-evaluate one's heretofore undervalued and devalued body in favor of the individual body as specific and as it is.

As a way of introducing the topic of reinhabiting the racialized body, let me begin with some reflections and commentary on a memoir that I use in my "Introduction to Buddhism" class entitled *Meeting Faith: The Forest Journals of a Black Buddhist Nun* by mixed raced author Faith Adiele. I use this text as one of the first books in the quarter precisely because Adiele's work connects Buddhist practice to issues of race, class, gender, and sexuality. Many of my students come to my classes because they are intrigued by the exoticism of Buddhism, but what this text reveals is that Buddhist meditation is beneficial for the precise instances of suffering that they themselves experience on an everyday level. As such, they come away with the understanding of meditation as strategy for everyday survival. I also chose this memoir because it begins when the author has a nervous breakdown while attending Harvard and students seem to relate to some of her struggles. Adiele begins her memoirs of living as a black Buddhist nun in Thailand with the following words: "Besides nearly killing me, college taught me several things. Namely, that external identity mattered. Being black mattered. It determined where to get off the Boston subway without receiving a baseball bat to the head. Being the biracial child of a single, white mother determined which whites would beg me, breezily to integrate certain spaces and which blacks would turn their backs, stage whispering about 'messed up Oreos.' Being female determined the number of times I would cross my professors' minds, and the number of men who would grope me, curious for integration of a sort."[11]

Faith Adiele's ordination and subsequent meditation can be interpreted as a process of stripping away the external layers of racialization and sexism that have come to define her identity. Hers is a narrative of putting back together the pieces of the self after having fallen apart through the unlikely process of meditative deconstruction. She muses rather insightfully in retrospect:

> If I had planned to start again, it certainly wouldn't have been in a world where the independent self did not exist. How could one plop oneself down amidst mendicants seeking to renounce their egos and find one's own. How could stripping possibly save one's life. If I'd been thinking, I wouldn't have chosen to erase all physical identifiers and

swaddle my body in sexless layers of white cloth. (Despite sharing the American girl's love-hate relationship with her body, I balk at punishing it; feeding weakness is more my style!) It wouldn't have occurred to me to try reconstruct an identity free of this troubling, marked body.[12]

It is the troubling vexing marked body—marked by race, gender, class, sex, and ableism—that I find most intriguing in terms of its relationship to meditation as liberatory practice. Rather than enabling one to transcend the body and all the suffering it endures through physical and mental sensations, seated meditation requires a kind of settling into the physical base of the body and engaging in the development of concentration and focus on the breath to free oneself from all the negative layers of judgment placed upon the body.

What is this meditative practice that Adiele experiences and how does it actually help? There are two main types found in the Theravada Buddhist tradition of Southeast Asia that Faith practices. First there is what is known as *samatha* or calming meditation, which can be seen as a way to calm the emotions and the pull of the three poisons of greed, ill will, and delusion that manifest in emotional states such as anger, frustration, impatience, and self-centeredness. If in Buddhist traditions the mind is seen as an ocean whose clear nature can only be discerned by calming the waves on top of the ocean, one must attend to the surface first. So in many ways, samatha can be seen as a way of gently bringing a sense of calm atop the ocean so that our experiences may not be so choppy, which will then lead to direct realization.

One very popular and well-known Buddhist practice of samatha is known as *metta* meditation or loving kindness meditation. This form of practice is particularly useful for moments of self-doubt, delusion, anger, hatred, etc. In many ways, this form of practice is quite useful and apropos for addressing the many layers of internalized white supremacy where one's racialized self is measured over and against something that it will never be. The meditation begins with self as object of loving kindness, which is of course akin to bell hooks's claim that self-acceptance and self-love are critical for any kind of justice work. Without cultivating and experiencing openness, love, and acceptance of and for ourselves, we are in many ways groundless despite our desire to be open, loving, and accepting of and for others. I myself am grateful to have a few dear *kalyana mitras*, or good spiritual friends, who remind me of this very fact.

I am not always the best teacher to myself but am fortunate to have others who are constant reminders of what hooks urges in her work *All about Love: New Visions* in which she writes: "Self-love is the foundation of our loving practice. Without it our other efforts to love fail. Giving ourselves love we provide our inner being with the opportunity to have the unconditional love we may have always longed to receive from someone else. . . . We can give ourselves the unconditional love that is the grounding for sustained acceptance and affirmation. When we give this precious gift to ourselves, we are able to reach out to others from a place of fulfillment and not from a place of lack."[13] hooks continues rather poignantly and honestly: "One of the best guides to how to be self-loving is to give ourselves the love we are often dreaming about receiving from others. There was a time when I felt lousy about my over-forty body, saw myself as too fat, too this, or too that. Yet I fantasized about finding a lover who would give me the gift of being loved as I am. It is silly, isn't it, that I would dream of someone else offering to me the acceptance and affirmation I was withholding from myself."[14] Thus, meditation is also deeply tied to an ethics of self-love, a way of being fully in the world, a means of cultivating wholeness, centeredness, and what vipassana teacher Sharon Salzberg refers to as "inner sufficiency" and "inner abundance."[15]

In loving kindness meditation one sits in meditative posture and takes as object of focus the self and wishes the following toward the self: "May I be safe. May I be happy. May I be healthy. May I live with ease." This meditation then extends from self as object to loved one to neutral person to one's enemy. The process of meditation intentionally rests upon the cultivation of self-love as well as a cultivation of love for one's purported enemy who is someone else's primary object of love. In traditional Theravada Buddhism, samatha is the preliminary practice where one calms the emotions to begin the process of deeply looking into the true nature of reality or vipassana described simply as insight meditation.

In vipassana meditation one learns to stabilize attention onto the present moment such that one is no longer haunted by specters past and future. Rather, one learns to gather one's attention and settle one's focus onto an object such as a mantra, a prayer, a sound, sensation in the body, an attribute or feeling of the breath. One of the most common object meditations focuses on the breath and the rising and falling of the breath as it moves through the body and tickles the nostrils. The aim is to recognize thoughts and feelings as they emerge during this meditation but to constantly return to the breath without judgment. The part that is most difficult is in fact this nonjudgment because we are conditioned to judge everything. Thus, the emphasis on the breath requires a gentle moving back to the mind whenever a thought arises and constant starting over rather than as

Salzberg notes "tying knots onto our experiences as good or bad." It is precisely this moment of letting go and starting over that prepares us for everyday life.

Included in this practice is a light awareness of sensations in the body as we explore where the body is right now, how it feels, how does the thing it feels feel? The idea is that we have a light awareness and recognition of the sensation rather than overloading the sensation with the add-ons of judgment. "I am too tired, can't do this, why can't I focus, everyone else looks so good in their focus . . ." Rather than trying to ignore negative emotions, we can learn "just to acknowledge that they are here again and to hold negative emotions with some tenderness." As Salzberg further advises, "in mindfulness, one looks for the add-ons, noting discomfort and what is added on. There is a choice and one can loosen the grasp of add-ons" while attending to how and what one feels and what it feels like. Such practice eventually leads to the ability to see more clearly the constructs imposed on reality such as race, gender, sexuality, and to freedom, "the ability to relate differently to our experience." The power of such practice is the ability to return to the present moment "more gracefully where all that dispersed energy" onto the past and future can be brought back and made more useful for healing and an integration of our being. I would contend that this process is very important to healing from racial stress because it allows a gathering and reforming of the continually assaulted self.

"Body as Skin Sack"

One aspect of insight meditation that has a rather fascinating yet unexpected impact on one's understanding of body is that of seeing the body as a "skin sack," which might initially appear revolting and counterproductive to self-love but I would encourage imagining otherwise. In the *Satipatthana* or the *Sutra on the Four Establishments of Mindfulness*, meditators are taught the following:

> Further, the practitioner meditates on his very own body from the soles of the feet upwards and then from the hair on top of the head downwards, a body contained inside the skin and full of all the impurities which belong to the body: "Here is the hair of the head, the hairs on the body, the nails, teeth, skin, flesh, sinews, bones, bone marrow, kidneys, heart, liver, diaphragm, spleen, lungs, intestines, bowels, excrement, bile, phlegm, pus, blood, sweat, fat, tears, grease, saliva, mucus, synovic fluid, and urine." Bhikkhus [monks], imagine a sack which can be

opened at both ends, containing a variety of grains: brown rice, wild
rice, mung beans, kidney beans, sesame seeds, and white rice. Just so the
practitioner passes in review the whole of his body from the soles of the
feet to the hair on the top of the head, a body enclosed in a layer of skin
and full of all the impurities which belong to the body.[16]

A Buddhist interpretation of body can be helpful insofar as it might allow
for a new space, a new terrain, a new site of identification not beyond, not
above, but within the body. Meditation can thus create a new discursive
space where the raced body can settle into itself, can reinhabit that space
that has been ravaged socially, the space that has rendered invisible or spectacle for many racialized bodies. I employ the term "skin sack," which is
borrowed from Faith Adiele's Thai meditation teacher, Maechi Roong-
duan, who refers to the body as a vehicle that one should not become overly
attached to lest one continue to suffer. While a meditation teacher who
comes from the forest tradition in Thailand utilizes this term in classical
Buddhist thinking as a means of detaching from desire, which leads to
suffering, I reconsider this term as a transformative gift that allows Adiele
to reinhabit the space of her body, a body that has, because of its mixed
race social markings, been the cause of much internal struggle.

The notion of body as skin sack gives rise to a mental revisioning, a
mental means for renegotiating the terms of how bodily inscription affects
the psyche. That is to say, the body as skin sack works to press restart, level
the playing field where one sees body as it is—a skin sack holding together
a complex panoply of blood, bones, organs. Yet, what happens through the
mental deconstruction of the body can be more than a simple detaching
from the desires of the self for permanence, beauty, and agelessness. What
happens is that through the mindful awareness of body as simply "body,"
a Buddhist neutral site emerges where phenomena arise and fall as many a
Buddhist teacher from Rahula to Thich Nhat Hanh teach. A space opens
for that socially vexing body that does not fit in with dominator culture's
vision of what body should be and is interpreted and racially neutralized
even if only for a specific moment in time.

My analysis of body as skin sack does not mean that the individual oblit-
erates racialization and the host of racist statements associated with that
body. Rather, meditation on body as skin sack can provide more than mere
hatred of the body as Buddhist literature might encourage the lustful monk
to adopt. Body as skin sack might allow us to simply look at body as body—a
skin sack or container that contains and holds together all the contents
that would otherwise spill out. Contents that, on the cellular level, are no

different from the bodily contents of all other beings. This notion of body as skin sack therefore can provide an alternative to the continual experience of the body as contents under pressure. There can be a way of cultivating a mindfulness of body through the *Satipatthana* practice where this body is ultimately no different from any other body. Such a process allows one to note where the notion of race emerges—it is an external phenomena or label placed upon a body that is at its core a skin sack holding together natural processes. If understood as such, then one also notes and creates space to allow for a divestment, even if temporarily, from the social stigmatization of certain kinds of bodies. What would happen if we allowed ourselves that temporary divestment and space to reimagine body as a skin sack? Would we venture off into the downward spiral of racial self-loathing? I think not.

The divestment of body from social inscription through meditation has the potential to lead to a reinhabiting of the skin sack we are in. Rather than avoiding or neutralizing race and experiences of racism, meditation allows a rejoining of the mind with the body as it is where the skin, bones, blood, organs are embraced as they are—a temporary constantly changing phenomenon whose energies create this person in this very moment. Perhaps Faith Adiele's conclusion to her memoir sums it up best. She offers the following observations in Thailand after being questioned by a Thai police officer who was confused by her biracial body swathed in Buddhist nun's clothing, "What are you?" Adiele reflects, "It is the first part of the policeman's question that haunts me, at first shaking and annoying me, and then pleasing me that for once identity can't be recognized, assumed, categorized, explained from the outside. That I have indeed accomplished my goal before returning to the West, establishing that there is no easy answer to the question. It's a good question and I honestly consider it, *What am I?*"[17]

One might want to argue that such meditational practices can lead to the obliteration of subjectivity but I would argue otherwise. The practice of mindfulness and notation of the body in its component parts allows for a shift in perception of self that leads to an internal respite from social labeling, race-making, gender-making, and sex-making. It is the relief that allows for the subject to reinhabit the body with a new strategy for living.

Concluding Remarks

As a Buddhist studies scholar, I am often baffled by the lack of discourse on Buddhism and race in the discipline since I believe that the tradition offers methods to peel off the external labels placed upon the bodied self, particularly for people of color whose very bodies have been racialized, rejected, critiqued, and excluded within American Buddhist communities themselves. Thus, I continue to draw attention to how a meditation practice that denies the solidity of the body can be utilized by practitioners whose very bodies have been under assault and whose well-being is in many ways deeply connected with inhabiting the body with agency and positive sense of self. Developing awareness of the elements of the body in transition can be an incredibly powerful and effective practice, yet one that is not ultimately aimed at transcending race as many a white Buddhist may proclaim as a benefit. To develop awareness and objectify the racialized body means to practice divorcing body from external stimuli and their constant bombardment of labels and judgment of being inferior, being exotic, being object for the taking, etc. In this way, Buddhist meditation is not an abstract practice allowing one to transcend dualities and ego self, nor is meditation viewed as a practice of the mind that has little regard for body. It is instead a practice of building a self rather than deconstructing a self even though deconstruction happens. My rereading of meditation removes it from the realm of exotic monks, nuns, *sifus*, and white practitioners aiming to let go of materialism, ego self, and attachment. As a form of resistance, I read meditation as a way of re-entering into a new relationship with the body with all of its glorious corporeal specificity. Such a practice is not exotic in the very least; it is a reparative, recuperative, political strategy for survival.

In concluding this essay, I cannot help but extend its meditative focus back on the field of Asian American studies and wonder what would happen if we began to rethink the field itself in order to revisit the origins and choices that contributed to the creation of what have been highlighted as the gems of the discipline with regard to focus and methodology. In other words, in what ways might the field find a more expansive and ever more creative focus if we engaged in a meditative revisioning of the discipline itself as a kind of reparative, recuperative, and political strategy? In what ways might we reimagine and reimage Asian American studies if we turned that meditative lens upon ourselves as scholars in a discipline whose very nature rests on disciplinary practices embedded in several modes of power. Would we be able to perhaps cling a bit less to our received notions of what constitutes appropriate scholarship in the same ways that meditation encourages us to reimagine ourselves and others? Such is my optative desire for Asian American studies where the perceived centers of what might be considered the darlings of Asian American studies might be transitioned from a position of vertical power to more horizontal positionings where they take their place among a variety of actors and subjects.

NOTES

1. See Joseph Cheah, *Race and Religion in American Buddhism: White Supremacy and Immigrant Adaptation* (Oxford: Oxford University Press, 2011), and Jane Iwamura, *Virtual Orientalism: Asian Religions and American Popular Culture* (Oxford: Oxford University Press, 2011), for in-depth studies of the intersections of Buddhism and race.

2. An Internet search of the term will generate over ten thousand references. These references include scholarly articles, "how to" YouTube videos, workshops and retreats, as well as institutions of higher educations that study the practice.

3. Laurie Cassidy, "Mindful Breathing: Creating Counterpublic Space in the Religious Studies Classroom," *Journal of Feminist Studies in Religion* 2, no.1 (2012): 164–77; bell hooks, "Women Changing Buddhism: Feminist Perspectives," in *Women Practicing Buddhism: American Experiences*, ed. Peter N. Gregory and Susanne Mrozik (Boston: Wisdom, 2008), 67–90; Ann Gleig, "Queering Buddhism or Buddhist De-Queering? Reflecting on Differences amongst Western LGBTQI Buddhists and the Limits of Liberal Convert Buddhism," *Theology and Sexuality* 18, no. 2 (2012): 198–214.

4. See David K. Yoo's special edited volume, "Racial Spirits: Religion & Race in Asian American Communities," *Amerasia Journal* 22, no. 1 (1996).

5. See Khyati Joshi and Sylvia Chan-Malik's coedited special follow-up volume to "Racial Spirits" found in "Asian American Religions in a Globalized World," *Amerasia Journal* 40, no.1 (2014).

6. See Pew Forum on Religion & Public Life, "Asian Americans: A Mosaic of Faiths," Pew Research Center, Washington, D.C., August 19, 2012, http://www.pewforum.org/2012/07/19/asian-americans-a-mosaic-of-faiths-overview/.

7. A noted exception is the East Bay Meditation Center in Oakland, California, and the People of Color and Allies Sangha associated with the Seattle Insight Meditation Center. Similarly, the renowned insight meditation center, Spirit Rock, hosts an annual People of Color Silent Meditation retreat.

8. See Sharon A. Suh, *Being Buddhist in a Christian World: Gender and Community in a Korean American Temple* (Seattle: University of Washington Press, 2004), and *Silver Screen Buddha: Buddhism in Asian and Western Film* (London: Bloomsbury Press, 2015).

9. bell hooks, *Writing beyond Race: Living Theory and Practice* (New York: Routledge, 2013), 11.

10. hooks, *Writing beyond Race*, 25.

11. Faith Adiele, *Meeting Faith: The Forest Journals of a Black Buddhist Nun* (New York: W.W. Norton, 2000), 24.

12. Ibid., 10.

13. bell hooks, *All about love: New Visions* (New York: Harper Collins, 2000), 66.

14. hooks, *All about love*, 66–67.

15. I had the fortune of attending a day-long meditation retreat with Sharon Salzberg in 2013 and have taken the liberty of inserting some of her own words into this essay.

16. I purposefully utilize Thich Nhat Hanh's translation of the *Satipat-thana Sutta* because its translation is aimed at a general public, thus his translation of the original texts is quite clear. Thich Nhat Hanh, *Awakening of the Heart: Essential Buddhist Sutras and Commentaries* (Berkeley, Calif.: Parallax, 2012),105.

17. Adiele, *Meeting Faith*, 280.

CHAPTER 16

What Is Passed On (Or, Why We Need Sweetened Condensed Milk for the Soul)

Brandy Liên Worrall-Soriano

I'm writing this book in another book. Both books have essentially the same story.

About the book in which I am writing: I made it in July 2005. It was my finished project for a bookbinding class I took one weekend at Emily Carr University of Art and Design in Vancouver. The instructor, to my absolute delight, was Wade Berridge, who makes the prototypes for Paperblanks journals. I am a total Paperblanks junkie. Paperblanks journals are beautiful things of mass-produced art. To me this class was like getting a guitar lesson from Prince.

In this particular class, we learned the technique for making an exposed-cord journal, where you can see the cords that run through the front cover, connect the folios, and run through the back cover, ends to ends, which in my journal are knotted off with thick beads resembling jade earrings.

By the time Wade had finished giving an overview of the history and technique of this type of bookbinding, I knew what my first handmade book would be. I took the postage stamp–sized, black-and-white picture from the journal in which I was writing at the time. I carried the tiny photo with me because I was writing a book about it, and I needed a reminder of the actual discoverable genesis of my mom's—and therefore, my—story. The picture is of my mother's mother—Ba ngoai—my "outside" grandmother. (*Ba noi* is the word for paternal grandmother or "inside" grandmother.) I don't even know her first name, but I do know she committed suicide in Vietnam by eating rat poison. Even after publishing my first memoir in 2014, about my family's trauma from the Vietnam/American War, I still don't know much about Ba ngoai beyond the facts that she killed herself and that my mother loved her very much.

I sit here, writing into this book I made more than a decade ago, drinking my coffee with sweetened condensed milk, a bit speechless. I look at Ba ngoai's face on the cover of my handmade book—The Book of My Outside Grandmother. I see the faint outline of the jagged edges of the photograph. I had put excruciating detail into the making of this book. I sewed a lot of meaning into it—its spine exposed, ten folios of pages ripped to mimic the frame around Ba ngoai's face. For years I hadn't written much in it, only this first paragraph:

> 21 September 2005
> Mom hesitates to write in here. She says she needs to think first. I tell her "Mom, just write. Just write about Ba ngoai, anything you can think of. Don't worry about it." It's no use. What I'd put in her hand was left in the computer room, next to a bunch of other paper products, as if she were trying to hide this book.

I had planned to find out more about Ba ngoai—the outside grandma I never knew. But over the years, I instead found out more about my mother, father, and older half-sister (and my secret older dead half-brother, and even very recently my secret older dead half-sister)—not about my grandmother who killed herself. The book I'm writing in this book is about how most of my immediate family, including myself, have attempted to kill themselves, sometimes with fatal consequences. And it's about other things we don't talk about.

It's about what some people call mental health, but what I call spirit, and how broken it is after forty-plus years since the end of the war. It's about how I'm trying to expose the spine, to see what's there so we can try to fix our broken spirit, individually and collectively.

As a young adult cancer survivor, I've often heard said to me that all the bad stuff that's happened in my life is to serve a purpose—so I can serve a purpose—to help people and inspire them to talk about their pain—whether that be about cancer or war. It's rare to meet someone whose life hasn't been affected by cancer or war, and that's unbelievably sad when you think about it. But all those people, most of the human race, they can't find the space to share their spirit break and trauma. It's excruciating.

When I was a girl, my mom would sometimes bring home a treat from her Saturday afternoon grocery trip. After putting away the twenty two-liter bottles of Pepsi and Diet Pepsi and eggs and milk, she and I would sit down with a warm loaf of crusty french bread and a can of sweetened condensed milk between us. I remember the first time she taught me her beloved Vietnamese treat, when I was about eight years old. She broke the loaf in half and dug her fingers and thumbs into the pillowy middle of the bread and tore out a soft, steamy ball. Then she dipped it into the can, or into the mug of coffee sweetened light brown by the same goopy milk. I remembered my first time doing it. It was one of those "first times" I'll always remember because it was so fucking amazing (I wonder how many Asians remember their first sweetened condensed milk experience).

Then Mom began to talk about Ba ngoai—another "first time" I'll never forget. About how her mother had beaten her so badly and how she made my mom give her all her money that she had made since she stopped going to school and went working as a maid at age eight, and how her lazy and abusive brother and father had never worked. But my mom still loved her mother and missed her a lot. My abusive/abused grandma who killed herself with rat poison (though that first time I heard about Ba ngoai, I only knew the abusive/abused part). I actually wasn't paying that much attention, other than it was strange that she was talking about her mom and that she loved her so much that she didn't care she never saw love from her mother other than abuse being seen as love. That's the kind of love she passed onto my sister, who is "full" Vietnamese, and to a lesser extent, me, the "American One."

When my dad passed away almost three years ago, we time-traveled back to the 1970s, from before I was born, until the 1990s, when I left home to go to college. It was the period in which my sister experienced most of the abuse, from our mother and my sister's first husband, sometimes so severe she'd end up in the hospital, and no one from my dad's family ever mentioned giving a damn. They said they thought it was Mom's "culture," so they didn't say anything or call police or child services. My sister recalls feeling that my dad's parents, aunts, uncles, and cousins were willing to let her die. That's what I'm thinking when my family tells me stories of when Mom took a hammer to the television set when she got home from work and saw my sister watching a show instead of making dinner. Or how they knew my mom made my sister go outside and find branches with thorns that my mom would use to beat her with. I'm stunned by the brutality and how no one ever intervened. And then I feel guilty because that would have never happened to me—everyone knew that. I was the American One; no one dared lay a hand on me. I didn't grow up with a knife under my pillow like my sister did.

While my sister had been fearing for her life, trying to make it from one day to the next until she got married and moved out before the end of high school, my father took classes at Harrisburg Area Community College (HACC). Dad never talked much about his time at HACC, where he got a higher education on the GI Bill. But before he died, I found an essay he wrote for his English composition class, dated June 23, 1975, five months and two days before I was born. His essay follows mine.

What's striking about his essay is how passionately and astutely my dad wrote about the refugee crisis at the time and how the U.S. government should take responsibility for this damaged population, just how the U.S. government (kind of) takes care of its soldiers and vets from the same war. He begins his essay with a personal anecdote, of the moment that he and my mom realized that the country was going to fall to communism. He wrote about that moment so artfully that I could see how he could have been a memoirist, if he had lived long enough, and with enough neurological and intellectual capacity left, which diminished quickly in large part due to the two decades of lithium that was for his supposed bipolar disorder—symptoms of which I had never seen in my father. He was never super high, elated, happy even. He was always depressed. He always sank in his chair and slouched from the sedative numbing effects of all the drugs the government sent him every month in big boxes driven up the long driveway by UPS, for twenty years up until he died from metastatic lung cancer due to his exposure to Agent Orange. But Dad loved the drugs. Anything to get him high or make him pass out so he didn't think about the graphic trauma he played out in his head everyday.

When he died, I found all of Dad's rehab and AA journals and handbooks. He tried—he really, really tried. But I was not prepared for what I read when he described the trauma he experienced in Vietnam. It was a nightmare worse than *Apocalypse Now*. Dad saw that shit, felt that—you could not get a more visceral experience than what my father had had. But he got help. He had a space where he got to talk about it—to connect with other human beings who experienced the same horrors and who therefore understood. My mother did not have that. I think about that all the time.

I do write in humorous ways how my mom is different—how weird and religiously fervent she is, the funny things she says, the things that get lost in translation between us. But when I *know* what my dad had experienced, I can only imagine what my mother had experienced at the same time. I've heard stories of how her uncle (her mother's brother) threatened to kill her mother when my mom married my dad. I heard about how her brother called her a whore, how she lost children and babies. The whole time she and my father were together until his sudden death, almost forty-five years, she kept her trauma under lock and key. No one offered my mom therapy—I don't think there was anyone even trained to deal with someone like her, a refugee isolated by language and culture, someone who's lost a lot of family and whose world was completely different and unwelcoming. It's only now that my father has been dead almost three years, and my sister and I have tried the best we can to teach Mom what it takes to live without him—he who was her translator and the only person who understood her best—only now am I seeing how Asian American studies fails refugees and other communities affected by war trauma. Both of my parents have experienced the same war trauma, but the disparity in benefits between the two demographics is alarming.

As a student interested in the social welfare and psychological challenges of the refugee population, my dad foresaw this and engaged in these issues in an anthropological insider, activist way. He knew the refugees would get the shaft. Headlines that have come across my newsfeed over the years make it sound like it's not going to get better. We hear of stories of Hmong immigrants with PTSD who murder their families or how Asian American university students have high suicide rates. We need to stop NOT talking about mental health or the Asian American spirit. When you read my dad's essay that follows, you will be struck by how his words of over forty years ago echo the refugee situation today. And what have we done? We have a chance to learn and say, "We need to tell each other stories about how our lives got fucked up. We need to support one another. This demon, it's real."

Since my father died, my sister and I have taken on various forms of depression, anxiety disorders, and substance abuse, as if we were taking turns being various pieces of Dad. Mom's trauma is so deep, she has so much distrust of everyone, including me and my sister, but she convinces herself she needs to trust us. According to our Vietnamese family, my sister and I are losers. One of us should be living with her and taking care of her 100 percent of the time, "like kids do in Vietnam," never mind that we have our own families. It's at moments like this when I'm thankful that I live across the continent from my mother.

But my sister is there, at Mom's beck and call. It's wearing her down so thin, my sister constantly tries to disappear herself by drinking a bottle of wine between noon and 3 P.M. everyday. She replays in her brain how she and her older brother were separated, and he ended up dying, homeless, from stepping on a poisoned spike. That's one of the stories being told. The other is that he killed himself because he couldn't take Uncle abusing him anymore. Or maybe a combination of those stories. I've heard that version. Whatever the truth—we won't know. It's driving my sister crazy. Mom is not helping, as she's finally talking about our brother, after Dad died and she felt free to talk about him. My dad didn't know Hieu existed until recently. He didn't know my mom had a son she left behind in Vietnam because she didn't think my dad would marry her if he knew she had two kids instead of just one. So she told Dad that Hieu was her nephew. He didn't know my mom had this son who was left behind and died, until the last few days he was alive. I don't know how much he did know, though. I doubt he knew about the first child she gave birth to when she was a teenager, a little girl who died when she was three. Mom casually brought up my dead half-sister, Xanh, before we went to Vietnam together for the first time a couple years ago.

So now I'm watching my sister and mother play out their trauma and torture each other everyday. And how, how do I get them help? All the training that I had in Asian American studies, getting my master's at UCLA and then becoming editor at *Amerasia Journal*, none of it has trained me to deal with this trauma.

When I did my book tour in 2015 (the fortieth anniversary of the Fall of Saigon), I was surprised by how many Asian American—Vietnamese American, mostly—students came up to me at the end of my readings and told me that they finally kind of understood why they felt these impressions of trauma without having experienced the trauma firsthand. Generational trauma. It was first studied using Holocaust survivors and their children. Why do children, or even grandchildren, who had not experience the Holocaust, have feelings of having been traumatized? My book isn't scientific, but my experiences coming from it and the connections I made tell me that genetically inherited trauma is real. When will the government begin to service the refugee population, in particular insofar as mental health goes?

My sister is getting help. I've convinced her it was worth it. I told her how I've been doing therapy for half my life, how I'm on antidepressants, how I began the process of loving detachment. So she started going. Her therapy is very much in its infancy, but it's a start.

A few months ago, my mother had a major psychotic breakdown and spent over a week involuntarily checked into a mental health facility. I flew to Pennsylvania to help put out these fires. My sister and I got blamed for putting our mother into this hospital, though it was solely Mom's present actions that got her there—that and her traumatic past that erupted. It sounds weird, but I am thankful for my mother's breakdown because I never ever had any hope that she would get the mental health care she so desperately needs and has needed. Her treatment is not perfect; her unfortunate translator who followed her from group to group and to our family meetings in the hospital was a college kid who just wanted to make some money, and who looked extremely uncomfortable when the doctor would ask him to translate questions in Vietnamese to my mother. Even that kid knew you can't ask "those types" of questions to an elder in your community, and especially not in front of a group of people. Alas, we navigated those waters, day by day, and continue to do so.

Forty-plus years, and where are we with seriously giving a damn about Asian American groups with disabilities, mental illness, and trauma? Over the last decade, I've looked to my own story, and those of my family, to confront that question, mostly because I have no choice. I've inherited depression, anxiety, PTSD, chronic pain/fatigue, and autoimmune illnesses from my parents, from my individual and collective history. I know my mom and sister won't read this essay. But if we, as activists, artists, and academics, are to continue our mission in Asian American studies, to address the social ills in our communities, we need to read more stories like mine and my family's.

We've made great strides in diagnosing and treating the social ills in our Asian American communities. But it's time we put disability, mental illness, and trauma on the radar, at the forefront, of Asian American studies and our communities. We need the recognition. We need the discussion. We need the release. We need the collective sigh. We need the support and the space to hold ourselves as we need to be held, and then to be able to let go.

"Refugees Today—Americans Tomorrow"[1]
    By Walter L. Worrall
    English Composition 102, Section 2333
    June 23, 1975
    I sensed that something was wrong when I walked in the house and
saw my wife sitting, staring out the window at nothing in particular.
The letter that she held in her hand was written in Vietnamese.
Although I could not read the contents of it, I was able to understand
what it contained by the expression on her face. After several seconds

of silence, she stated with disbelief in her voice, "It's all over. There's no hope left." I searched for a way to comfort her, but it was very hard because I also realized that the fall of her country was going to take place in the near future.

This was the last letter we received from her parents, and it forced me to face what most Americans were denying—that communist victory was certain to come in Vietnam. And come it did, less than three weeks later.

When the end of the war came, the United States was left to make the decision to aid the refugees of Vietnam or to turn their backs on them. Most of the citizens of Vietnam felt that the Americans had let them down in wartime, as the following statement from a Vietnamese soldier points out: "Vietnamese soldiers and Vietnamese people hate the Americans so much—the Americans have left us without notice, without aid."[2] With these thoughts in mind, most citizens began to wonder if America would be of any help after the war. "My God, said an anguished old Vietnamese gentleman in Oxford English as he passed some foreigners in street, are you Americans really going to let this happen to us?"[3] With this question, he spoke for many.

As it turned out, the United States did decide to aid as many refugees of Vietnam as it possibly could. This decision brought dissent from people all over the country. In a *Time* magazine interview many persons voiced the opinion that we should forget about Vietnam, and act as though it was nothing more than a nightmare. One man stated, "People are drained. They want to bury the memory of Indochina. They regard it as a tragic chapter in American life, but they want no further part of it."[4] The words of another person interviewed were similar: "The feeling is that we have made a considerable contribution to Cambodia and South Vietnam and that we've done enough."[5] I think that all persons who have this "we don't owe them anything" attitude should evaluate the circumstances surrounding their forced flight from their own country.

When the communists gained control of Vietnam, many of the refugees who fled to this country would have been executed in a matter of days had they remained in their homeland. Why? Because they believed in the Americans: not only the ones who had direct dealings with the Americans would be murdered, but the ones who were involved with us indirectly would also have been killed. This adds up to many individuals, and a large number of them were not able to make it out of the country. It took money or pull to get on a refugee flight, and these were things most of the Vietnamese people did not possess. As one friend told me on her arrival in the United States: "It cost some folks as much as five hundred dollars just to get inside the airport, and then they weren't guaranteed on a flight out."[6]

Having lived in Vietnam for four years, both as a soldier and a civilian, I honestly feel that what happened to the Vietnamese people can be blamed on the American government. And since the government supposedly is run by the people, everyone should accept their share of the blame. We promised them victory over the enemy, corrupted their young, showed them a new way of life which we said was better than what they had, and in general, we raised their hopes and expectations beyond their wildest dreams. After all of this, we just pulled out and said, "We want nothing more to do with you and *your* war." Taking all of this into consideration, I don't see how anybody can say that we don't owe them anything.

I fear that many people are against the Vietnamese not for economic reasons, but just because they are blind racists. This is indicated by an elected official from California: "Republican Representative Burt L. Talcott suggested that, damn it, we have too many Orientals already. If they gravitate to California, the tax and welfare rolls will get overburdened and we already have our share of illegal aliens."[7] I wonder what nation Mr. Talcott's family tree leads to? And how can he say that they are illegal aliens when Immigration Services has a record of each and every one of them? I think that he need not fear, because no one in his right mind would want to settle in an area where the politicians are dumb and ignorant of the world around them! Perhaps the citizens of California should elect a refugee to replace Mr. Talcott in the next election. The West Coast wasn't the only area heard from. Representative William Randall of Independence, Missouri, said that he had received dozens of calls from constituents saying: "We want no part of them in our area."[8] It seems as though an emphasis was placed on the number of persons against the refugee program, but the number of people in favor of aiding them was kept quiet.

Like it or not, there are 130,000 Vietnamese refugees in the United States, and they have enough problems to face without the added burden of racists jumping on their backs every time they make a move.

Many of the Vietnamese refugees are still trying to figure out what has happened to their lives in the last couple of months. As was stated in *Newsweek*, ". . . echoing a charge by fellow Democrat George McGovern, Kennedy also declared that the evacuation had swept up hundreds of Vietnamese who fled in panic—not fully understanding where they are now or how they got there."[9]

The refugees are going to face many trying situations in the months ahead. They have been thrown in a culture which is entirely different from the one they have been living in. Our customs and way of life are the complete reverse of theirs, and it is going to be a very hard adjustment for some of them to make, especially the peasants who never associated with the Americans before coming to this country. Adding a language barrier to this problem, many of them will be ready to throw in the towel before they give their new life a chance.

In addition to these problems, employment will be next to impossible for some to secure. Many of the refugees are uneducated, and they have never done any type of work but fishing and farming. How much of a demand is there for fishermen in the country? Not much, I'm afraid. The only hope for these people might come from places other than the United States. Julia Taft has stated, "Guam is showing a particular interest in having qualified fishermen settle there."[10] Ex-Premier Ky has plans for the farmers: "We will plant rice and stay out of your cities. We want to avoid trouble for the American people. We will be quiet—and far, far away from your cities."[11] This idea to buy farming land sounds like a good, workable plan, but will the Americans let them live in a world of their own? It will be difficult for the educated to find employment also. They might end up taking a job that requires much less skill and knowledge than they are capable of producing in order to support their families. This will be a difficult transition for some to make.

The problems of racism, culture difference, language barriers, and employment would be enough to make any adult feel uncertain of his life, and the Vietnamese are no different than anyone else. These problems have already caused some to express a desire to return to Vietnam, whatever evils might be waiting for them on their return. "A total of 1,264 has said that they want to go back home, and the number of those who would privately like to return is doubtless much higher," a *Time* article stated.[12] There are other reasons that make some want to return to Vietnam, other than the ones I have already stated. *Time* reported, "Some elderly Vietnamese have expressed the desire to return with the classic outcasts' plaint: I want to die in my own country."[13] This is a request that has been made by people from all societies at one time or another.

Julia Taft, Head of the Refugee Program, has said that the refugees are facing a difficult situation, and if the American people refuse to accept and aid them, the situation will be impossible for them to cope with. "Some of the refugees, particularly the elderly, will meet many psychological problems in the months ahead, and they will need our support to survive."[14]

In addition to all the human problems they are facing, the refugees are being confronted with processing difficulties. It seems like a never-ending process that one must complete before obtaining a release from a refugee center. *Newsweek* reported, "Red tape, the search for sponsors, and special screening procedures for 'undesirables' slow the flow of refugees into the civilian world to a trickle."[15] Before their processing is completed, a refugee must complete paperwork for six federal agencies. The most difficult stage of the processing is the issuance of a security clearance. A person must be thoroughly scrutinized before a security clearance is issued, and this process takes anywhere from three to six weeks.

After the processing is completed, a refugee cannot leave the center until sponsorship is received. There is a shortage of sponsors, and some refugees might never get out of the centers. In order to sponsor a Vietnamese, several requirements must be agreed to. Among these requirements is the agreement to support the refugee until he receives employment and becomes self-supporting. This is more than most people are willing or able to do, especially since the economic outlook is not very bright in most parts of the country.

However, time spent in the refugee center is not a complete loss for most. The government is utilising this time to educate and train those refugees who need it. They are being taught basic English and job skills by qualified instructors. The Head of the Refugee Program offered, "We have hopes of training the refugees so that most can become self-supporting within one year."[16]

While the emphasis has been placed on the difficulties that the refugees are facing, one important fact has been overlooked by most people. The fact is the number of children who are among the refugees. This figure has been placed at sixty percent, and not all of the problems facing the adults will affect them.

Most of these Vietnamese children will easily adapt to the American way of life. Within one year, most will consider themselves Americans, and they will have forgotten most of what they learned as citizens of Vietnam. Language and culture changes will not be major problems to them. On a recent visit to Fort Indiantown Gap Military Reservation, I observed many Vietnamese children playing tag, baseball, and other games. And this was after only several weeks in this country! Also, I have a Vietnamese daughter whom I adopted and brought to this country four years ago. She is a straight "A" student, and is as much of an American as any other youngster in her class. A friend has just returned from Saigon with two of his wife's nieces. As he complained to me, "The girls have only been here for two weeks, and already they prefer hamburger to rice! My wife just doesn't understand this change, and it upsets her to no end."[17]

These few examples should serve to illustrate that while life is going to be a trial for the adult refugees, the children among them are going to adjust pretty fast. After taking away the children from their numbers, that only leaves forty percent to be dealt with. That should make the odds sound a little better to those folks who are full of doubt about the whole program.

Since we chose to retreat and allowed the communists to gain power in Indochina, I think that it is only fair that we help those people to whom we have brought so much suffering. The average citizen of Vietnam could not have prevented the takeover anymore than you or I could have, so why should they have to pay? The way I see it, most of the burden for defeat rests not on their shoulders, but on ours.

The refugees are not going to cause any major disaster to our troubled economy as some fear, due to the fact that most of them will be forced to take jobs that the average American refuses to accept. Any employment agency will tell you that there are many of these jobs open, but they cannot find people to fill them.

Considering the whole situation, I feel that the refugees can become an asset to this country of ours. While many people would disagree with me on this point, if they had a better understanding of what the Vietnamese are really like, some would certainly change their opinions. Given a fair chance, most of the refugees will prove themselves in more ways than one, and they will become proud citizens of America. Would the average American want this chance if the situation was reversed, and they were on the receiving end? Speaking for myself, the answer is definitely yes.

NOTES

Dedicated to Walter "Walt" Lee Worrall and Don Nakanishi, two of my biggest influences in the field of Asian American studies.

1. On the last page of my father's typewritten essay, the professor wrote: "A. A worthwhile subject well researched!"

2. "Is This What America Has Left?" *Time*, April 7, 1975, 33–34.

3. "The Yanks Are Going," *Newsweek*, April 14, 1975, 33.

4. "Why They Flee," *Time*, April 14, 1975, 22.

5. Ibid.

6. Nga (Vietnamese refugee), interview by Walter L. Worrall, June 8, 1975.

7. "The New Americans," *Newsweek*, May 5, 1975, 37–38.

8. "The Last Exit from Saigon," *Newsweek*, May 5, 1975, 33.

9. "Red Tape," *Newsweek*, May 26, 1975, 34.

10. Julia Taft, television interview on the refugee program, CBS, *Morning News*, May 27, 1975.

11. Jeff Werner, "Ex-Premier Ky: We Will Plant Rice and Stay out of Your Cities," *People*, May 26, 1975, 14–15.

12. "Some Yearn to Return Home," *Time*, June 9, 1975, 17.

13. Ibid.

14. Taft interview, May 27, 1975.

15. David M. Alpern, "Hail from the Chief," *Newsweek*, May 19, 1975, 16.

16. Taft interview, May 27, 1975.

17. Nick Gallagos (former contractor employee in Saigon), interview by Walter L. Worrall, June 6, 1975.

CHAPTER 17

An Ethics of Generosity

Min Hyoung Song

1.1

An ethics of generosity is called for because so much of contemporary life is being filtered through a dominant system of beliefs that is often referred to loosely as "neoliberalism." This system privileges individuals and their right to maximize self-interest regardless of consequences to others. This habit of thought deliberately undervalues the enormous generosity that we are all beneficiaries of. Everyday, someone picks up our trash, tends the food we eat, makes the clothes that keep us warm, treats us when we get sick, creates stories that entertain us, produces new knowledge that expands what we can know about the world. For some of us, or for all of us on some days, acts of extraordinary generosity are all that keep us from falling into despair or dropping out of life altogether. Generosity is everywhere. And yet it can be difficult to acknowledge. We are somehow ignorant to it. What I am offering in this document is highly speculative, in that it seeks to make visible something that is operating all around us in near invisibility. I intentionally do not mention any critics by name or cite any specific scholarly sources because I do not want this document to personalize issues that feel to me to transcend individual persons. Personalizing works against my goal of making generosity more visible.

1.2

Although I have rarely come across this argument in scholarly writing, I have heard informally from many people I respect that they no longer want anyone to use the word "neoliberalism." The argument goes something like this: It is a trendy term that takes the place of other trendy terms, like "globalization," "postmodernism," and "late capitalism." It may have had a precise meaning at one time, but it has morphed into a term that is asked to mean too many different things; it has, in essence, become a way to disparage phenomenon we don't like. It also allows us to position ourselves always ever leftward to another, so that no matter what another might try to argue or present or narrate he or she betrays complicity with neoliberalism. It is a totalizing term from which there is no escape, and as such leads to a paradoxically conservative position.

1.3

This argument continues: If there is no alternative, if we remain always neoliberal no matter what we think we believe, its ubiquity leads us either to submit to the inevitable or to participate in a constant critique. If we accept the former, we rationalize acceptance of the status quo as inevitable. This is a kind of realism that says what we have is all we can have. Maybe it's even the best of all possible worlds. If we choose the latter, we end up engaged in a routinized and predictable critical activity. X claims to be Y but is in fact really neoliberal deep down. We find everywhere a duplicity that must be uncovered. If these become our only options, perhaps we are better off eschewing the use of the term? Might such eschewal allow us to develop a more precise and sophisticated vocabulary that can help us to understand the present better? What if all of this talk about neoliberalism is actually a way not to talk about capitalism and the kinds of exploitation on which it has always depended?

1.4

The flipside of this argument, much more explicitly written about, is that neoliberalism is on everyone's lips because it is everywhere. It is the very horizon that defines the present, and to ignore it would be to do so delib-

erately. The insistence on the importance of keeping the term in our critical vocabulary is largely premised on the idea that the present has entered
into some novel phase of capitalism, or maybe simply history itself. The
social heterogeneity that once could be taken for granted has been lost to
us. What remains is a singular model of being, sometimes describes as a
homo economicus, when before we had other models that were exempt from
the demands of the market. The present is thus a kind of postlapsarian moment that exists ever in the shadow of a time before, when—despite whatever limitations defined it—liberalism and the state worked together to
promote economic and wealth parity, liberty of inquiry, and spaces for ex-
perimentation that actively accepted failure as a precondition for any possibility for genuine innovation.

1.5

The argument in favor of keeping neoliberalism in critical circulation continues: Politics as we once understood it has been replaced by the language of governance. Governmentality, as it is sometimes referred to, is
in part an administration through consensus, best practices, and accumulation of metrics rather than a reaching of decisions through democratic
participation and active debate. It is how a for-profit corporation might
operate. As the logic of the marketplace invades all facets of human interaction that heretofore was somehow exempt from thinking in this way,
language is contorted and mangled so that we end up always speaking the
validity of this logic. We seek greater efficiency, inclusivity by identifying
and involving stakeholders, effective management of diversity, and civility
as a precondition to free speech. We value reason, if by "reason" we mean
what best guarantees a status quo where buying and selling are our most
important activities. If neoliberalism names a total phenomenon, as many
critics fear it does, we may have reached a moment when critique itself has
found its limits. The marketplace is now everything and everywhere. To
point this out is merely to point out something we are powerless to change.
We may instead want to seek some hybrid deformity within this discourse
that can lead us not beyond its horizons, which is impossible, but to a kind
of turning inside-out or a making monstrous.

1.6

Confronted by such opposing arguments, it is difficult to know how to
think about a term like *neoliberalism*—especially when we consider that the

presentation here is itself simplifying a much larger, more byzantine set of concepts with many different genealogies. Those critical of its continued usage understandably do not use it much in their writings. We might wonder, should we give up on it because it has lost its precision or hold fast to it because it names something important about the present? Neoliberalism almost certainly has become a catchall term for disparaging what we do not like and for making easy critiques that cannot offer genuine alternatives to whatever is being critiqued. It can too easily depend on an uncritical nostalgia for a golden age that has somehow just come to an end. It has on frequent occasion led discussion outside the realm of political economy into more cultural or discursive byways and in doing so perhaps become a more polite way of talking about a much longer existing system of profit-making based on exploitation. It is, in other words, a way of talking about capitalism when we do not want to use that word or to contend with the red-baiting that often accompanies it. At the same time, neoliberalism seems to name something important about the present, so that completely forsaking it feels unattractive. We *are* in a crucial moment of crisis. Much of this crisis is exacerbated by a pervasive tendency to reduce all social relationships to the logic of market exchanges. This kind of reduction endangers what were once semiautonomous spheres of social activity.

1.7

Asian Americans have a special interest in this debate about the utility of "neoliberalism." Because they are so frequently cast as members of a model minority, they are also viewed as being singularly focused on their individual gain. Such a focus precludes concern for the struggles of others. All that matters is that they maximize their economic self-interest and wrest from the status quo a privileged place among its elites. Asian Americans are becoming, in other words, the premier neoliberal subject, a *homo economicus* devoid of any motivation other than personal gain. We can see how the most visible Asian American political struggles reinforce this view. For instance, an Asian American student, with the support of like-minded civic institutions, sued Harvard for discrimination. The lawsuit claimed that its policies were deliberately limiting the number of Asian Americans on their campus by taking a holistic approach to admissions rather than focusing on the more objective measures of grades and standardized test scores. As critics—many of whom were Asian American—argued, this lawsuit replicates antiaffirmative action claims that disadvantage other minorities. This argument is made in lockstep with cases such as *Abigail Fisher v. University of Texas*, in that like the claims made in these other cases it hides the pursuit of selfish goals behind a guise of abstract meritocracy.

2.1

When we try to adjudicate the question of the term's usefulness, it's helpful to ask, why has neoliberalism become so ubiquitous now? Why is the phenomenon so visible and easy to name? One possible response is that the strategy for capital accumulation we call neoliberalism is reaching its own moment of crisis after having enjoyed a period of strengthening dominance. As it reaches saturation, where the easiest profits have all been fully exploited, it must necessarily turn its logic onto other forms of social activity that have not before been completely brought under its regime and are therefore still available for the extraction of profit.

2.2

The value of a university education is now being actively turned into a question of simple return on investment because it has until recently not been exclusively valued in this manner. If a way could be found to lower the cost of investment—such as converting labor-intensive brick-and-mortar universities serving a few thousand students to virtual sites run by a much smaller number of poorly paid technicians and overseen by well-paid administrators that can serve hundreds of thousands of students—investors could then reap the rewards of operating such educational sites on a massive economy of scale. In the process, other universities that cannot make this kind of transition must be phased out because they will be at a competitive disadvantage. What was once understood to be a public service that by its very nature could not directly produce profit might thus become a source of enormous profit for a few. This process of bringing the university more explicitly into the market is accompanied by the language of customer-centered satisfaction, robust competition, increasing efficiency, and disruption for its own sake. Students are made into consumers, and maybe even products.

2.3

As neoliberalism turns to these kinds of ventures, profits are not as high or as easy to get as investors might hope, and the application of this logic becomes more visible and produces more opposition. There is a reason why universities cannot easily be converted into a profitable business venture. A university education, much like elementary school and high school (and the practice of medicine and legal work), requires a lot of labor that cannot be simply automated. If costs are to be brought down so that money is available to be extracted as profit, highly skilled workers need to be paid less and less-skilled workers must increasingly be substituted for more-skilled workers. The quality of the service inevitably goes down. At the same time, since generating profit is the primary objective, tuition must continue to go up. Students are thus constantly being asked to pay more for less, especially at public schools that are most directly affected by the harsh application of this logic. Moreover, the attempt to make the university a primarily for-profit business enterprise necessarily demonizes ideas of education that view it as more than an investment seeking high returns, such as enabling opportunities for greater civic involvement, thoughtful and guided inquiry into abstract existential questions, and acquiring greater independence of thought. Such ideas, long cherished, are not easily demonized.

2.4

What all of this means is that neoliberalism as a strategy for generating profit for investors, while continuing to be destructive of anything that isn't operated completely in terms of market competitiveness, is breaking down and losing its capacity to produce what is most sought after. If true, we can speak so easily about neoliberalism because neoliberalism does not work as quietly and as well as it once did, and new strategies for the accumulation of wealth must be found. I am speaking about neoliberalism mostly in relation to the wealth it might be capable of producing to highlight how, even by this narrowly defined measure, what is becoming increasingly evident is that it is failing.

2.5

Perhaps neoliberalism has always been a failure, even when defined solely in economic terms, since the profit it produces is more often than not just a redistribution of wealth rather than the actual production of new wealth. The enormous global inequalities in income and especially wealth that have marked the last several decades should therefore be understood as a feature of neoliberalism, for it makes profits for an elite group of investors by extracting wealth from everyone else. Lack and austerity are all signs of an economic situation where enormous amounts of capital seeking ever-higher rates of return are stymied by the paucity of investment opportunities. When every avenue for profit has been maximized and exploited to its fullest potential, capital is forced to create opportunities where there were none by shuffling wealth around. Capital cannibalizes itself.

2.6

One reason to keep neoliberalism on our list of keywords is that it provides a highly visible name for how social relatedness is now so dominated by the mediation of market logic. This dominance is not a permanent state of affairs but better thought of as a stage of capitalism. The growing ease with which we talk about neoliberalism might thus signal the approach of a coming crisis in meaning-making in capitalism, when accepted ways of doing things are becoming more and more unacceptable. What was once largely taken for granted becomes available for widespread and more public scrutiny. What was excluded or marginalized in discourse has an opportunity to be re-examined. The range of ideas we can talk about widens. Ideas connected to socialism and fascism in the United States (and elsewhere), for example, are making an appearance in public discourse and, in the process, are losing some of the stigma that were once attached to them.

2.7

This is the moment to fight like hell for the ideas we believe in and despaired were consigned permanently to the outer bounds of acceptable discourse. This is also the moment to fight like hell to make sure ideas that belong in the dustbin of history stay there. What are the ideas that are most important to us? How can those ideas be connected so they amplify each other rather than cancel each other out? What strategies draw others to find solidarity with these ideas and see in them a truth they want to champion? An important intellectual task at the present moment is the imagination of alternatives to neoliberalism and a passionate resolve to explain why some alternatives are better than others. This is a difficult task because, even as the range of ideas being considered widens, ideas that favor greater authoritarianism, more law and order, and heightened exploitation of natural resources are heavily favored by those who currently benefit most from the existing social order and even by those who, often hurt deeply by this social order, fear what the alternatives might be. Proponents of more democracy, greater wealth equity, redress of social injustices, and acknowledgment of ecological limits face a steep uphill struggle.

3.1

In its contemporary usage, generosity refers to a kind of excess. It means giving more than we need to. It is doing more than is expected of us. Someone asks for a dollar; we give them ten. Someone asks for directions; we take the time to show them on a map exactly how to get to where they are going and then walk part of the way there with them, or perhaps all the way. Someone who doesn't speak the local language asks if anyone speaks his or hers; we do or we don't, but we nevertheless take the time to try to communicate and to find out what we can do to help. Someone suddenly starts to cry; we spend the next hour or two letting him and listening to whatever he feels comfortable sharing. We give money. We give time. We give labor. We give our attention. We do more than what others feel comfortable asking of us or what others believe possible.

3.2

What is noteworthy about generosity as excess is that it involves acting in a way that is contrary to maximizing self-interest. In doing more, we may get an affective thrill—the satisfaction of knowing that we helped someone out—but at the cost of resources that we could use on ourselves. It is of course possible that acting generous *is* a way to refocus attention on ourselves. It can be a kind of self-branding and therefore an extension of thinking of ourselves as human capital. We may also act generously because we like the way it makes us feel. Regardless of what generosity does for us, it also aids others, and usually at our expense in one way or another. There is in this excess a reversal of a logic that views all social interaction as lack. If everyone engages with each other with the thought of getting the most out of this engagement, an exchange of goods and services in the marketplace where each is seeking to benefit the most, then a condition of austerity is necessarily produced. There can never be enough of whatever is being traded because everyone is trying to get the most they can get.

3.3

The more we delve into the roots of the word, the more we are confronted by the issue of class and lineage. Generosity once used to mean that one was of aristocratic birth. One's generosity was a sign of one's good breeding. This idea of ancestry connecting to behavior later yielded another meaning, largely out of use today, that animals who are easy to take care of, are beautiful to look at, and do the work we tasked them with exceptionally well were marked by generosity. Good breeding shows. Perhaps this root meaning casts an unshakeable shadow on contemporary usage? Perhaps generosity depends on the idea that doing more for others flows from the kind of family one is born into and the kind of affluence and reputation one's family enjoys? We cannot be generous, in other words, if we do not already have an abundance to share with others.

3.4

For racial minorities and women, a focus on generosity is fraught with peril because so many expectations exist that minorities and women will be the ones who provide their services with an agreeable affect, little compensation, and tireless activity. Much is expected of them. They have much to prove. And their workload increases with demands that aren't strictly in the description of their duties. It is not enough simply to do the jobs for which they are being paid. They are also expected to do additional work, to do it in particular ways, and to do it without expectation of extra compensation. At the university, for example, anecdotes abound of minority faculty being asked to serve on numerous diversity-related committees, to hold extra office hours with minority students who are struggling with their place at school, and to participate in planning for initiatives that often will never go anywhere.

3.5

These anecdotes are, in turn, stories of relative privilege, for the problem compounds when we consider how race and gender affect the treatment of other kinds of workers who are already under enormous stress. Consider workers in the service industries, so many of whom are racial minorities of every kind. They are the most visible members of the working class in many economies. Go to any shop or restaurant and pay attention to the workers who do their jobs with focused intensity. They are a blur of activity. Their bodies do not rest. Their labor is physically exhausting. They work long hours. Their compensation is small. They are expected to blend into the background, if not disappear from view as much as possible. When they are visible, they greet the public with a smile and an agreeable affect.

They try to make everyone feel at ease, welcome, respected. Such a cheery affect is increasingly becoming compulsory. In this way, their visibility is yet another form of invisibility.

3.6

It is not accurate to describe these examples as a problem with generosity. They are, rather, indicative of the opposite. They are a sign of a lack of generosity, where one's willingness to give is overwhelmed by others who want simply to take. Nevertheless, even in a situation of lack, generosity is necessary for constructing a sense of the everyday that refuses the destruction of the commons that neoliberalism encourages. Recognizing the work of others who do more than simply what is necessary to be paid, such as those who try to be friendly when not strictly required, is itself generous. Even when a clerk is friendly to us because she is required to be does not mean that she does not enjoy the brief social encounter or that her friendliness is not also a sign of genuine camaraderie. Generosity is everywhere. Just as important, as a colleague taught me, we need to recognize that saying "no" is also often a profoundly generous act, especially when one is expected to give without any hope of a compensatory return. If we do not say no, we will have nothing to give to those who we care deeply about saying yes to.

3.7

Generosity flourishes in an economy of excess and must be more sparing when all social interactions are predicated on the marketplace and hence on lack. We need to be able to say "no." But lack also requires excess. Without generosity, it is difficult to survive in austerity. Generosity thus names an underground economy or perhaps, as some have suggested, an undercommons. When neoliberalism is orthodox, generosity in its myriad forms and instances becomes heterodox. This heterodoxy endures and remains embedded in our social relations. This means, if we are looking for alternatives to what is orthodox, we have many ready-made and concrete examples of what those alternatives can look like.

4.1

Another meaning of generosity that is a little less frequently used than the one that depends on acts of excess refers to a willingness to forgive. This meaning entails giving others the benefit of the doubt, being slow to injury, and difficult to fill with resentment. All of these, too, are examples of excess, but of thought rather than action. In addition to a generosity of acts, then, we can also talk about a generosity of opinion (although I would also want to add that the line between action and thought is not easily drawn). What is noteworthy about the *OED* entry for the latter usage is how the examples gradually make use of this kind of generosity as an absence starting in the nineteenth century. The very first example, from the sixteenth century, posits generosity as a quality that exists in an almost tangible way and that must be protected from harm: "Thou hurtest generositie, when yu prayest or intreatest the vnworthy." Also from the sixteenth century: "And such generositie was in the heartes of those theeues, that they rather chose to dye then to liue slaues." And from the seventeenth: "Their generosity is remarkable, in regard they grudge not to give praise to the vertue even of their enemies, when they deserve it." In the nineteenth (from Melville's *White-jacket*), a shift toward a negative usage occurs: "That peculiar noble-heartedness and exaggerated generosity of disposition fictitiously imputed to him." And the twentieth: "I don't think Eliot has in the least justified your generosity in his review of Pound . . . for there is no doubt Pound is a cheat and a charlatan." The final example is from the *Cape Times*, in 2001: "South Africans lack a generosity of spirit and would much rather actively resent the success of others than be happy that success means one less lumpen pissing on the pavement."

4.2

What a bad feeling the last example leaves in the mind. In the name of generosity, it impugns a nation of people and renders their complaints, which may give testimony to the difficulty of their lives, a null value. In the two immediately previous examples, generosity is associated with illusion or mistake. It is used to describe someone who is not in fact generous. Being generous is less a reliable characterization and more a cover for what truly lies underneath. We cannot, of course, generalize too much about the development of a word's specific meaning on the basis of a handful of examples. These examples in their chronological order are, however, suggestive that as we move through time motivations become murkier, more complexly self-involved, and somehow different than what has been reputed. Such a chronological order should strike us as similar to other stories about the progression of time into the present. As we approach the modern era, appearances become increasingly suspect. The world becomes one of false seeming. If we are to survive in this world, we must seek to unmask the guise of generosity to find out what we are underneath so that we are better prepared to exist with this reality. What we are underneath this guise, as it invariably turns out, is selfish. We are, in short, the very kind of person that neoliberalism says we should be. Modernity and neoliberalism seem to meet in agreement around a universal, inner-core of self-regarding and other-loathing, and in this way provide meaning and comprehension to a situation that seems constantly shifting, constantly obscuring what there is to be seen and known. Maybe we are all selfish deep down, but we may also simultaneously be deeply generous. It's the latter possibility that neoliberalism in particular is keen to deny.

4.3

Here is a way in which belief can create its own reality. If we truly believe that everyone is selfish, this is a license to be selfish. Maybe it is even more than a license; it is a demand. You must always be knowing since you live in a world where every face is a mask. Any attempt at generosity in your opinion of others is an exercise in naïveté, and hence a making vulnerable to the predation of others. You must therefore live with the assumption that others are out for themselves, and if you do not strike first to maximize your interests they will take away everything from you in the natural pursuit of their interests. You can only ever act alone to secure what is yours and to get everything that you can get, because if you do not you will lose everything that you already have. You would become, in the common vernacular of the present, a loser. The only virtue you can know is being a winner. There is no in-between or alternative.

4.4

Many people do not have to believe this for this belief to wreak havoc on social relations and on communities of persons. Even the presence of just a few such persons who hold this belief completely can do great damage. Such persons in the short term can succeed in grabbing everything of worth for their use, but in their wake they leave distrust and greater selfishness and a weakening of a sense of togetherness. This belief can easily spread, as one gets burned by the presence of such a person and learns that being trusting can be a sure way to getting played. The best-case scenario is that such persons ostracize themselves and become isolated so the harm they can do is minimized. The worst-case scenario is that this belief spreads and becomes a new norm. It is not difficult to imagine what this worst-case scenario looks like because in many ways this *is* the norm that neoliberalism names. The mantra of this belief is simple and has a hallowed place in our contemporary cultures: Greed is good.

4.5

We cannot simply decide that the belief in our innate selfishness is itself an illusion that must be cast away. When this belief is the norm, we are—all of us—vulnerable to the kind of predation it encourages. We must be wary of each other, for we do not know what the other believes. This is true for the poor of every race, whose economic vulnerability make them prey to the greed of others. This is also true for racial minorities and recent immigrants, whose marginality in their countries of residence makes them vulnerable to being taken advantage of. They have every reason to be suspicious about the motivations of others because so much of daily life and lived experience amply validate the wisdom of such suspicion. Such peoples cannot afford to give up their practices of questioning appearances, looking into the depths, and seeking out truths that remain insistently hidden, even if often in plain sight.

4.6

Elected officials with the collusion of agencies that are supposed to watch out for the common good approved the use of water that poisoned the residents of the city of Flint, Michigan, and then covered up the consequences of their actions for two years. In an era when something like this can happen, calls for greater generosity of opinion sound a sour note. We have an ethical duty to refuse what is presented to us and to penetrate deeply into the selfish thinking that rationalizes such atrocity. The residents of Flint cannot afford to be generous toward the governor of Michigan, who denies culpability in the very breath with which he apologizes for what has happened. To say that there is no longer any great surprise in discovering that an elected official turns out not to have his constituent's best interests in mind does little to lessen the need to insist on making this discovery over and over again whenever elected officials betray the duties of their office. If we view this discovery as self-evident, we accede to the belief that all we ever are is selfish.

4.7

Claims of racial microaggression are also premised on the need to question appearances and get at what lies underneath. Asian Americans have often resorted to such claims because the kind of discrimination they often face is subtle and quotidian. While there are those who of course experience outrageous incidents of police mistreatment or violence born of racial hate, as when a Sikh man in Arizona was killed by someone seeking retribution for the September 11 terrorist attacks only four days after the event, there are many more cases of dismissal, minor mistreatment, words used to demean that make daily social interactions a minefield of painful suspicion. To demand generosity of opinion from people who experience this kind of daily withering away of the spirit is itself a grossly selfish demand.

4.8

We are in a conundrum. The very belief that makes us vulnerable, and prey to each other, is also the belief we must insist on as a truth that is kept hidden from us and must be discovered. How do we break out of this cycle? How do we critique those who deserve criticism, hold those in suspicion who act in ways that deserve special scrutiny, challenge surfaces when they lie baldly about what lies underneath, while refusing the idea that all that can motivate us is self-gain? How can we encourage a generosity of opinion to flourish when there are so many good, and often necessary, reasons to be skeptical about the motivations of others?

5.1

There are no easy answers to this conundrum. One possibility we might explore is a re-evaluation of our dislike of social norms. They are, to be sure, routinely oppressive and restrictive. The critique of norms around race, gender, sexuality, and able-bodiedness has made it possible for many of us to imagine a more inclusive social world in many places and to breathe a little freer in actually existing social worlds that are welcoming of nonconformists. Such worlds may be tentative and vulnerable, and every gain may always be susceptible to reversal, but they persist. Indeed, the critique of normativity may even have moved public opinion so that, for instance, being openly racist or sexist or homophobic or intolerant of disability are now less easily tolerated. There is much work to be done to further this kind of critique and to alter public opinion even more. Every gain is greeted with reaction and is at risk of being lost. Often what is gained feels simply discursive, even while the lived experiences of many remain unchanged or, even more disturbing, made more endangered.

5.2

If public opinion has indeed changed somehow over the past several decades, no matter how incompletely or in what precarious state, it follows that critique itself already operates not only through the questioning and dismantling of norms but also in the creation of new norms. When I was in college, a professor once commented that she did not like the phrase "common sense." It assumed too much about what could be held in common and excluded too many who might not see things in the same way. As valid as these points are, and as much as I agreed with her at the time, I find myself now thinking that critique operates both as the dismantling of what once seemed like common sense and the struggle to create in its place a new common sense—or better yet, a new sense of the commons that more and more of us can share. A re-evaluation of our attitude toward normativity might thus be making explicit what has been implicit to critique, the positing of alternative values we wish to make ordinary and widely accepted. This is what I am thinking of as an ethics, a self-critical and dynamic but nevertheless strong sense of what is not only wrong but also right. If we critique the governor of Michigan and his administration and the ideas they govern by for their culpability in the Flint water tragedy, we do so because we believe this tragedy reveals yet again the failures of neoliberalism. We also do so because we believe that alternatives to neoliberalism, which do not view water solely as belonging to those who can pay for it, are ethically more attractive. Likewise, if we insist on the existence of racial microaggression, we do so because we feel the everyday can be something more welcoming. In critique, we posit these alternatives as norms that should center the political spectrum and push out ideas associated with neoliberalism into the fringe while banishing fascism from political discourse altogether. We also need to remember that any alternative, in order to be viable, must have the ability to call new publics into being.

5.3

Too often, those who care deeply about class look with skepticism on those who care deeply about social justice. The latter seem, from such a perspective, too concerned with identity and difference and other concerns that leave them numb to alarming and ever-increasing inequalities of wealth. Those who care deeply about social justice fear that those who care deeply about class only care about class and may as a result be too eager to sacrifice other concerns as less consequential. The most vocal proponents on each side of this divide exacerbate this tension and add fuel to the worry that each side is, in fact, actively hostile to the other. The fear lingers, and is even encouraged by some, that those who only pay attention to class or social justice do so because what they really care about is denying social justice to others or maintaining their own class privileges. Such thinking is very much a part of the gothic world we call neoliberalism. In this world, selfishness is everyone's motivations, and trust in others leave us prey to their betrayal. One possibility that's been pointed out to me is that this fear can crush what we can imagine or hope for as generous beings. Because others seem selfish and we must guard against the consequence of this selfishness, many of us are stuck in a state of foreclosed potential.

5.4

The opposite of such fear is to see in others the very generosity of opinion we wish was more commonplace. We might take a chance sometimes and not portray everyone as deserving our suspicion. What if those who care deeply about class do so because they genuinely care about the injustices created by widening inequalities of wealth? What if those who care deeply about social justice do so with an awareness that addressing the problem of wealth inequality is only part of a larger set of problems? What if we just cut each other some slack? How do we know when to do this and who to trust?

5.5

I do not know the answer to this last question. What I do know is that there are many scholars and activists whose deeds seem to match up with their professed beliefs. Their arguments that wealth inequality and social injustices are intertwined seem to me to be genuine. They seem actively hard at work addressing multiple concerns together in their myriad complexity and in their lived obduracy. They seem thoughtful about what others care about. In the process, they seem admirable in their striving to forge worlds of mutual care. So much seeming might prove only an illusion, a mask that hides mere selfishness, but it might also prove to be what it appears.

5.6

I have formally mixed the unfamiliar (numbered paragraphs) with the familiar (an homage to the five-paragraph essay) to stress the importance of both shaking up and putting back together. I am tempering my usual caution with willful enthusiasm for the idea of generosity. What I hope I have at least gestured toward is the fact that if we are looking for attractive alternatives to neoliberalism, there are many models to be found readily at hand. I know that I have benefited enormously from the generosity of others, whether in act or thought, and that I am not alone in this. I am guided by my ethical conviction that such generosity needs to be acknowledged, and encouraged, if we are to contest the idea that our current social order, so modeled on selfishness, is immutable. It isn't, and it mustn't be.

Becoming Bilingual, or Notes on Numbness and Feeling

Viet Thanh Nguyen

Let me take a different direction. Let me shed, one by one, the plates of paper armor I put on over the years, the hardened layers of professional habit and posturing, the densely printed sheets of my thick curriculum vita. Let me lay down the weaponry I acquired in finishing school, the accoutrement of the doctorate, the magic sword of theoretical language that I wrestled from academia's stone. It served me well, but every weapon has its cost. I no longer want to pay it.

As a novice in academia, I was not aware of my profession's price. I entered graduate school as an idealist, a convert to the cause of theory and a loyalist to a newly discovered country, Asian America. As befitting a former Catholic, steeped in the blood of sacrifice and the Jesuit mantra of service to others, I was ready to believe. The university became my church and my temple, my professors became my priests. They held the key to the sacred knowledge that could answer my questions and alleviate the numbness of which I was not even aware until I came to college.

I was a refugee and even though my passage to this new American world had been undertaken thirteen years before college, something in me hurt. Perhaps it was losing an old world and an adopted sister, both left behind, both beyond my memory. Perhaps it was watching my parents work and suffer, our family living the tired immigrant story of the shopkeepers and their lonely child. Perhaps it was hearing that they got shot on Christmas Eve and not feeling a thing except a child's bewilderment. Perhaps it was the gun aimed in my face by a gunman who broke into our house, looking for gold. Perhaps it was losing my mother tongue and knowing I had cut it off myself. Because I did not want to feel any of those things and many more, I became numb.

What I discovered in the university's secular temple was that Kafka's claim for literature applied to theory as well—both were axes to smash the ice covering one's frozen soul. At nineteen, I was dizzy with the passion released from the blows of both axes. I underlined my books using a ruler and red ink, I covered my precious books in clear plastic, I exercised the art of exegesis with the finesse of an inquisitor. I learned the histories of the railroad, the internment, and exclusion. I wrote on the other, orientalism, and American wars in Asia. I marched, I protested, I was arrested. My lawyer had helped win redress and reparations for Japanese Americans, his office had a view of the San Francisco skyline, he drove a Porsche. I read semiotics and deconstruction, minority discourse and postcolonial theory, psychoanalysis and Marxism. Believing that something should be done, and that criticism was the way to do it, I wrote to the graduate admissions committees of my belief that criticism could change the world. I did not know that my criticism could never hope to do so if I did not also change myself.

A professor had already signaled that I was not feeling enough, that those blows of theory and literature had only cracked the ice, not broken it. She was a famous writer who admitted me to her class on nonfiction writing. At nineteen, I took this privilege for granted. Fourteen students, and I fell asleep at every single meeting, sometimes two or three feet away from the famous writer. At the end of the semester, she wrote me a letter. You don't ask questions. You don't give to your fellow students. You seem alienated. You are not awake. I want you to be awake. I was awake enough to keep the letter, dormant in a box of my college papers. One day I will frame it on my wall and show it to my own students. The professor was Maxine Hong Kingston.

Can one be both awake and asleep at the same time? That might have been me in graduate school. The power of learning theory was heady. I thought I understood more and more of how the world operated and my place in it as a critic. Like the theorists I admired, I passionately believed that theory, criticism, and literature were political and that in practice all could be radical. But the power of the institution that I had committed myself to worked its own persuasion, its own inexorable discipline that I and some of my fellow students tried to resist. I registered what a classmate said, that she wanted to write something that her mother could understand, but that was improbable for me. To write in a language my mother would understand would be enormously difficult, for cutting off my mother tongue also meant breaking away from my mother. Now I hardly ever spoke to my mother, and I mistook a limit for an impossibility. There was only room for one kind of language in academia, or so it seemed to me, and that was the difficult language of theory chosen by my subfield of the humanities, of which my niche in Asian American studies was a part. So it was that the idealist who dared arrest withered and the professional who yearned for tenure took over.

If I could be both awake and asleep at the same time, if I could both feel theory and be numb to my own emotions, blind to my own memories, could theory both provoke and die at the same time? Let's not rehearse the tired debates of the pro- and anti-theory camps. Both submit to the binary of false choices, as if an artfully written essay could not be theoretical, or a theoretical meditation not poetic. These mergers and crossovers were rare to find, their practitioners existing as iconoclasts. In academia, people built careers and reputations by fostering mentees, acolytes, fields, cliques. Knowledge and power could not be separated, greatness and pettiness sometimes coexisted. In my corner of the academic world, a career could be made on a book few could understand, and so why would a young academic contest the system of reward, recognition, and privilege? One could profess rebellion in theory and be a conformist in practice. One could be a star whose light was only visible through a telescope. Or perhaps it was only I that lacked imagination and daring.

In some cases, obscurity mattered not—the power of the ideas being such that the theory could transcend its initially limited readership. This is why theory still matters for me, why I would not renounce it, because the most powerful theory transcends the vast array of mediocrities populating fiction and poetry. But in most of those cases called theory or even just criticism, the ideas were relatively paltry, the effort needed to understand the prose not commensurate to what could be extracted. (Read the introduction and conclusion, a professor told me. Skim the rest. He was mostly right.) Academia was not exceptional, after all, to the general rule of life that most things in any category were not very good. This was true for Asian American studies and Asian American literature, the subjects of my dissertation. The price of being an expert meant that I would spend

my life mostly dealing with dull axes. This was the nobility and the futility of academia, the subterranean work of excavation and living in the foot-
notes that no one besides an academic would want to do.

For a decade, as a graduate student and assistant professor, I gave in to
the scholarly work, first willingly and excitedly, then grudgingly and with
resignation, and finally with hopelessness. This was not because my writer's
self had died, or my critic's self. They survived, if beaten down, and led me
to think that if literature was committed to originality in language, what
did it mean to exercise theory that was often ridden with clichés at the
level of both language and idea? My writer's self cringed every time I read
those most pious of genuflections before Derrida, "always already." There
was also the variation on the reliable "future yet to come," usually uttered
as the concluding note to a rousing book calling for justice. Quoting him
reflexively was jargon, but some defend the necessity of jargon as a technical language. If scientists could have their jargon, why could not the hu-
manists or the antihumanists, as the case may be? The defense is false.
Scientists do not work in language. For those who work with language,
jargon was also cliché, and cliché is a failure of thought. For writers, cliché
is almost a moral lapse, an offense against the very nature of being a writer.
But it appears to be the case that many scholars are not writers except in
the technical sense, as was I.

Derrida is simply a sign here that stands for the double bind of theory,
how it illuminates and blinds at the same time, how claiming a theory can
also short-circuit the very thing that theory claims, to be critical. The trend
now is to put the word "critical" before a school of thought, as if invoking
that word would call its meaning into being, when it is already a banality
(I await the rise of the school of critical criticism in twenty years' time, as
soon as this generation of graduate students ascends and calls attention to
the arthritic thinking of the full professors). Nevertheless, the axe of theory that I picked up sometimes did break through smudged glass, opened
a window to help me see the world with clarity. By the end of my first decade in academia, I thought that I had achieved some clarity as to the plati-
tudes of Asian American studies and Asian American literature. Asian
American literature was too often saturated with the anxiety to please the
white majority, too eager to translate, to accommodate. Conversely, Asian
American studies believed that Asian Americans always resisted what was
done to them and that Asian Americans stood for justice and the future
yet to come. What justice and the future meant need never be defined, so
that the scholar could avoid the uncomfortable reality that conflicting
notions of justice existed or that Asian Americans could sometimes act

unjustly. Sometimes it seemed to me, fairly or not, that I could predict the arguments of Asian American scholars and the stories of Asian American literature before reading them.

The chore of reading dull work lead more and more to a dull soul, or whatever illusion of a soul that lent me feeling. I did not object to the hard work of using the axes of theory or literature to chop wood rather than smash ice. My refugee parents had imparted, through their exhausting example, the belief that working constantly was beneficial, good for the soul and the bank account. What I objected to was the boredom of being a technical writer. Perhaps it's an unfair criticism of the state of criticism or Asian American writing. Most professions may be tedious, their moments of illumination and inspiration rare. But having achieved the habits and rewards of the professional, having been crowned with tenure, having contributed my book to a growing heap, I no longer wanted to be a professional. Being a professional made me feel like I could no longer stand my profession. After the tedium of writing the book I had just written, steeped in the jargon of a profession that it had taken me a decade to master, it seemed to me the most awful fate I could imagine to write another technical manual just like it.

I was luckier than many. I could leave academia, at least for a while. My university paid my salary so that I could live for seven months in Paris and another seven months in Saigon. I carried a box of the most recent and praised critical works to both cities and could not bring myself to read a single book. I wrote fiction full-time, which I had promised myself in graduate school that I would do when I got tenure. I was happy. I was going to be a writer. I wrote short stories and they looked good. An arts center granted me a fellowship to live on the eastern tip of Cape Cod for seven months. The fellowship paid nearly nothing but included a room. I studied the roll call of famous and prize-winning writers who had received this fellowship and wondered who might have lived in this room before me. I was tremendously confident and wrote more stories and felt that I was on the cusp of greatness. I still had the box of theory and I still could not read a single book. I did not have a car, but I had plenty of cheap whiskey. I read novels. I read short stories. I had a wonderful time until the blizzard decked the cape in snow and insomnia arrived and I was trapped for months within a short story that would eventually take a decade and fifty drafts to complete and publish.

I spent the dispiriting decade that followed as a continuing academic, laboring in the middle rank of my profession. I did not have the courage to leave academia and try myself as a writer. I liked academia's paycheck, and being the good student I was and am, I was comforted by academia's conformity and its system of reward. But something in me had changed—the ice was breaking if not fully broken. I could feel my extremities if not my entire body and soul. My vision was clear enough for me to see that I could not be an original critic if I wrote in an unoriginal language. I hoped that I could take criticism and theory and make them my own, use the liveliest of their ideas but excise the gangrenous language. As a writer and a critic, I could not give up the idea that the language mattered as much as the thinking, that the form was as important as the content, and that submitting to the language of others had changed me and would change me in ways that I did not want. In looking at Asian American studies, it appeared to me that the field's wholesale adoption of the most conventional of theoretical language, at least in the humanities, had transformed it in ways both positive and negative. No longer could Asian American studies be accused of being untheoretical, as it once was. New insights arose and the field moved in some new directions. But in giving itself over to theory, Asian American studies also inadvertently proved that it was another manifestation of the model minority, theorizing like white people and with their authority, speaking in their language even as it tried to make that language its own.

Not that I was any different. In turning to fiction, I discovered new depths of vulnerability and of my desire for approval. As an academic and critic, because I had mastered the language and therefore could obtain my rewards, I had also tamed, to some extent, my neediness. I could project invulnerability, the armor needed to survive in academia. But as a fiction writer, I was back to being an apprentice, only I had no teachers. I struggled to write short stories that imitated, in form, the style of middle-brow realism that dominates American literary fiction. If I was successful, I, too, could become a model minority Asian American writer of the kind produced from the MFA programs, the beneficiaries of a century of Asian American struggle who had sublimated the violence and anger of Asian American history into the paperweights of industrial standard fiction. Rejecting the jargon of theoretical and Asian American scholarship, I found myself in danger of adopting the clichés of a certain kind of literary form.

The decade of learning to be a writer was nearly as difficult as the decade of learning to be an academic, except that tenure's guaranteed salary cushioned my bruised ego. Still, writing short stories was mostly an exercise in being miserable. The rewards for writing were few and the rewards accrued for being a scholar amounted to little more, since my attention was divided. Along with writing a short story collection, I was also working on a scholarly book about war and memory whose scale grew with every year. The professional in me was in despair over not publishing a book for a decade. But my capacity for feeling was growing, and despair foreshadowed something greater. The idealist in me was still alive and quickening, and the ideal that I held before myself was that perhaps it would be possible to write fiction like criticism and criticism like fiction.

It is not an ideal that I have achieved, even if the novel I eventually wrote seems to me to approximate criticism. In creating that novel over a span of two years, I finally broke through the numbness of both mind and spirit and wrote with utter feeling. By "feeling" I mean passion and joy, even moments of ecstasy, words I had never used to describe my academic work. I abandoned myself to the writing and wrote mostly without fear, except when I talked to my agent and the professional in me returned, worried about whether the novel would ever sell. I reminded myself constantly that while I wrote my first book for academia and my short stories for the literary world, I was writing the novel for myself. I finally understood the idea that only by moving myself could I possibly hope to move a reader.

In order to move myself, I had to shed the weight of all that armor. I had to smash the ice that had frozen my soul. The armor and the ice were the accumulation of my refugee childhood and my academic career. They existed to protect me from the emotions and the memories that threatened me, the inarticulate pain of arriving in America and separating from my parents. My memories begin in the summer of 1975, somewhere between Fort Indiantown Gap, Pennsylvania, where we were housed in a refugee camp with thousands of others, and Harrisburg, where we were resettled. Except that no sponsor would take our entire family. My parents went to one sponsor, my brother to another, myself to a third. My four-year-old self experienced these months of separation as abandonment and loss. I suppressed those feelings in order to live. I grew to fear being alone even as I was used to being alone, living in a world of books while my parents worked twelve to fourteen hour days. I contained myself except for those rare moments when the ice melted and flooded through the armor. Once, well into my adulthood, realizing that my mother would never recover from an illness and ever be herself again, I burst into tears. This was the woman who had carried me or dragged me as a four-year-old nearly two hundred kilometers to escape the communist army, from our hometown of Ban Me Thuot to Nha Trang. At least our trek was downhill. At least I don't remember the dead paratroopers hanging from the trees, as my brother did. I was driving the car in which my father and brother were sitting as we talked about my mother. Neither of them said a word as I gripped the wheel and struggled to see through the tears. Once I had recovered myself, they resumed their conversation as if nothing had happened. I resumed my life as if nothing had happened.

This moment did not make its way into the scholarly book on which I spent over a decade, *Nothing Ever Dies: Vietnam and the Memory of War*, but its memory lurks behind the pages. In the epilogue, I wrote this about my mother: "Her memories are vanishing and her body is slow to obey her. She will not be counted as one of war's casualties, but what else do you call someone who lost her country, her wealth, her family, her parents, her daughter, and her peace of mind because of the war?" This was a departure for me. I had published several articles over the previous decade where I worked through different ideas in the book, but almost all of them were written in the academic way, even though I had pushed myself with each article to break down the ingrained habit of jargon and stiff syntax. I struggled to melt the ice, to ease the tone of coldness and hardness that marked my academic writing. In the end, I had to throw away most of the words in those articles and write my book on war and memory afresh, from the beginning, as a story that began with me and ended with my family. "I was born in Vietnam but made in America" are the book's first words. The last deal with the fate of the bones of the dead, from those belonging to my grandfather to those belonging to all of the Vietnamese people.

In between the beginning and ending, this book on war and memory is recognizably a scholarly one. There are theoretical arguments and critical readings. There are accounts of fieldwork and the citation of famous or influential scholars. But there is also emotion on my part, a claim to the power of my own subjectivity and history that had driven me to be an objective scholar. One way to put this is that this book on war and memory makes explicit what is implicitly personal in the theoretical. I thought back to the naïve young man I once was, a college student full of braggadocio and angst, yearning to be awake and stricken with sleep, who believed wholeheartedly in the power of criticism and a country called Asian America. I could not reclaim that self and would not want to, but I could be inspired by the passion I had forgotten and hidden away under my professionalism. I cannot say that I loved writing my book on war and memory in the way that I loved writing my novel. But I was moved. That gave me hope that the reader of this book on war and memory would be moved as well, that my critical insights would achieve more force when carried along by the flow of prose and narrative. I wanted to convince the reader through what I had to say and how I said it, in a book that was informed by the lessons of fiction about the power of emotion, passion, and intuition.

Letting myself feel through language saved me as a scholar, an academic, and a writer. It saved me as an Asian American, too. Once or twice over the hard decade of learning to write I would say in public that I was no longer an Asian Americanist. The commonplaces and conformity of thinking and practice in Asian American studies dismayed me. But I have not yet been able to leave Asian American studies and perhaps never will. What I love about Asian American studies and the Asian American culture that has been influenced by it—and vice versa—is the sense of duty, service, community, solidarity, and justice. I share those values, even if I think that in their exercise they can sometimes be unimaginative. Failures of imagination and the pleasures of conformity are not restricted to the conservative. They are human failings, and Asian Americans have sought to prove their humanity in all ways. I have come to recognize and accept these failings and this flawed humanity. Now, with a measure of renewed enthusiasm, I teach Asian American studies because I see the need among my students for that same blow of the axe that cracked the white ice that had frozen me.

I am certain that there is still a core of ice inside of me that I have not yet touched. The problem with being numb is that one can get used to it. I even learned to live with the pain of cutting off my mother tongue. Learning other languages was how I made up for that absence. First the language of theory, now the language of fiction. Like all languages worth knowing besides one's mother tongue, both have taken years of patient practice. Oftentimes I felt like a fool, an idiot, a child, a student, anything but an authority. Giving up authority for a scholar, a professor, or a theorist can be hard. It can be costly. But I was willing to pay that price in order to say, in more ways than one, that I was bilingual again.

ACKNOWLEDGMENTS

From the outset, Richard Morrison at Fordham University Press was incredibly supportive of *Flashpoints for Asian American Studies*; indeed, he saw the potential of the project in a way that extended well beyond my original vision of it. Such critical support incontrovertibly carried with it the unmatched expertise of someone whose work in academic publishing has consistently accentuated the ongoing relevance of Asian American studies as a significant and urgent field of interdisciplinary inquiry. To say that this project could not have reached fruition without his astute advice and capacious comprehension would be an absolute understatement—*Flashpoints for Asian American Studies* is entirely indebted to him. I want to also thank the anonymous readers who—at various phases and stages of the project—offered detailed suggestions that dramatically helped clarify the overarching stakes of the manuscript. Last, but certainly not least, Fordham University Press has proven to be an ideal *Flashpoints* home. I appreciate greatly the dedication, commitment, and patience of the staff who, without complaint, answered numerous queries and concerns.

Admittedly, *Flashpoints for Asian American Studies* is very much a "conversational" endeavor, and the essays contained within this volume assume, to varying degrees and wonderfully divergent ends, the starting and end points of multiple discussions. In recollecting the genesis of the project, I must necessarily go back to March 2013, when I had the opportunity to give a talk at the University of Southern California. Following the talk, I had what would emerge as a crucial tête-à-tête with Viet Thanh Nguyen over dinner and drinks. Despite engaging a variety of topics that ranged from the personal to the familial to the professional, our conversation kept cycling back to the current "state" of Asian American studies as an institutionalized ethnic studies interdiscipline. Integral to that discussion was the question of whether Asian American studies "mattered" in a contemporary political imaginary marked by indiscriminate multiculturalism (in various governmental echelons and legal machinations) and diversity management (which militated against claims of systemic racism by stressing the singularity of racist actors). Likewise significant was the extent to which the "neoliberal university" as a central site of racially inflected knowledge production represented a profound impediment to the work of a field born out of midcentury social movement and antiwar protest.

This discussion of field history, interdisciplinary viability, and critical legibility in many ways served as the impetus for bringing *Flashpoints for Asian American Studies* "into being." Such dialogues about disciplinary place and space are at the forefront of the chapters included in the volume, and I am humbled by each contributor's willingness to take seriously the need to re-evaluate, reassess, and recalibrate a field that for many has served as a generative intellectual home. Envisioned as equal parts manifesto and critique, *Flashpoints for Asian American Studies* is truly the "sum of its parts," and I am eternally grateful to those who—armed with an unparalleled generosity of work and aspirational spirit—contributed to it. This sense of collegiality vis-à-vis dialogue and debate was analogously at the forefront of exchanges I had over the years with Janet Francendese, Linda Trinh Vo, and K. Scott Wong, whom I credit as significant mentors over the course of what has proven in many ways to be an unexpected academic career.

Whereas *Flashpoints for Asian American Studies* is undeniably a multivalent work of (inter)disciplinary reflection, it is also a volume that makes visible the oft-accessed adage in ethnic studies and women's, gender, and sexualities studies that the personal is indeed political. Situated accordingly, I owe much to my parents, Charles and Ginko Schlund, who, because of history and circumstance, instilled in me an interest in civil rights and engendered a long-lasting genealogical respect. My twin brother—also named Charles—has always kept me grounded via much-needed humor at pivotal moments. Last, but certainly not least, I am forever grateful to Chris Vials, my best friend and interlocutor, whose activist work and impressive research constantly remind me why the work we do—inside and outside the classroom—matters.

YOONMEE CHANG is associate professor of English at George Mason University. She received her PhD from the University of Pennsylvania and was awarded a Mellon postdoctoral fellowship at Northwestern University. She was previously an assistant professor of English and American studies at Indiana University. Chang specializes in Asian American literature and culture and is the author of *Writing the Ghetto: Class, Authorship, and the Asian American Ethnic Enclave.* Her current projects include a study of Asian Americans and disability, research on North Korea, and some dabbling in writing poetry. Chang's work has been published in the *Journal of Asian American Studies, Modern Fiction Studies,* and *Beltway Poetry Quarterly.* She has an article on disability and storytelling forthcoming in *Twentieth Century Literature.*

KANDICE CHUH is professor of English and American studies at the CUNY Graduate Center, where she is also a core member of the Mellon Interdisciplinary Committee on Globalization and Social Change. The author of *Imagine Otherwise: On Asian Americanist Critique* and the editor, with Karen Shimakawa, of *Orientations: Mapping Studies in the Asian Diaspora,* Chuh's most recent project, *The Difference Aesthetics Makes: On the Humanities 'after Man,'* reflects her research and teaching interests in the relationships among the politics of knowledge and social transformation. She teaches in such areas as critical race studies. U.S. cultural studies, queer theory, aesthetics, and literatures of the United States.

YÊN LÊ ESPIRITU is distinguished professor and former chair of the Department of Ethnic Studies at the University of California, San Diego. She has published widely on Asian American panethnicity, gender and migration, and U.S. colonialism and wars in Asia. Her most recent book is *Body Counts: The Vietnam War and Militarized Refuge(es).*

CANDACE FUJIKANE is associate professor of English at the University of Hawai'i (Manoa). In addition to a number of articles and book chapters,

Professor Fujikane coedited *Asian Settler Colonialism: From Local Governance to the Habits of Everyday Life in Hawai'i*. She is presently completing a book manuscript titled *Mapping Abundance: Indigenous and Settler Cartographies in Hawai'i*, which articulates a practice of anticolonial mapping as one that provides evidence of the ways in which the settler state never completely captures the occupied territory, making possible the enactment of a future beyond that state.

LISA LOWE is professor of English and American studies at Tufts University. She is the author of *Critical Terrains: French and British Orientalisms*, *Immigrant Acts: On Asian American Cultural Politics*, and coeditor of *The Politics of Culture in the Shadow of Capital*. Her most recent book is *The Intimacies of Four Continents*.

MARTIN F. MANALANSAN IV is associate professor of anthropology and Asian American studies and a Conrad Humanities Professorial Scholar at the University of Illinois, Urbana-Champaign. He is an affiliate faculty in the Department of Gender and Women's Studies, the Global Studies Program, and the Unit for Criticism and Interpretive Theory. He is the author of *Global Divas: Filipino Gay Men in the Diaspora*, which was awarded the Ruth Benedict Prize in 2003. He is editor/co-editor of three anthologies: *Cultural Compass: Ethnographic Explorations of Asian America*, *Queer Globalizations: Citizenship and the Afterlife of Colonialism*, *Eating Asian America: A Food Studies Reader*, as well as a special issue of *International Migration Review* on gender and migration. Presently, he is social science review editor of *GLQ: A Journal of Gay and Lesbian Studies*. His current book projects include the ethical and embodied dimensions of the lives and struggles of undocumented queer immigrants, Asian American immigrant culinary cultures, sensory and affective dimensions of race and difference, and Filipino return migration.

ANITA MANNUR is associate professor of English and Asian/Asian American studies at Miami University; she recently served as the director of the Women's, Gender, and Sexuality Studies Program at Miami University. She is the current editor of the *Journal of Asian American Studies* and the recipient of the 2012 Association for Asian American Studies' Early Career Award. She is the author of *Culinary Fictions: Food in South Asian Diasporic Culture* and a coeditor of *Eating Asian America: A Food Studies Reader*.

ASHA NADKARNI is associate professor of English at the University of Massachusetts, Amherst. Her work has appeared in *Novel: A Forum on Fiction*, *American Quarterly*, and *Feminist Studies* and she is a contributor to *The*

Cambridge History of Asian American Literature and *Oxford Bibliographies in Literary and Critical Theory*. Her book *Eugenic Feminism: Reproductive Nationalism in the United States and India* traces connections between U.S. and Indian nationalist feminisms to suggest that both launch their claims to feminist citizenship based on modernist constructions of the reproductive body as the origin of the nation. She is working on a second book project, tentatively titled *From Opium to Outsourcing*, that focuses on representations of South Asian labor in a global context.

VIET THANH NGUYEN is professor of English and American studies and ethnicity at the University of Southern California, as well as a member of the steering committee for the Center for Transpacific Studies. He is the author of *Race and Resistance: Literature and Politics in Asian America* and the 2016 Pulitzer Prize–winning novel *The Sympathizer*. His most recently published nonfiction work, *Nothing Ever Dies: Vietnam and the Memory of War*, was a finalist for the 2016 National Book Award. His articles have appeared in numerous journals and books, including *PMLA*, *American Literary History*, *Western American Literature*, *positions: east asia cultures critique*, *The New Centennial Review*, *Postmodern Culture*, *The Japanese Journal of American Studies*, and *Asian American Studies after Critical Mass*. His most recent work is an acclaimed short story collection, *The Refugees*.

JUNAID RANA is associate professor of Asian American studies at the University of Illinois at Urbana-Champaign with appointments in the Department of Anthropology, the Center for South Asian and Middle Eastern Studies, and the Unit for Criticism and Interpretive Theory. His publications have appeared in *Cultural Dynamics*, *Souls*, and the edited anthologies *Pakistani Diasporas*, *State of White Supremacy*, *Reinventing Race*, *Reinventing Racism*, *Dispatches from Pakistan*, *Between the Middle East and the Americas*, and *The Sun Never Sets*. He is the author of the book *Terrifying Muslims: Race and Labor in the South Asian Diaspora*, winner of the 2013 Association of Asian American Studies Book Award in the Social Sciences.

CATHY J. SCHLUND-VIALS is professor of English and Asian/Asian American studies at the University of Connecticut (Storrs); she is also the director of the UConn Asian and Asian American Studies Institute. In addition to published book chapters, articles, reviews, and edited collections, she is the author of two monographs: *Modeling Citizenship: Jewish and Asian American Writing* and *War, Genocide, and Justice: Cambodian American Memory Work*. She has edited and coedited a number of anthologies and collections, which include *Disability, Human Rights, and the Limits of Humanitarianism*,

Keywords for Asian American Studies, Interrogating the Perpetrator: Violation, Culpability, and Human Rights, and *Asian America: A Primary Source Reader,* among others. She is a coeditor for Temple University Press's Asian American History and Culture series and is the current president of the Association for Asian American Studies (AAAS, 2016–2018).

Nitasha Tamar Sharma is associate professor of African American studies and Asian American studies at Northwestern University, where she is also an affiliate of performance studies. She is the author of *Hip Hop Desis: South Asian Americans, Blackness, and a Global Race Consciousness.* She is currently writing a book on Blacks and mixed race Blacks in Hawai'i.

Min Hyoung Song is professor of English at Boston College, where he directs the Asian American Studies Program. He is former editor of the *Journal of Asian American Studies* and the former director of the English MA program at Boston College. Song is the author of two books, *The Children of 1965: On Writing, and Not Writing, as an Asian American* and *Strange Future: Pessimism and the 1992 Los Angeles Riots,* as well as the coeditor of *Asian American Studies: A Reader.* He has published academic articles in the journals *Mosaic, Twentieth-Century Literature, American Literary History, LIT,* and *Legacy,* and in numerous edited volumes of essays. He is currently coediting (with Rajini Srikanth) the *Cambridge History of Asian American Literature* and has started work on a new book project tentatively entitled *The Elusive Aesthetics of the Present.* His most recently published essay, on Chang-rae Lee's career so far, appeared in the *LA Review of Books.*

Rajini Srikanth is professor of English and affiliated faculty of Asian American studies at the University of Massachusetts, Boston. She is the author of, among other things, the award-winning book *The World Next Door: South Asian American Literature and the Idea of America* and the book *Constructing the Enemy: Empathy/Antipathy in US Literature and Law.* She is coeditor of the forthcoming *Cambridge History of Asian American Literature.* Her research interests include American literature, human rights, comparative race and ethnic studies, and international American studies. Srikanth is past president of the Asian American Studies Association.

Sharon A. Suh is professor of Buddhism and chair of the Department of Theology and Religious Studies at Seattle University. She is the author of *Being Buddhist in a Christian World: Gender and Community at a Korean American Temple* and *Silver Screen Buddha: Buddhism in Asian and Western Film.*

AMY UYEMATSU was raised in southern California by parents who had been interned in American camps during World War II. She earned her undergraduate degree in mathematics at the University of California, Los Angeles. A renowned poet, her work considers the intersection of politics, mathematics, spirituality, and the natural world. She is the author of several poetry collections, including *Stone Bow Prayer*, *Nights of Fire, Nights of Rain*, and *30 Miles from J-Town*, which won the Nicholas Roerich Poetry Prize. She coedited the seminal anthology *Roots: An Asian American Reader* and her own work has been included in numerous anthologies. She has collaborated with multimedia artists Joan Watanabe and Roger Shimomura; her most recent collection of poems is *The Yellow Door* and includes work that reflects upon her activism in the Yellow Power movement.

BRANDY LIÊN WORRALL-SORIANO is author of *What Doesn't Kill Us*, a groundbreaking memoir about growing up in the din of her Vietnamese mother and American father's trauma from the Vietnam War and how it related to her breast cancer experience as a young adult. She is also the author of eight collections of poetry (the *podBrandy* series), as well as having served as editor of numerous magazines, journals, and anthologies. She is the owner and editor of Rabbit Fool Press, a small family-owned-and-operated publishing company based in Vancouver. Brandy received her MA in Asian American studies from UCLA in 2002 and her MFA in creative writing from the University of British Columbia in 2012. She was formerly the editor of *Amerasia Journal*.

CYNTHIA WU is associate professor of transnational studies at the University of Buffalo (SUNY-Buffalo). Professor Wu specializes in Asian American and critical ethnic studies, U.S. literatures after 1865, disability studies, and queer of color analysis. She is the author of *Chang and Eng Reconnected: The Original Siamese Twins in American Culture*. Currently, she is at work on two projects—one that examines military service among Asian Americans and the other on intraracial same-sex desire in Asian American literature. Excerpts from these manuscripts have appeared in *Amerasia Journal*, *Meridians*, and *Signs*. In addition to her scholarly work, Wu has written for *The Chronicle of Higher Education*, *Inside Higher Ed*, and *The Los Angeles Review of Books*. She has held leadership positions in the Association for Asian American Studies, the Modern Language Association, and the Society for Disability Studies. She has served on the editorial boards of *Disability Studies Quarterly*, *The Journal of Asian American Studies*, and *Text and Performance Quarterly*. She is a past recipient of the Milton Plesur Excellence in Teaching Award at the University at Buffalo, and she credits her students with keeping her desire for learning strong.

Lisa Yoneyama is professor of women and gender studies and East Asian studies at the University of Toronto. She is the author of *Hiroshima Traces: Time, Space, and the Dialectics of Memory, Violence, War, Redress: The Politics of Multiculturalism (Boryoku senso, ridoresu: tabunkashugi no poritikusu)*, and coeditor of *Perilous Memories: Politics of Remembering the Asia-Pacific War(s)*. Her most recent book, *Cold War Ruins*, is from Duke University Press.

Timothy Yu is professor of English and Asian American studies and director of the Asian American Studies Program at the University of Wisconsin-Madison. He is the author of *Race and the Avant-Garde: Experimental and Asian American Poetry since 1965*. He is also the author of an acclaimed collection of poetry, *100 Chinese Silences*.